Healthy Living Lifestyle Eradicating Illness Naturally

Volume II

Salim Rahim Rana

Dr. Jyothi Shenoy

Dr. Mervin Leo

Copyright © 2022

All Rights Reserved

Disclaimer

This book is meant to provide information about natural treatments. It is not meant to replace physician's advice, treatments, or counseling. The author does not hold any responsibility for any liabilities arising due to the use of the content provided in this book in any form. Readers are advised to consult their healthcare physician for advice and treatment of their health issues.

All royalties received by the author of this book will be donated to a Foundation providing knowledge to people in rural communities. Therefore in purchasing this book, you too are aiding in support of further education and encouragement of living a healthy lifestyle!

Contents

Dedication 1

Acknowledgements 2

About the Authors 4

   First Aid Agents and Antidotes in Ayurveda 6

      Overindulgences and Their Antidotes 6

      The Ayurvedic First Aid Kit 8

      Hydration and Its Importance for Maintaining Health 12

      What Is the Right Way of Drinking Water According to Ayurveda? 13

      How Much Water Should You Drink Every Day to Meet the Body's Hydration Requirements? 13

      Maintaining the Body's Hydration Based on Your Constitution or Dosha 15

      What Are the Benefits of Drinking Lemon Water? 17

      What Are the Health Benefits of Green Tea? 18

   Electrolyte Homeostasis 22

      What Is Electrolyte Imbalance? 23

      What Are Electrolytes? 23

      What Are the Causes of Electrolyte Imbalances? 24

      What Are the Signs and Symptoms of Electrolyte Imbalances? 24

      Electrolyte Imbalance in Children 25

      Electrolyte Imbalances in Older Adults 25

      Treatment of Electrolyte Imbalance 26

      Management of Electrolyte Imbalances 26

      Home Remedies for the Management of Electrolyte Imbalances 27

      Conclusion 28

   Vitamin Deficiencies 29

      Bleeding Gums 29

- Brittle Nails and Hair ... 30
- Poor Night Vision ... 31
- Mouth Ulcers ... 31
- Scaly Patches ... 32
- Red Bumps on the Skin ... 32
- Hair Loss ... 33
- Conclusion ... 33

What Is Anaemia? ... 35
- What Are the Predisposing Factors for Anaemia? ... 35
- Common Signs and Symptoms of Anaemia ... 36
- What Are the Risk Factors or Causes of Anaemia? ... 36
- How Can You Diagnose Anaemia? ... 37
- The Possible Complications of Anaemia ... 38
- Treatment Options Available for Anaemia ... 38
- Is it Possible to Prevent Anaemia? ... 39

Anticoagulant Effect and Blood Coagulation ... 41
- What Is Blood Coagulation? ... 41
- What Are the Stages of Coagulation? ... 42
- The Coagulation of Blood ... 42
- What Are the Symptoms of Coagulation Disorders and Difficulty in Clotting? ... 46
- What Are the Common Symptoms of Coagulation Disorders and Increased Clotting? ... 46
- Pulmonary Embolism ... 46
- Which Are the Test Ayurvedic Herbal Remedies for the Treatment of Clotting and Bleeding Disorders? ... 47
- Conclusion ... 48

Ayurvedic Approach to the Treatment of Diabetes ... 49
- What Are the Types of Diabetes? ... 49
- What Are the Common Causes of Diabetes? ... 50
- What Are the Signs and Symptoms of Diabetes? ... 50

- What Are the Complications of Diabetes? 52
- Lifestyle Choices Recommended by Ayurveda for the Treatment of Diabetes 53
- How Does Obesity Lead to Type 2 Diabetes? 53
- The Safe and Natural Herbs for Treating Diabetes 54
- Safe and Effective Exercises for Controlling Your Blood Sugar Levels 58
- How Does Yoga Help Fight Diabetes? 58
- How Can Meditation Help Control Blood Sugar Levels? 60
- How to practise Mindfulness Meditation? 61
- How to practise Transcendental Meditation? 61
- Conclusion 61

Ayurvedic Approach for the Treatment of Hypercholesterolemia 62
- What Are the Common Causes of Hypercholesterolemia? 63
- What Are the Signs and Symptoms of Hypercholesterolemia? 63
- What Are the Complications of Hypercholesterolemia? 63
- Ayurvedic Treatment for Managing Cholesterol Disorders 64
- The Do's and Don'ts for Healthy Cholesterol Levels 67
- Dietary and Lifestyle Changes for Managing High Cholesterol 68
- Conclusion 68

Treatment and Prevention of Malaria Based on the Ayurvedic System of Medicine 70
- What Are the Common Causes of Malaria? 71
- What Are the Common Signs and Symptoms of Malaria? 71
- What Are the Complications Caused Due to Malaria? 72
- Tips to Prevent Malaria 72
- Things to Avoid while Suffering from Malaria 76
- Conclusion 76

Ayurvedic Treatments for the Management of Respiratory Disorders 76
- Respiratory Disorders 77
- Structure and Functions of the Respiratory System 78

Common Conditions Affecting the Respiratory System 80
Conditions Affecting the Upper Respiratory Tract 80
Common Conditions Affecting the Lower Respiratory Tract 80
Ayurvedic Treatments for the Management of Respiratory Disorders 82
Ayurvedic Treatments for Respiratory Disorders 85
Ayurvedic Herbal Drinks 85
Ayurvedic Treatments for the Management of Snoring Linked to Respiratory Problems.... 86
Effective Natural Remedies to Avoid Snoring and Restore Optimum Respiratory Health.. 87
Conclusion 88

Ayurvedic Treatments for Respiratory Infections 90

Acute Respiratory Infections 91
What Are the Common Signs and Symptoms of Acute Respiratory Infections? 91
What Are the Causes of Acute Respiratory Infections? 92
Who Is at a Higher Risk of Developing Acute Respiratory Tract Infections? 92
How Are Acute Respiratory Infections Diagnosed? 92
What Are the Potential Complications of Acute Respiratory Infections? 93
Prevention of Acute Respiratory Infections 93
What Are Chronic Lung Infections? 94
What Are the Causes of Chronic Lung Infections? 94
Chronic Respiratory Infections in Institutionalised Settings 95
What Are the Common Symptoms of Chronic Respiratory Tract Infections? 96
Diagnosis of Chronic Respiratory Tract Infections 96
Treatment of Chronic Respiratory Infections 96
Prevention of Chronic Respiratory Infections 97
Ayurvedic Treatment for the Management of Respiratory Tract Infections 98
Ayurvedic Treatment for Unproductive (Dry) Cough 98
Ayurvedic Medicines for the Treatment of Productive Cough (Cough With Phlegm) 99
Ayurvedic Medicine for the Treatment of Sore Throat and Cough 99

- Ayurvedic Medicines for the Treatment of Cough with Fever 100
- Ayurvedic Medicines for the Treatment of Running Nose with Cough 100
- Other Effective Home Remedies for Treating Cough and Cold 101
- Conclusion 102

Ayurvedic Treatments for Relief From Asthma Attacks 103
- What Are the Common Signs and Symptoms of Asthma? 103
- What to Do During a Severe Asthma Attack? 106
- A Four-Step Approach for Preventing a Severe Asthma Attack 106
- Use Salt and Water Treatment to Relieve Severe Asthma Attacks 107
- Apple Cider Vinegar 107
- Take Steam Inhalation 108
- How to Manage Asthma Naturally? 108
- Personalised Approach for the Natural and More Efficient Treatment of Asthma 109
- Identifying the Root Cause 109
- Preventing Infections 110
- Natural Herbs for Asthma Treatments 110
- Diagnostic Approach to the Treatment of Asthma 110
- Conclusion 111

Ayurvedic Treatment for Respiratory Infections Such As Tuberculosis 112
- What Is Tuberculosis? 113
- Latent TB (or TB Infection) 113
- Active TB (or TB Disease) 114
- What Are the Early Warning Signs of TB? 114
- Symptoms of Specific Forms of TB 115
- Diagnosis of TB 115
- Treatment of TB 116
- Prevention of TB 117
- TB Vaccination 117

- Risk Factors for TB 117
- Complications of TB 118
- Ayurvedic Treatment for TB 118
- Herbal Remedies for Preventing and Treating TB 119
- Conclusion 120

Cardiovascular Disorders (Hypertension, Arrhythmia, Atherosclerosis) 121
- What Is Hypertension? 121
- Ayurvedic Remedies for Lowering Blood Pressure 122
- Diet and Lifestyle Recommendations by Ayurveda for the Comprehensive Management of Hypertension 123
- Meditation and Breath Therapy for Hypertension: 123
- How to Control Hypertension Safely and Naturally? 123
- Treatment and Approach of Ayurveda for Cholesterol Disorders 126
- Dangers of High Cholesterol 126
- Ayurvedic Treatments for Managing Cholesterol Disorders 126
- Herbal Remedies 127
- Managing Arrhythmias 128
- The Ten Most Common Lifestyle Factors That Can Aggravate Arrhythmias 129
- Conclusion 130

Natural Ayurvedic Remedies to Support the Healing of Varicose Veins 131
- Maintain Healthy Weight 131
- Conclusion 134

Ayurvedic Medications for the Treatment of Cancer 135
- What Is Cancer? 135
- What Is the Difference Between Healthy Cells and Cancer Cells? 136
- Ayurvedic Cancer-Fighting Remedies 137
- Conclusion 140

What Leukaemia Is and Ayurveda's Role in Managing Leukaemia 141
- What Are the Signs and Symptoms of Leukaemia? 142

- What Are the Common Causes of Leukaemia? ... 142
- How Does Leukaemia Form? ... 142
- How Is Leukaemia Classified? ... 143
- What Are the Different Types of Leukaemia? ... 143
- What Are the Risk Factors for Leukaemia? ... 144
- Treatment of Leukaemia ... 145
- Coping and Support ... 145
- Ayurvedic Treatment for Patients with Leukaemia ... 146
- Supplements and Nutrition ... 146
- The Advantages of Herbal Therapies ... 147
- Conclusion ... 148

Treatment and Prevention of Skin Cancer through a Comprehensive Plan ... 150
- Cells Commonly Involved in Skin Cancers ... 151
- What Are the Symptoms of Skin Cancer? ... 151
- Common Causes of Skin Cancers ... 153
- Potential Causes of Skin Cancer ... 153
- Prevention of Skin Cancers ... 154
- The Most Effective Natural Remedies for Preventing Skin Cancer ... 155
- Simple Home Remedies for Relieving the Symptoms of Skin Cancers ... 156
- Conclusion ... 158

What Is Thyroid Cancer and the Most Effective Natural Remedies to Manage It? ... 159
- What Are the Different Types of Thyroid Cancer? ... 160
- What Are the Symptoms of Thyroid Cancer? ... 160
- What Are the Causes of Thyroid Cancer? ... 161
- What Are the Risk Factors for Thyroid Cancer? ... 162
- Natural Ways to Control Thyroid Diseases ... 162
- Conclusion ... 164

Management of Colorectal Cancer With Ayurvedic Remedies ... 165

- What Are the Signs and Symptoms of Colorectal Cancer? 165
- Treatment of Colorectal Cancer 166
- What Are the Causes and Risk Factors for Colorectal Cancer? 166
- Diagnosis of Colorectal Cancer 167
- Prevention of Colorectal Cancer 168
- Conclusion 168

The Safe and Natural Treatment Methods for Cervical Cancer 170

- What Are the Signs and Symptoms of Cervical Cancer? 171
- What Are the Common Causes of Cervical Cancer? 171
- What Are the Different Types of Cervical Cancers? 172
- Risk Factors of Cervical Cancer 172
- How to Prevent Cervical Cancer? 173
- Diagnosis of Cervical Cancer 173
- Modern Treatments for Cervical Cancer 174
- Ayurvedic Treatment for Cervical Cancer 174
- Conclusion 176

Management of Prostate Cancer With Safe and Effective Ayurvedic Remedies 178

- What Are the Signs and Symptoms of Prostate Cancer? 178
- What Are the Causes of Prostate Cancer? 179
- What Are the Risk Factors for Prostate Cancer? 179
- What Are the Complications of Prostate Cancer? 180
- Screening for Prostate Cancer 180
- Prevention of Prostate Cancer 181
- Choosing a Healthy and Nutritious Diet Full of Fruits and Vegetables 181
- Choosing Healthy Foods and Avoiding Junk Foods 181
- Exercising Regularly 181
- Maintaining a Healthy Weight 181
- Medications for Prostate Cancer 182

- Natural Ayurvedic Remedies for the Management of Prostate Cancer 182
- Conclusion 184

What Is Bone Cancer and How to Manage It With the Help of Natural Treatments? 185
- What Are the Common Types of Bone Cancers? 186
- What Are the Symptoms of Bone Cancer? 186
- What Are the Causes of Bone Cancer? 187
- What Are the Risk Factors for Bone Cancers? 187
- Diagnosis of Bone Cancers 187
- Ayurvedic Treatments Recommended for the Management of Bone Cancers 188
- Best Foods for the Management of Bone Cancers 188
- Conclusion 191

Ayurvedic Treatments for Patients with Alzheimer's Disease 192
- What Is Alzheimer's Disease? 192
- Treatments of Alzheimer's Disease 193
- How to Practice Meditation to Improve Your Concentration, Memory, and Attention Span? . 193
- Natural Remedies for Improving Your Memory and Reducing Anxiety Associated With Alzheimer's Disease 196
- Conclusion 198

What Is a Headache or Migraine, and How to Manage It? 199
- What Are the Risk Factors for Migraines or Recurring Headaches? 199
- Natural Ayurvedic Remedies to Get Rid of Migraines Quickly 201
- Conclusion 204

Depression and Its Management Using Natural Methods 205
- What Are the Causes of Depression? 205
- What Are the Signs and Symptoms of Depression? 206
- What Are the Hidden Signs and Symptoms of Depression? 207
- Importance of Timely Diagnosis and Treatment of Depression 207
- Food and Mood: How Diet Relates to Your Mental Health and Depression 208

- Depression and Nutrition 208
- Positive Role of Specific Nutrients in Managing Depression 209
- Know the Effect of Junk Food on Depression 210
- Foods to Avoid to Prevent and Treat Depression More Effectively 212
- How Can a Nutritional Imbalance Lead to Depression? 212
- Popular Nutritional Supplements for Depression 213
- 'Good' Nutrients for the Brain 213
- Ayurvedic Herbs You Must Include in Your Diet to Protect Yourself From Depression.... 214
- Anti-Depression Herbs... 214
- Aromatherapy for Depression 216
- Happiness: A Key to Unlocking and Getting Rid of Negative Thoughts 216
- How Do Meditation, Pranayama, and Yoga Help You Control Your Thought Process and Overcome Depression? 217
- Helpful Yoga Postures.. 218
- Conclusion 219

Treatment of Chronic Fatigue Syndrome Using Natural Methods 220
- Treatment of Chronic Fatigue Syndrome 221
- Prevention of Complications 221
- Daily Limitations and Fears of Patients with Chronic Fatigue Syndrome 222
- What Are the Psychological Effects of Chronic Fatigue Syndrome? 222
- Foods that Can Worsen the Symptoms of Chronic Fatigue Syndrome 222
- The Best Foods to Eat for Relieving Symptoms of Chronic Fatigue Syndrome 225
- Conclusion 226

What Is Insomnia and How to Avoid Its Consequences on Your Health? 227
- Common Consequences of Sleep Deprivation for Your Health and Future Life 228
- What Are the Health Benefits of Sleep? 231
- Seven Best Yoga Poses You Should Practice to Fight Insomnia and Get a Sound Sleep ... 234
- Foods That Can Keep You Awake and Prevent a Good Night's Sleep 238
- How to Put Your Sleep Schedule Back in Sync.. 241

- Conclusion 243

What Is Multiple Sclerosis and the Most Effective Ways to Manage It 244
- What Are the Signs and Symptoms of Multiple Sclerosis? 245
- Disease Course or Pathogenesis of Multiple Sclerosis 245
- What Are the Causes of Multiple Sclerosis? 246
- What Are the Risk Factors for Multiple Sclerosis? 246
- What Are the Complications of Multiple Sclerosis? 248
- Diagnosis of Multiple Sclerosis 248
- Treatment of Multiple Sclerosis 248
- Treatments for Modifying the Progression 249
- Ayurvedic Treatments for the Management of Multiple Sclerosis 250
- Conclusion 251

What Are the Symptoms, Root Causes, and Treatments for Dementia? 252
- What Are the Symptoms of Senile Dementia? 252
- What Are the Causes of Dementia? 253
- Treatment of Dementia 253
- Conclusion 254

The Adverse Effects of Nicotine Consumption on Your Body and How to Get Rid of the Addiction 255
- Some Facts About Nicotine 256
- Adverse Effects of Nicotine Intake 256
- Pharmacologic Effect of Nicotine 256
- Side Effects of Nicotine 257
- What Are the Effects of Smoking on the Skin? 259
- Treatment of Nicotine Addiction 261
- Medications for Nicotine Addiction 261
- Psychological Support and Counselling 261
- Conclusion 262

Alcohol Hangover and the Best Detox Mechanisms to Overcome It 263

- Direct Effects of Alcohol Intake 263
- Biochemical Processes Responsible for Symptoms of Alcoholic Hangover 264
- How Do Your Body's Organs React to the Increased Level of Acetaldehyde? 264
- What Are the Common Signs and Symptoms of an Alcoholic Hangover? 265
- Detoxification for Reducing Alcohol Hangover Symptoms 265
- What Is a Detox Diet? 265
- What Are Toxins, and How Does a Detox Diet Help Get Rid of Them? 266
- Foods to Avoid During a Detox Diet 266
- Conclusion 266

Natural Ayurvedic Therapies for Improving Memory and Cognitive Functions 268
- The Role of Sound Sleep in Memory 268
- Effect of Lack of Sleep on Memory and Other Cognitive Functions of the Brain 269
- How Does Lack of Sleep Affect Cognitive Functions? 270
- Dementia 270
- Herbal Remedies for Improving Memory and Attention Span 271
- Conclusion 271

Learning to Cope With the Challenges Posed by ADHD to Lead a Normal Social, Personal and Academic Life 273
- Introduction: What Is ADHD? 273
- What Are the Common Causes of ADHD? 274
- What Are the Early Warning Symptoms of ADHD? 274
- The Types of ADHD 276
- Challenges Associated with ADHD 276
- Effective Methods for Minimising the Effect of ADHD on a Child's Daily Activities 277
- Some Dos to Be Followed by Parents and Teachers 278
- Strategies at Workplace or School for Overcoming ADHD Challenges 279
- Effective Conventional Treatment Options and Counselling methods to Prevent Your ADHD Traits from Decreasing Your Effectiveness 282
- Holistic Approach to ADHD Management 284

- The Benefits of Yoga for ADHD Patients: 284
- The Role of Meditation and Breathing Exercises in Managing ADHD 284
- Exercises to Sharpen Your Mental Skill and Reduce Your Anxiety and Impulsiveness 285
- How to Improve Your Child's Self-Confidence and Prepare Them to Be a Capable Adult 286
- Conclusion 288

Symptoms, Causes, and Treatment for Duchenne Muscular Dystrophy 290
- What Is Duchenne Muscular Dystrophy? 290
- What Are the Symptoms of DMD? 291
- How Is DMD Diagnosed? 292
- Treatment of Duchenne Muscular Dystrophy 292
- Ayurvedic Treatment of Muscular Dystrophy 292
- Conclusion 293

What Is Down Syndrome and Can It be Treated? 295
- What Are the Symptoms of Down Syndrome? 295
- Intellectual Disabilities in Patients With Down Syndrome 296
- What Are the Causes of Down Syndrome? 296
- Is Down Syndrome Inherited? 297
- What Are the Risk Factors of Down Syndrome? 297
- What Are the Complications Linked to Down Syndrome? 298
- Prevention and Treatment of Down Syndrome 299
- Ayurvedic Treatment for Down Syndrome 299
- Down Syndrome Concepts in Ayurveda 299
- Conclusion 300

Can Ayurveda Provide Relief From the Symptoms of Parkinson's Disease? 301
- Early Signs of Parkinson's Disease 301
- What Are the Causes of Parkinson's Disease? 302
- Prevention of Parkinson's Disease 303
- Conclusion 305

- [What Is Indigestion and Acid Reflux? Ayurvedic Treatments for Improving Digestion ... 306](#)
  - [What Are the Common Symptoms of Acid Reflux? ... 306](#)
  - [Complications of Indigestion and Acid Reflux ... 307](#)
  - [Diet Recommendations for Patients with Indigestion and Acid Reflux Disease ... 308](#)
  - [Effective Natural Herbs and Home Remedies for Treating Acid Reflux ... 311](#)
  - [Natural Ways to Treat Chronic Acid Reflux ... 312](#)
  - [How Can Ayurveda Help Improve Your Gut Health and Reduce Indigestion? ... 315](#)
  - [The Concept of Gut Health in Ayurveda ... 315](#)
  - [Conclusion ... 317](#)
- [Common Signs, Causes, and Treatments for Gluten Intolerance ... 318](#)
  - [What Is Gluten Intolerance? ... 319](#)
  - [What Is Food Intolerance? ... 319](#)
  - [What Are the Symptoms of Food Sensitivities? ... 319](#)
  - [What Causes Gluten Intolerance and Why Is Gluten so Harmful to Your Health? ... 320](#)
  - [Conclusion ... 321](#)
- [Ayurvedic Treatment for Diarrhoea and the Common Causes of Loose Motions ... 323](#)
  - [What Are the Common Signs and Symptoms of Diarrhoea? ... 323](#)
  - [What Are the Causes of Diarrhoea? ... 324](#)
  - [Ayurvedic Treatments for Children with Diarrhoea ... 324](#)
  - [Dietary Advance for the Prevention of Diarrhoea ... 325](#)
  - [Lifestyle Habits Recommended by Ayurveda for the Prevention of Diarrhoea ... 325](#)
  - [Treatment of Diarrhoea ... 325](#)
  - [Home Remedies for Diarrhoea Management ... 325](#)
  - [Conclusion ... 326](#)
- [Ayurvedic Treatment for Vomiting ... 327](#)
  - [What Is Vomiting? ... 327](#)
  - [What Are the Causes of Vomiting? ... 328](#)
  - [Vomiting Emergencies ... 328](#)

- What Are the Complications of Vomiting? 329
- Treatment of Vomiting 329
- Prevention of Vomiting 330
- Ayurvedic Treatment for the Management of Vomiting 330
- Conclusion 331

What Is Inflammatory Bowel Disease and How to Manage It Naturally? 332
- What Is Inflammatory Bowel Disease? 332
- What Are the Types of Inflammatory Bowel Diseases? 333
- What Are the Causes of Inflammatory Bowel Disease? 334
- What Are the Signs and Symptoms of Inflammatory Bowel Disease? 335
- What Are the Complications of Inflammatory Bowel Disease? 336
- Ayurvedic Concepts for IBD Management 336
- Ayurvedic Approach to IBD Management 337
- Conclusion 338

Management of Intestinal Parasites Using Ayurvedic Remedies 339
- What Are the Symptoms of Parasitic Infections? 339
- Diagnosis of Parasitic Infections 340
- Treatment of Parasitic Infections 340
- Home Remedies for Parasitic Cleanse 341
- Parasitic Cleanse Diet 341
- Ayurvedic Home Remedies for Parasitic Infection Management 342
- Dietary Recommendations for Parasitic Infection Management 343
- Lifestyle Modifications for Parasitic Infection Management 343
- Conclusion 343

Management of Peptic Ulcers Using Natural Ayurvedic Remedies 344
- What Are Peptic Ulcers? 344
- What Are the Symptoms of Peptic Ulcers? 344
- What Are the Causes of Peptic Ulcers? 345

- What Are the Common Complications of Peptic Ulcers? 345
- Treatment of Peptic Ulcers 345
- Conclusion 346

Weight Loss Strategies Recommended by Ayurveda 347
- What Is Obesity? 347
- How Is Obesity Measured? 347
- Why Is It Important to Lose Weight? 348
- Economic Consequences of Abnormal Weight Gain 349
- Common Mistakes Made by People While Trying to Lose Weight 349
- Why Do Most People Gain Back the Weight They Have Lost? 350
- The Right Attitude for Weight Loss 351
- The Critical Role Nutrition Plays in Losing Weight 353
- What Is a Nutritious Diet? 354
- What Is Meant by "Eating the Rainbow"? 354
- Does the Term 'Fat-Free' Mean No Calories? 355
- Tips to Make Sure You Eat a Nutritious Diet: 355
- Conclusion 355

What Is Metabolic Syndrome and the Best Natural Ways to Manage It 357
- What Are the Symptoms of Metabolic Syndrome? 357
- What Are the Causes of Metabolic Syndrome? 357
- What Are the Risk Factors for Metabolic Syndrome? 358
- Ayurvedic Treatment for Metabolic Syndrome Prevention 358
- Foods You Should Eat to Prevent Metabolic Syndrome: 360
- Conclusion 361

Ayurvedic Treatment and Prevention for Gallbladder Stones 362
- What Are the Causes of Gallstones? 362
- What Are the Different Types of Gallstones? 363
- What Are the Risk Factors for Gallstones? 363

- What Are the Symptoms of Gallstones? 364
- What Are the Possible Complications of Gallstones? 364
- Diagnosis of Gallstones 365
- Ayurvedic Recommendations for Gallstone Prevention 365
- Herbal Remedies for Gallstone Treatment 366
- Conclusion 366

The Best Ayurvedic Herbal Remedies for Liver Health 367
- Turmeric 367
- Green Tea 368
- Liquorice 368
- Milk Thistle 368
- Ginseng 369
- Ginger 369
- Danshen 369
- Garlic 369
- Astragalus 369
- Ginkgo biloba 370
- Conclusion 370

The Natural Remedies for the Treatment and Prevention of Liver Cirrhosis 371
- What Is Liver Cirrhosis? 371
- What Are the Causes of Cirrhosis? 372
- What Are the Symptoms of Cirrhosis? 372
- Treatment of Cirrhosis 374
- Ayurvedic Herbs for the Treatment of Cirrhosis 374
- Conclusion 375

Best Ayurvedic Remedies for the Management of Arthritis and Other Bone Diseases 376
- What Causes Arthritis and Back Pain? 376
- Modifiable Causes of Arthritis and Back Pain 378

- Simple Exercises to Prevent Arthritis and Back Pain 380
- Ayurvedic Remedies for the Treatment of Arthritis and Backache 382
- Exercise Your Joints 384
- Conclusion 384

Benefits of Ayurvedic Herbs for Maintaining Dental Health 386
- Ayurvedic Methods of Maintaining Oral and Dental Health 386
- How to Use a Twig? 386
- Effective Home Remedies to Whiten Your Teeth 387
- What Else Can You Do? 389
- Conclusion 389

Ayurvedic Remedies for Fighting Bad Breath 390
- Neem 390
- Apple Cider Vinegar 391
- Fennel Seeds 391
- Ginger 392
- Cardamom 392
- Eucalyptus Oil 392
- Mint and Tulsi Leaves 393
- Lemon Juice 393
- Conclusion 394

What Is Sinusitis and How Can It Be Treated With Ayurvedic Remedies? 395
- What Is Sinusitis? 396
- What are the Signs and Symptoms of Sinusitis? 396
- What Are the Causes of Sinusitis? 397
- What Are the Risk Factors for Sinusitis? 397
- Home Remedies for Managing Sinusitis 397
- Treatment of Acute and Chronic Sinusitis 398
- Acute and Subacute Sinusitis 398

- Chronic Sinusitis 398
- Conclusion 399

Natural Ways to Improve Your Eyesight 400
- Kale 400
- Fish Oil 400
- Spinach 401
- Corn 401
- Exercise Your Eyes 401
- Give Adequate Rest to Your Eyes 402
- Keep Your Environment Safe 402
- Ginkgo Biloba 402
- Bilberry 402
- Conclusion 403

Natural Treatment for Macular Degeneration 404
- What Is Macular Degeneration? 404
- What Are the Symptoms of Macular Degeneration? 405
- What Are the Causes of Macular Degeneration? 405
- How Is Macular Degeneration Diagnosed? 405
- What Are the Treatments for Macular Degeneration? 406
- Prevention of Macular Degeneration 406
- Conclusion 407

Common Skin Conditions and Their Natural Treatments 408
- What Is Eczema? 408
- What Are the Symptoms of Eczema? 409
- What Are the Causes of Eczema? 409
- Factors That Can Provide Relief From Eczema 410
- Natural Treatments for Eczema 412
- Home Remedies for Relieving the Symptoms of Eczema 412

Conclusion 413

What Are the Symptoms, Causes, Risk Factors, and Treatment for Herpes 415

    What Are the Symptoms of Herpes Infection? 416

    Symptoms of Oral Herpes 416

    Symptoms of Genital Herpes 416

    What Are the Primary Symptoms of Herpes Infection? 416

    What Are the Recurring Symptoms of Herpes Infection? 417

    What Are the Causes of Herpes Infection? 417

    The Association Between HSV and HIV 417

    Treatment of Herpes Infection 418

    Home Remedies for Herpes Infection 418

    Medications 419

    Prevention Tips for Herpes Infection 419

    Conclusion 419

How To Manage the Symptoms of Allergies in a Safe and Natural Way? 421

    Identifying the Allergens 422

    Probiotics 422

    Quercetin 422

    Avoid Pollen 422

    Conclusion 422

Symptoms, Causes, Treatment, and Home Remedies for Candidiasis 424

    What Is Candidiasis? 424

    What Are the Symptoms of Candidiasis? 424

    What Are the Causes of Candidiasis? 425

    Treatment of Fungal Infections, Including Candidiasis 426

    Treatment of Uncomplicated Candidiasis or Yeast Infections 426

    Treatment of Complicated Yeast Infections 426

    Home Remedies for Candidiasis 427

- Prevention of Candidiasis 427
- Conclusion 427

What Are the Causes of Hair Loss and How to Manage It Naturally? 429
- What Are the Causes of Hair Loss? 429
- Side Effects of Medications 431
- Best Natural Ways to Prevent Hair Fall Naturally! 431
- Some More Tips to Reduce Hair Loss 433
- Conclusion 433

What to Expect During Wound Healing and Natural Ways to Accelerate Healing 435
- What Are the Different Types of Wounds? 436
- What Are the Stages of the Wound Healing Process? 436
- Natural Methods to Support Wound Healing Processes 438
- Conclusion 438

What Is Constipation and What Are the Natural Remedies to Avoid It? 439
- What Are the Common Symptoms Associated With Constipation? 440
- What Are the Causes of Constipation? 440
- Management of Constipation Using Natural Home Remedies 442
- Conclusion 442

Natural Treatments for Haemorrhoids 443
- What Are the Causes of Haemorrhoids? 443
- What Are the Symptoms of Haemorrhoids? 444
- What Are the Possible Complications of Haemorrhoids? 445
- Prevention of Haemorrhoids 445
- Treatment of Piles 446
- Conclusion 446

Natural Home Remedies for the Management of Urinary Tract Infections 447
- Drink Plenty of Water 448
- Celery Seeds 448

- Parsley 448
- Baking Soda 448
- Indian Gooseberry 449
- Ginger Tea 449
- Blueberries 449
- Cucumbers 449
- Use Heating Pads 450
- 4 C's You Must Avoid While Suffering From Urinary Infections: 450
- Conclusion 450

Treatment of Kidney Stones Using Natural Remedies 451
- What Are the Common Causes of Kidney Stones? 451
- What Are the Types of Kidney Stones? 452
- What Are the Risk Factors for Renal Stones? 453
- What Are the Symptoms of Kidneys Stones? 453
- Prevention and Treatment of Kidney Stones Using Simple Natural Remedies 454
- Conclusion 455

What Are the Causes, Symptoms, and Treatments for Gout? 456
- Why Does Gout Occur? 456
- What Are the Symptoms of Gout? 456
- What Are the Risk Factors for Gout? 457
- How Is Gout Diagnosed? 457
- Effective Herbal Ingredients for the Treatment and Prevention of Gout 457
- Bets Natural Herbs for Managing Gout 458
- How to Prevent Gout? 462
- Conclusion 464

What Are Diuretic Agents? 465
- What Are Diuretics Used For? 465
- What Are the Different Types of Diuretics? 466

- What Are the Side Effects of Diuretics? 467
  - Natural Herbs That Can Produce a Diuretic Action 467
  - Conclusion 469
- Postoperative Care 470
  - Preparing for Surgery Ahead of Time 470
  - Postoperative Care in Hospital Settings 471
  - Postoperative Care at Home 473
  - Conclusion 473
- Management of HIV Infections 474
  - What Are the Symptoms of HIV Infection? 474
  - Transmission of the HIV Infection 475
  - What Are the Risk Factors for the HIV Infection? 475
  - Prevention of the HIV Infection 475
  - Treatment of the HIV Infection 476
  - Ayurvedic Treatment for the HIV infection 476
  - Conclusion 476
- Management and Treatment of Influenza 478
  - What Are the Symptoms of Influenza? 478
  - What Are the Risk Factors for Influenza? 479
  - What Are the Common Causes of Influenza? 479
  - Prevention of Influenza 480
  - How to Manage Influenza at Home Using Ayurvedic Remedies? 480
  - Tulsi 480
  - Honey 480
  - Mulethi 480
  - Cinnamon 480
  - Conclusion 481
- Female Hormonal Status 482

- The Types of Female Hormones 482
- What Happens When the Hormonal Levels Become Unbalanced? 483
- Conclusion 484

Fertility Boost for Men and Women With Infertility 485
- What Is Infertility? 486
- What Are the Causes of Male Infertility? 486
- What Are the Causes of Female Infertility? 487
- Some Other Common Causes of Infertility in Men and Women 488
- The Importance of the Time of Intercourse While Trying to Conceive 488
- Changes in the Basal Body Temperature 489
- Treatment Approach: Medications, IUI and IVF, Surrogacy 493
- Effective Herbs and Spices to Boost Fertility 496
- Conclusion 499

Importance of Improving Nutritional Support and General Health Before and During Pregnancy 500
- Check Your Weight 500
- Clean Up Your Diet 501
- Eat Iron-Rich Foods 501
- Exercise Regularly 501
- Limit Your Exposure to Toxins 502
- Make Space in Your Life 502
- Curb Caffeine 502
- Avoid Alcohol 502
- Manage Your Current Medical Conditions 503
- Essential Nutrients for a Smooth and Healthy Pregnancy 503
- Essential Nutrients for a Healthy Pregnancy 503
- Some More Guidelines for Healthy Conception and Smooth Pregnancy 504
- Other Fitness Considerations 505
- Conclusion 506

- Pregnancy and Birth Defects 507
  - Plan in Advance 507
  - Avoid Harmful Substances 508
  - Quit Smoking 508
  - Avoid Marijuana 509
  - Protect Against Infections 509
  - Avoid Overheating 509
  - Maintain Normal Blood Sugar Levels 509
  - Maintain a Healthy Weight 509
  - Talk With the Healthcare Provider 510
  - Take Vaccinations 510
  - Conclusion 511
- Best Natural Herbs That Can Reduce the Signs of Ageing 512
  - Protect From the Sun 512
  - Retinoids 513
  - Moisturiser 513
  - Herbal Remedies for Reducing Wrinkles 513
  - Conclusion 514
- Common Ailments Affecting Children 515
  - Sore Throat 515
  - Ear Pain 516
  - Urinary Tract Infections 516
  - Skin Infections 516
  - Bronchitis 516
  - Bronchiolitis 516
  - Other Respiratory Infections 517
  - Pain 517
  - Conclusion 517

References 518

Dedication

'I would like to dedicate this book to those of you who would like to have the opportunity to access information on living healthily through the natural resources and treatments that our earth has to offer. May you find, within the pages of this book, the knowledge and ray of hope that will allow you to dedicate your life to living healthily and to its fullest potential.'

- Salim Rahim Rana, Author

'This book is dedicated to those individuals who suffer from acute and chronic illness. The best health care should be accessible to all the people in this world irrespective of their geographical location.'

- Dr. Jyothi Shenoy, Writer and Researcher

'I dedicate this book to my teachers who not only provided me with the knowledge needed to grow successful in my line of work, but also who provided me with the inspiration to live a healthier and happier life which I hope you readers shall gain in reading this book. Special thanks must go to the most inspirational of all, my Guru and legend of nature cure, Dr Jay Kumar M. Sanghvi – an angel to many patients and a mentor for all Naturopaths.'

- Dr. Mervin Leo, Naturopath

Acknowledgements

'To my parents, Rahim Rana and Gulzar Rana, I must thank you for the dedication and support you have shown in raising me. Without your guidance and nourishment, I would not be doing what I am today and though I forever work to make you both proud, I can say with deepest sincerity that I am proud to be called your son.

To Dr. Jyothi Shenoy, who researched and wrote this book. Thank you for the time and dedication you took in assisting me with the writing and for sharing your knowledge with me and the readers.

And to Dr Mervin Leo, who I owe more thanks that I can perhaps ever give and without whom I would not be here today to have this book written. Thank you Dr. Leo for sharing your knowledge of Naturopathy. I can honestly say in the literal sense, you saved my life.'

- Salim Rahim Rana, Author

'Firstly, I would like to take this opportunity to thank the author Salim Rana for allowing me to assist in the writing of this book and sharing my knowledge with him and the readers;

To the editorial team, who provided their input on the editing of this manuscript and ensuring that the text within its pages read clearly;

To my parents, who I can never thank enough for always being there in my times of need and showing endless patience and support while writing this book;

And to my dear husband, Ananth, who assisted me in the beta-reading of this book and ensured that the technical and medical terms used were easy to comprehend to any who may wish to read the book but have no greater understanding of the medical field.'

- Dr. Jyothi Shenoy, Researcher

'I would like to give thanks to all those who contributed to the making of this book, from teachers, parents and well-wishers alike. A special thanks must be given to Dr. Jay Kumar M. Sanghvi; by Dr Bhimsi Savla, whose guidelines allowed for him to recover naturally after his tongue was cut in two and whose help inspired him to become a follower of Nature cure and Shree Satya Narayana Goenkaji.

To Dr. Sanghvi, who has founded many nature cure and wellness centres worldwide. Every man has his destination. After a long silence in his life, Dr. Sanghvi entered glory leaving his remembrance behind. I, as one of his students, cannot forget the great things he has taught us. He will always remain in our hearts forever.'

- Dr. Mervin Leo, Naturopath

About the Authors

Salim Rahim Rana

Born in Kenya, Africa, Salim Rana lived there until the age of thirteen when he moved to the UK and then a number of other countries. This move from his homeland triggered within Salim a complexity in his immune system that saw him grow severely ill despite the aid of antibiotics. Despite the intake of medication, Salim's health continued to travel on a downward spiral until he tried a more natural way of regaining control over his diet. Through the guidance of those at Jindal, a facility near Bangalore, Salim was able to develop and benefit from living a healthier lifestyle that saw him eating naturally and exercising daily to improve his physical health. A sudden bout of tragedy struck in 2019 when Salim fell ill once again… However, it was with the help of Dr. Mervin – a naturopath based in Nashik – that he was able to turn his life around and live to complete this book. With the experience and dedication shown by Salim, he decided to write this book in order to spread awareness of the benefits of naturopathy and has kindly arranged for all the royalties of this book to be donated to the foundation for humanitarian causes.

Dr Jyothi Shenoy, Researcher

As a doctor who has 15+ experience in alternative medicine, Dr. Jyothi Shenoy believes that all patients should be treated in a holistic manner. Her aim in educating patients about their illnesses and providing lifestyle advice stems from her desire to ensure that they are able to thrive and achieve long-term relief from their ailments. With experience in treating acute and chronic diseases like obesity, IBS, asthma, allergies, autoimmune disorders, arthritis, cancer, skin diseases, and many more… Dr Jyothi's insight and knowledge of medicine and these illnesses proved too invaluable, and therefore was a must-have to be included within this work.

Dr. Mervin Susairaj Leo, Naturopath

Born in 1980, Dr. Leo grew up in the central part of southern India and suffered from a variety of health conditions from his infancy. It was in his years of studying further education that Mr. Leo came across Naturopathy during his search for something to help with healing and it was with the support of his teachers that he started to develop an understanding of the science of nature. This journey has led Dr. Mervin to help a great number of individuals recuperate from their diseases and suffering, and even saved the life of the author of this book. He lived to this day and his story continues as he proceeds to dedicate the life the Almighty God has gifted him with to use his knowledge in aiding others.

First Aid Agents and Antidotes in Ayurveda

Antidotes can help counteract the effects of a particular medicine or even an unpleasant sensation. Sometimes, the foods we eat can cause problems such as nausea, vomiting, diarrhoea, skin rashes, and asthma. These adverse effects may occur due to a person's hypersensitivity or overindulgence to the particular substance.

It is ideal to avoid overindulging too often. However, it is usually too hard to get away from the temptation.

Besides food items, other factors such as excessive exposure to the sun or travelling may affect our sense of wellbeing. These factors need to be tackled appropriately.

You can avoid the negative effect of these things by using herbal remedies recommended by Ayurveda that act as natural antidotes.

Below, some of the most potent natural antidotes have been listed that can be used to offset the 'not-so-healthy' effect of the factors your body might be hypersensitive to.

Overindulgences and Their Antidotes

Chocolate

Chocolate is the perfect example of a 'Srota Blocker'. Srotas refer to the 'channels' in the body, which must be kept free and clear to ensure you can maintain optimum health with improved vitality.

If these channels are blocked, you may develop unpleasant signs and symptoms. It may put you at risk of major diseases.

The primary culprits in chocolates are the higher levels of carbohydrates, especially in the form of simple sugars and milk solids.

It is possible to counter chocolate's harmful effects by drinking hot or warm water with two or three cardamom pods. The hot water would 'melt' the improperly digested carbs and other foodstuffs, while the cardamom pods would help by re-opening the channels or srotas.

Alcohol

The worst effects of excessive alcohol consumption produce on the liver cells. Alcohol is known to have a severely detrimental effect on hepatic functions. The risk of diseases like hepatitis, ascites, alcoholic liver diseases, and liver cancer can increase substantially.

Though these effects of alcohol cannot be completely reversed, a significant reduction in alcohol-induced liver damage could be achieved through the use of herbs like turmeric.

It is advised to take one or two pinches of this medicinal herb in a glass of warm water or milk to minimise the harmful effect of alcohol. You can also add turmeric to your regular cooking as a part of a healthy routine to protect your liver.

Drinking warm water with half or one full spoon of turmeric may also provide relief from the symptoms of a hangover.

The combination of the depressing and stimulatory effects of alcohol could be avoided by eating one or two cardamom seeds and chewing a spoonful of cumin seeds.

Another herbal remedy that can help treat a hangover is Ojas. Eating dried-out ojas would improve your digestion. Ojas is also believed to enhance the link between our consciousness and the body. It is considered the material equivalent of bliss that can give us mental clarity and improve our resistance against disease development.

Red Eyes

Redness and soreness of the eyes may occur due to several factors such as infections, overuse, and sun exposure.

A rosewater eye spray could be an effective, time-tested antidote for sore eyes caused due to excessive exposure to the sun. You can add two to three spoons of rose water to a glass of water, then splash it on your eyes.

Alternatively, an eye bath using cold milk may also relieve the signs of red-eye. Additionally, putting sliced cucumbers on the eyelids would help counter the effects of harsh sun rays on your eyes.

Seafood

Seafood is considered 'hot' by nature. It can cause symptoms related to increased digestive heat, such as heartburn, gastritis, acid reflux, and indigestion.

The best antidote to neutralise or minimise the effects of seafood is peppermint tea. It would reduce stomach heat and prevent unpleasant symptoms. Ayurvedic experts believe that the custom of eating 'peppermint' after lunch or dinner came from eating seafood.

Sunburn

One of the best antidotes for relieving symptoms of sunburn would be aloe vera. Extracting fresh aloe vera gel from the leaves and applying it to the affected part could be highly therapeutic for the sun-damaged skin. You can apply the gel regularly to protect your skin from sun damage and speed up repair.

Motion Sickness

Ayurveda recommends consuming the juice of fresh ginger squeeze for reducing travel sickness. Take $1/4^{th}$ tablespoon of the freshly squeezed ginger juice. You may add a few drops of lemon juice and a pinch of salt to it. Simply licking the spoon dipped in the mixture would help you eliminate the unpleasant sensation.

Coffee

It is common for people to be surprised when they know that excessive coffee or other caffeinated beverages like cola and tea can cause unpleasant signs and symptoms.

Coffee contains caffeine that can over-stimulate our nervous system resulting in restlessness and insomnia.

You may drink a glass of warm milk or two to three glasses of hot water to counter the effects of excess caffeine in the body. This step would also help you get a peaceful and undisturbed sleep. These ill-effects of coffee could also be avoided by using nutmeg powder.

The Ayurvedic First Aid Kit

Children and adults are susceptible to incidents that can harm them and even result in minor or major injuries. So, we all keep a first aid kit ready at home packed with bandages, antiseptic cream, plasters, wipes, drugs like painkillers, and antacids.

But what if you want to achieve quick first aid relief naturally?

With just a little patience and proper knowledge, you can easily find a natural remedy from your own kitchen for administering first aid in case of emergencies.

Here are some of the best first aid natural herbal remedies that you can use in such case:

Cuts

Applying a turmeric paste and honey on the wound would stop the bleeding within a few seconds. Just make the paste and press it on the wound. It also acts as an antiseptic and prevents any infection. It will also help the wound to heal faster.

This natural tip is beneficial even for diabetic patients whose injuries can take longer to heal and even trigger infections.

Sore Throat

The classic combination of turmeric and honey works fast and effectively for relieving a sore throat. Just mix a spoonful of these natural remedies and suck the mixture on the spoon. Alternatively, you can add turmeric and rock salt in warm water and gargle. It will help you derive instant relief from the problem.

Burn

In the case of burns, the first thing to do is run the part through cold water immediately. Let the water flow over the region as long as the burning sensation remains. This tip will not only relieve the pain but also prevent blisters from forming.

Then, apply a paste of aloe vera gel with a pinch of turmeric powder. You can leave it until the initial stinging and burning sensations subside. You may continue applying aloe vera gel or coconut oil with sandalwood or rose water to enhance the cooling effect.

Headache

Apply a paste of ginger on the forehead and lie down for about five to ten minutes. Then, remove the paste. You will find your headache disappearing miraculously after this. The aroma of ginger will also make you feel refreshed.

Headaches can also be a sign of dehydration. So, drink one or two glasses of water, especially if you start getting a headache after a workout or due to travelling under the harsh sun. A gentle massage of the forehead, temples, shoulders, and neck with eucalyptus oil can also help loosen up the muscles and relieve headaches.

Sinus headaches can be relieved by applying gingelly oil mixed with camphor oil on the forehead.

Acid Reflux

Acid reflux is usually a result of an increase in or imbalance in the pitta dosha. A pitta-pacifying diet can help correct this problem quickly. You can try chewing fennel seeds or drinking aloe vera juice to relieve the pain.

You can also drink a glass of buttermilk with a pinch of fenugreek powder and asafetida. This mixture will help neutralise the stomach acid and prevent regurgitation and the resulting heartburn.

Cold and Cough

Dry cough can be treated by taking a decoction of liquorice root. If you suffer from a cough with a lot of mucous secretion, take a decoction of ginger, turmeric, a pinch of black pepper, lemon, and a squeeze of honey.

You may eat a paste of garlic or chew on a ginger root. You will be able to derive significant relief by boiling some ginger powder in water and inhaling the steam. Applying a few drops of eucalyptus oil on the sides of the nose will help relieve nose block. Inhaling the powder of calamus root into each nostril can reduce congestion.

Indigestion

The best natural quick fix for this common problem is drinking a glass of pomegranate juice. You can also try drinking hot water infused with lemon juice.

Drinking buttermilk with cumin seeds and a little salt can also help instantly relieve flatulence and abdominal discomfort.

Diarrhoea

If diarrhoea results from indigestion or overeating, drink a glass of buttermilk with a pinch of salt and asafetida. Another excellent remedy for treating loose motions is powdered mango seed taken with honey. A mix of rock salt, dry ginger, and jaggery is also effective for relieving diarrhoea caused due to indigestion.

Asthma

Combine ginger herb with liquorice and drink it as tea. The recommended proportion is about one teaspoon of both herbs for one cup of water. Drinking onion juice mixed with one or two teaspoons of honey and a pinch of black pepper can also relieve an asthma attack.

Backache

A gentle back massage using ginger paste and eucalyptus oil can help relieve back muscle spasms and reduce back pain. You can relieve backache resulting from bone-related disorders by massaging with coconut oil. However, it can only lessen the pain for a short duration and not cure the disease completely.

Acne

Acne can be an emergency sometimes. A small pimple here or there on your face can send you in a tizzy, especially when it crops up before a special event.

Though the pimple will not disappear entirely within just a day, it can reduce in intensity and appear less visible by if you apply a paste of sandalwood powder and turmeric on it. Take about one teaspoon of each of these powders and mix them with rose water to make a paste. Apply it on the affected part and leave it for 10 to 15 minutes before washing it off.

For internal treatment, drink one cup of fresh aloe vera juice twice a day until the acne clears.

Toothache

The toothache can be instantly relieved by applying two to three drops of clove oil to the affected tooth. You can also put the drops on a piece of sterilised cotton ball and press it between the teeth. Gargling with salt water or slightly warm sesame oil can also relieve toothache.

Bad Breath

Drinking half a cup of aloe vera juice and eating a teaspoonful of fennel seeds can help reduce bad breath. You can also chew on peppermint or ginger to avoid this problem.

Bleeding

External bleeding can be arrested by applying ice or sandalwood paste. For stopping internal bleeding, patients are advised to drink warm milk with half a teaspoon of saffron and turmeric powder. This tip should be followed by consultation with a medical professional to ascertain the cause of bleeding so that appropriate measures can be taken.

Burning in the Eyes

Put four drops of rosewater or fresh aloe vera juice into the affected eye. You can also apply castor oil to the soles of the feet.

Boils

Applying a paste of ginger and turmeric powder directly on the boil or using cooked onions as a poultice can help a boil heal quickly.

These home remedies can work as effective antidotes and first aid treatments. You can try these therapies in the event of symptoms we discussed above to derive relief. It is advisable to consult an expert Ayurvedic physician for further treatment to identify and correct the underlying imbalances to restore optimum health.

Hydration and Its Importance for Maintaining Health

Ayurveda considers the quality of the water, its temperature, the time, and the way you drink it, to ensure you can achieve optimum body hydration.

Medical professionals across the world often advise people to drink at least 2 litres of water every day, leaving them the option to arbitrate between drinking water that flows from taps and drinking mineral water, the physicochemical composition of which is not always known.

It also counts all the liquids, including teas, coffee, fruit juices, carbonated beverages, herbal teas, and even the water contained in vegetables, while considering the total fluid intake needed to maintain the body's hydration.

Generally, no details are provided on how these liquids need to be consumed, when, and at what temperatures.

However, Ayurveda goes into the details of maintaining the body's hydration to teach us how much exactly you should be consuming, the exact types of fluids your body needs, the right time to drink water, and so on.

What Is the Right Way of Drinking Water According to Ayurveda?

Drinking water the right way is vital for maintaining hydration. Our body is made up of 50 to 70% water.

Here are some facts related to the body's water content that will help you realise why drinking water in optimum quantities is essential for maintaining health:

- The brain is comprised of nearly 74% of water
- Blood is composed of 83% of water
- Bones are made of 22% of water
- Lean muscles contain almost 75% of water

All the organs of the body need water to ensure proper hydration and functioning of the cells and tissues. Water also helps to regulate the body temperature. The body uses up water consumed by us during various digestive, metabolic, and other physiological processes such as breathing, absorption of foods, minerals, nutrients, sweating, etc.

This reason why rehydrating your body is significant is for ensuring the healthy functioning of the complete body system.

Now that you have realised the importance of drinking water for maintaining good health, let us learn what Ayurveda recommends for keeping ourselves well hydrated.

How Much Water Should You Drink Every Day to Meet the Body's Hydration Requirements?

According to Ayurveda, several rules need to be followed to ensure proper water intake to maintain the body's hydration. These rules also aim to maximise the benefits you would achieve through this healthy habit.

Read on to learn the proper ways to improve the body's hydration by increasing your fluid intake.

- The daily recommended intake of water for men is about 2.5 litres a day, while for women, it is 2 litres a day.
- Ayurveda recommends drinking water at room temperature or warm/hot. According to Ayurveda, drinking warm or hot water can help raise the body temperature, thus supporting the body's metabolic activities.
- Ayurveda does not advise drinking ice-cold water. The logic here is that the ice-cold water might put out your digestive fire, to which you may develop disturbances in the digestion

process.

Also, drinking cold water may cause several health issues in the short and long run. It may put you at risk of respiratory problems such as asthma, nasal congestion, common cold, sinusitis, and pharyngitis. It may also disturb your digestion and increase your chances of developing severe constipation, kidney failure, and heart issues.

- You should preferably consume water when seated instead of while standing. This posture would help in efficient absorption as well as distribution of water throughout the body.

- You should drink water in small sips. It should not be gulped down in bigger volumes or quick small breaths. Drinking water in small sips can help prevent gastric juice and blood dilution.

- Ayurveda advises us to drink water as and when we feel thirsty. Any person's daily water intake will be fulfilled if they drink sufficient water whenever the body asks for it. You may stop drinking more water once your thirst has been quenched and you feel satisfied.

- The urine colour can indicate if you are adequately hydrated or not. If the urine is dark yellow, it means you need to drink more water to hydrate the body. If your body is sufficiently hydrated, urine colour would be light yellow or relatively clear.

- Your lips may also become dry and appear chapped if your body is not sufficiently hydrated. Being aware of these signs and modifying your water intake accordingly can be a great way to ensure your body is well hydrated.

It is good to have a gap of at least 45 minutes between your food and water intake. If you feel thirsty immediately after eating food, you can have the following fluids:

- After breakfast or mid-meal snack: Fresh fruit juice, preferably without sugar
- After lunch: Buttermilk, or yoghurt
- After dinner: Milk

These fluids do not contain a very high water amount, and they can also support your digestion.

- According to Ayurveda, water should be drunk between meals and not just before or after eating your meals. Drinking water just before or after meals can result in some ill effects. For example, drinking water before food may reduce digestion, while drinking water after food could increase assimilation and make you obese.

- Warm water should be consumed first in the morning before brushing your teeth. Drinking water on an empty stomach is believed to provide a high medicinal value.

You can drink at least two glasses of water every day the first thing in the morning. This step is particularly recommended for young and middle-aged people between 18 to 60 years.

This tip would aid digestion, improve your alertness levels, increase your energy levels, and help you be more active.

Maintaining the Body's Hydration Based on Your Constitution or Dosha

Discovering your dominant Ayurvedic dosha would allow you to understand your body's constitution and tendencies in a better way.

Even without turning to holistic medicine or Ayurveda, we all know when we experience water retention and when we tend to become easily dehydrated.

A person who has a tendency for water retention may need to balance their body's fluid levels by modifying their food habits, exercising more, and drinking less water; these strategies can work as natural and healthy diuretics.

At the same time, a person who tends to be dehydrated might benefit from supporting the body's absorption processes linked to water and fluids.

Being watchful of when your body tends to get dehydrated or overhydrated is the key to regulating your water intake to maintain the optimum hydration needed for supporting the physiological and metabolic processes.

The goal of identifying the doshas is also critical in this regard.

It can help you create a deeper level of self-awareness. It can allow you to discover a balanced approach to maintaining hydration and assessing its impact on your general health and wellbeing.

Once you understand how your constitution or tendencies affect your hydration, you can start adopting healthy water intake habits that would benefit your health in numerous ways.

Here are the recommendations by Ayurveda related to water intake based on the dominant dosha or Prakriti:

Vata Dosha

People with a dominant vata dosha usually tend to develop recurrent dehydration. They need to drink plenty of water and other fluids like herbal tea, green tea, and fruit juices throughout the day.

As the basic qualities of the vata dosha are dry, cool, and rough, sipping warm liquids and adding hydrating oils to the skin every day is also recommended for creating and maintaining fluid balance.

Some of the best beverages for pacifying the vata dosha include fresh ginger juice and green tea. You can add some freshly squeezed ginger juice to a glass of water. Sip the water throughout the day, preferably with chia seeds, to maintain hydration and help with absorption. To improve flavours, you may add sliced raspberries or strawberries.

Pitta Dosha

People with a dominant pitta dosha tend to run hot. They tend to sweat profusely and metabolise foods quickly, in which they lose liquids at a rapid speed.

To stay in balance, they can consume liquids at room temperature or eat cooling foods like watermelon, especially during the summer and hot spring months.

Also, when the body seems to be overheating, they need to cool the entire body by taking dips in water or taking a cold shower.

Some of the best beverages and foods for pacifying the pitta dosha include sipping on cucumber and watermelon juice. You can add a few drops of lemon juice and sprigs of mint to the water to enhance its flavours and soothe digestive processes.

Kapha Dosha

People with a dominant kapha dosha tend to retain more water and metabolise foods slowly. The qualities of kapha include cool, smooth, slow, soft, and stability.

To increase the digestive fire and stay in balance, you can consume warm liquids or add heating spices like ginger and cayenne to create spiced water that you can sip all day long.

As the body tends to retain water, it is also advisable to try yoga asana, saunas, and exercises to help water move throughout the body and prevent stagnation.

One of the best beverages for pacifying the kapha dosha is a steaming decaffeinated tea. You can also add ginger, a splash of cayenne, and a few drops of lemon juice to water and sip it throughout the day.

Ayurveda also recommends drinking lemon water and green tea to derive better benefits. Lemon water and green tea possess a very high medicinal potential owing to their therapeutic properties.

Let us look at the benefits of drinking green tea and lemon water and how they would help improve your hydration and general health.

What Are the Benefits of Drinking Lemon Water?

Nothing can be as refreshing as drinking a glass of lemon water on a hot sunny day. It can make you feel rejuvenated and help you forget the vows of summer. But, should you be restricting drinking lemon water only to the summer months?

Of course, not!

Lemon is such a wonderful gift by nature that you must drink lemon water every day irrespective of the season to stay healthy and feel fresh! Here are some more reasons why you must drink lemon water:

Improves Digestion

The main benefits of lemon water could be attributed to its ability to boost your digestion. Drinking lemon water, especially warm water, consumed first thing in the morning, is a perfect remedy to flush out all the toxins from your digestive system and rehydrate your body.

It will also enhance your body's digestive functions like the breakdown of food, assimilation, and absorption. You can feel ease in symptoms of digestive troubles too, like constipation, indigestion, bloating, and nausea.

The last one reminds me that lemon water is also a good recipe for countering the disgusting morning sickness that pregnant women feel!

Boosts the Immune System

Do you know what gives lemon its sour taste? It's citric acid rich in vitamin C! Lemons also provide a high amount of potassium. Both of these nutrients play an essential role in modulating your immune system.

Vitamin C strengthens the immune system's response against toxins and allergens and reduces the frequency and intensity of allergic diseases like asthma and dermatitis.

Drinking lemon water in the morning can enhance these benefits as this is the best time

of the day to give your digestive system a chance to absorb these nutrients efficiently. Plus, vitamin C is excellent for your adrenals. It can help reduce the harmful effects of mental and physical stress.

Improves Mineral Absorption

Vitamin C in lemon juice can enhance the absorption of minerals including iron, magnesium, sodium, calcium, and phosphorus, each of which performs a unique function in the body.

So, by simply drinking lemon water, you can ensure your body gets more benefits from what you eat!

Protects the Liver

The main functions of the liver, which include the digestion of foods and detoxification of your body, could be significantly enhanced by drinking lemon water. Interestingly, the liver gets extremely busy during sleep as sleeping allows the body enough time to restore and regenerate. In other words, the liver is better prepared in the morning to get the maximum benefits from lemon water.

So, the conclusion is drinking lemon water, especially in the morning, can help your liver perform its function most efficiently.

Weight Management

Drinking lemon water is an easy way to lose weight. It would create a sense of satiety in the stomach and reduce your calorie intake. The weight loss property of lemons could be attributed to their high pectin content. Pectin is a type of fibre that helps you feel fuller for longer.

You may add a spoonful of honey to your lemon water for better results.

Lemon water also raves up your metabolism, ensuring your body can burn up calories faster, allowing you to lose more weight in a shorter time span.

Plus, staying well dehydrated by drinking lemon juice can also reduce your risk of developing fatigue, headaches, and an overall low mood, common in dieters eating very low-calorie foods to lose weight.

This effect means drinking lemon water will help you stick to your healthy and nutritious weight loss diet and allow you to shed those extra pounds with ease.

What Are the Health Benefits of Green Tea?

Green tea is a "complete" beverage that encloses within itself a whole of your health. Such is the power of this drink that it can keep you healthy even in your older age, and prevent a range of acute and chronic disorders such as diabetes, hypertension, and even cancer.

Let us have a look at the health benefits of green tea.

Natural Antioxidant

Green tea is loaded with powerful free-radical fighting antioxidants like catechins and polyphenols. These substances increase the ability of the body to ward off diseases by slowing down the degeneration caused by advancing age.

Catechins and polyphenols from green tea stop the processes that can cause damage to the DNA, raise your cholesterol levels, and even lead to cancer. These antioxidants would also act as a natural vasodilator for blood vessels and improve their elasticity, thus reducing the risk of clogging.

Moreover, since green tea does not have to undergo processing, the natural antioxidants remain concentrated and intact, making it much more potent than other antioxidant-rich foods.

However, you must remember that adding milk to your green tea can reduce its antioxidant value. And since most of the health benefits of green tea come from its antioxidant activity, you must consume it without adding milk.

Boosts Immunity

Green tea is a perfect immunity booster. The chemicals in green tea could promote a person's health by enhancing the immune system's response against toxins in the environment like dust and pollutants and chemicals in food like preservatives and pesticides.

Green tea would also help relieve symptoms of allergic diseases like dermatitis, asthma, and rhinitis by strengthening the immune system's reaction against these allergens.

Green tea would provide considerable relief from autoimmune diseases like rheumatoid arthritis, psoriasis, and lupus.

Prevents Cancer

Green tea has immense potential to fight several forms of cancer. The antioxidants present in green tea have been found to shrink tumours' size. Green tea consumption would also lower the risk of lung cancer by almost 18%.

Regular consumption of green tea would also prevent stomach, oesophagal, pancreatic, prostate, and colon cancer.

Supports Heart Functions

Green tea possesses cardioprotective properties. It would protect the heart from damages caused by free radicals, preventing the risk of hypertension, heart attacks, and cardiac failure.

It might lower the level of cholesterol in the blood. Green tea would also burn off the harmful fats stored in the body and prevent them from forming deposits in the blood vessels.

These beneficial properties could help prevent heart attacks that can occur due to the narrowing of the arteries and the resulting loss of blood flow to the heart.

Controls Diabetes

Green tea has the potential to regulate the metabolic processes of the body. It would alter the metabolism of carbohydrates and keep blood sugar levels within normal limits.

Drinking green tea twice a day would prevent sudden spikes in blood sugar levels. Green tea may also control diabetes complications, such as diabetes nephropathy, diabetic neuropathy, and stroke.

These preventive benefits could be attributed to green tea's antioxidant action, which helps protect the kidneys, nerves, and other body tissues from damages caused by free radicals and high blood sugar levels.

Improves Digestion

Green tea works as a digestive stimulant. It would boost the functions of the digestive tract and reduce bloating and intestinal gas. It may also help reduce the symptoms of digestive disorders like ulcerative colitis and Crohn's disease.

Aids in Weight-Loss

Green tea is a perfect natural aid for losing weight. The fat oxidation properties of green tea can help a person lose several pounds in a short period.

The polyphenols in green tea create a fat-burning effect and also increase the metabolic rate. Both these actions can help improve the utilisation of calories by the body, thus reducing your weight.

Healthier Skin

The effect of advancing age on the skin could be reversed to a great extent by drinking green tea. This effect is perhaps the best health benefit of this drink!

Green tea would reduce or delay the appearance of wrinkles and fine lines and make the skin smoother and firmer. It would also provide a natural glow to the face and make a person look younger and more attractive.

It is thought to work by preventing the harmful effect of toxins on the skin by producing an antioxidant action and increasing the production of skin-protective collagen. The bioactive compounds in green tea would help you enjoy a youthful glow, even as you age!

There's still more!

- Green tea would improve the functions of your nervous system and boost your memory and intelligence, making you smarter
- It would improve your physical performance by increasing your stamina and strengthening

- the muscles
- It would act as a stimulant and help you feel fresh and rejuvenated
- Green tea may reduce your risk of Alzheimer's disease
- It would act as an antibacterial agent and lower your risk of infections
- It would delay the progression of Parkinson's disease

It's incredible to know how simple-looking drinks like water, green tea, and lemon water have such a vast treasure of health benefits and healing properties.

Electrolyte Homeostasis

Electrolytes play a crucial role in maintaining balance and homeostasis in the body. They help regulate neurological and myocardial functions, oxygen delivery, fluid balance, and acid-base balance while supporting other biological processes.

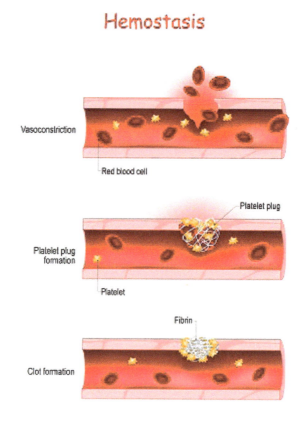

Electrolytes are critical as they are what the cells (particularly those of the nerves, heart, and muscles) use to maintain optimum voltages across the cell membranes to carry electrical impulses (muscle contractions and nerve impulses) across themselves as well as to other cells.

Electrolyte imbalances may develop due to diminished or increased ingestion and the high or reduced elimination of the electrolyte. The common cause of electrolyte imbalance is renal failure. The most severe disturbances in electrolyte levels could be abnormalities in the concentration of sodium, potassium, and calcium in the blood.

It is important to learn various minerals that play a role in sustaining the fluid and electrolyte balance in the body, as well as the signs and symptoms that can occur due to these minerals' increased or decreased levels to maintain electrolytes.

Read on to learn more about electrolyte imbalances, their causes and symptoms, and the proper ways to treat or prevent the abnormalities arising due to the same.

What Is Electrolyte Imbalance?

An electrolyte imbalance occurs when the body experiences an increase or a decrease the amount of water in circulation in blood or tissue fluids.

Electrolytes are minerals present in the blood and the organs and tissues of the body. The name electrolyte refers to minerals that tend to have an electrical charge, either positive or negative.

Consuming a rehydration drink often helps to rebalance the electrolyte levels in the body.

Let us now learn what electrolyte imbalances feel like, the signs to watch out for, and the Ayurvedic recommendations for preventing and treating electrolyte imbalances.

What Are Electrolytes?

Electrolytes are minerals in which the body needs to perform certain functions, such as:

- Balance its water level
- Remove waste products like toxins and by-products of metabolism
- Move nutrients like vitamins and antioxidants into the cells
- Enable muscles to contract and relax normally
- Allow nerves to carry signals
- Support the functions of the brain and heart

The body gets electrolytes from the foods and drinks we consume. The liver and kidneys play a crucial role in keeping the levels of electrolytes in balance to maintain homeostasis.

Eating a variety of foods, especially fresh fruits, and drinking adequate fluids are considered the best ways to maintain normal electrolytes levels in the blood and body tissues.

The typical examples of electrolytes in our body include:

- Sodium
- Calcium

- Potassium
- Phosphate
- Magnesium
- Bicarbonate
- Chloride

When the level of one or more of these electrolytes becomes too high or low, it leads to an electrolyte imbalance.

Electrolyte imbalance is not a disease. In fact, it is a sign of an underlying abnormality in the body.

What Are the Causes of Electrolyte Imbalances?

An electrolyte imbalance may occur when a person is dehydrated or has consumed too much water.

The factors that commonly cause electrolyte imbalances include:

- Severe vomiting
- Diarrhoea within frequent watery loose stools
- Not eating enough or fasting
- Not drinking enough fluids
- Excessive sweating
- Use of certain medications, like diuretics and laxatives
- Liver and kidney problems
- Eating disorders such as bulimia nervosa
- Congestive cardiac failure
- Undergoing cancer treatment

What Are the Signs and Symptoms of Electrolyte Imbalances?

The body responds to the imbalance in electrolyte levels in various ways. The effect may depend on the particular electrolytes in imbalance and the severity of the imbalance.

The person's pre-existing health conditions can also determine the symptoms they may develop.

The most common symptoms of electrolyte imbalance include:

- Fever, usually low grade
- Shortness of breath
- Swelling in the face, legs, and hands
- Confusion and lack of clarity in thinking
- Bloating
- An irregular heartbeat
- A rapid heart rate

Some other rare symptoms of electrolyte imbalance include:

- Fatigue
- Irritability
- Numbness and tingling in the hands and legs
- Rapid changes in the blood pressure
- Twitching and spasms of the muscles
- Muscle weakness
- Seizures

Electrolyte Imbalance in Children

Children tend to have a higher risk of developing dehydration than adults due to their smaller size and the faster rate of metabolism of electrolytes and fluids.

Suppose a child contracts an infection of the digestive system and gets sick, resulting in severe vomiting and diarrhoea. In that case, they may develop electrolyte imbalances that require immediate medical intervention. Children suffering from an underlying health condition affecting the functions of the thyroid gland, heart, and kidney often have a very high risk of developing an electrolyte imbalance.

If a child is at risk of developing dehydration and electrolyte imbalances, it is crucial to seek medical attention and follow the Ayurvedic treatment to maintain homeostasis.

Electrolyte Imbalances in Older Adults

Older adults are usually more susceptible to developing dehydration and an electrolyte imbalance than younger adults.

There are several reasons responsible for this, such as:

- The kidneys tend to lose some of their functioning with advancing age.
- Older adults usually have to take multiple medications, like diuretics, to modify their fluid and electrolyte levels.
- Older people may not eat enough food or drink enough liquids due to disability, reduced appetite, thirst, or lack of regular access to foods and drinks.

Close family members, caregivers, and loved ones are advised to closely watch older adults for the signs of dehydration. They might need to monitor whether the person is eating enough food and drinking enough fluids.

The common signs of dehydration in older adults may include:

- Dryness of the mouth, especially of the lips or tongue
- Drowsiness
- Sunken eyes
- Skin that looks too dry and less stretchy or firm
- Disorientation
- Confusion
- Low blood pressure
- Dizziness

Treatment of Electrolyte Imbalance

The treatment of electrolyte imbalances should aim to replenish the electrolytes that are deficient and eliminating those in excess. Ayurveda recommends maintaining an optimum balance of fluids and electrolytes in the body for maintaining homeostasis.

Let us learn more about the concept of electrolytic homeostasis and imbalances as recommended by Ayurveda.

Management of Electrolyte Imbalances

- If a person becomes sick due to a short bout of vomiting and loose motion or has been sweating profusely, drinking plenty of water or an over-the-counter electrolyte solution could help restore the balance of critical electrolytes.

- There are several oral rehydration drinks available in stores. In most cases, the intake of these drinks is sufficient for relieving the signs of a mild electrolyte imbalance, with minimal or mild symptoms.

- Some patients may develop electrolyte imbalance due to a health condition affecting the kidneys or heart.

- In such cases, it is still possible to correct the imbalance over a few days to weeks by adopting healthy dietary habits and modifying the intake of foods and drinks based on the specific deficiency or excess of minerals.

- It is also essential to monitor the progress to ensure the person receives the correct amounts of electrolytes through dietary sources.

- It should be noted that taking in a very high amount of electrolytes may create an imbalance of other electrolytes and lead to severe complications.

- Also, some patients may require additional treatments such as herbal remedies to address the underlying disorder affecting the vital organs.

- If a person has severe kidney disease, they may also need dialysis to correct the electrolyte imbalance.

Home Remedies for the Management of Electrolyte Imbalances

If a person is mildly dehydrated, they can consume a rehydration drink to restore the balance of electrolyte levels.

You can also prepare your oral rehydration solution at home using ingredients commonly available in your kitchen.

The oral rehydration drink can be prepared at home by mixing one litre of water in one teaspoon of salt and two tablespoons of sugar. You can drink this liquid several times a day to restore fluid balance, mainly if the imbalance has occurred due to severe vomiting and loose motions.

Ayurveda also offers a host of natural remedies that you can try when you lose electrolytes like sodium, chloride, and potassium to replenish them faster and effectively!

Here are some recommendations that would help you avoid electrolyte imbalances:

- The first cup of water you drink in the morning should be slightly warm. You may squeeze in a spoonful of lime juice and add a pinch of Himalayan salt

- Drink one glass of pomegranate juice with a spoonful of cardamom powder and a squeeze of lime

- Drink one glass of coconut water every day to support detoxification and elimination of unwanted toxins and excess minerals

- Steep mint leaves in boiled water, add lime juice, maple syrup, and a pinch of Himalayan salt

- Drink warm milk with a pinch of cardamom, a little maple syrup, coconut sugar, and rose water

- Drink cilantro juice added with chopped or blended cucumbers, and apple chunks

- Drink a glass of cucumber juice after lunch

- Drink a glass of cold milk after dinner

- Avoid using ice in your beverages! Drinking icy liquids can make it difficult for your intestine to absorb them. If you use ice, you might feel like you did not drink enough water, making you drink excessively.

Conclusion

Healthy adults and children with mild dehydration often find that drinking a homemade rehydration solution helps to replenish their electrolyte levels.

Suppose the imbalance is caused due to a health condition. In that case, you can use appropriate herbal remedies that possess the medicinal properties needed to correct the underlying dosha and restore the affected organs' optimum functioning.

Vitamin Deficiencies

A well-balanced, nutritious diet offers several benefits. On the other hand, people who consume a diet lacking essential nutrients often develop several unpleasant signs and symptoms.

Ayurveda believes that these symptoms could be the body's way of communicating the potential vitamins and minerals deficiencies to make you aware of the same. Recognising these signs, some of which could be subtle, would help you adjust your dietary habits accordingly.

Ayurveda strongly recommends eating a healthy and nutritious diet. Such a diet is complete, comprising essential vitamins, minerals, and other nutrients to maintain good health.

Let us look at the most common signs of nutritional deficiencies and the proper ways to address them as recommended by the Ayurvedic system of medicine.

Bleeding Gums

Most often, a rough technique of brushing teeth is the primary cause of bleeding gums. However, a diet deficient in vitamin C may also be blamed.

Vitamin C plays a vital role in immunity and wound healing. It also acts as an antioxidant and helps to prevent cellular damage. The body does not make its own vitamin C. Hence, the only way to ensure your body gets adequate nutrient levels is through dietary sources.

Vitamin C deficiencies are rare in people who consume fresh fruits and vegetables. However, it is common for the routine screenings of healthy people to show a low vitamin C level. Nearly 13 to 30% of the population has lower levels of vitamin C. In comparison, five to 17% of them have severe deficiency of this nutrient.

Ayurveda strongly advises consuming vitamin C-rich foods like fresh citrus fruits.

Eating minimal vitamin C through your diet for extended periods may bring on severe deficiency symptoms, such as bleeding gums and tooth loss. Another serious complication of severe vitamin C deficiency is scurvy which suppresses the immune system and weakens muscles. It can also affect the health and strength of the muscles and bones, making you feel sluggish and fatigued all the time.

Other common signs of vitamin C deficiency include easy bruising, dry, scaly skin, slow wound healing, and frequent nosebleed.

You can avoid these symptoms by ensuring you consume enough foods containing vitamin C.

Ayurveda advises people to eat at least two pieces of fresh fruit and 3 to 4 portions of vegetables every day.

Brittle Nails and Hair

A variety of factors can cause brittleness of the hair and nails, and one of the most common among them is the lack of vitamin B7 (biotin).

Biotin can help the body convert foods into a usable source of energy.

A biotin deficiency is rare. However, it can cause brittleness, thinning, and splitting of the hair and nails when it occurs. Some other symptoms of biotin deficiency include fatigue, muscle pains, cramps, and tingling in the hands and legs.

Pregnant women, people with digestive disorders such as Crohn's disease, and heavy smokers and drinkers are at a higher risk of developing biotin deficiency. Moreover, prolonged use of anti-seizure medications and antibiotics could also be a risk factor.

Surprisingly, people who eat raw egg whites regularly can also develop biotin deficiency as they contain avidin, a protein that can bind to biotin, thus reducing its absorption.

Ayurveda advises people to eat foods rich in biotic such as egg yolks, broccoli, cauliflower, dairy, nuts, seeds, spinach, sweet potatoes, yeast, bananas, and whole grains.

Poor Night Vision

Poor night vision coupled with the abnormal white growths on the eyes' surface is a sign of a deficiency of some nutrients. A nutrient-poor diet may also cause severe vision problems.

For example, a lower intake of vitamin A often links to a disorder called night blindness that reduces the ability of a person to see in dim lights and darkness. This state is because vitamin A is essential for the production of rhodopsin, a pigment found in the eye's retina. This pigment helps us see at night.

If left untreated, night blindness may progress, resulting in complications like xerophthalmia, a disorder that occurs due to the damage to the cornea, ultimately leading to blindness.

Another early sign of xerophthalmia is Bitot's spots. These are slightly raised, white, foamy growths occurring on the conjunctiva or the white part of the eye. These growths can be removed only to a certain extent. They can disappear entirely only once the deficiency of vitamin A is corrected.

Fortunately, vitamin A deficiency is rare nowadays, especially in developed countries. People who suspect their intake of vitamin A is inadequate may eat more vitamin-A-rich foods, like dark leafy greens, dairy, eggs, or yellow or orange-coloured vegetables.

Also, unless diagnosed with a deficiency of vitamin A, you should avoid using vitamin A supplements because it is a fat-soluble vitamin. If consumed in excess, it can accumulate in your body's fat stores, causing toxicity. The signs of vitamin A toxicity could be severe and include headaches, nausea, joint and bone pains, skin irritation, and sometimes, even coma and death.

Mouth Ulcers

Ulcers in the mouth or cracks at the corners of the mouth can show nutritional deficiencies. Lesions in the oral cavity or around the mouth may be linked to insufficient intake of some vitamins or minerals.

For example, mouth ulcers, commonly referred to as canker sores, are usually the result of a deficiency in B vitamins and iron.

Also, it has been observed that patients with oral ulcers tend to be more prone to have lower iron levels. Additionally, around 28% of people with mouth ulcers have deficiencies of one or more B vitamins, including thiamine (vitamin B1), pyridoxine (vitamin B6), and riboflavin (vitamin B2).

Angular cheilitis, a disorder that causes cracks at the corners of the mouth and splitting or bleeding, usually occurs due to excess salivation and dehydration. However, it may also occur due to insufficient B vitamins, especially riboflavin and iron.

Ayurvedic recommendations for managing these signs include eating iron-rich foods such as dark leafy greens, legumes, nuts, whole grains, and seeds. You can also increase your intake of healthy natural sources of riboflavin, thiamine, and pyridoxine like whole grains, eggs, dairy, starchy vegetables, legumes, green vegetables, nuts, and seeds.

Scaly Patches

Dandruff and scaly patches can occur in people who lack skin-friendly nutrients.

Seborrhoeic dermatitis (SB) and dandruff are part of the same category of skin diseases that affect the oil-producing tissues of the body. Both these diseases involve itching and flaking of the skin. Dandruff is usually restricted to the scalp, while seborrheic dermatitis may also affect the skin of the face, armpits, upper chest, and groin.

The chances of developing these skin disorders are higher within the first three months of life and during mid-adulthood and puberty. It is estimated that nearly 50% of adults and 42% of infants tend to develop seborrheic dermatitis or dandruff at one point of time in their life.

Dandruff and seborrheic dermatitis can occur due to many causes. The nutrient-poor diet is the most common among them. For instance, a low blood level of zinc, riboflavin (vitamin B2), and pyridoxine (vitamin B6) might play a role.

As the close link between these skin conditions and the nutrient-poor diet has been established, it would be advisable to consume more of the nutrients you are deficient in to restore the healthy appearance of the skin and reduce flakiness and itching.

Foods rich in niacin, pyridoxine, and riboflavin include whole grains, eggs, legumes, green vegetables, dairy, starchy vegetables, seeds, and nuts. Dairy, nuts, legumes, and whole grains are some excellent sources of zinc mineral.

Red Bumps on the Skin

Red or white bumps on the skin could be a sign of keratosis pilaris. This condition results in the appearance of goosebump-like bumps on the cheeks, thighs, arms, or buttocks. Ingrown or corkscrew hairs often accompany these tiny bumps. This condition usually appears in childhood and disappears naturally in adulthood.

The common cause of these bumps is too much keratin production in the hair follicles. Keratosis pilaris may also have a genetic component, which means a person is more likely to develop it if their family member has it. It has also been observed that people eating a diet low in vitamins A and C are more likely to develop these symptoms.

Hence, in addition to the traditional treatments with soothing Ayurvedic creams and lotions, patients with keratosis pilaris can also consider including foods rich in vitamins A and C in their diet. These foods may include dairy, eggs, dark leafy greens, fruits, and yellow- or orange-coloured vegetables.

Hair Loss

Hair loss is a common symptom affecting nearly 50% of the adult population worldwide.

Ayurveda recommends eating a diet rich in the following essential nutrients to prevent or slow down hair loss:

- Iron: This mineral helps in DNA synthesis, including the DNA synthesis in the hair follicles. The iron deficiency may cause hair to stop growing and fall out.

- Zinc: This mineral is needed for cell division and protein synthesis. These two processes play a crucial role in hair growth. As such, the deficiency of zinc may cause severe hair loss.

- Alpha-linolenic acid (ALA): It is one of the essential fatty acids required for supporting hair growth and preventing hair loss.

- Biotin (vitamin B7): This is another vitamin B, which, when deficient, could be linked to severe hair loss.

- Niacin (vitamin B3): This nutrient is essential for keeping your hair healthy. Alopecia, a disease in which the hairs tend to fall out in patches, could be one of the expected consequences of niacin deficiency.

Foods rich in iron and zinc include eggs, nuts, seeds, legumes, dark leafy greens, and whole grains. Some of the best niacin-rich foods are legumes, nuts, dairy, whole grains, seeds, and leafy greens, while foods rich in biotin include egg yolk and organ meat. Nuts, leafy vegetables, walnuts, chia seeds, flaxseeds, soy nuts, vegetable oils, and whole grains are all rich in ALA.

Conclusion

A diet providing sufficient vitamins and minerals could protect you against several symptoms linked to nutrient deficiencies. Ayurveda strongly recommends increasing your intake of healthy foods rich in vitamins and minerals to resolve or reduce your symptoms.

What Is Anaemia?

Anaemia is a common disorder caused due to reduced red blood cell count and lower haemoglobin levels.

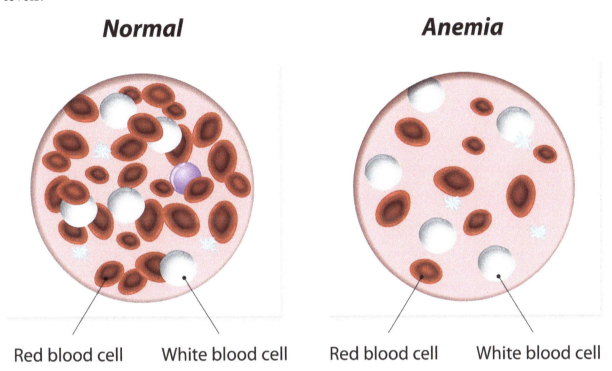

For men, it can be is defined as a haemoglobin level of fewer than thirteen grams per 100 ml. It can be defined as a haemoglobin level of fewer than twelve grams per 100 ml in women. Here is a detailed description of the causes, symptoms, complications, and diagnosis of anaemia and ways to prevent and treat it.

What Are the Predisposing Factors for Anaemia?

The risk of this disease is higher in females compared to males. The higher risk in women could be attributed to the loss of blood during normal menstruation. Other factors that can worsen anaemia include recurring internal bleeding from the organs such as the colon and stomach due to disorders like colon cancer and peptic ulcers.

The treatment of anaemia must be aimed at detecting the exact cause or predisposing factor. It is essential to identify if the low haemoglobin level is due to recurring bleeding, as in the case of peptic ulcers or colon cancer. Appropriate treatment must be administered according to the cause of anaemia combined with the primary therapy for replenishing haemoglobin levels to derive long-term results.

If the root cause of bleeding is unattended, the patient may continue to suffer from anaemia despite receiving treatment.

Common Signs and Symptoms of Anaemia

Patients with mild anaemia usually do not develop any noticeable symptoms. However, in severe cases, this disease may cause signs and symptoms such as unusual tiredness, extreme weakness, pallor of the skin or nails, shortness of breath, or palpitations.

What Are the Risk Factors or Causes of Anaemia?

The common causes of anaemia include reduced production of red blood cells (RBCs) in the body.

A lower level of haemoglobin is also a common risk factor for anaemia. This condition may also occur due to the loss of haemoglobin or RBCs due to excessive internal bleeding, wounds, or external injuries. Here are some more risk factors that can increase the risk of anaemia:

- Deficiency of nutrients in the diet: people who consume a diet consistently low in nutrients like iron, folate, and vitamin B12 are at a higher risk of developing anaemia.

- Iron deficiency is one of the most typical causes of anaemia because iron is an essential component needed for haemoglobin synthesis. Loss of blood and a shortage of this nutrient in your regular diet could also reduce the iron level in the blood and worsen the risk of developing anaemia. Hence, patients diagnosed with this illness are advised to improve their iron intake by consuming foods rich in this mineral.

- Age: the incidence of anaemia is higher in people above the age of 65 years.

- Menstruation: It has been found that women at premenopausal age or those having late menopause have a higher risk of iron deficiency anaemia than postmenopausal women and men. This situation could be attributed to the regular menstrual cycles that cause the loss of RBCs or red blood cells.

- Pregnancy: Pregnancy is one of the leading causes of anaemia in women. The risk is even higher in women who do not consume a balanced diet with natural iron and folic acid sources.

- Intestinal disorders: a pre-existing intestinal condition that interferes with the absorption of nutrients in the small intestine like Crohn's disease or celiac disease can increase the likelihood of developing anaemia.

- Chronic conditions: patients with cancer or renal failure are at risk of anaemia. These conditions cause anaemia by creating a shortage of RBCs.

- Ulcerations: ulcer formation in the body tissues such as the intestine, stomach, or oral cavity could lead to slow and continuous blood loss from the affected site. This ailment can deplete your body's reserves of iron, thus increasing the risk of iron deficiency anaemia.

- Family history: anaemia is higher in patients with a family history of the same disease. Some forms of anaemia, like sickle cell anaemia, are known to run in families as these are genetically-linked disorders.

- Other factors: the risk of anaemia may worsen temporarily during an acute bout of infections. Other diseases known to cause anaemia include blood disorders, autoimmune disorders, exposure to toxins such as harmful chemicals, and alcoholism. The use of certain medications can also cause anaemia by affecting the production of red blood cells.

- Bone marrow dysfunction: Aplastic anaemia, another common form of anaemia, occurs due to bone marrow failure. It may also result from an inadequate formation of red blood cells, platelets, and white blood cells by the tissues of the bone marrow.

Depending on their causes or characteristics, some other types of anaemia include sickle cell anaemia and pernicious anaemia.

How Can You Diagnose Anaemia?

Anaemia is often diagnosed when a person visits a doctor due to systemic complaints like weakness and fatigue. It is also diagnosed during a routine examination of pregnant women. The general symptoms like fatigue, weakness, and the medical and family history of the patient, and the physical examination that reveals pallor and blood tests can help diagnose anaemia. The following tests may be performed for the diagnosis of this condition.

- Complete blood count (CBC): This test is performed to count the number of blood cells in the sample of your blood. Anaemia can be diagnosed when red blood cells, hematocrit, and haemoglobin levels are lower than average.

    In normal adults, hematocrit values are between 40% and 52% for men and 35% and 47% for women. The average haemoglobin values are 14-18 grams per deciliter and 12-16 grams per deciliter for men and women, respectively.

- Other tests can also be performed to determine the size and shape of the red blood cells. An unusual size, colour, and shape of the blood cells can help diagnose the type of anaemia.

- Additional diagnostic tests may be recommended to detect the cause of bleeding. For example, an esophagogastroduodenoscopy is performed to diagnose stomach ulcers, while a colonoscopy with biopsy can help detect colon cancer and ulcerative colitis.

The Possible Complications of Anaemia

Haemoglobin plays a role in the transportation of oxygen to the cells, organs, and tissues in the body. It can combine with oxygen to form oxyhaemoglobin. The haemoglobin present in the cells later releases oxygen as the blood circulates to different organs.

Therefore, normal haemoglobin levels must be maintained to ensure an adequate oxygen supply to organs and tissues. However, this function could be hampered when the patients develop iron deficiency anaemia.

Lower haemoglobin levels may affect oxygen supply to vital tissues like the heart, kidneys, and brain. If this condition is not managed correctly, it could lead to unpleasant symptoms, including chest pain, a decline in cognitive functions, confusion, and a reduced attention span or ability to focus.

The reduced oxygen supply to the skin, scalp, and hair roots may also lead to additional symptoms such as hair loss, the appearance of wrinkles and fine lines, greying of hair, split ends, and so on at an earlier age. It may also worsen breathing difficulties leading to life-threatening situations.

Treatment Options Available for Anaemia

The best and the most effective way to manage anaemia is to ensure the body receives a good supply of nutrients, such as iron, folate, and vitamin Bs. You may also use herbal remedies that possess a rich iron content to replenish the depleting iron reserves in your body. Regular use of herbs containing iron and folate is recommended for females who suffer from increased menstrual flow due to conditions such as polymenorrhea or menorrhagia. It can help prevent anaemia caused due to the excessive loss of blood during menses.

Aplastic anaemia can be managed well by using herbs that can improve the functions of the bone marrow.

Finding suitable herbal remedies that can manage the primary cause of anaemia forms the basis of the natural treatments recommended by Ayurveda. It can allow patients to avoid the signs and complications of anaemia safely and effectively.

Here is the list of herbs you can use to manage anaemia. These herbs possess various medicinal properties that can help improve your RBC and haemoglobin levels and provide relief from the symptoms of this disease.

- **Mustak:** Ayurvedic treatment using herbs like Mustak could inhibit the complications of this disease with its rich iron content.

- **Amala:** It is an effective herbal medicine for anaemia that is caused due to the damage or destruction of the RBCs due to exposure to toxins, pollutants in the air, and free radicals.

- **Draksha:** Patients diagnosed with myelodysplastic anaemia may use Draksha to derive relief from the signs and symptoms like pallor, breathlessness, unusual bleeding, and palpitations.

- **Punarnava:** this herb is specifically recommended for the management of autoimmune anaemia. It is believed to work by regulating and improving the functions of the immune cells.

- **Kumari:** Ayurvedic herbal remedies like Kumari could help arrest bleeding and prevent anaemia by promoting the ability of the blood to form clots.

- **Haritaki:** the symptoms of Pernicious anaemia can be managed effectively by using Haritaki. It is particularly recommended for patients who suffer from gastric ulcers characterised by persistent blood loss from the lesions.

- **Shatavari:** Shatavari may improve the prognosis of patients diagnosed with aplastic anaemia by enhancing RBC production by the bone marrow.

- **Guduchi:** Guduchi offers a safe and natural treatment for patients with sickle cell anaemia. It is believed to work by supplying a higher amount of iron to your body and improving haemoglobin level.

Is it Possible to Prevent Anaemia?

One of the most effective ways to prevent anaemia is to ensure the body receives an adequate supply of iron and folate through a balanced diet.

Some dietary sources of iron and folate include:

- Dark green leafy vegetables like chard and spinach
- Meat
- Tofu
- Poultry
- Beans

- Dried fruits
- Fish
- Iron-fortified foods like cereals and bread

It is also important to undergo routine tests and appropriate treatment for conditions that worsen anaemia, such as peptic ulcers.

Anticoagulant Effect and Blood Coagulation

Blood coagulation is one of the body's defence mechanisms that help prevent excessive blood loss. However, it happens to be a double-edged weapon as abnormal blood clotting may put you at risk of developing disorders like heart attacks and stroke.

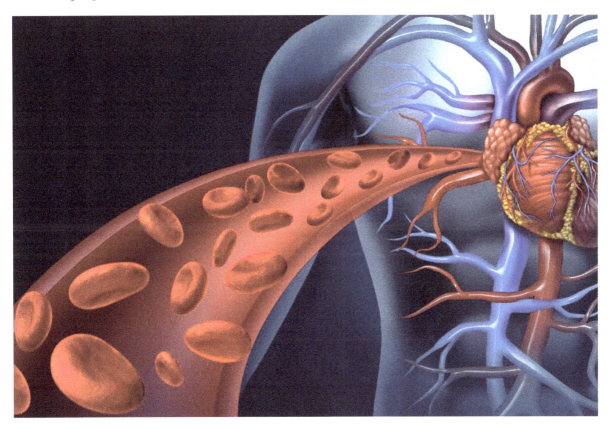

The body also has an inherent mechanism aimed at preventing abnormal blood clotting. Hence, we can prevent the formation of a clot inside a healthy blood vessel having a regular blood flow through it.

There is a need to understand the normal blood coagulation and anticoagulation processes and why both coagulation and anticoagulation are essential defence mechanisms.

Keep reading to learn more about the coagulation effect and the natural Ayurvedic remedies that can be used to restore healthy clotting mechanisms to protect yourself against the diseases linked to abnormal clotting or bleeding.

What Is Blood Coagulation?

Coagulation is a physiological process, which involves the formation of a blood clot. The appearance of the blood clot is usually referred to as the secondary haemostasis, as it makes up the second phase in the process of arresting blood loss from a ruptured blood vessel in the event of trauma, injury, or accident.

What Are the Stages of Coagulation?

The first stage of coagulation, called primary haemostasis, is characterised by the constriction of the blood vessels (vasoconstriction) and aggregation of platelets at the site of trauma, injury, or rupture.

Under abnormal circumstances, a clot may form in a blood vessel that has not been damaged or breached. Such abnormal clots can cause an occlusion or blockage in the blood vessel, resulting in thrombosis.

Clotting is the sequential process, which involves the interactions between numerous blood components known as the coagulation factors. There are thirteen main coagulation factors, each designated with a Roman numeral, starting from I to XIII.

Coagulation is initiated when two separate pathways are activated, called the extrinsic and intrinsic pathways.

Keep reading to learn more about these pathways and the processes involved in blood coagulation.

The Coagulation of Blood

Blood coagulation refers to a process that converts the substances circulating within the blood vessel into an insoluble gel-like plug. The gel plugs can leak into the damaged blood vessels causing the bleeding to stop. These processes occur in the presence of coagulation factors, phospholipids, and calcium.

The coagulation factors are nothing but proteins. They are primarily manufactured in the liver. Ionized calcium (Ca++) available in the blood and intracellular sources can also support these processes.

Phospholipids are the prominent components of platelet and cellular membranes. They help in the coagulation by providing a surface on which a chemical reaction of coagulation can occur.

As discussed earlier, coagulation is initiated by either of the two distinct pathways called the intrinsic and extrinsic pathways. Events taking place inside the lumen of the blood vessel activate the intrinsic pathway. This pathway can occur only in the presence of elements such as clotting factors, calcium ions, and platelets that are inherent to (within) the vascular system.

On the other hand, the extrinsic pathway is another route to activate coagulation. It occurs in the presence of the Tissue Factor (called tissue thromboplastin), a substance extrinsic to or outside the blood vessel. This behaviour means it is not usually found circulating in a blood vessel. The Tissue Factor is released only when the vessel wall is damaged or ruptured.

Irrespective of whether it is the intrinsic or the extrinsic pathway starting the coagulation process, the completion of the process tends to follow a common course. This standard course or path involves stimulating factors including X, V, XIII, II, and I.

Both these pathways play critical roles in maintaining normal haemostasis in the body.

Positive feedback loops exist between these two pathways, which amplify the reactions to produce an adequate amount of fibrin needed to form a life-saving plug or clot. A deficiency or abnormalities in one or more factors can slow down the overall coagulation process, thus increasing the risk of excessive blood loss or haemorrhage.

The coagulation factors have been numbered in the order of they were discovered.

Though there are 13 roman numerals for coagulation factors, there are only 12 factors. Factor VI was later found to be just a part of another factor and hence, excluded from the list of coagulation factors.

The following are the coagulation factors along with their common names:

- Factor XIII (or fibrin-stabilizing factor)
- Factor XII (or Hageman factor)
- Factor XI (or plasma thromboplastin antecedent)
- Factor X (or Stuart-Prower factor)
- Factor IX (or Christmas factor, plasma thromboplastin component)
- Factor VIII (or antihemophilic factor)
- Factor VII (or proconvertin, stable factor)
- Factor V (or proaccelerin, labile factor)
- Factor IV (or ionized calcium)
- Factor III (or tissue thromboplastin)
- Factor II (or prothrombin)
- Factor I (or fibrinogen)

A person's liver must be in good health to use vitamin K to produce clotting factors IX, II, VII, and X.

Vitamin K is readily available in several dietary sources, including plant and animal sources. This nutrient is also produced in the intestinal gut flora. A deficiency of vitamin K is rare, though it may occur in some cases as described below:

- In newborns, they must have to first develop normal gut flora to form vitamin K
- When the gut flora is disrupted due to the excessive or recurrent use of broad-spectrum antibiotics

At birth and later during childhood, Factor VIII levels are the same as those in adults. The levels of several other factors tend to be below the adult levels at birth, with some of them being as low as just 10% of the adult values. These levels slowly increase toward the adult values by the age of six months. However, they remain slightly below the adult average values throughout childhood.

Children and newborn babies do not usually develop excessive blood loss despite having lower levels. This matter confers some extent of anti-thrombotic protection during adolescence.

During pregnancy, the levels of Factor XI may decrease, though the levels of factor VIII and fibrinogen rise.

It is crucial to understand how clotting levels factor change during different phases of life to learn the risk of specific clotting and bleeding disorders at different ages.

Coagulation disorders occur due to disruptions in the ability of the body to control the blood clotting processes. Coagulation disorders often result in a haemorrhage (too little clotting resulting in an increased chance of excessive bleeding) and thrombosis (too much clotting, which causes abnormal blood clots to be formed in the blood vessels resulting in the obstruction to the blood flow). These clotting disorders may develop due to several underlying conditions.

Common causes of coagulation disorders that can result in bleeding include:

- Von Willebrand disease: This disorder derives from the clotting factor protein in the blood known as the von Willebrand factor. This condition is usually genetic and often passed down from one or both the parents to the child. It results in excessive bleeding due to the low levels of the von Willebrand factor in the blood.
- Haemophilia: It is a bleeding disorder, which occurs due to the inability of the blood to clot normally. It usually affects children. Children with haemophilia tend to have a low level of a clotting factor protein that is necessary for the process of clot formation.

- Disseminated intravascular coagulation: This disorder is known to cause excessive abnormal clotting in the blood vessel. This leads to obstruction of the flow of blood through them.

- Other clotting factor deficiencies: A lower than the expected level of clotting factor proteins excluding those responsible for the development of haemophilia can also result in excessive bleeding.

- Increased secretion of anticoagulants: This state can cause diminished blood clotting, resulting in a condition characterised by similar symptoms to haemophilia.

- Liver diseases: Liver diseases comprise several conditions that impair hepatic functions. The organ is unable to use vitamin K to form clotting factors.

- Platelet dysfunctions: Platelets play a vital role in forming blood clots. Excessive bleeding and bruising may occur if the platelet count is too low or if these cells are not working correctly.

- Vitamin K deficiency: The deficiency in vitamin K, which is common in breast-fed infants, may impair blood clotting processes.

Common causes of coagulation disorders that lead to excessive clotting include:

- Protein S or Protein C deficiency: Protein S and protein C help regulate the clotting and bleeding systems. The lower levels of these proteins can cause the blood to form clots too often.

- Antithrombin III deficiency: Antithrombin III can help regulate the clotting and bleeding systems. Antithrombin III deficiency is a genetic disorder caused due to the lower levels of antithrombin III, resulting in excessive blood clotting.

- Factor V Leiden stimulation: It is a genetic disorder characterised by the overstimulation of the blood-clotting protei. Sometimes called the factor V Leiden, it results in the excessive or frequent clotting of the blood.

- Antiphospholipid antibody syndrome: It is an autoimmune disorder that causes an increase in the levels of specific blood proteins that can worsen the risk of abnormal clotting.

- Prothrombin gene mutation: This is sometimes called a factor II mutation. A prothrombin gene mutation is a rare genetic disorder – the mutation results in excessive clotting factors being produced in the body resulting in increased abnormal clotting.

What Are the Symptoms of Coagulation Disorders and Difficulty in Clotting?

- Presence of blood in the stools or urine
- Bruising excessively and easily
- An injury that takes longer to stop bleeding
- Nosebleeds without any apparent cause
- Extreme fatigue
- Joint pains caused due to internal bleeding
- Prolonged bleeding from minor cuts or dental work or surgery
- A severe headache that does not go away
- Vision problems, like double vision
- Sudden pain, warmth, and swelling in the muscles and joints
- Repeated vomiting

What Are the Common Symptoms of Coagulation Disorders and Increased Clotting?

- A Stroke or Heart Attack at a Very Young Age
- Recurrent Stillbirth or Miscarriages
- Deep Vein Thrombosis

A blood clot in the body's deep veins is sometimes called deep vein thrombosis (DVT). The symptoms of DVT include:

- Pain in the affected area of the body
- Redness of the affected part
- Swelling in one hand or leg
- Warmth of the skin

Pulmonary Embolism

An abnormal blood clot that has travelled to the lung tissues. The symptoms of a pulmonary embolism include:

- Fast heartbeat
- Shortness of breath
- Chest pain

Which Are the Test Ayurvedic Herbal Remedies for the Treatment of Clotting and Bleeding Disorders?

Turmeric

Curcumin, an active compound in turmeric, is known to help regulate the functions of the platelets and prevent abnormal clotting.

The medicinal properties of curcumin can also help relieve the pain in the muscles and joints caused due to the formation of clots.

The bioactive properties of turmeric can be attributed to the various therapeutic components obtained from its rhizome. This herb acts as a natural anti-thrombotic agent and supports the modulation of several factors, which aid in clotting.

Garlic

Garlic has a rich content of sulfur compounds that can melt or disintegrate abnormal blood clots.

Consuming one raw clove of garlic every morning can effectively regulate blood clotting and prevent excessive bleeding.

Garlic also works on the smooth muscles of the blood vessels causing them to dilate and relax, thus lowering blood pressure. It also acts as a natural blood thinner and prevents blood clots in the patients at a higher risk for stroke and heart attacks due to abnormal clotting.

Cayenne

Cayenne pepper acts as a natural blood thinner. Thanks to medicinal compounds like salicylates and capsaicin, it has a practical impact on the body.

Capsaicin in cayenne pepper can help promote blood circulation, thus preventing blood clots formation. These compounds also help clear away the artery-narrowing cholesterol deposits and dilate the arteries and small blood vessels, thereby clearing away the clots.

Arjun ki Chhaal

Arjun ki Chhaal, also called Terminalia Arjuna, is an effective natural remedy for managing blood clotting. It is a blood thinner that can ensure the smooth flow of blood through all organs by preventing abnormal clotting of blood.

All you need to do is soak a small piece of Arjun ki Chhaal bark in warm water for a few minutes and drink this water once every morning.

This herb can promote stronger contractions of the cardiac muscles, allowing the heart to pump blood more efficiently, thereby preventing stagnation, which is responsible for triggering abnormal clotting.

Chia Seeds and Flax Seeds

These are tiny seeds full of healthy fats such as omega-3 fatty acids, which can help in preventing abnormal blood clotting and improving blood circulation.

Flaxseeds also help in the formation of platelets that are involved in clotting. It also makes the platelets less sticky, thus preventing clotting. These seeds might also reduce risks of atherosclerosis; a condition caused by the hardening of the arteries due to cholesterol plaques deposited along the walls of the blood vessels.

Chia seeds are known to act as natural blood thinners. They are packed with essential nutrients, like omega-3 fatty acids, considered healthy for the heart.

Conclusion

It is essential to ensure your body is protected against the risk of both abnormal clotting as well as bleeding. Regular use of these natural herbs would optimise these processes, thus protecting you against the risk of excessive blood loss, heart attacks, stroke, DVT, and other diseases caused due to increased clotting or bleeding.

Ayurvedic Approach to the Treatment of Diabetes

Diabetes mellitus is a metabolic disorder that causes an increase in blood sugar levels. A hormone called insulin is responsible for moving the carbohydrates from the blood into the cells for energy or storage. Diabetes develops when the body can neither produce enough insulin nor use the insulin it creates effectively.

If left untreated, the high blood sugar level caused due to diabetes may result in damage to the nerves, kidneys, eyes, and other vital organs of the body, resulting in serious complications.

What Are the Types of Diabetes?

Type 1 Diabetes

It is an autoimmune disorder. This description means it occurs when the immune cells attack and destroy the healthy cells in the tissues of the pancreas, called the islets of Langerhans, where insulin is secreted. However, it is unclear what causes this form of abnormal response or attack by the immune cells. Nearly 10% of patients with diabetes have this form.

Type 2 Diabetes

It occurs when the body's cells and tissues become resistant to insulin, causing the sugar levels to build up in the blood.

Prediabetes

It is a form of diabetes in which the blood sugar levels are higher than the normal range, though they are not high enough for the diagnosis of diabetes.

Gestational Diabetes

This form of diabetes occurs due to increased blood sugar levels during pregnancy. The insulin-blocking hormones produced by the placenta are responsible for causing gestational diabetes.

Additionally, a rare condition, diabetes insipidus – though not directly related to diabetes mellitus – shares a similar name. It is a different condition wherein the kidneys remove too many fluids from the body.

Every form of diabetes has its own set of unique symptoms, causes, risk factors, and treatments. Read on to learn more about how these forms differ from one another.

What Are the Common Causes of Diabetes?

- Advancing age
- Obesity
- Family history of diabetes
- Sedentary lifestyle
- Lack of adequate physical activities
- History of gestational diabetes
- Pre-existing high blood pressure, high triglycerides, or high cholesterol
- Unhealthy dietary habits such as increased intake of sugars and fatty foods

What Are the Signs and Symptoms of Diabetes?

Most people know that diabetes causes increased frequency of urination, non-healing wounds, change in appetite, and others.

However, it is not like you wake up one day and suddenly feel thirsty or hungry. These symptoms pick up gradually and hence, are difficult to notice. That is why you need to learn to apply the knowledge of the symptoms into practice.

Here are some silent symptoms of diabetes and ways to know you have them.

You Feel More Thirsty

The best way to know how much water you drink every day is to keep a bottle at your desk and sip from it whenever you feel thirsty. This routine will help you keep track of how much water you are drinking to make any increase in your thirst noticeable.

Another way to help you notice a change in your thirst is a shift to cold beverages other than water. When you feel thirsty, you prefer something cold over your regular tea and coffee. Hence, if you think you have switched to juices or soda to quench your thirst and have been drinking less tea and coffee, it could be diabetes.

You Feel Hungry All The Time

Increased hunger is a common warning sign of diabetes. You may find yourself feeling extremely tired with an immediate need to reach out for high-carb foods like candies, pastries, and chocolates.

This symptom occurs because the high blood sugar level reduces the ability of your body to regulate its insulin production. It passes through cycles of low and increased production of insulin. So, each time there is an increase in insulin production, your sugar level drops, prompting you to reach out to carbs quickly.

So, get your blood sugar level tested if you have been getting hunger pangs too frequently with a feeling of urgency to eat high-carb foods.

Increased Frequency of Urination

When you have diabetes, your body loses the ability to break down the foods into sugars, because of which you may have more sugar flowing in your bloodstream. Your body tries to eliminate this excess sugar by flushing it out via urination.

This condition is why you may have an increased frequency of urination. However, you may not notice this symptom during the daytime. Hence, the better way would be to keep a watch on your night-time urination frequency.

If you are getting up at night more than once, your ability to sleep peacefully is affected; it is time to get your blood sugar test done.

You've Lost a Little Weight

Losing weight is considered a sign of good health nowadays. But, sometimes, it can be a sign of diabetes as well. Since obesity is the most common risk factor for diabetes, it sounds strange that shedding weight could signify this disease.

When you have diabetes, you may lose weight primarily due to the loss of water from urinating.

Secondarily, you may experience weight loss from losing calories as your body does not absorb all the calories from the foods.

So, if you are losing weight steadily over more than two months without making any conscious efforts like dieting or exercising, it might not be something to rejoice. Instead, you should get your blood sugar levels checked to rule out diabetes.

Some more signs and symptoms to look out for:

- You behave in a grumpy and moody manner
- You develop frequent urinary tract infections
- Your vision seems blurry
- You feel exhausted all the time
- Your scrapes and cuts take a longer time to heal

The basic idea behind learning these silent symptoms is being able to identify them. They won't come together or suddenly in high intensity for you to take notice. They often develop slowly over some time. You might get used to your increased frequency of urination or increased thirst without feeling anything unusual about them.

The tips given above will let you introspect whether you have any of these symptoms.

What Are the Complications of Diabetes?

- Heart diseases, heart attack, or stroke
- Nephropathy
- Neuropathy
- Retinopathy
- Hearing loss
- Vision loss
- Skin conditions like bacterial or fungal infections
- Foot damage due to infections or sores that do not heal
- Dementia
- Depression

Lifestyle Choices Recommended by Ayurveda for the Treatment of Diabetes

Obesity is the single most significant factor responsible for the development of type 2 diabetes. The excess fat that you have accumulated in your body over several years can bring you closer to the doors of diabetes.

Ayurveda recommends a few simple strategies that can help you reduce your risk of obesity-linked type 2 diabetes.

But, before that, let us learn how obesity is linked to type 2 diabetes:

How Does Obesity Lead to Type 2 Diabetes?

Insulin resistance is the critical factor involved in developing type 2 diabetes. It reduces the ability of the body's cells and tissues to respond to insulin, due to which carbohydrates are not metabolised effectively, leading to high blood sugar levels.

Obesity can cause type 2 diabetes by inducing insulin resistance. The pro-inflammatory cells in the fats stored in your body can trigger inflammation, which results in the release of proteins called cytokines. The release of cytokines makes the cells resistant to insulin, thus setting the stage for developing type 2 diabetes.

To prevent these developments, you must break the progressive cycle of diabetes. Let us learn some practical ways for preventing obesity-linked diabetes:

A Very Low-Calorie Diet

The first and the most effective method to achieve your goal is to follow a Very-Low-Calorie diet. It can help you achieve significant weight loss. As your waist gets thinner by every inch, your body cells would start responding to insulin favourably, thus preventing diabetes or improving your diabetes control.

Your diet should include whole grains, fresh fruits, vegetables, and plenty of fibres. Avoid fried and fatty foods, high-carb foods, and packaged or processed foods. The faster you lose weight, the quicker you will be able to notice the results.

Avoid Simple Carbs

Simple carbohydrates that we consume in plenty are known to cause sharp spikes in blood sugar levels and increase the risk of obesity.

On the other hand, a low carbohydrate diet can reduce your pancreas' insulin level to produce to metabolise the sugars. This effect would help minimise the strain on this organ and thus, result in decreased insulin resistance.

Physical Activities

Increasing your physical activities is the key to losing weight faster and preventing type 2 diabetes. The deposition of fats around your belly could result from a sedentary lifestyle.

Without regular exercises, the other tips mentioned above will not be effective enough.

If you are new to the world of exercise, start slowly. Begin with simple activities like walking, cycling, or swimming. Exercise for at least 20 minutes every day. Increase the intensity and duration gradually.

Regular exercises will help your body to become more sensitive to insulin. When combined with a healthy diet, it can also reduce the demand for insulin by the body and help prevent or even reverse diabetes.

Sleep Well

Getting a sound sleep of eight hours every day is an essential factor that can help you prevent diabetes. When you do not get enough sleep, your mind and body are stressed out. Mental stress can result in an imbalance of hormones, affecting insulin production.

Lack of sleep does not allow enough time for the body to repair and thus, reduces its ability to perform various functions, including responding to the insulin. So, make no compromise on your sleep.

With every higher number shown by your weighing scale, you are brought closer and closer to diabetes. Luckily, the vice versa is also true. A fall in your weight by every kilogram will take you away from the risk of diabetes.

Follow the tips given above to maintain a healthy weight and protect yourself against type 2 diabetes.

The Safe and Natural Herbs for Treating Diabetes

Herbs have immense potential to keep you healthy and fit. They are considered a gift from Mother Nature to help us prevent and treat almost every disease. Herbs also offer safe and natural treatments for patients with diabetes.

Here are some herbs that have been proven to benefit patients with diabetes help them control their blood sugar level and prevent complications:

Mucuna prureins

Mucuna prureins is believed to be one of the most effective natural remedies for type 2 diabetes since it can inhibit insulin resistance. It could help lower your blood sugar levels and lessen the risk of complications.

It could also delay the signs of ageing by producing an antioxidant, adaptogenic, and anti-degenerative effect. These effects would help you avoid your bodily functions declining due to age.

The significant anti-diabetic benefits of mucuna prureins are linked to its ability to improve insulin production. This herb can enhance the number of beta cells of Langerhans in the pancreas. These cells are responsible for ensuring your body receives an adequate amount of insulin.

When your pancreas has a higher number of these insulin-producing cells, it would naturally lead to more increased secretion of the hormone and thus, enable you to achieve better control over your blood sugar levels.

Diabetes is one of the most typical causes of stress and depression. Nowadays, stress-linked problems aggravated due to diabetes such as depression, hypertension, and heart attacks have become too frequent primarily due to the lowered average age at which diabetes strikes men. Our unhealthy lifestyle has also led us to develop diabetes at a much earlier age, the age at which you should be enjoying your life and not taking insulin injections or anti-diabetic medicines!

The sudden need to take more care of your health after the diabetic diagnosis can contribute to stress and further worsen your glycemic control.

The adaptogenic and stress-relieving properties of mucuna pruriens could help reverse the damage caused at the physical and emotional levels.

This herb would protect you against the effect of diabetes-induced stress by improving the secretion of feel-good hormones called dopamine and serotonin and controlling the synthesis of the stress hormone called cortisol in the brain.

This herb also has the potential to stimulate the functions of the adrenal glands and restore a healthy secretion of hormones.

Mucuna prureins also has antioxidant properties that could efficiently destroy the free radicals responsible for causing damage to your vital organs – including the pancreas – thus allowing you to regain optimum glycaemic control.

This bodily response is how mucuna prureins, with its numerous medicinal properties, could help you avoid the consequences of diabetes and enhance your mental, physical, and emotional health.

Gynostemma Tea

The anti-diabetic effect of Gynostemma tea could help restore bodily functions. It can lessen insulin resistance. It would make the cells in the vital organs such as the brain, kidneys, eyes, and other body parts more receptive to the insulin secreted in your pancreas. This positive effect would enhance this hormone's efficiency and help control your blood sugar levels.

It would also inhibit the development of diabetic complications, including neuralgia, neuropathy, and others.

Regularly using Gynostemma tea could also help you regain your bodily functions by producing an antioxidant and detoxifying effect. It would stimulate the elimination of toxins from your body and protect your vital organs against future damage.

The anti-diabetic properties of Gynostemma tea are beneficial for patients suffering from type 1 and type 2 diabetes. It can support a higher production of insulin in the pancreas. This effect would help avoid fluctuating blood sugar levels during and after meals, as the controlled release of insulin would enable an efficient metabolism of carbs present in your food.

This herb may also help lower the blood sugar level by enhancing the insulin sensitivity of the cells in the body. Research has shown that this herb can inhibit insulin resistance. It might promote the effectiveness of insulin by making the cells and tissues of the body react to it more favourably.

It would enhance your glycaemic control and ensure your blood sugar levels stay within the normal range. These anti-diabetic benefits of Gynostemma tea may benefit patients struggling with severe complications like diabetic nephropathy. When diabetes has indirectly affected your health, Gynostemma tea might help you restore it.

Also, diabetes, which is a significant cause of mental stress, can contribute to several health issues like heart attacks, high cholesterol, and stroke by increasing inflammation and stress hormones like cortisol.

However, these effects of diabetes could be inhibited by the regular use of Gynostemma tea, which works by producing an adaptogenic effect. It could enhance your ability to easily accept and adapt to the lifestyle changes essential for controlling diabetes. It might relieve your mental stress and restore your health.

Gynostemma tea may also produce a natural antioxidant effect on your pancreas and protect it against the oxidative damage caused by free radicals. It would inhibit the weakening of the functions of this organ and protect your general health.

The attributes of Gynostemma tea may also prevent diabetic complications like heart attacks and hypertension. These conditions are not only dangerous for your physical health but even for your emotional state.

Hypertension can directly impact the functions of the vital organs by reducing the blood flow through the body. Regular use of Gynostemma tea may inhibit the development of these ailments by ensuring a higher secretion of Nitric Oxide. The vasodilatory effect of this chemical compound could support normal heart functions and lower the tension within the blood vessels, thus inhibiting heart attacks and hypertension, respectively.

Fenugreek (Methi)

Fenugreek seeds contain a high amount of soluble fibre, which could help lower your blood sugar level by slowing down the breakdown and absorption of carbohydrates. Several clinical trials have indicated that fenugreek seeds could be potent in improving the symptoms of diabetes by reducing blood glucose levels and boosting glucose tolerance.

Bitter Gourd (Karela)

This veggie contains at least three strong anti-diabetic properties, including vicine, charantin, and polypeptide-p, an insulin-like component. These substances work together and individually to help reduce your blood sugar levels.

Bitter gourd also contains lectin, reducing your blood glucose level by acting on the peripheral tissues and reducing your appetite. Additionally, karela is rich in vitamins A, B, C, and minerals like Iron.

Regular intake of this vegetable would prevent the complications associated with people who have diabetes, including diabetic retinopathy and neuralgias.

Jambu Fruit (Jamun)

The seeds of Jamun contain jamboline, which could regulate the conversion of starch into sugar, thus keeping your blood sugar levels within normal limits. The seed powder can be consumed by adding one teaspoonful to a glass of water or buttermilk.

Garlic

Garlic contains a substance called Allicin, which is a potent anti-diabetic agent. It would also protect the organs and tissues of your body from the spiralling effect of the high blood sugar level and thus, help prevent its complications.

Bael Leaves

Bael leaves have been scientifically proven to possess anti-diabetic properties. Drinking fresh juice of Bael leaves with a pinch of pepper once every day would keep your blood sugar level in control.

Curry Leaves

Curry leaves have anti-diabetic properties, which help in reducing blood sugar levels. Patients should eat 10 to 12 curry leaves every morning for at least three months to notice a significant improvement in their blood sugar levels.

Aloe Vera

Most people consider aloe vera to be beneficial only for the skin. However, this is not true. This all-around herb can also help patients with diabetes. It would act as a liver tonic and regulate metabolic processes. Regular use of aloe vera also would tone up and increase the efficiency of the hepatic-biliary system, which would lead to improved carbohydrate metabolism.

Cabbage

It has been found that cabbage works similarly to insulin and would help prevent spikes in blood sugar levels. Diabetic patients may include cabbage in their regular diet in salads, soups, or curries to derive its health benefits.

Cinnamon (Dalchini)

A clinical study has proven that cinnamon bark would improve blood sugar and cholesterol levels in patients with type 2 diabetes. It would also reduce the risk factors associated with diabetes, such as obesity. It is, hence, considered a natural way to prevent this illness.

Including these herbs in your regular diet can ensure your blood sugar levels stay within the normal range. These herbs can also protect the vital organs in your body and prevent the complications of diabetes.

Safe and Effective Exercises for Controlling Your Blood Sugar Levels

Exercises are the key to staying fit and healthy. Not just the patients with diabetes, but even those who seem to be in good health, can benefit significantly by exercising regularly.

However, a few exercises are specially meant for patients with diabetes to help them keep their blood sugar levels in control. Some simple yoga poses and relaxation techniques like meditation can profoundly affect your efforts to keep diabetic complications at bay.

Let us now learn how to practise the yoga poses to keep diabetes in control.

How Does Yoga Help Fight Diabetes?

Yoga can help reduce the glucose level in the blood while keeping your blood pressure and weight within normal limits. It can reduce the severity of the symptoms of diabetes and slow down or prevent the progression of the complications.

Yoga can also lessen the risk of severe complications by reducing stress, one of the major causes of diabetes. It works by increasing the secretion of glucagon, which is responsible for regulating blood glucose levels.

The practice of yoga has been proven to help with weight loss. Since obesity is the major contributing factor leading to diabetes, doing yoga is highly recommended for keeping your weight in check.

Below are the best yoga poses that can help diabetic patients to keep their blood sugar levels in control and prevent complications:

Pranayam

Deep breathing through pranayama can help oxygenate the blood and improve circulation in different body parts. It also relaxes the mind and calms the nerves.

To practise:

Sit on a yoga mat with your legs folded or cross-legged. Close your eyes. Then, straighten your back, keeping the chin parallel to the floor. Place your hands on your knees. Make sure your palms are facing upwards. Take a deep breath and hold your breath for five seconds. Exhale slowly.

Repeat the same at least ten times. Then, rub your palms against each other till they feel warm, and place them on the eyes. Now, open your eyes and smile.

Balasana

This pose is an excellent stress-buster for patients with diabetes. It gently stretches the hips, ankles, and thighs and calms the mind, thereby relieving stress and tiredness.

To practise:

Sit on the floor, putting the weight of your body on your knees. Then, flatten your feet onto the floor to sit on your heels while spreading your thighs apart. Exhale deeply and bend forward from the waist. Make sure your stomach rests on your thighs. Extend your back and stretch out your arms in front to elongate your back.

Rest the forehead on the floor. However, make sure you don't push yourself beyond your natural flexibility. You will be able to do it better with regular practice. It is a resting pose so breathe ideally at a normal pace. Stay in this pose for two to three minutes.

Setubandhasana

This asana can keep your blood sugar level in control and help you feel calm and relaxed. It can also improve digestion and glycaemic control.

To practise:

Lie down flat on the yoga mat, with your feet flat on the floor. Then, slowly exhale and push yourself up and off the floor, keeping your feet firmly touching the ground. While raising your body, make sure your neck and head lay flat on the mat. You may use your hands for added support. If you are flexible, clasp your fingers below your raised back for an added stretch. The key is not to hurt yourself or overexert while doing the pose.

How Can Meditation Help Control Blood Sugar Levels?

Meditation offers a perfectly natural way to relax your mind and body through controlled breathing and focusing techniques. It can help reduce stress and prevent diabetes complications by correcting the body's metabolic practices.

Below is a brief discussion about how meditation can help control diabetes and how best to practise this method.

Meditation can help you achieve a peaceful state of mind and spirit. It takes practice and focus to reach the meditative state. However, no special equipment is needed to practise meditation.

There are different types of meditation; Mindfulness meditation and transcendental meditation are found to be the most beneficial for patients with diabetes.

The quiet contemplation and the state of serenity achieved through the practice of mindfulness meditation can help you put aside your worries and anxieties about the future. The breathing motion helps bring you to the present moment while removing the thoughts about the future and past, thus preventing a wavering state of mind.

How to practise Mindfulness Meditation?

Mindfulness meditation can be practised sitting on the floor or a chair. You may also lie on the floor.

This practice aims to bring you, physically, spiritually, and emotionally, into the present moment by achieving a complete focus on the breathing process.

Wear comfortable and loose-fitting clothing while meditating. If you are a beginner, start with 10 minutes of practice a day and gradually work up to 20 minutes a day.

Mindfulness meditation can help minimise stress and lower blood pressure. It can also reduce levels of stress hormones such as cortisol.

Cortisol contributes to belly fat, weight gain, and insulin resistance. Excess weight can further increase your risk of diabetic complications like high blood pressure and heart problems.

How to practise Transcendental Meditation?

Another form of meditation beneficial for diabetic patients is transcendental meditation. It is typically practised sitting on the floor and focusing on a phrase or word called a 'mantra.'

The mantra can be a simple word like 'One' or 'Om.'

In this practice, you need to focus on your breathing and chant the word. You may begin by practising it for 10 minutes each day. After one week, you can practise it for 15 minutes a day and work up to about 20 minutes every day.

Transcendental meditation can help diabetic patients control their blood sugar levels. It works by reducing insulin resistance and improving carbohydrate metabolism.

Conclusion

Diabetes occurs when the tissues and cells in the body do not respond to the insulin produced in the pancreas. When you practise meditation and these yoga asanas regularly, your body begins to respond to insulin appropriately, thus helping reduce the blood glucose level. These exercises also help improve blood circulation in different parts of your body, particularly the heart, brain, arms, legs, eyes, and nervous system, where diabetic patients encounter problems.

Using herbal remedies, practising meditation and yoga also offers an excellent way to fight stress at the physical and mental levels, thus keeping your glucose levels within normal limits.

Ayurvedic Approach for the Treatment of Hypercholesterolemia

Hypercholesterolemia is a disorder characterised by a high level of cholesterol. Cholesterol is a soft, waxy substance found in the fatty tissues of all of the body's cells, especially in the bloodstream.

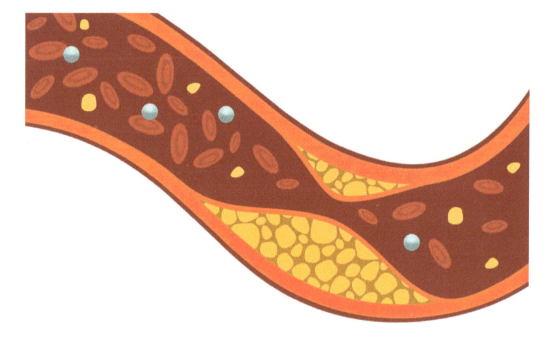

It is present in small quantities and forms a part of the nerve coverings, cell walls, and brain cells.

Hence, it has an essential function in the body. However, when this substance is present in excess quantities, it can cause blockages in the arteries resulting in severe consequences.

What Is Hypercholesterolemia?

Cholesterol has rightfully earned a bad name in the dictionary of health and fitness. There are so many diseases whose occurrence is attributed to high cholesterol levels. This fatty substance can make you prone to heart attacks, diabetes, hypertension, cancer, stroke, and many more diseases.

Here, the cholesterol we are talking about is the 'bad' cholesterol or the low-density lipoprotein form of cholesterol. It is this cholesterol that is the real culprit affecting your health.

On the contrary, the other form of cholesterol, the 'good' or high-density lipoprotein form of cholesterol, is a fatty substance present in the blood of all normal individuals. You need this for carrying out specific functions and maintaining the cell membranes.

But, when we say cholesterol and its negative effect on our health, we mean LDL or 'bad' cholesterol. The level of LDL cholesterol must be lowered to keep in good health.

What Are the Common Causes of Hypercholesterolemia?

Excess cholesterol in the blood tends to form fatty plaques along the walls of the arteries, veins, and the large vessels supplying blood to the heart.

As the cholesterol continues to accumulate, it can cause larger atherosclerotic plaques to form. The arterial walls thus become narrow and more rigid. This phenomenon is known as atherosclerosis.

Eventually, the plaques block the arteries and limit the flow of oxygen-rich blood to the heart. This issue can increase your risk of developing angina and heart attacks. For example, if the artery supplying blood flow to the brain is narrowed or hardened, it would increase the risk of a stroke.

The common risk factors for developing high cholesterol include:

- Having one or both parents with a history of high cholesterol
- A high-fat diet
- Pre-existing hypertension or diabetes
- Sedentary lifestyle
- Lack of essential nutrients in the diet

What Are the Signs and Symptoms of Hypercholesterolemia?

Most patients with hypercholesterolemia experience mild chest pain, though occasionally. In some forms of high cholesterol, the patient may experience the effect later in life as the condition affects the blood flow to the vital organs.

Although most patients do not develop any evident symptoms pointing specifically to the diagnosis of hypercholesterolemia, there could be some subtle signs that should raise the suspicion, such as:

- Occasional chest discomfort
- Small bumps on the skin, usually on the hands, elbows, or knees
- Xanthomas, waxy deposits of cholesterol in the tendons or skin
- Small yellowing deposits of cholesterol built up under and around the eyelids

What Are the Complications of Hypercholesterolemia?

An excessive amount of cholesterol circulating in the blood can lead to a slow build-up of this substance in the walls of arteries of the heart and brain. It combines with other substances and forms thick, hard deposits called plaques that can clog those arteries. This condition is called atherosclerosis.

If the plaque breaks away in pieces and circulates in the blood, it can travel to distant organs like the heart or the brain, causing heart attacks or stroke, respectively.

Common complications of high cholesterol linked to the compromised blood flow to the vital organs include:

- Heart attack
- Strokes
- Peripheral vascular disease

Here are the safe and effective remedies recommended by Ayurveda that will help you keep 'bad' cholesterol in check.

Ayurvedic Treatment for Managing Cholesterol Disorders

The Ayurvedic approach for treating this condition includes eliminating toxins and excess cholesterol from the blood vessels and restoring the digestive fire to burn excess fats more efficiently.

Following are the herbs that have potent medicinal properties for lowering cholesterol:

Onions

Onions, especially red onions, are highly beneficial for managing high cholesterol levels.

They would reduce the level of bad cholesterol and elevate the level of good cholesterol. This turn of events can help lower your risk of heart diseases.

You can mix two teaspoons of onion juice in one teaspoon of honey and drink it once every day. You can also add a finely chopped onion and half a teaspoon of pepper in one cup of buttermilk and consume it once daily to keep your cholesterol levels in control.

Ginger

Ginger is a potent herb that would help you reduce your cholesterol levels while protecting you from heart, stomach, and liver diseases. It would also add a unique flavour to your foods.

You can prepare ginger tea by boiling grated ginger into your regular tea. It can also provide relief from sore throat and the common cold. You may also add ginger to your food while cooking.

Coriander Seeds

Coriander has the potential to lower the level of LDL. It would protect you from heart attacks and stroke and produce a hypoglycaemic effect, thus reducing your risk of diabetes.

To use, make a powder of coriander seeds by roasting and grinding them. Add two teaspoonfuls of this powder to one cup of water. Let this mixture boil for a few minutes, and then strain it. Drink this at least once every day.

You may add milk and cardamom to it for an added flavour. This mixture makes up for a refreshing and healthier replacement for your morning cup of tea.

Coriander also works as an excellent diuretic. It would help control cholesterol by boosting the functions of the kidneys. It would also ensure that the kidneys can efficiently flush out the excess cholesterol from the body via urine, thereby reducing blood cholesterol levels.

Amla

Amla, or Indian gooseberry, is a natural hypolipemic agent. It would promote the utilisation of fats by the body, thus lowering cholesterol levels in the blood.

This fruit may also produce anti-atherogenic and antioxidant effects. The anti-atherogenic effect would inhibit the development of a condition called atherosclerosis, which is characterised by the deposition of cholesterol plaques in the arteries and thus, prevent their narrowing. This will help to prevent the abnormalities that can lead to a heart attack or stroke.

Simply mix one teaspoon of Amla powder in a glass of warm water and drink it once daily, preferably in the morning.

Apple Cider Vinegar

Apple cider vinegar could lower your cholesterol and triglyceride levels. Additionally, it is an excellent natural remedy for several other ailments like high blood pressure, acid reflux, upper respiratory infections, and gout.

Mix one teaspoon of apple cider vinegar in a glass of water and drink it two to three times a day for a month. You may increase the amount of apple cider vinegar after a month to two tablespoons per glass. If you do not like the taste of vinegar, you can also add fresh orange juice or grape juice to this drink.

Orange Juice

Oranges contain a high amount of vitamin C, a powerful antioxidant. It would prevent the ill effects of cholesterol on your blood vessels, heart, and brain.

It is also rich in folate and flavonoids, which further help lower cholesterol levels and reduce your risk of heart attack, stroke, and atherosclerosis.

Drink two cups of orange juice daily to keep your cholesterol levels in check naturally.

Oatmeal

Eating oatmeal for your breakfast or other meal times is an easy yet powerful way to control your cholesterol levels. Oatmeal is full of fibres, reducing fat absorption and cholesterol, thus lowering the harmful cholesterol levels.

You may add fruits and nuts like apples, strawberries, bananas, walnuts, or almonds to your oatmeal for better flavours and a more powerful punch of nutrition.

Coconut Oil

Surprisingly, coconut oil, a form of unhealthy fat called saturated fat, has been found to reduce cholesterol levels, thanks to the high amount of lauric acid present in it.

Lauric acid would increase the high density 'good' cholesterol. This would improve the low-density lipoprotein/high-density lipoprotein ratio, which is favourable for the heart and the brain.

Add coconut oil to your diet in moderate amounts. Adding just one to two tablespoons of coconut oil to your daily diet would suffice to extract its beneficial effect while preventing its negative influence linked due to its saturated fat content.

Alfalfa

Alfalfa would clear the arteries congested by cholesterol by producing a disintegrating effect on the plaques. Regular consumption of this herb would help people control their cholesterol levels and avoid complications like stroke and peripheral vascular disease.

Arjuna

Arjuna has been used for centuries to manage cardiac problems like heart attacks. The bark of this herb, when taken in powder form, has beneficial medicinal properties. It would dissolve the cholesterol plaques deposited in the coronary arteries and reduce the risk of heart attacks.

Garlic

Garlic is highly beneficial for people with cholesterol problems. Experts recommend eating two to three cloves of garlic every day, first thing in the morning. You can chew it raw if the sharp taste can be tolerated or simply gulped down with a glass of water.

It would help eliminate excess cholesterol from the blood by disintegrating the plaques and free up the arteries.

Guggulu

Guggulu is a popular Indian herb with potent medicinal properties that treat cholesterol-related heart problems. It contains guggulsterone that could help reduce cholesterol levels. It can also dissolve the cholesterol plaques in the arteries to be excreted via urine.

The Do's and Don'ts for Healthy Cholesterol Levels

- Do consume fresh fruits and vegetables
- Don't smoke
- Do exercise regularly
- Don't eat foods containing trans or saturated fats
- Do maintain a healthy weight
- Don't consume butter and processed foods
- Do eat frequent small meals in a day

Dietary and Lifestyle Changes for Managing High Cholesterol

Ayurveda suggests following a disciplined diet and a regular exercise plan for achieving healthy cholesterol levels.

Here are a few time-tested measures that can help patients bring their cholesterol levels to normal:

- Start your day with a breakfast containing high fibre grains like oats and fresh fruits. Eat plenty of dried beans or legumes.

- Eat lots of fruits rich in natural antioxidant compounds like citrus fruits, apples, and strawberries. Nuts like almonds and walnut and vegetables like spinach, broccoli, and carrots are also rich in antioxidant compounds.

- Keep a watch on the number of calories you consume. Say 'no' to red meats, chocolates, ice creams, and other foods that can increase your calorie count. Also avoid foods rich in fats, like fried foods.

- Drink plenty of water. This routine causes increased excretion of water and the toxins and excess fats from the body.

- Do regular exercises like brisk walking for at least 40 minutes every day, five days a week. Everyday physical activities can help control obesity and improve the body's metabolic rate, which, in turn, accelerates the utilisation of excess fats.

- Practise deep breathing exercises and meditation for 15-20 minutes daily. It helps refresh your mind and body and also works as an effective de-stress technique.

- Avoid excessive intake of alcohol. People, who consume moderate amounts of alcohol, have a lower risk of cardiac complications than non-drinkers. However, increased alcohol consumption can bring about other health dangers like high blood pressure, stroke, and obesity.

- Quit smoking. Smoking increases the tendency of the blood to clot and worsens atherosclerosis. It also causes damage to the walls of the arteries. Besides this, recovery of patients who have suffered a heart attack due to high cholesterol levels is much slower in smokers than in non-smokers.

Conclusion

Ayurvedic treatments, including dietary modifications and herbal remedies, may help reduce your cholesterol levels to a great extent.

Ayurvedic herbs are safe as they do not cause any severe side effects. It is possible to avoid the life-threatening complications of high cholesterol by making dietary and lifestyle changes recommended by Ayurveda and including natural antilipemic herbs in the treatment plan.

Treatment and Prevention of Malaria Based on the Ayurvedic System of Medicine

Malaria is a life-threatening disorder. It is typically transmitted due to the bite of infected Anopheles mosquitos. The infected mosquitoes carry the parasites called Plasmodium, responsible for malaria, a parasitic infection.

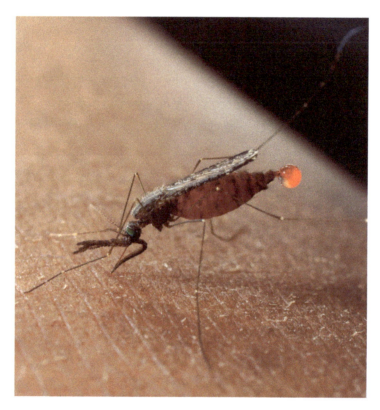

When the infected mosquito bites you, the parasites are released into the bloodstream, thus triggering the development of the symptoms of malaria.

Once the parasites are inside the body, they travel through the bloodstream to reach the liver, undergoing various stages of maturation. After a few days, mature parasites are again passed into the bloodstream, infecting the red blood cells.

After about 48 to 72 hours, parasites inside the red blood cells multiply, causing these infected cells to swell and burst. The parasites will continue to infect more red blood cells, resulting in widespread signs and symptoms that occur in repeating cycles, each of which usually lasts for about 2 to 3 days.

Malaria is most common in regions with a tropical or subtropical climate where these parasites can thrive. It is one of the most common infective disorders across the globe. In the United States alone, the Centres for Disease Control and Prevention (CDC) reports more than 1500 cases of malaria every year. Patients with malaria often include those who have travelled to the countries where this infection is widespread.

What Are the Common Causes of Malaria?

Malaria occurs when a mosquito infected with the parasite Plasmodium bites you. There are four kinds of malarial parasites known to infect humans: Plasmodium vivax, P. malariae, P. ovale, and P. falciparum.

Among these, P. falciparum can cause a more severe form of this disease. Also, those who contract this form of malaria usually have a higher risk of complications, including death. Moreover, an infected mother may pass the infections to her baby during labour. This incident is called congenital malaria.

The parasites that cause malaria transmit in the body through the bloodstream. In addition, these parasites can spread via an infected mosquito bite to a human through the passage of blood. Consequently, malaria can get transmitted through other routes involving the exposure of a person to an infected sample of blood, such as during:

- An organ transplant
- A blood transfusion
- The use of shared syringes and needles
- Entry of blood from an infected person into the bloodstream of another person can result in the spread of malaria.

What Are the Common Signs and Symptoms of Malaria?

The typical symptoms of malaria usually develop within the first ten days of the mosquito bite or exposure to the infected sample of blood. In some cases, it may take up to four weeks following the infection for the full-blown symptoms of malaria to occur. In some patients, the symptoms may not develop for several weeks to months. Some malarial parasites can enter the body of a healthy human, though they may lie dormant for a prolonged period leaving the patients completely asymptomatic.

The common signs and symptoms of malaria include:

- High fever, usually with severe chills

- Shaking chills that often range from moderate to severe in intensity
- Profuse sweating
- Severe headaches
- Nausea and vomiting
- Pain in the abdomen
- Loose motions
- Anaemia due to the destruction of the red blood cells
- Muscle and bone pain
- Convulsions, especially if the malarial parasites have travelled to the brain or meninges and infected these tissues resulting in cerebral malaria or meningitis
- Coma
- Blood in stools

What Are the Complications Caused Due to Malaria?

Malaria may cause several life-threatening complications such as:

- Swelling of the blood vessels in the brain resulting in cerebral malaria
- The accumulation of fluids in the lung tissues that causes difficulty in breathing or pulmonary oedema
- Organ failure of the liver, kidneys, and the spleen
- Anaemia due to the rapid destruction of red blood cells
- Very low blood sugar

Tips to Prevent Malaria

There are no vaccines available for the prevention of malaria. Hence, it is important to follow other preventive measures, including hygienic habits, to protect yourself against this infection. It is also advisable to take optimum precautions, especially if you are travelling to the area where malaria is more prevalent or if you reside in such an area.

You might be prescribed herbal supplements that can boost your immunity, help prevent the infection, or minimise the intensity of the symptoms it can cause. Long-term prevention for people who live in areas where malaria is more common includes protecting themselves against mosquito bites. Sleeping under a mosquito net might help prevent infected mosquitoes bites. Covering your skin and using bug sprays containing DEET can also help prevent this infection.

Ayurvedic Remedies for Malaria

While this infection can be treated effectively with various anti-malarial medications, some natural home remedies would also help more efficiently deal with malaria's signs and symptoms.

Ayurveda advises people to use some herbs to help patients recover from fever, inflammation, and excess weakness.

Here is a list of a few natural Ayurvedic remedies that can support patients with malaria:

Saptparna ki Chhaal

The bark of the Saptparna, a tropical tree, could be used effectively to treat and prevent malaria. This tree has been used in Ayurveda and traditional Chinese medicine to treat headaches, malaria, influenza, bronchitis, and pneumonia. Various alkaloids present in the bark and leaves of this tree have been known to possess active ingredients that could help relieve the symptoms of these diseases.

You can make a Kadha with the bark or leaves of the Saptparna ki Chhaal and drink it to feel fresh and energetic and reduce fever.

Dhaniya Paani

Consuming the concoction of coriander seeds (Dhaniya ka Paani) could help relieve the fever and other symptoms that you may experience due to malaria. The anti-inflammatory properties of coriander would help in reducing the heat generated inside your body and bring down your body temperature.

To use, simply boil a spoonful of fresh coriander seeds or leaves in a glass of water and strain the concoction. Drink this coriander concoction every day until the symptoms have resolved entirely.

Drink Lots of Water

This one may not sound like an extraordinary remedy, but its effects are extraordinary! In fact, drinking plenty of water is what you must do to prevent and treat your infections.

When you drink more water, your kidneys secrete more urine to be thrown out of the body. Along with this extra amount of urine goes the bacteria, parasites, viruses, and other toxins that cause the infection and affect your health!

Drink 8 to 10 glasses of water or even more to flush out the parasites, viruses, and bacteria from your body system and bounce back to good health rather quickly.

Parsley

Parsley not just makes a wonderfully refreshing drink but can also relieve the symptoms of parasitic infections like malaria. It can promote the healing processes by working as an immunity booster, which speeds up the body's repair processes, thus restoring health in a shorter duration.

Increased urine secretion would help flush out bacteria and malaria parasites from the body and relieve your symptoms. All you need to do is add about half a cup of fresh parsley leaves in one or two cups of water and bring this to a boil. You may also use dried parsley leaves if the fresh leaves are unavailable.

Reduce the heat and allow it to simmer. Let parsley infuse the water for 6 to 10 minutes. Then, strain out the leaves and drink the water.

Celery Seeds

Celery seeds act as a natural immunity booster and an antioxidant, mainly due to phenols and polyphenols present. Chewing a handful of these seeds would increase the body's natural defence processes against the malarial parasites and help relieve the symptoms.

Boil a handful of celery seeds in one or two cups of water on medium heat until the liquid is reduced to half. Strain it and drink the liquid one or two times a day. Alternatively, you can snack on celery seeds. Apart from relieving the symptom of malaria or any other infection, it would also help improve your digestion.

Drink 'Soda'

The soda we are talking about here is not a sugary soft drink but baking soda. This miraculous substance can cure ailments arising from the acidic pH balance in the body fluids, including infections, heartburn, and gastritis.

The alkaline nature of baking soda can neutralise the acidity that allows the parasites to thrive. It can ease the discomfort caused by recurrent fever and body aches and hasten your recovery by creating an unfavourable environment that prevents the malarial parasites from surviving.

Stir in one teaspoon of baking soda in a glass of water and drink this once or twice daily for five to seven days. You may drink this once every day in the morning regularly if you tend to develop repeated infections such as malaria or dengue.

Ginger Tea

When dealing with an infective or inflammatory condition, ginger is the ingredient you cannot leave behind. The chemical make-up of this root helps block the prostaglandin synthesis, thus reducing pain, inflammation, body aches, headaches, and fever.

You can make ginger tea by boiling grated ginger with your regular tea. Consume this drink two to three times a day.

Indian Gooseberry

Indian Gooseberry contains a high amount of vitamin C, which helps treat malaria infection by inhibiting the growth of parasites.

Simply add one teaspoon of Indian gooseberry powder and a pinch of turmeric powder in a cup of water and boil this solution for 10 minutes. Drink the concoction twice a day for about four to five days.

Cucumbers

Cucumbers are bland vegetables with no particular taste other than a slightly sour and watery finish. But, it is the liquid content of cucumbers that can come in handy for improving your energy levels, especially while you are recovering.

The high water content of cucumbers would help you feel more energetic and also aid in flushing out the malarial parasites and bacteria from your body system. You can add cucumber slices to your sandwiches, salads or eat it raw.

Heating Pads

The best way to reduce the body pain, headaches, and joint discomfort caused due to malaria is to use heating pads. The inflammation that accompanies the symptoms of malaria can cause a continuous, nagging discomfort, which can make you feel irritable at all times.

Applying a heating pad over your aching joints and muscles would provide significant relief when this happens. The warmth will melt away the pain caused due to inflammation and also release the spasm or stiffness of the muscles.

Blueberries

If you feel 'blue' due to the pain and fever caused by malaria infection, fight it off with rich blueberries. Blueberries possess anti-bacterial, anti-parasitic, anti-inflammatory, and antioxidant properties, which would help reduce inflammation and infection.

You can munch on berries for your snacking or breakfast, add them to a smoothie, or top your oatmeal with chopped berries.

Things to Avoid while Suffering from Malaria

- Chocolate: The high-carb chocolates can create a favourable environment for the parasites and bacteria to grow, thus worsening your infection.

- Carbonation: Fizzy carbonated drinks can aggravate your symptoms by creating an imbalance in the body's pH levels.

- Caffeine: Caffeine might relieve body aches temporarily. However, an increased intake of caffeinated beverages might worsen inflammation and fever, making you feel weaker and uncomfortable.

Conclusion

These home remedies are highly effective and can help you get rid of parasitic infections like malaria and dengue with ease. You can also use some of these remedies routinely to prevent these infections in the future.

Ayurvedic Treatments for the Management of Respiratory Disorders

It is not uncommon for people to take their respiratory health and breathing for granted. However, the lungs are vital organs of the body that are highly sensitive to injuries, airborne infections. They can be vulnerable to damage from the external environment in case of constant exposure to pollutants, toxic particles, chemicals, and infectious organisms in the ambient air.

Respiratory symptoms are also a significant cause of consultation at most primary healthcare centres. Respiratory diseases are estimated to affect millions of people worldwide, including nearly 235 million patients who have asthma and 64 million who suffer from COPD.

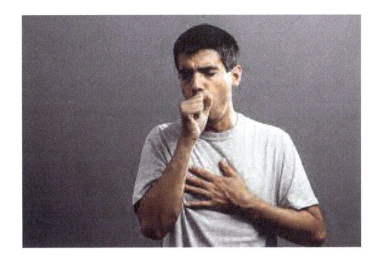

This issue marks the need to be aware of the common respiratory disorders and how to prevent or treat them to ensure the critical respiratory functions are not hampered.

Respiratory Disorders

A respiratory disorder is a term that encompasses many pathogenic conditions that can affect the breathing and respiration in living organisms. Respiration supports the process of the exchange of gases in the body, which involves taking in oxygen and expelling carbon dioxide from the body.

Respiratory diseases occur in the respiratory tract tissues, including the nose, larynx, bronchi, bronchioles, trachea, alveoli, pleura, pleural cavity, and the blood vessels, nerves, and muscles involved in the process of breathing.

There are three primary forms of respiratory disease: lung tissue diseases, airway diseases, and lung circulation diseases.

- Airway diseases affect the tubular passages that carry oxygen, carbon dioxide, and other gases in and out of the tissues of the lungs. Airway diseases often result in the narrowing and blockage of the air passages.

- Lung tissue diseases include those that affect the vital structures of the lungs and result in inflammation or scarring of the tissues. This affliction, in turn, can make breathing difficult, resulting in serious complications.

- Lung circulation diseases occur when the essential blood vessels supplying blood to the lungs are clotted, scarred, or inflamed. These diseases tend to affect the ability of the lung tissues to receive oxygen and produce carbon dioxide. They may also affect the vital functions of the heart.

A common cold is the most common example of mild respiratory disease. The more severe and life-threatening respiratory disorders include lung cancer, bacterial pneumonia, and pulmonary embolism. Other common disorders affecting the lungs are asthma, chronic obstructive pulmonary disease (COPD), bronchiectasis, influenza, pulmonary hypertension, obstructive sleep apnoea syndrome, and tuberculosis. Some lung disorders may lead to respiratory failure.

Exposure to allergens, tobacco smoking, indoor air pollution, and outdoor air pollution are the common risk factors that can trigger the development of these respiratory disorders.

The two major parts of the respiratory system are the upper respiratory tract and the lower respiratory tract. Let us explore more about the respiratory system, bringing into discussion the functions, parts, and common conditions known to affect it.

Structure and Functions of the Respiratory System

The respiratory system is responsible for supporting the exchange of oxygen and carbon dioxide in our bodies. This system also allows for the removal of metabolic waste products, thus keeping the pH levels in the boy tissues in control.

The respiratory system contains the upper respiratory tract and the lower respiratory tract. The names imply that the upper respiratory tract is made of the structures above the vocal folds, while the lower respiratory tract includes the structures below our vocal folds. These two tracts work together to perform the process of respiration that provides for the exchange of carbon dioxide and oxygen between the body and the external atmosphere.

From the nose to the alveoli in the lungs, various elements of the respiratory system play equally important though different roles in the process of breathing and respiration.

Upper Respiratory Tract

The upper respiratory tract begins at the nasal cavity and the sinuses, forming the area just behind our nose.

The nasal cavity is an area located directly behind the nose. It allows the outside air to enter the body. As the air enters through the nose, it passes through the hair-like structure called the cilia lining the inner surface of the nasal cavity. These cilia help trap and dispose of the foreign particles, thus preventing them from entering the respiratory tract's more delicate and vital structures.

The sinuses are small air spaces located behind the front of the skull, on both sides of the nose, and behind the forehead. These sinuses help in regulating air temperature while we breathe.

In addition to air entry through the nasal cavity, air can also enter the body through our mouth.

Once the air enters the body, it passes to the upper respiratory system's lower part, including the larynx and pharynx. The pharynx, or the throat, allows air passage from the mouth or nasal cavity to the larynx and then to the trachea.

The larynx, also called the voice box, contains vocal folds necessary to make sounds or speak. As air enters the larynx, it flows down into the lower respiratory passages that begin with the trachea.

Lower Respiratory Tract

The trachea, also called the windpipe, refers to the passage, allowing the air to flow directly to the lungs. This tube is highly rigid. It is composed of multiple hard rings called the tracheal rings. Anything that can cause the trachea to become narrow, like inflammation and obstruction, can restrict oxygen flow into the lungs.

The primary function of the lungs is to support the exchange of oxygen and carbon dioxide. The lungs inhale or take in oxygen during breathing and exhale or eliminate carbon dioxide from the body.

The trachea divides or branches off to form two tubular passages called the bronchi, leading to the right and the left lung in the lungs. Then, these bronchi continue to branch off to form smaller passageways called the bronchioles. Finally, the bronchioles end into air sacs called the alveoli that play a vital role in exchanging gases like oxygen and carbon dioxide.

Oxygen and carbon dioxide are exchanged in the alveoli of the lungs through the steps mentioned below:

1. The heart pumps the deoxygenated blood carried to the lungs by a large pulmonary artery. This deoxygenated blood comprises carbon dioxide, a by-product of the cellular metabolism continuously occurring in all the organs and tissues of the body.

2. Once the deoxygenated blood flows toward the lungs, carbon dioxide is released into the alveoli in exchange for oxygen that has been breathed in through the air. The blood now becomes oxygenated.

3. Now, the oxygenated blood travels from the lungs to the heart, which is released into the circulatory system to supply oxygen and other nutrients to all the cells.

The exchange of minerals and other metabolites in the kidneys, coupled with the exchange of oxygen and carbon dioxide in the pulmonary tissues, is responsible for helping the body maintain the optimum balance of pH in the blood.

Common Conditions Affecting the Respiratory System

Viruses, bacteria, and even autoimmune conditions can affect the respiratory system and cause illnesses. Some respiratory diseases affect only the upper tract, while some others affect the lower tract primarily.

Conditions Affecting the Upper Respiratory Tract

Allergies

There are several forms of allergies, such as food allergies, skin allergies, and seasonal allergies, that can affect the tissues of the upper respiratory tract. Some allergic conditions can cause mild symptoms, like running nose, congestion in the nose, or itching in the throat. Some severe allergies may lead to anaphylaxis, closing the airways, leading to severe breathlessness.

Common Cold

A common cold is one of the most prevalent upper respiratory tract infections that is known to be triggered by more than 200 viruses. Common cold symptoms usually include running nose, stuffy nose, congestion in the nose, pressure and pain in the sinuses, fever, sore throat, and others.

Laryngitis

Laryngitis is a common condition that occurs when the larynx or the vocal cords are inflamed. This condition may also be caused due to an infection, irritation, or overuse of the vocal cords. The most common symptoms of this condition are throat irritation, hoarseness of voice, or the loss of voice.

Pharyngitis

Pharyngitis, also known as the sore throat, refers to the inflammation of the tissues of the pharynx usually caused due to a bacterial or viral infection. A sore, dry, scratchy throat is one of the primary symptoms of pharyngitis. These symptoms may also be accompanied by flu or cold symptoms like runny nose, cough, fever, and wheezing sounds in the chest while breathing.

Sinusitis

Sinusitis can be acute as well as chronic. This disorder is characterised by the swollen and inflamed membranes of the sinuses and nasal cavity. The common symptoms of this disease include congestion, mucous drainage, sinus pressure, and fever.

Common Conditions Affecting the Lower Respiratory Tract

Asthma

It is a chronic inflammatory disorder, which affects the air passages. Asthma occurs due to the inflammation in the airways, causing them to become narrow, and in turn, obstruct breathing. The common signs and symptoms of asthma include coughing, shortness of breath, and wheezing sounds in the chest. In case these symptoms become severe, the patient may develop an attack of asthma that must be attended to immediately.

Bronchitis

Bronchitis is a respiratory disorder characterised by inflammation in the bronchial tubes. The initial symptoms of this condition are usually similar to those of a common cold. If the condition persists, the patient may develop fever, severe mucous-producing cough, and a mild to moderate difficulty in breathing. Bronchitis may be acute (lasting for less than ten days) or chronic (lasting for several weeks to months and recurring frequently).

Pneumonia

It is an infective disorder that causes the alveoli in the lungs to become inflamed with the accumulation of fluids and pus. Both SARS (severe acute respiratory syndrome) and COVID-19, which are caused due to the coronaviruses, result in the development of pneumonia-like symptoms. This family of viruses links to several other respiratory infections such as MERS. If left untreated, these conditions can lead to fatal consequences.

The common symptoms of pneumonia include shortness of breath, cough with mucous, chest pain, blood in sputum, and fever.

Chronic Obstructive Pulmonary Disease (COPD)

COPD is an umbrella term comprising a group of chronic or long-lasting progressive lung disorders, the most common among them are emphysema and bronchitis. Over time, these diseases may lead to the deterioration of health and the functioning of the lungs and airways.

If not managed properly, this condition may progress, causing other chronic respiratory diseases, including lung cancer.

The common signs and symptoms of COPD are:

- Cough
- Shortness of breath
- Wheezing
- Chest tightness
- Frequent lower respiratory infections

Emphysema

It is a pulmonary condition that occurs due to damage to the alveoli in the lungs resulting in the reduction in the amount of oxygen circulating in these tissues. Emphysema is a chronic condition, which, unfortunately, has no cure. The common symptoms of this condition include exhaustion, increased heart rate, and weight loss.

Lung Cancer

It is a form of cancer affecting the lungs. Lung cancer differs among patients, depending on the exact site where cancerous changes have occurred, such as in the alveoli or airways. The symptoms of lung carcinoma include wheezing and shortness of breath that are often accompanied by chest pain, coughing blood, loss of appetite, and drastic or unexplained weight loss.

Several other conditions can affect the upper and lower respiratory tracts. However, the conditions we discussed so far are more severe and mobile.

Ayurvedic Treatments for the Management of Respiratory Disorders

The description of respiration as suggested by the Ayurvedic system of medicine is brief and even somewhat poetic. It says that the Prana Vayu, one of the five types of Vatha, tends to traverse from the navel region through our throat and then passes out to receive the nectar from the outside air in the atmosphere. It then ultimately comes back to nourish our body.

Ayurveda diagnoses respiratory disorders not according to the infections caused by the microorganisms, but in terms of the nature of systemic imbalances caused due to the form of respiratory distress.

Physicians believe that the respiratory system is influenced, to some extent, by our state of mind and also by excretory functions and body metabolism.

According to Ayurveda, respiratory disorders could be classified into different categories: such as Kasa (Cough), Peenasa (Sinusitis), Shwasa (Breathing difficulties), and Pratishyaya (Rhinitis).

Kasa

These diseases have their origins in the digestive organs, considered to be the sites for the aggravation and accumulation of the doshas. Kasa usually starts over the vitiation of the Apana Vayu (one of the five forms of vathas that govern eliminating waste from the body) in the intestine. Once this happens, the flow of vatha tends to get obstructed. Eventually, the vatha overflows into the circulation, thus relocating into the respiratory system.

Any additional dosha may mix with the excess vatha. The vitiation of Udana Vayu (vatha, which governs expiration, hiccough, sneezing, and spitting) can result in the flow of the air upward and then out from the body. However, it might start residing in the lungs, chest, back, and head in this process, resulting in cough, mucous secretion, and even pain.

There are five types of Kasa: pitta, kapha, vatha, ksaya, and ksataja

- Cough caused due to the pitta vitiation is called the 'Pittaja Kasa'. It is usually continuous. The infection is deep-rooted (like pneumonia) and indicated by more mucous (typically yellow in colour, mixed with blood) and fever.

- Cough caused due to the kapha vitiation is called the 'Kaphaja Kasa'. A large amount of white, sticky, thick mucous accumulates and other symptoms such as nausea, vomiting, and running nose. Cough is often continuous in this form.

- The vitiation of the vatha dosha causes 'Vataja Kasa'. Also, the nature of cough includes dryness with limited mucous secretions. Hence, loss of voice and chest pain cough might be accompanied by the. The frequency of cough would be intermittent such that it occurs in fits.

- Cough caused due to ksaya occurs with conditions such as tuberculosis. Additionally, the condition may result in dryness and tissue loss (ksaya). The Vata dosha plays an essential role in this form of cough. Yet, it may also occur due to the vitiation of all three doshas.

- Cough, known as the 'Ksataja Kasa,' shows the symptoms of vatha as well as pitta vitiations. Bleeding and infection may make the mucous reddish, yellowish, and black. Joint pains and fever may follow with blood appearing in the urine.

Acute Bronchitis

In Ayurveda, bronchitis is called the Kasa Roga. It denotes the inflammation of the bronchial tubes, carrying air to the lungs. It usually occurs due to a viral infection in the respiratory tract.

The phlegm is sticky and adheres to the mucous membranes, making it difficult to expel. The semi-fluid sticky phlegm is often purulent. The phlegm sticking to the bronchi walls may cause breathing difficulties, thereby starving the lungs and alveoli of air.

Air pollution, smoking, and emphysema usually tend to be the causes behind this condition. Furthermore, advancing age may also influence the development and progress of bronchitis. The main symptoms include dry or productive cough, mild fever, shortness of breath, fatigue, and chest pain.

Shwasa

Disorders that affect breathing (called dyspnoea) are also referred to as "Shwasa." These disorders are characterised by the types of breaths they create.

There are five forms of Shwasas called Ksudra, Tamaka, Urdhva, Chinna, and Mahan.

- Ksudra Shwasa (also called heavy breathing) occurs due to factors that can distress the respiratory system, such as physical activities like exercises and even heavy meals.

- Tamaka Shwasa involves forceful respiration. It is commonly referred to as bronchial asthma. It is an allergic condition that usually results from our body's reaction to one or more allergens.

  It is one of the most intense respiratory diseases. According to Ayurveda, asthma is caused by the vitiation of Vatha dosha and Kapha dosha, and its seat of pathogenesis is located in the digestive tract. It may be triggered due to multiple genetic and environmental factors.

  It is characterised by chronic inflammation in the airways and an increase in the hyperresponsiveness of the air passages. Some of the primary symptoms of this condition include breathlessness, tightness in the chest, wheezing, and accumulation of mucous in the pathways like bronchi.

  Asthma attacks typically occur in the morning, causing the patient to wake up with a sense of alarm or apprehension, associated with difficulty breathing in the lying down position.

- Chinna svasa is characterised by interrupted and disturbed breathing. Chinna svasa occurs when there is a downward eye gaze with one eye appearing red. It often marks the onset of severe conditions such as coma.

- Urdhva svasa refers to the prolonged expiration with the inability to inhale. Just like in tamaka svasa, patients with urdhva svasa may have an upward eye gaze, and their eyeballs may roll back.

- Mahan svasa refers to the state of 'The Great Dyspnoea'. It is the most severe form of breathing disorder.

Peenasa

Peenasa or sinusitis refers to a condition wherein the air spaces called the sinuses lined by the mucous membranes get impeded due to the accumulation of the purulent phlegm. Sinusitis is usually caused due to an infection, primarily viral or bacterial, spreading to the sinuses from the nose. Allergies can also be responsible for causing the development of sinusitis.

The primary symptoms include severe headache, tenderness on the affected sinuses, nasal stuffiness, heaviness in the head, bad breath, sore throat, facial pain, and swelling around the eyes.

Ayurvedic Treatments for Respiratory Disorders

Diseases such as upper respiratory tract infection, cough, dyspnoea, bronchial asthma, bronchitis, sinusitis, allergic rhinitis, deviated nasal septum, and nasal polyps can effectively be managed in Ayurveda with the help of appropriate herbal remedies discussed below:

Asparagus

It is an incredible medicinal herb commonly used in Ayurveda and Chinese traditional medicine for several centuries for its lubricating and strengthening properties. It can also bolster your immune system. The immune-boosting action of asparagus effectively manages a common cold, flu, other respiratory infections, asthma, and seasonal allergies.

Liquorice

It would work as an effective herbal demulcent, which would shield your respiratory system and soothe the irritated sinuses and throat. Liquorice is one of the effective herbal remedies that help secrete healthy mucous and release excess phlegm, thus clearing the nasal passages.

Chewing a twig of liquorice or drinking a mixture of liquorice and grated ginger boiled in water for a few minutes would help you get instant relief from the symptoms of a sore throat, cough, a common cold, and other respiratory infections.

Kalmegh

Kalmegh leaf and root are the well-proven Ayurvedic remedies commonly used for treating respiratory ailments. The natural anti-inflammatory, anti-bacterial, anti-viral, antioxidant, and immunity-boosting properties of kalmegh would be beneficial in the treatment of infections, fever, cough, common cold, and other respiratory disorders.

Ayurvedic Herbal Drinks

Eating healthy and the right foods can play a crucial role in strengthening and healing lung functions. According to Ayurveda, adding specific foods to your diet could support normal respiratory functions.

The herbal drinks given below could also uplift your lung functions.

Turmeric

Consuming turmeric drinks daily would reduce the inflammation in the airways. The medicinal properties of the active compound called curcumin in turmeric would support the cleansing of the lungs and flushing out of the toxins from the body, thus strengthening the immune response. You can have this drink with water or milk to keep respiratory infections at bay.

Peppermint Tea

It is a time-tested natural remedy for treating respiratory problems. The rich medicinal value of the bioactive compounds in peppermint would relieve sore throat symptoms by clearing away the mucous and lessening inflammation caused by infections in the lungs.

Ginger Tea

Ginger tea is prized for its potent antioxidant and anti-inflammatory properties that help relieve the symptoms of common cold and cough. This herb can also support the clearing of toxins from the respiratory passages. Laden with magnesium, potassium, and zinc, ginger tea would build a robust immune system and help you fight seasonal infections like flu.

Ayurvedic Treatments for the Management of Snoring Linked to Respiratory Problems

Snoring is a kind of shuddering sound that comes from your nose or throat while sleeping. Instead of normal silent breathing, the person who snores tends to produce a highly disruptive noise, disturbing their own and their partner's sleep.

When you lie down to sleep, the muscle tissues in the upper airways relax to allow you to breathe well. This response is what happens or should happen in typical cases.

But, sometimes, these muscles relax excessively, in which the flow of air through the respiratory passages in the nose or throat becomes restricted, resulting in airflow turbulence.

And it is this turbulence that is responsible for the snoring sound, which is produced when the air passes through these restricted or narrowed passages.

Now, let's see why the relaxation of the muscles which is responsible for causing snoring occurs. Some of the common causes of snoring include:

- Sleep apnoea
- Obesity
- Seasonal allergies
- An unsuitable sleeping position
- Swelling of the tonsils
- Sleep deprivation
- A structural abnormality of your mouth, throat, or nose

- The use of sedative drugs
- Consumption of alcohol
- Excessive smoking

Effective Natural Remedies to Avoid Snoring and Restore Optimum Respiratory Health

Maintain a Healthy Weight

Research studies have proven obesity as a common cause of snoring. If you are overweight, you are likely to have an excess of fatty deposits around your throat region. This excess fat obstructs the airflow and results in snoring.

If you have realised this, take steps to lose those extra unwanted pounds. You can reduce your calorie intake and exercise regularly to maintain a healthy weight so that your airways are cleared off of obstructing fats.

Avoid Sleeping on the Back

When you sleep on your back, the tongue is forced to move toward the back of your throat, thus blocking air passages to some extent.

If this is how you sleep, changing your position to the sides may prove helpful. This position will prevent the fall back of the tongue and allow the air to flow through the air passages without causing turbulence and snoring.

Take Care of Allergens

If your snoring is often accompanied by recurrent sneezing, it could be due to the allergens like dust and bacteria harboured into your mattress.

Your old and worn-out mattress may have, over the years, harboured much dust within itself. And now these dust particles are triggering allergies, in which you are developing snoring and sneezing.

When you sleep on such a mattress, your nasal passages are exposed to the dust particles. Your immune system reacts to them by producing excessive mucous and triggering sneezing episodes. And this excessive mucous is responsible for obstructing the air passages and causing snoring.

Snoring in patients with allergic rhinitis due to dust mites can effectively be managed by tackling the allergen itself. Just changing your mattress or regularly cleaning it might do the trick to stop snoring in such cases.

Identify the Triggers

Two triggers, namely, alcohol and smoking, must be avoided if you want to prevent snoring.

The excessive relaxation of the muscles in the airways is primarily responsible for snoring, and alcohol can induce this excessive relaxation, which is why it must be avoided. You should avoid alcohol consumption, especially for the 2 hours before bedtime.

Similarly, chronic smoking can also result in an obstruction in the air passages by causing long-term damage to the tissues of the airways. That's why it is vital to quit smoking at the earliest if you want to avoid snoring and improve respiratory health.

Drink Lots of Water

Drinking plenty of water throughout the day will liquefy the mucous accumulated in your air passages. Dehydration or a reduced water intake, on the other hand, would cause thickening of the mucous in the throat. This deficiency can worsen snoring due to the obstruction created by the thick secretions.

That is why keeping yourself well-hydrated by drinking lots of water is recommended to avoid snoring. However, water intake must be limited, not beyond the evening hours. While drinking water can help you sleep well by reducing snoring, it won't let you sleep if you drink it after the evening hours. You would likely want to get up again and again for bathroom visits.

Avoid Stress

Ayurveda recommends trying meditation, yoga, and deep breathing exercises to improve the quality of your sleep. This practice might snap the chain connecting insomnia with snoring and help you avoid these unhealthy habits.

Address Structural Problems

If none of the above treatments works, you might need to explore deeper to check if the problem is linked to a structural abnormality in the air passages like a deviated nasal septum.

A deviated nasal septum refers to the misalignment of the nasal septum, which can lead to restricted airflow. If the root cause of your snoring is the deviated nasal septum, you might need to undergo a surgical correction to restore the septum's alignment.

Conclusion

The therapeutic healing properties of herbal remedies are believed to be highly beneficial for treating common respiratory problems. These herbs can protect the lungs against harmful toxins, allergens, and pollutants, improve your overall health, and bolster your immunity.

As discussed, snoring can also signify an underlying health problem affecting the lungs. If you choose to ignore it, you, as well as your partner, will have to bear the consequences.

So, if you suffer from snoring and other respiratory symptoms, try to identify the root cause. Then follow appropriate tips and tricks to improve your respiratory health to avoid the risk of developing more severe complications.

Ayurvedic Treatments for Respiratory Infections

Respiratory infections include all the infective conditions that affect the respiratory system, including the lungs, chest, sinuses, throat, and nose. Chronic diseases include those that repeatedly occur over a period, especially during the months of winter and fall seasons. This time period is when patients are more likely to spend time indoors or in groups.

The increased exposure to germs during these seasons and the higher chances of coming in close contact with an infected person make it easier for these organisms to spread and cause respiratory infections.

Many respiratory pathogens can quickly be passed from one person to another while breathing, coughing, or sneezing. The spread of these infections usually occurs through the respiratory droplets released from an infected person while coughing or sneezing or touching the nose, eyes, and mouth after coming in contact with someone with a respiratory infection. Touching any object exposed to bacteria and viruses can also result in the spread of these infections.

Respiratory infections are usually caused due to bacteria or viruses, though other germs like parasites and fungi can also cause infections in the lungs and air passages.

Bacterial respiratory infections are often treated with antibiotics. However, viral infections cannot be treated with antibiotics. Anti-viral drugs may be used in these cases. However, both antibiotics and anti-viral drugs are known to cause serious side effects. Also, the effectiveness of these medications tends to reduce with repeated or inadvertent use. Hence, there is a need to adopt alternative therapies that are safer and more effective for managing respiratory infections.

The treatment for most chronic respiratory infections needs to be based on the specific symptoms the person is suffering from, the exact diagnosis, and the underlying dosha responsible for triggering the events preceding the infections.

The common examples of respiratory infections are the common cold, chronic sinusitis, pneumonia, chronic bronchitis, rhinitis, influenza (flu), and strep throat.

Let us develop a clear understanding of what happens when a person develops these infections, followed by the best ways to treat these conditions without risking side effects associated with antibiotics or anti-viral drugs.

Acute Respiratory Infections

Acute respiratory infections include infective conditions that tend to interfere with the normal process of breathing. It may only affect the upper respiratory system that starts at the sinuses and ends at the vocal cords or only the lower respiratory tract that begins at the vocal cords and ends at the lungs.

This infection is more dangerous for older adults, children, and patients with immunological disorders.

What Are the Common Signs and Symptoms of Acute Respiratory Infections?

The symptoms a patient may experience would be different if it is a lower or an upper respiratory tract infection.

The symptoms often include:

- Congestion in the nasal sinuses and the lungs
- Cough
- Running nose
- Sore throat
- Fatigue
- Difficulty in breathing
- Body aches
- A mild to moderate fever over 39°C (103°F) usually with chills

- Loss of consciousness
- Dizziness

What Are the Causes of Acute Respiratory Infections?

- Acute ear infections
- Acute pharyngitis
- Common cold
- Pneumonia
- Bronchitis
- Bronchiolitis

Who Is at a Higher Risk of Developing Acute Respiratory Tract Infections?

It is nearly impossible to avoid exposure to bacteria and viruses. Hence, any person can develop respiratory infections. However, certain risk factors can increase the chances of developing acute respiratory infections, as explained below:

- The immune system of older adults and children is more vulnerable to viruses.
- Children are particularly at a higher risk due to their increased likelihood of coming in contact with other children who could be the carriers of viruses.
- Children often do not wash their hands properly. They are also likely to rub their nose and eyes or put their fingers in their mouths, thus resulting in a faster viral spread.
- Patients with heart diseases and pre-existing lung problems are more likely to develop recurrent acute respiratory tract infections.
- Any person whose immune system has become weaker due to other diseases is also at risk. It reduces the ability of the immune cells to attack and destroy viruses, thus allowing the infection to develop into full-blown symptoms and the infectious organism to thrive easily into the respiratory passages.
- Smokers also are at very high risk and have more difficulty in recovering.

How Are Acute Respiratory Infections Diagnosed?

The physician focuses on assessing breathing and other respiratory functions during a respiratory examination. They would check for the accumulation of fluids or inflammation in the lung tissues by listening for the abnormal sounds in the lungs while you are breathing. The doctor might also examine the nose and ears and check the throat for the possible signs of inflammation and infections.

If the physician believes that the infection has affected the lower respiratory tract, a chest X-ray and CT scan might be necessary to assess the condition of the pulmonary tissues.

Lung function tests can also be helpful for the diagnosis of infections in the lungs. Pulse oximetry, also called pulse ox, can check how much oxygen can get into the lungs. A physician might also take a swab from the nose and mouth or ask the patient to cough up a sputum sample (secretions coughed up from the throat and lungs) to check for the specific type of viruses or bacteria responsible for causing the disease.

What Are the Potential Complications of Acute Respiratory Infections?

The complications of acute respiratory infections are extremely severe. They may permanently damage the lung tissues and even result in death.

The complications linked to the infections in the respiratory tract include:

- Respiratory arrest that occurs when the breathing ceases or the lungs stop working
- Respiratory failure that occurs due to the rise in the levels of carbon dioxide (CO_2) in the blood as a result of the lungs not functioning efficiently
- Congestive cardiac failure

Prevention of Acute Respiratory Infections

Most causes of acute respiratory infections are not avoidable. Hence, prevention is considered the best way to ward off harmful acute respiratory infections.

Practising good hygiene through the following habits is highly recommended for protecting yourself against acute respiratory infections:

- **Wash your hands regularly**, especially after being at a public place such as schools, offices, parks, or malls.
- Always sneeze into a handkerchief, in a tissue, or the arm of your shirt. Though this may not help ease your symptoms, it would prevent you from spreading the infection-causing germs to others.
- Avoid touching your nose, eyes, and other parts of the face, including your mouth. This prevents introducing viruses and bacteria into your body system.

- Avoid smoking.
- Make sure you include essential vitamins in your diet, like vitamin C, which can strengthen your immune system.

What Are Chronic Lung Infections?

Chronic respiratory infections or chronic lung infections include those that do not resolve quickly or do not go away at all despite regular conventional treatments such as antibiotics or anti-viral drugs.

The most common causes of these infections include chronic obstructive pulmonary disease (COPD), bronchiectasis, and cystic fibrosis, all of which involve an inability to clear the mucous secretions accumulated in the lungs. All persistent or chronic lung infections tend to have alternate periods of stability followed by periods of exacerbations (with changes in cough, sputum, dyspnoea, and fatigue).

Chronic respiratory infections usually occur due to the compromised state in the dynamic action of ventilation in the lungs and air passages. Moreover, immunocompromised patients and those already suffering from the dysfunctions and tissue destruction linked to chronic obstructive pulmonary disease (COPD) are also more likely to develop these infections recently.

Some examples of the underlying mechanisms responsible for causing chronic lung infections include:

- Bronchiectasis-related pneumonia (with an inability to clear mucous and secretions)
- Pneumonia due to COPD or aspiration
- Cystic fibrosis-related pneumonia
- Tuberculosis

What Are the Causes of Chronic Lung Infections?

Depending on the specific illnesses or the extent of debilitation, respiratory changes that might lead to chronic lung infections may include:

- Loss of or damage to the alveoli in the lungs
- Loss of elastic recoil of the chest wall leading to trapping of air and an increase in the residual volume of the lungs
- Diminished respiratory muscle endurance and strength

- Inability to increase the rate of respiratory efforts to compensate for the loss of pulmonary functions
- Reduction in the process of exchange of gases like oxygen and carbon dioxide in the lungs
- Reduced ability of the cilia to move bacterial debris and mucous upward
- Decreased cough and the gag reflex (often leading to reduced clearance and aspiration pneumonia)

The common causes of chronic respiratory infections are discussed in detail below:

Chronic Respiratory Infections in Institutionalised Settings

The aforementioned risk factors may get extensively compounded in closed settings. This is especially for the immunocompromised patients who need to get admitted to a nursing home, or other healthcare facilities, and institutions for a prolonged period or short periods frequently.

These infections are considered hospital-acquired infections as they occur in institutionalised settings. Hence, they are more likely to affect patients who need to get admitted to a hospital frequently due to any pre-existing illness.

Hospital-acquired pneumonia is also likely to have a drug-resistant nature. Co-morbidities are also the strongest independent predictors of mortality risk in patients with chronic lung infections.

Smoking

Smoking can lead to most of the respiratory changes cited above. The upward or the elevating movements of the cilia to move the inhaled particles, like viruses and bacteria, out from the pulmonary passage may become inert in smokers.

Smoking is also the primary cause of COPD. The damage or inflammatory destruction of the alveoli occurring due to COPD in smokers may decrease the surface area that can be used for the process of respiration.

These changes could be so severe in smokers that any infection may already become synergistic for compromise during the gaseous exchange.

Stroke

One of the most severe stroke complications is losing the swallowing or gag reflex. This difficulty can create a scenario in which foods and drinks passing into the oesophagus while eating can pass into the lungs, providing a suitable medium of growth for bacteria, thus triggering the risk of repeated infections.

Immunocompromised State

Patients who are immunocompromised (for example, due to infections such as HIV and those who are immunocompromised pharmacologically due to the long-term use of systemic corticosteroids) are more vulnerable to developing recurrent chronic respiratory tract infections.

Even commonly used medications, including antibiotics, might be ineffective in these cases. The body may also be deprived of its first lines of defence via limitations imposed on the innate immune system due to the immunocompromised state.

What Are the Common Symptoms of Chronic Respiratory Tract Infections?

- Cough
- Shortness of breath
- Mucous production
- Fatigue
- Sore throat
- Fever
- Postnasal drip with nasal discharge
- Bad breath

These symptoms may vary depending on the specific underlying cause.

Diagnosis of Chronic Respiratory Tract Infections

A healthcare provider would take a detailed history and perform a physical examination to diagnose these infections. Specific laboratory testing and imaging studies such as X-rays of the chest, CT scan of the chest, and MRI may also be needed to confirm the diagnosis.

Treatment of Chronic Respiratory Infections

The treatment for most chronic respiratory infections is based on the specific symptoms the patient is having and the diagnosis. Your Ayurvedic physician may recommend a particular treatment for you depending on the underlying dosha and the imbalances in the body's physiological mechanisms.

The possible treatments that might be recommended include:

- Methods to clear mucous such as a nasal wash are often recommended for patients with chronic sinus problems.

- Effective coughing techniques with or without airway clearance devices may also be recommended to clear the chronic respiratory infections in the lower air passages.

- Herbal medications may be prescribed for treating the infection.

- Smoke avoidance is highly advisable for clearing the infection, improving lung functions, and restoring the ability of the pulmonary tissues to protect themselves against infectious pathogens.

- In case one or more of your family member or work colleague smokes, it is advisable to request that person/s quit smoking or smoke outside and not in your presence.

Prevention of Chronic Respiratory Infections

There are several ways that can help you avoid infections in the respiratory tract, as explained below:

- Wash your hands regularly with soap, and plenty of water, especially before eating food and after you have had a bout of coughing or sneezing.

- Alcohol-based hand sanitisers could be more effective for cleaning your hands when soap and water are unavailable.

- Cover your mouth and nose with a tissue or a handkerchief when you cough and sneeze. Throw the tissue into the trash bin after using it.

- Avoid touching the eyes, nose, and mouth as germs are more likely to spread in this manner.

- Stay at home when you are sick. This approach would keep you from infecting others and prevent the further spread of the infection.

- Try to avoid close direct contact with people already sick with a respiratory infection.

- The use of vaccines is also recommended for protecting yourself against infections. For example, the influenza vaccine (flu vaccine) is to be taken yearly, often before or during the months of fall.

In case you notice any bothersome symptoms that could be linked to respiratory infections, consult your Ayurvedic physician to help detect the possible cause, get a diagnosis, and begin the treatment at the earliest before the full-blown symptoms of the infection occur.

Ayurvedic Treatment for the Management of Respiratory Tract Infections

Ayurveda is one of the oldest and the most effective medical systems globally. The earliest account of Ayurvedic treatments comes from the collection of Hindu religious texts known as the Vedas, which are believed to be written nearly 3,000 years ago.

Even today, the Ayurvedic system of medicine is practised widely across the world as one of the most effective and the safest form of alternative medicine, especially for the management of acute and chronic respiratory infections. The practitioners of the Ayurvedic system of medicine can recommend the best herbal remedies to treating your health issues. As this book has demonstrated, they follow a holistic approach that often includes correcting nutritional deficiencies, balancing the underlying dosha, exercising, and making healthy lifestyle changes.

There is ample scientific evidence suggesting the effectiveness of Ayurvedic medications for treating respiratory health problems, including common infections such as the cold, bronchitis, sinusitis, and flu.

However, some herbs are more commonly used in Ayurvedic medicine as they possess specific medicinal properties, which can improve the functions of the respiratory system and restore health in a much shorter duration.

Ayurveda also recommends making healthy additions to your lifestyle and diet to help you manage and prevent respiratory infections like a common cold or flu more efficiently.

Here are some of the most effective herbal treatments you can adopt to overcome the symptoms of common respiratory infections:

Ayurvedic Treatment for Unproductive (Dry) Cough

A dry cough refers to a form of cough that does not produce mucous or phlegm. It could be a symptom of a common cold or even asthma. Allergens and pollutants in the air are also known to cause a dry or unproductive cough.

Tulsi (holy basil) is one of the common remedies effective in treating dry cough, throat irritation, and fever. In Ayurveda, Tulsi is also known as the 'queen of herbal remedies' for the powerful therapeutic and preventive potential this herb possesses.

Tulsi tea is also touted as an effective and fast-acting home remedy against cough, including both the dry cough and the productive cough that results in mucous production.

Tulsi may help liquefy phlegm and improve the symptoms of respiratory infections such as cough and breathing difficulties that are usually caused due to bronchitis, pneumonia, and sinusitis. This herb is also effective for relieving allergies, asthma, and other lung diseases like COPD and emphysema.

The potential health benefits of Tulsi tea also include prompt relief from breathlessness caused due to respiratory infections as well as allergic conditions like asthma. It has been found that this herb can improve lung capacity. It can produce less laboured breathing by clearing the air passages through its action of liquefying the mucous secretions accumulated as a result of the infections.

Holy basil also seems much safer than most other commonly used drugs like antibiotics. This herb may help normalise blood pressure, sugar, and lipid levels. These attributes make this herb one of the best holistic medicines for improving your overall health. It can relieve the symptoms of respiratory infections and improve your general health by protecting you against other common chronic diseases such as diabetes, hypertension, and hyperlipidaemia.

You can use this herb by making Tulsi tea at home. You need to brew about four to six leaves of Tulsi in a glass of water for about 5 to 10 minutes. Strain the liquid and drink it immediately while it is still warm to enjoy the soothing effect of this herb on the air passages to relieve cough and reduce mucous.

Ayurvedic Medicines for the Treatment of Productive Cough (Cough With Phlegm)

Ginger is one of the widely used herbs in the Ayurvedic system of medicine. Modern research has found that this herb contains several active ingredients that provide anti-inflammatory and antioxidant benefits.

The ginger's potential benefits that could be effective for the treatment of productive cough caused due to respiratory infections are linked to its ability to reduce swelling and inflammation in the air passages.

The active ingredients in ginger, such as 6-gingerol, 6-shogaol, and 8-gingerol, possess the potential to relax the smooth muscles in the throat. These effects of ginger would improve the cough caused due to common respiratory infections like a cold, pneumonia, and flu.

You can make warm ginger tea at home by grating a small piece of ginger and adding it to a cup of hot water. Let it steep for about 5 to 10 minutes and then, strain and drink the liquid. It is best to drink it in small sips to let the soothing effect created by the warmth last for longer.

Ayurvedic Medicine for the Treatment of Sore Throat and Cough

Liquorice root possesses anti-inflammatory compounds. The effectiveness of applying the extracts of the liquorice root topically to the sore throat caused due to surgery has been highly valued in

Ayurvedic medicine. Liquorice root can reduce throat pain by creating a natural anti-inflammatory effect.

Additionally, the pain-relieving effects of the liquorice gargle could effectively prevent respiratory infections and throat pain in patients who have undergone thoracic surgery.

Gargling with the solution made by diluting the liquorice root extract in 30 ml of water could provide significant relief from these symptoms. Several cases have reported instant relief from the post-operative sore throat following this simple remedy.

Ayurvedic Medicines for the Treatment of Cough with Fever

Sudarshana powder is a commonly used Ayurvedic medicine for the treatment of fever caused due to respiratory infection. It contains a combination of more than 50 herbal ingredients. This herb has a sharp, bitter taste.

It might also help reduce fever associated with other symptoms of chronic respiratory infections like anorexia, severe fatigue, an upset stomach, and nausea.

Ayurvedic Medicines for the Treatment of Running Nose with Cough

Garlic is believed to have potent anti-viral and antimicrobial properties that could reduce the risk of developing cold or more serious respiratory infections like pneumonia and bronchitis.

It is estimated that adults tend to have nearly two to four episodes of a common cold per year on average. Regular use of garlic could improve your immunity and protect you against the germs known to cause respiratory infections, thus reducing your chances of developing these issues.

Regular use of garlic in a dose of about 180 milligrams a day could protect the respiratory passages against infection-causing germs, thanks to the presence of allicin in this herb. This active ingredient is responsible for the strong smell of garlic. However, this compound is also revered for its natural anti-inflammatory and antioxidant potential to protect you against the risk of repeated respiratory infections throughout the year.

You can add garlic to your regular diet or try consuming 1 to 2 raw cloves of this herb every day.

Some other herbs that you can try to obtain relief from the symptoms of respiratory infections include:

Turmeric (Curcuma longa)

Known to have strong anti-inflammatory properties, turmeric would help you get relief from the inflammation in your lungs and avoid chest congestion and breathing problems as well.

Tumeric can manage most viral and bacterial infections. It also has several other health benefits. It can prevent heart diseases and reduce the risk of Alzheimer's disease and cancer, owing to the high amount of a medicinal compound called curcumin present in it.

Ashwagandha (Withania somnifera)

This herb offers numerous health benefits. It would help your body manage mental and physical stress and lead a happy and healthy life. It would also aid in managing respiratory tract infections, as well as quickly rejuvenate the body's cells and heal lung infections.

This herb's natural antioxidant and anti-inflammatory properties would help manage inflammation in the air passages caused due to infections. This fantastic herb may also boost your immunity.

Neem (Azadirachta indica)

This herb possesses antimicrobial and anti-inflammatory properties that would help you deal with infections, allergies, and other respiratory diseases that might have occurred due to bacteria and viruses in general. Neem is also revered for its antioxidant properties.

Other Effective Home Remedies for Treating Cough and Cold

Honey Tea

You can prepare honey tea by adding about two or three teaspoons of honey to a cup of warm water, milk, or tea. Drink it while it's warm to soothe your irritated and inflamed throat to derive instant relief from the symptoms of respiratory infections.

Saltwater Gargle

Saltwater is known to help with reducing mucous secretions and phlegm accumulated in the throat. You can prepare a saltwater gargle by adding 1/4th to half a teaspoon of salt in a glass of water.

Steam

Taking steam inhalations is a popular and effective technique in helping clear mucous and phlegm from your lungs. You can take steam inhalation at home by simply filling a bowl with hot water or even by having a warm shower or bath. Consider adding a few drops of eucalyptus oil to the water for bath or inhalation for better results.

Bromelain

This is an enzyme present in pineapple. Consuming pineapple or bromelain supplements would help break down the mucous in the throat and clear the infection in a shorter duration.

Peppermint

Peppermint tends to help soothe the throat and break down the phlegm and mucous. You can try drinking peppermint tea or even adding peppermint oil to your steam bath.

Conclusion

Ayurveda offers some of the most effective natural remedies for managing respiratory infections. The herbs used in the Ayurvedic system of medicine would help you manage the symptoms of cold and flu relatively immediately.

Ayurvedic Treatments for Relief From Asthma Attacks

Asthma is a chronic disorder characterised by recurrent episodes of difficulties in breathing that exposure to an allergen triggers. The symptoms of an asthma attack, such as wheezing, cough, breathlessness, and constriction in the chest, occur due to the inflammatory changes occurring in the air passages and increased production of mucous secretions in the bronchi and bronchioles. These abnormal changes are attributed to the exaggerated reaction of the immune system.

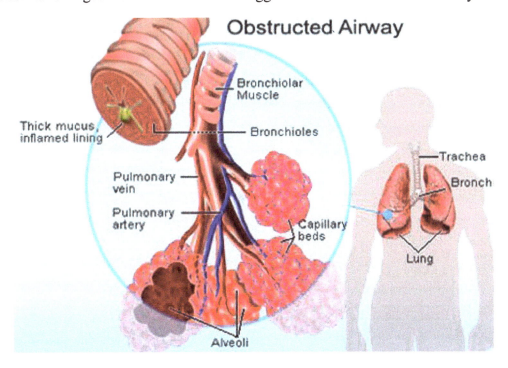

Let us look at the symptoms of an asthma attack and abnormal changes occurring in the body before and during an episode of breathlessness.

What Are the Common Signs and Symptoms of Asthma?

Breathlessness

This primary symptom characterises asthma attacks. Breathing difficulties may also occur due to other disorders such as congestive cardiac failure, myocardial infarction, pneumonia, and bronchitis. However, when breathlessness repeatedly occurs, when the body is exposed to a substance to which a person is hypersensitive, it could be considered a sign of asthma.

The substances to which the hypersensitive reaction occurs are known as allergens. Allergens can vary among different patients. However, some of the common allergens that can precipitate an attack of asthma include:

- Dust
- Fur of animals
- The smell of deodorants, perfumes, and flowers
- Weather changes
- Frigid weather
- Food additives, colouring agents, and preservatives

The reaction of each patient to any of these allergens could vary. While some patients may develop a severe asthma attack due to dust particles, some may not experience any symptoms at all.

Hence, it is crucial to identify the substances to which you are allergic. This approach will help you avoid factors that can cause an asthma attack and reduce the frequency of episodes.

Wheezing

Wheezing is not precisely a symptom, but it is a sound that commonly occurs when air passes through constricted passages. The sound is similar to what we hear when we whistle or blow air through a narrow pipe.

The abnormal immune response triggered following the exposure to the allergen results in a constriction of the bronchi and bronchioles. As a result, these air passages tend to become narrow. So, when you breathe in air, it passes through these narrow air passages producing a wheezing sound.

However, wheezing can be heard only in severe cases of asthma attacks. Often, the wheezing sound is not loud enough to be heard by bare ears. However, a doctor can detect this sign through the auscultation of the chest. Auscultation by placing a stethoscope over the chest would enable a doctor to hear the wheezing sound even in mild cases of asthma.

Cough

Cough is a common symptom that may occur before and during an attack of breathlessness. It occurs when the body is exposed to an allergen such as the fur of animals, pollutants, dust, or pollens. When these particles enter the lungs through the nose, the immune system recognises them as a foreign body. It reacts exaggeratedly to remove them from the system. These efforts increase mucous production in the lungs and the air passages like bronchi and bronchioles so that the perceived foreign object can be expelled from the body through coughing.

However, excessive mucous production may also worsen asthma symptoms as they cause the narrowing of the airways. The collection of mucous secretions in the air passages obstructs airflow and, thus, precipitates breathlessness. The body's effort to remove the allergens or the foreign body through the production of mucous results in coughing.

Cough associated with asthma attacks usually occurs at night. The exact cause of the higher incidence of cough at night is unknown. However, it is believed to occur due to the colder weather during night hours or the chest's compression due to the diaphragm's upward shifting in the lying down position.

When you lie down, the diaphragm – a thick muscular wall that separates the chest and the abdominal cavities – shifts upwards, resulting in the compression of the lungs. This motion could reduce the capacity of the lungs resulting in breathing difficulties.

You can avoid the risk of cough and the consequent asthma attacks by maintaining an appropriate room temperature and keeping one or two pillows under your head while sleeping.

Tiredness

You may feel extreme weakness and exhaustion a few hours before the attacks of breathlessness. These warning signs tend to be more common when the attacks occur during winter or fall months or weather changes.

It suggests that the body is trying hard to cope with the changes in its surroundings. This symptom may also occur when the triggering factor is not strong enough to cause a sudden attack of breathlessness.

Some patients experience being easily worn out after minimal physical activities or exercising. These symptoms suggest that the body is putting in efforts to counter the effect of the allergens on your body. These efforts could work out the body excessively, due to which the patient tends to feel weak and severely exhausted.

Some other symptoms of asthma attacks include:

- Feelings of anxiety, restlessness, and panic
- Pain, pressure, or a sense of constriction in your chest
- Rapid breathing
- Difficulty in talking

- Excessive sweating
- Inability to exhale fully
- Pale face
- Blue lips and fingernails

A diagnosis of asthma often brings about several changes in the patient's life. It could harm your decisions related to dietary habits and vacation plans, especially if you are sensitive to food additives and weather changes.

It is prevalent for asthma patients to experience some warning signs that begin a few hours or even a day or two before the actual episode of breathlessness. These early symptoms may vary among different patients.

Being aware of the symptoms of an asthma attack and what exactly happens during the attack is imperative. It would help you stay alarmed about an upcoming episode of breathlessness. This action would give you enough time to prepare yourself to minimise the symptoms and overcome the breathlessness with ease.

What to Do During a Severe Asthma Attack?

All asthma patients dread being caught with a severe asthma attack! An asthma attack can come at any time and cause considerable disturbances in the activities you are performing. Perhaps, it is this uncertainty related to asthma attacks that make patients more anxious.

It can strike you at any time and any place! Hence, it is highly advisable to be armed with different ways to control breathlessness through natural methods.

When you develop a severe asthma attack, keeping calm would be the key to controlling the symptoms. Several natural ways can help you minimise the symptoms of an asthma attack and ease your breathing.

Let us look at the most effective natural methods to relieve breathlessness during a severe asthma attack.

A Four-Step Approach for Preventing a Severe Asthma Attack

If you get an asthma attack, the first thing you must avoid is panic. If you panic or become more anxious, the state created would generate signals sent to the brain indicating you are trapped in a dangerous situation. Your brain, in turn, would respond by stimulating the production and release of some enzymes and hormones to prepare you to fight or escape the adverse situation.

This response might increase heart rate and breathing, trigger high blood pressure, and excessive sweating. This reaction is called the 'fight and flight' response triggered by the body. It enables your body to be quick and reactive instead of being thoughtful and critical of your actions or thinking.

This reaction would make you act emotionally or impulsively instead of rationally, which could significantly inhibit your recovery.

That is why it is crucial to avoid getting panicky during a severe asthma attack. Instead, it is advisable to follow the strategies described below:

1. Stay calm. This step would prevent symptoms from worsening by avoiding the tightening of the chest muscles and thus, ease the breathing.

2. If you are lying down, get up and sit upright. An upright position would make the air passages straight without any curvatures and allow for improved or smoother airflow through them.

3. Take deep breaths. Breathing in deeply through the nose and breathing slowly through the mouth would slow down the breathing rate and inhibit hyperventilation.

4. Move away from the possible triggers. Several factors, including dust, perfumes, deodorants, and cigarette smoke, trigger an attack of breathlessness in patients with an allergy. Move away from the sources of the allergens to get faster relief from breathlessness.

Use Salt and Water Treatment to Relieve Severe Asthma Attacks

When an asthma attack strikes, you can try some simple remedies conveniently found in your home. Salt and water treatment often works as a perfect home remedy for relieving asthma attacks.

Simply take a pinch of sea salt and place it under the tongue. Do not gulp it. Let it dissolve on its own. Drink two to three glasses of water while the salt is dissolving.

Placing the salt under the tongue would open up the airways and allow you to breathe more easily. However, avoid drinking cold water. Also, make sure you use sea salt instead of the common table salt.

Apple Cider Vinegar

This concoction is another natural remedy you may try during a severe asthma attack. You would be able to obtain considerable relief from breathlessness within just one hour of using this remedy.

Apple cider vinegar would boost the natural ability of the body's immune system to fight the effects of allergens. It may also help maintain the balance between the body's acidic/alkaline levels, thus quickly reducing inflammation and swelling in the air passages. It would also liquefy the mucous secretions accumulated in the respiratory passages and thus, prevent the obstruction to breathing.

To use, mix one or two tablespoons of apple cider vinegar in a glass of warm water and drink it.

Take Steam Inhalation

Taking steam inhalation could offer a quick way to obtain relief from breathlessness during an asthma attack. Steam inhalation produces a tremendous therapeutic and soothing effect on your airways.

It may enhance the blood circulation in the lungs, bronchi, and bronchioles. This attribute would allow for the faster absorption of the mucous accumulated in the airways and clear these passages for easy breathing.

Steam inhalation would also increase the humidity in the bronchi and bronchioles and thus, lubricate them. This method might help reduce the dryness in the airways, a common precursor to a severe asthma attack.

Steam inhalation can produce an anti-inflammatory effect and reduce swelling in the airways. It would ensure a free flow of air through them and allow you to breathe easily.

How to Manage Asthma Naturally?

Most patients with asthma are advised to use bronchodilators, steroidal drugs, and inhalers containing these medications. However, you should be aware that bronchodilators can only temporarily relieve the problem. They do not provide any long-term relief or prevent these attacks.

Additionally, bronchodilators and steroidal medications cause serious side effects, primarily when you use them over several months to years. That is why it is crucial to be aware of the natural remedies for asthma.

Natural asthma treatment involves alternative therapies, the use of herbs, and changes in your lifestyle to support the body's functions and the ability to prevent or relieve the attacks of breathlessness.

Being aware of the ways to treat asthma naturally could improve the quality of your life by minimising the intensity and frequency of the attacks of this disease.

Let us have a look at some of the best natural ways to manage asthma through a personalised approach.

Personalised Approach for the Natural and More Efficient Treatment of Asthma

A personalised approach holds the key to the successful management of asthma. Asthma is not an acute disease that presents with any typical symptoms similar in all patients. Even the causes of asthma vary among different patients. Some patients suffer from this disease due to their genetic makeup; others develop it due to a faulty lifestyle or occupational factors such as smoking or working in a bakery (Baker's asthma).

Also, different asthma patients have allergies to various substances. The common allergens include animal fur, the smell of perfumes and deodorants, and additives and colouring agents in foods.

So, it makes sense to treat each patient differently when a person has asthma due to various causes and allergens and differing symptoms. That is why a personalised approach is ideal for asthma management. This approach is devised after the Ayurvedic physician's complete physical health check-up and consultation that involves questions related to the patient's dietary habits, occupation, lifestyle, and other factors that might have played a role in developing asthma attacks.

The patients are advised to follow a specific regimen customised based on the information provided. This approach includes avoiding allergens, making healthy changes in the lifestyle, improving dietary habits, and supporting the natural ability of the body to counter the effect of allergens.

This natural and customised approach can help asthma patients avoid breathlessness attacks and live stress-free lives.

Identifying the Root Cause

There are two methods for treating asthma. The first is the simple method, and the other is deeper. The simple approach is often more accessible as it aims to relieve the symptoms visible to us by just taking bronchodilators and inhalers. However, the results with these treatments are also superficial and too short-lasting!

If you want to enjoy long-lasting results, you must follow the more difficult route and go deeper to identify the real cause of your asthma. You have to find the exact substances to which you are allergic or hypersensitive.

Considering the long list of allergens, you may think of this as an impossible task. But, with little effort, it is possible to shortlist the potential triggers and arrive at the exact allergens. All you need to do is maintain a diary of your routine in which you can note down the foods you ate, the changes made in your soaps or perfumes, and the weather changes.

In short, you have to note everything that you suspect could cause asthma. The next step involves correlating this information with the actual attacks of asthma. This approach would help you short-list a few substances exposed to that have repeatedly coincided with breathlessness attacks.

Once you have crossed this step, you can identify the exact allergens with the trial-and-error method. Finding the exact allergens would help you make appropriate changes in your diet and lifestyle. This way your exposure to them will be minimised, and so will be the asthma attacks!

Preventing Infections

Infections in the respiratory tract affect the functions of the lungs, bronchi, and bronchioles. They cause severe irritation and inflammation in the airways, which would precipitate an asthma attack.

Natural asthma treatments aim to prevent bacterial, viral, and fungal infections to ensure optimum health of the respiratory tract. The treatment should be focused on avoiding infections by strengthening the functions of the immune system and allowing it to destroy the disease-causing germs efficiently.

Natural Herbs for Asthma Treatments

A personalised treatment containing natural herbs could help you prevent asthma attacks. Herbs are Mother Nature's gifts that possess potent medicinal properties. They would help regulate the functions of your immune system and thus, prevent an exaggerated reaction of the immune cells to the allergens while also preventing the infections.

Some of the commonly used herbs for treating asthma include:

- Garlic
- Ginger
- Turmeric
- Oregano
- Holy basil
- Gingko Biloba

These natural herbs contain pure medicinal compounds that can cleanse your body and eliminate the root cause of asthma.

Diagnostic Approach to the Treatment of Asthma

A complete medical history would help your Ayurvedic physician recommend a personalised herbal formula. The personalised treatment will be based on the combination of bacteria, viruses, fungi, parasites, and toxic substances you are exposed to. It would also help detect the underlying causes of asthma specific to you. This process is a natural, unique, and non-invasive method that will help you keep asthma in control.

Conclusion

Ayurvedic treatments aim to ease the life of patients who have asthma by educating them about the safe and natural ways to manage this disease. Being aware of the dangerous side effects of using steroids and bronchodilators for longer is also an integral part of asthma treatment. A personalised approach to treating asthma for each patient based on their lifestyle habits, dietary needs, and the specific substances they are allergic to is the best way of countering this ail. It would allow asthma patients to achieve better control over the disease and help them prevent episodes of breathlessness.

Ayurvedic Treatment for Respiratory Infections Such As Tuberculosis

Tuberculosis (TB) is a common infectious disease that affects the lungs. However, it can also affect other organs in the body. It may develop when the bacteria spread through the droplets in the air. TB can sometimes be fatal; however, it is treatable and preventable in most cases.

In the past, TB was the primary cause of mortality around the globe. Following improved living conditions and the development of effective antibiotics, the prevalence of TB has fallen dramatically, especially in industrialised countries.

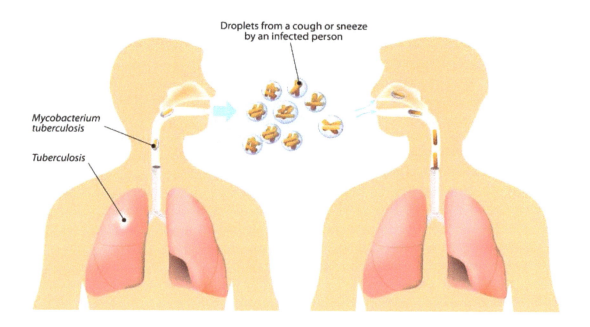

Still, in the last few decades, the incidence of this infection has started to increase again. The World Health Organization (WHO) had then described TB as a possible 'epidemic.' In the later part of the 20th century, the WHO reported TB to be among the most common causes of death worldwide and a leading cause of death due to a single infectious pathogen.

WHO had estimated that in 2018, more than 10 million people around the globe developed TB, and nearly 1.5 million patients have died from this disease, including those who also had severe viral infections like Human Immunodeficiency Virus or (HIV).

A vast majority of the patients affected with TB were in Asian countries. However, TB remains a significant cause of concern in most other areas, including the developed nations like the UK and the US.

Currently, antibiotic resistance contributes to the renewed concerns about the reduced chances of complete recovery of patients with TB. Some strains of this disease are not responding even to the most effective antibiotics and other treatment options. In such cases, TB can become extremely difficult to treat.

This incidence is why it is critical to focus on the alternative therapies that could strengthen immunity against bacteria and promote faster healing of the affected tissues, ultimately improving the patient's chances of complete recovery and prevent the risk of death.

Please keep reading to learn the common symptoms of TB, its causes, and treatment options.

What Is Tuberculosis?

A patient with TB often experiences swollen lymph nodes. It is the characteristic sign of this infection.

Patients may develop TB due to the inhalation of the bacteria called Mycobacterium tuberculosis. The disease is the most contagious when it affects the lungs. However, a person would usually become sick only after close contact with another patient with this form of TB.

Latent TB (or TB Infection)

In this form, a patient may have the TB bacteria in their body and never develop the symptoms. In these patients, the body contains the bacteria, though they do not replicate to cause the full-blown symptoms of the disease. In such cases, the patients would still have a TB infection, though not active infections. This disease is called latent TB.

In latent TB, the patient may never experience any symptoms. They would be unaware that they have the infection. There would also be no risk of passing the latent infection to other people.

However, the patient with latent TB would still require to undergo treatment.

The CDC has estimated that nearly 13 million patients in the US have the latent form of TB.

Active TB (or TB Disease)

The body may fail to suppress the TB bacteria in this form of TB infection. This circumstance tends to be more common in patients whose immune systems have become weak due to an illness and the use of some medications.

The bacteria might replicate and cause severe symptoms when this occurs, resulting in active TB or TB disease. Patients with the active form of TB can spread this infection to others.

Without active medical intervention, TB can become active in about 5-10% of patients with this infection. In nearly 50% of patients, the progression to a more severe state may occur within the first two to five years of getting the initial infection.

The chances of developing active TB disease are higher in some groups of people, like:

- Those with a weak immune system
- People who have first developed this infection in the last 2 to 5 years
- Young children
- Older adults
- People who have not received any appropriate treatment for managing TB infection in the past
- People who use the injected recreational drugs

What Are the Early Warning Signs of TB?

- A persistent cough, which lasts for at least three weeks
- Phlegm that may have blood in it, when the patient coughs
- Loss of appetite
- Loss of weight
- Recurrent low-grade fever
- Swelling in the neck
- A general feeling of being unwell and fatigue

- Chest pain
- Night sweats

Symptoms of Specific Forms of TB

Latent TB

A patient with latent TB would have no signs. Also, no damage can be seen in the lungs on the chest X-ray. But, a blood test or skin prick test might help reveal that they have a TB infection.

Active TB

A patient with TB disease might experience a cough producing phlegm with fatigue, fever, chills, loss of appetite, and weight loss. These symptoms typically become worse over time. However, they can also go away spontaneously and return repeatedly.

TB Infection Beyond the Lungs

TB usually affects the lungs, though the symptoms may develop in the body's other organs. This issue tends to be more common in patients with a weak immune system.

TB affecting the organs other than the lungs is known to cause symptoms like:

- Persistently 'swollen glands' or swollen lymph nodes
- Abdominal pain
- Confusion
- Joint pain
- Bone pain
- Seizures
- Persistent headaches

Diagnosis of TB

A patient with latent TB would have no symptoms, though the infection might show up in some tests. Patients should ask for the TB test if they:

- Have been in close contact with or have spent time with a patient who has TB or is at risk of developing TB
- Work in the environment where TB might be present

- Have visited a country having a high prevention rate of TB

A doctor can make a diagnosis based on the symptoms and the patient's medical history. They may also perform the complete physical examination that involves listening to the sounds in the lungs with the help of a stethoscope and checking for any swollen lymph nodes.

Two tests can help detect the presence of TB bacteria. These tests include the TB skin test and the TB blood test.

However, these tests cannot indicate whether the TB is latent or active. The physician might advise a chest X-ray and a sputum test to test for the active TB disease.

All patients with TB need to undergo proper treatment, irrespective of whether the condition is latent or active.

Treatment of TB

With early detection and the use of appropriate medications, including antibiotics and herbal remedies, TB is treatable.

The suitable types of antibiotics and the length of the treatment usually depend on:

- The age and the overall health of the patient
- The site of the infection
- Whether they have latent TB or active TB
- Whether the strain of TB infecting the tissues is drug-resistant

Treatment of latent TB may vary depending on the patient's specific signs. It may also involve taking a course of antibiotics once a week for about 12 weeks, or once every day for about nine months.

The treatment of active TB often involves using several drugs for six to nine months. When a patient has a drug-resistant strain of TB, the treatment needs to be more intense and complex.

Also, it is essential to complete the entire course of the treatment, even after the symptoms have resolved. If a patient stops taking the medications early, some bacteria may survive and become resistant to the antibiotics. The patient may develop a more severe or drug-resistant form of TB in such cases.

Depending on the body's tissues affected due to TB, a physician may also recommend systemic corticosteroids.

The modern treatment of TB involves the usage of antibiotics and other medications. However, these treatments have multiple limitations, such as the risk of incomplete recovery due to antibiotic resistance, side effects like gastritis, and the like. This predicament emphasises the need to complement these treatments with herbal remedies to support faster recovery and avoid unpleasant side effects.

Prevention of TB

There are several ways to prevent TB and inhibit it from infecting others, as recommended by the Ayurvedic and the modern systems of medicine. Some of the most effective methods for the prevention of TB include:

- Getting the treatment and diagnosis early by being watchful for the possible signs
- Staying away from people, if you are already infected, until there is no risk of infecting others
- Wearing a mask at all times while being in the presence of others to prevent the spread
- Covering the mouth while speaking, coughing, or sneezing
- Staying or working in the well-ventilated rooms

TB Vaccination

In most countries, children receive the anti-TB vaccination called the BCG (Bacillus Calmette–Guérin) vaccine as a part of the regular immunisation program. Vaccination can help build immunity against the TB bacteria and reduce the risk of developing this condition.

Risk Factors for TB

Patients with a weak immune system are more likely to develop active TB. The following are some common issues that can make the immune system vulnerable:

Human Immunodeficiency Virus (HIV)

For a patient with HIV, TB is considered one of the most common susceptible infections. It means that patients with HIV have a much higher chance of developing TB and experiencing severe symptoms than those with a healthy immune system.

The treatment of TB is often complex in patients with HIV. However, it is possible to develop a comprehensive treatment plan aimed at addressing both these issues.

Smoking

Active smoking, second-hand smoke, and tobacco use can increase the risk of TB. These factors can make the disease harder to treat and even more likely to return even after the treatment. Avoiding smoking and minimising contact with smoke can help reduce the risk of TB.

Other Conditions

Some health issues that can weaken the immune system and increase the risk of TB include:

- Extremely light body weight
- Diabetes
- Substance abuse disorders
- Silicosis
- Head and neck cancer
- Severe kidney disease

Also, some forms of medical treatments, like an organ transplant, may impede the functions of the immune system, making it weaker, thus putting the patient at risk of infections like TB.

Spending time in a country where TB is prevalent can also raise the risk of developing this infection.

Complications of TB

If not managed properly, TB can lead to fatal consequences. If it spreads from the lungs to the other body parts, the infection may cause diseases affecting the cardiovascular system, urinary system, and metabolic dysfunctions.

TB may also lead to sepsis, a potentially life-threatening form of most infections.

Ayurvedic Treatment for TB

Charaka, the great sage of Ayurveda, has dedicated an entire chapter to the treatment (Chikitsa) of Tuberculosis (Rajyakshma).

TB can be treated more effectively by combining modern medications and alternative therapies. The patient must be treated with antibiotics and other relevant prescription medications to cure TB and avoid spreading to other people. Some alternative and complementary therapies may help support the recovery.

Even when complementary therapies are included in the treatment plan, conventional drugs must strictly be used as directed.

Here are some treatments recommended by the Ayurveda for effective management of TB:

- Eliminate all the suspected food groups that could lower immunity or cause allergies, including cheese, ice cream, eggs, wheat (gluten), soy, preservatives, and chemical food additives.

- Eat foods rich in iron and B-vitamins like whole grains, and dark leafy greens like spinach or kale.

- Eat antioxidant-rich foods like fruits (including cherries, blueberries, and tomatoes), and vegetables like bell pepper and squash.

- Avoid refined foods, like white bread, sugars, and pasta.

- Reduce your intake of red meats, lean meats, and cold-water fish.

- Use healthy cooking oils, like olive oil.

- Eliminate or reduce the intake of trans-fatty acids found in most commercially-baked foods like cookies, French fries, margarine, onion rings, crackers, cakes, doughnuts, and processed foods.

- Avoid the consumption of coffee and other stimulants like tobacco and alcohol.

You may address nutritional deficiencies by using the following supplements:

- Consider using multivitamin supplements containing nutrients and antioxidant vitamins like vitamins A, C, E, the B-complex, and D, and trace minerals like magnesium, calcium, selenium, and zinc

- Eat probiotic foods or use supplements containing Lactobacillus acidophilus or other beneficial bacteria for the maintenance of the digestive and immune health

- Consider using alpha-lipoic acid supplements for added antioxidant and immunological support, especially if your immune system is weak.

Herbal Remedies for Preventing and Treating TB

We talked about herbs being readily available in kitchen in the form of spices, or others in the form of pills, capsules, tablets, teas, and tinctures/liquid extracts in the market.

Some herbs might help relieve the symptoms of TB and support the prognosis when used in combination with the conventional medical treatments as given below:

- Turmeric
- Ginger
- Holy basil
- Aged Garlic (Allium sativum)
- Astragalus (Astragalus membranaceu)
- Rhodiola (Rhodiola rosea)

Conclusion

The active TB infection could be contagious and even life-threatening, especially when the patient does not receive proper treatment. As highlighted, most cases of TB are treatable. The most ideal case would be early diagnosis and medical intervention, which can considerably improve the prognosis and help the patient completely recover in a shorter duration.

Cardiovascular Disorders (Hypertension, Arrhythmia, Atherosclerosis)

Hypertension or high blood pressure has become a significant cause of disability and death worldwide. If neglected, it can result in several complications like heart attacks, cerebrovascular stroke, and kidney failure. In some cases, it may not cause any apparent symptoms until these complications occur. It also plays the role of a silent killer in the body.

Hence, it is essential to keep in mind that you may have hypertension even if you are seemingly healthy. The only way you can know about it is to get your blood pressure checked at regular intervals.

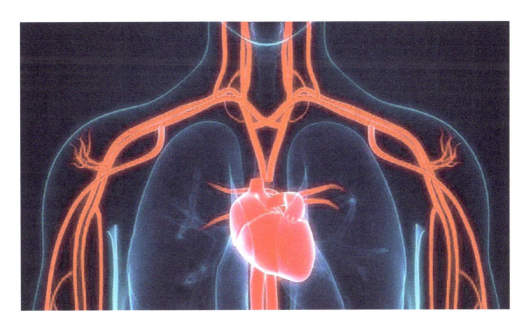

What Is Hypertension?

Hypertension means elevated blood pressure in the arteries. It is known as Rakta Gata Vata in Ayurveda. The normal blood pressure of a healthy adult is 120 mm of Hg systolic and 80 mm of Hg diastolic. The rise in blood pressure depends on age, gender, family history, physical activities, and diet.

Here are a few Ayurvedic remedies that can effectively lower blood pressure naturally.

Ayurvedic Remedies for Lowering Blood Pressure

Ashwagandha

Ashwagandha is a popular Ayurvedic herb known for its adaptogenic properties. It keeps the blood pressure within normal limits and reduces inflammation and damage in the arteries caused due to the persistently high blood pressure. It would strengthen the mind and body and improve a person's ability to handle psychological and physical stress, thus tackling the root cause of this illness. It would also increase vitality and resistance and produce a strengthening effect on bodily functions.

Stress is one of the most typical causes of high blood pressure. The increase in the production of stress hormones like cortisol would further elevate the blood pressure. Ashwagandha increases the person's ability to cope with emotional stress, creating greater inner calmness. This practice, in turn, would reduce the levels of cortisol circulating in the body and control the blood pressure.

Triphala

Triphala has been used for centuries for rejuvenating the body. It consists of three herbs that form a powerful combination, which works profoundly, though gentle. The three herbs are Haritaki (Terminalia chebula), Amla (Emblica officinalis), and Bibhitaki (Terminalia bellirica).

Triphala reduces hypertension and normalises blood circulation. It would also lower cholesterol, another common cause of hypertension, and prevent atherosclerosis. This formula's anti-inflammatory and anti-obesity effects may help control hypertension by tackling the other two causes of the illness, namely inflammation and obesity.

Jatamansi

Jatamansi protects the arteries from damage caused by free radicals. It might repair the arterial damage caused due to cholesterol plaques and thereby improve the inner diameter of the blood vessels. It can allow the blood to flow freely through the arteries, ensuring a lower force created by the blood on the walls of arteries.

This herb also creates a calming effect on the mind and body and hence, is highly effective in reducing psychological stress.

Arjuna

Arjuna is a powerful herb for treating high blood pressure. It reduces the low-density lipoprotein (bad) cholesterol level in the liver and increases the high-density lipoprotein (good) cholesterol, thereby reducing the risk of atherosclerosis.

It also reduces the effects of stress and anxiety on the heart functions by reducing the stress hormones production and protecting the blood vessels from the damage caused by them.

These herbal remedies are based on the healing principles of Ayurveda. These herbs are safe and natural and do not cause harmful side effects.

Diet and Lifestyle Recommendations by Ayurveda for the Comprehensive Management of Hypertension

For better control of the illness and for preventing complications, patients are advised to follow some dietary and lifestyle recommendations as given below:

- Avoid meat and eggs.
- Reduce the intake of table salt and other food items high in salts like pickles.
- Increase your protein intake.
- Eat lots of fruits like melons and vegetables like Garlic, lemon, and parsley.
- Avoid smoking as it increases heart rate. Smoking also worsens atherosclerosis resulting in further aggravation of the problem.
- Nurture love and affection. Love and an affectionate touch would drop your blood pressure significantly.
- Laugh more. It is the best medicine for laughter helps relieve anxiety and stress. It also emits positive energy and helps you keep negative energies at bay. Laughter also works as a good relaxation therapy. It controls the production of stress hormones. If you are frustrated, angry or sad, just laugh, and you will find yourself away from the rage. It is a very effective medicine that is always with you, without spending a penny for it.

Meditation and Breath Therapy for Hypertension:

You can achieve complete tranquillity of the mind and soul by meditating in the Corpse Pose. To practice this, take slow deep breaths and concentrate on the puffs. Focus on the temperature of the breaths while inhaling and exhaling. You may notice that the inhaled air is slightly colder than the exhaled air. Do this for about 10 minutes daily to get rid of mental and physical stress and the resulting high blood pressure. It is commonly observed that the people, who practice Corpse Pose, regularly have better control of their blood pressure.

How to Control Hypertension Safely and Naturally?

Hypertension, or high blood pressure, is associated with a risk of serious complications such as myocardial infarction and cerebrovascular stroke. Most patients with hypertension are prescribed anti-hypertensive drugs such as Amlodipine to control their blood pressure.

However, the use of these drugs may lead to serious side effects. Hence, patients are advised to follow the natural ways below to control their blood pressure. These natural ways would help keep your blood pressure within normal limits without the risk of any severe side effects.

Exercise Regularly

The best way to control your blood pressure is to exercise regularly. Simple exercises like walking, jogging, swimming, or doing household chores would lower your blood pressure. You may also incorporate cardiovascular exercises into your daily routine to improve circulation, cardiac efficiency, and lung capacity.

However, if you are a beginner and not ready for strenuous cardiovascular exercises, you can begin with simple stretching exercises. Pilates are also an excellent place to start with. All you need is half an hour of moderate physical activity five days a week.

Exercising would also help control obesity, which is a common precursor of hypertension. Avoid strenuous activities if your blood pressure is very high.

Take Power Walks

Taking a fitness walk at a brisk pace every day would help achieve better control over your blood pressure. Start with a walk of 30 minutes every day and gradually increase to an hour a day, instead of starting with a bang. A slow and steady approach is critical to allowing your body enough time to get used to any new exercise routine.

Reduce Your Salt Intake

As discussed earlier, sodium is the fiercest enemy of hypertensive patients. Hence, it is crucial to reduce your salt intake as it is high in sodium.

Sodium is also hygroscopic. It means it can pull water along with it. So, if sodium levels in your blood are high, there would be a higher amount of water retention in the body, resulting in a blood pressure increase.

Check the sodium content on the label of processed foods. It would be helpful to remove the salt shaker from your dining area. You can also use spices, lemon, herbs, and salt-free seasoning blends for seasoning your dishes.

Maintain a Healthy Weight

Obesity can increase the risk of developing hypertension and worsen the condition if you already suffer from it. Obesity may also cause more strain on the heart and result in poor blood circulation.

That is why losing excess weight is highly essential for lowering blood pressure. Maintaining a healthy weight would also help in preventing the complications of hypertension.

Breathe Deeply

Since stress is a significant cause of hypertension, the best way to prevent hypertension is to control stress. Deep breathing and meditation practices like yoga, tai chi, and qi-gong would reduce stress by allowing you to relax and feel calm. These practices may also regulate the stress hormones and renin, a kidney enzyme that raises blood pressure.

You can meditate for about 10 minutes in the morning and at night. Breathe in deeply and then exhale slowly to release all of your worries and tension.

When your blood pressure is under control, a proper blood supply to the vital organs like the heart, kidneys, and brain is ensured. Make sure you follow these natural ways and enter the safe zone of health and long life.

Treatment and Approach of Ayurveda for Cholesterol Disorders

Hypercholesterolemia is a disorder characterised by high levels of cholesterol. Cholesterol is a soft, waxy substance found among the fats in all body's cells, especially in the bloodstream. It is present in smaller quantities and forms a part of the nerve coverings, cell walls, and brain cells. Hence, it has an essential function in our body.

However, when this substance is present in the blood in excess quantities, it can cause blockages in the arteries resulting in severe consequences.

Dangers of High Cholesterol

An excessive amount of cholesterol circulating in the blood would lead to a slow build-up along the walls of the arteries of the heart and brain. It may combine with other substances and form thick, hard plaque deposits that can clog these arteries. This condition is called atherosclerosis.

In case the plaque breaks away in pieces and circulates in the blood, it can travel to distant organs like the heart or the brain, causing heart attacks and stroke, respectively.

Ayurvedic Treatments for Managing Cholesterol Disorders

The Ayurvedic approach for treating this condition includes eliminating the toxins and mucus from the blood vessels. This helps restore the digestive fire to allow the liver and intestine to perform optimally and burn excess fats.

The heightened cholesterol level would increase your risk of heart attack, diabetes, and hypertension. An unhealthy lifestyle coupled with sedentary habits and the increased consumption of junk foods has resulted in the rising incidence of hypercholesterolemia, a disorder characterised by high levels of lipids.

As a result, there is also a rise in the use of cholesterol-lowering drugs such as Atorvastatin.

However, these medications are known to cause serious side effects and affect the health of vital organs such as the liver, kidneys, heart, and eyes. You can easily prevent your dependency on these anti-lipemic drugs and avoid their side effects by following some simple natural ways to keep your cholesterol levels in control. Let us look at the natural methods to reduce your cholesterol levels.

Limit Your Consumption of Saturated and Trans Fats

Foods containing a high amount of saturated fats such as butter and red meat can increase your risk of hypercholesterolemia. Even low-fat dairy products and coconut oil have a very high amount of saturated and trans-fats. Avoiding these foods would control your cholesterol levels significantly.

Make sure you read the label of the ingredients before buying any product. If the label has partially hydrogenated fat as one of its ingredients, it means the product has trans-fats and must, hence, be avoided.

Increase Your Intake of Omega-3 Fatty Acids

Omega-3 fatty acids offer excellent protection to the heart by reducing LDL or bad cholesterol and increasing HDL or good cholesterol. Some of the best sources of omega-3 fatty acids include cold-water fishes such as halibut, salmon, mackerel, sardines, trout, and herring. Moreover, omega-3 fatty acids would also help reduce triglyceride levels.

Eat Fibre-Rich Foods

Foods containing soluble fibres like oats, barley, beans, and fresh fruits offer an effective natural way to control your cholesterol levels. You can also consume vegetables containing a high amount of soluble fibres such as carrots, beets, okra, eggplants, and Brussels sprouts and fruits like berries, oranges, pears, apricots, nectarines, and apples. These foods also help by preventing cholesterol absorption from the intestine into the blood.

Maintain a Healthy Weight

Obesity results from unhealthy dietary choices and a lack of physical activity. A higher cholesterol level would result in the build-up of fats in the abdominal region leading to central obesity.

Hence, losing excess weight is highly recommended for maintaining normal cholesterol levels. It would also help prevent high cholesterol complications such as diabetes, heart attacks, stroke, high blood pressure, and several forms of cancers.

Herbal Remedies

Herbal remedies such as onions, Amla, and oranges possess a natural anti-lipemic property. Onions, especially red onions, are effective in dealing with hypercholesterolemia. They would reduce the bad cholesterol levels and elevate the good cholesterol levels in the blood.

Some other natural ways to maintain healthy cholesterol levels are:

- Consume fresh fruits, whole grains, cereals, and vegetables

- Don't smoke
- Don't consume butter and processed foods
- Eat frequent small meals in a day

Keeping yourself armed with these natural home remedies would help you fight the worst enemy of your health, cholesterol, effortlessly. Try these home remedies to keep your cholesterol levels in control and prevent the risk of heart diseases.

Managing Arrhythmias

Several Small Meals

Having large meals increases the heartbeat, as all the blood is redirected to aid digestion. This mechanism aggravates the symptoms of arrhythmias. Therefore, you should consider having several small meals spaced out evenly in a day. Additionally, it will help you prevent arrhythmias and is also beneficial for your overall health.

Exercise

Exercise is considered an essential part of treating the most acute and chronic disorders. Doctors recommend reclined aerobic activities such as swimming, rowing and cycling to regulate the heart rate.

Reaction to Gluten

You should check your body's gluten sensitivity. Certain diseases need the patient to eat gluten for several weeks before the test. If your body is susceptible to gluten, it is better to avoid gluten. It may significantly increase your heart rate.

Healthy Diet

Diet is one of the crucial factors that would promote the body's well-being and healing. It plays a curative role in chronic diseases. Include lots of fruits, vegetables, fibres, and protein in your diet. Avoid caffeine, preservatives, processed foods, and artificial flavours to prevent arrhythmias.

Healthy Schedule

Hectic schedule and stress are the most significant reasons behind several health conditions. You must reduce the activity load and get more sleep by changing your schedule. Plan your activities at specific times that are more comfortable for you to prevent arrhythmias symptoms.

Quit Smoking and Avoid Alcohol

If you have the habit of smoking and consuming alcohol, you should quit them as soon as possible.

Both these habits increase your chances of arrhythmias. They can even worsen arrhythmias symptoms, as cigarettes and alcohol cause hypotension through the dilation of veins.

Supplements

There are certain supplements such as calcium, magnesium, and B-Complex that could help you compensate for the deficiencies in your body. Remember that the nutritional requirement of one person may not be the same as that of others; hence, it is essential to consult a physician before taking these supplements.

Positive Attitude

Living with a positive attitude will help you live a stress-free life. The more you think of negative things, the worse you will feel. Your mind and body are very much connected. If you do your best to stay happy, you will feel better physically and mentally.

The Ten Most Common Lifestyle Factors That Can Aggravate Arrhythmias

Smoking

Smoking can clog your arteries and damage the heart and the lungs, thereby affecting the functions of these vital organs. In the long-term, the damaging effect caused by smoking can become irreversible. Hence, you must quit this habit at the earliest.

Recreational Drugs

Recreational drugs like marijuana can alter how your body responds to blood pressure and heart rate changes. It can also cause several other health issues and also affect your mental health. Hence, it is best to avoid these harmful substances to prevent the symptoms of arrhythmias.

Heavy Meals

Eating heavy meals can worsen the symptoms of hypotension in individuals suffering from arrhythmias. This effect comes from the excessive pooling of blood in the abdomen to aid digestion. Eating large meals would shunt the blood towards the gut, which results in a reduced blood supply to the heart. To avoid this, you should have several smaller meals at regular intervals.

Carbonated Drinks

Individuals with arrhythmias should avoid carbonated drinks as excessive consumption of the same is associated with a vasovagal reaction. An excess intake of carbonated beverages can aggravate arrhythmias symptoms and may even lead to life-threatening complications.

Avoiding these drinks can help you reduce arrhythmias symptoms and live an active life.

Rigorous Exercises

Rigorous exercises may make arrhythmia patients feel worse. It is better to avoid strenuous and exhausting workouts. Some individuals will experience symptoms that last for a day or more, especially if they have any other cardiac disease. Before starting any exercise program, patients should check with their doctor and work accordingly.

Conclusion

Taking care of your heart by following healthy dietary habits and using herbal remedies would restore normal cardiac functions and protect you against the risk of heart diseases.

Natural Ayurvedic Remedies to Support the Healing of Varicose Veins

Varicose veins are a common problem that can occur due to the abnormally enlarged veins of the legs appearing close to the skin's surface. It usually affects the veins in the region of the calves and thighs. Varicose veins develop when the valves in these veins have weakened or are not functioning well, by which there is a backflow of blood.

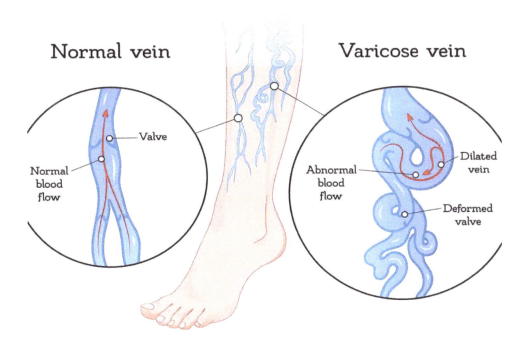

As a result, blood tends to stagnate into these veins instead of being pushed by the force of the calf muscles or vein walls. Due to this, these veins become enlarged and lax over time, leading to a state of varicosity.

The common symptoms of varicose veins are pain in the legs, fatigue, restlessness, and burning, or throbbing pain in the legs. Patients experiencing these symptoms may use the natural remedies given below to manage varicose veins effectively.

Maintain Healthy Weight

Obesity is one of the major contributing factors to varicose veins. Carrying excess weight can put a higher amount of pressure and strain on the veins of the legs, causing them to become lax and inflamed.

Hence, it is highly essential to reduce weight to get relief from varicose veins. You can lose weight by following a healthy, nutritious diet and exercising regularly.

Exercises

Regular exercises can ensure a proper flow of blood through the muscles of the legs and strengthen them. This method can increase the muscles ability to push blood from the legs against gravity toward the heart, thus reducing varicosity.

Also, sitting with a poor posture such as the forward head posture, sitting with your legs crossed, and standing for prolonged hours could result in the stagnation of the blood. As a result, blood could pool in the legs and thus worsen the varicose veins.

Exercises like leg lifts, bicycle legs, calf raises, and side lunges would prevent blood stagnation by strengthening these veins. Low-impact exercises like walking and bicycling are also ideal for patients with varicose veins as they help alleviate pressure.

Compression

Applying pressure on the legs with the help of specially designed stockings is one of the best ways to prevent the progression of varicose veins and obtain relief from the symptoms. The gentle and uniform pressure exerted by these stockings would result in the compression of the veins, thus reducing their diameter. This method may also increase the ability of valves to work more effectively and, therefore, prevent the backflow of blood.

The stockings would provide additional support for the walls of the veins, which facilitates the smooth flow of blood, and reduces the chances of stagnation.

Garlic

Garlic is a powerful herb that possesses excellent anti-inflammatory and antioxidant properties. It would help reduce the symptoms of varicose veins and prevent damage to the valves by protecting them from free radicals.

Garlic may also strengthen the muscles and walls of the veins, thus preventing laxity. Garlic also helps break down the harmful toxins in the blood vessels and improves blood circulation.

Slice up five to six garlic cloves by making a vertical slit and putting them in a glass jar. Add two orange extracts and three tablespoons of olive oil. Allow the mixture to sit for at least 12 hours. Gently massage the inflamed veins with this solution for 15 minutes. Repeat daily for two to three months.

Olive Oil

Improved blood circulation in the legs is the key to managing varicosity. Massaging the calf muscles using olive oil would help increase blood circulation and reduce pain and inflammation.

Olive oil would penetrate through the skin and strengthen the walls of the blood vessels by producing an anti-inflammatory action.

Mix one-fourth cup of olive oil in an equal quantity of vitamin E oil and warm it slightly. Massage the legs with this mixture for a few minutes. Do this twice every day for one or two months.

Grape Seed Extract

The tiny seeds inside the grapes are rich in antioxidant compounds and vitamin E. They would protect the walls of the blood vessels against the free radical damage and promote collagen production, which would help maintain the elasticity of the walls of the blood vessels. Grapeseed oil can be consumed orally or even used topically to massage the legs.

An Anti-Inflammatory Diet

A poor diet high in foods containing trans-fats, sugars, caffeine, processed foods, and alcohol can contribute to the development of varicose veins by causing vascular damage, poor circulation, elevated blood pressure, and weight gain.

On the contrary, certain foods can reverse the inflammation in the veins and improve the blood flow, thus making it possible to heal the varicose veins faster. Hence, it makes sense to ditch the unhealthy foods and switch to the anti-inflammatory foods given below for reducing the appearance of varicose veins:

- Antioxidant foods like berries, green veggies, and citrus fruits.

- High-fibre foods like chia seeds, flaxseeds, vegetables, fresh fruits, and legumes

- Natural diuretics such as parsley, basil, cucumber, dandelion greens, cilantro, fennel, asparagus, and celery.

- Foods with spices like cayenne pepper.

- Magnesium-rich foods like leafy greens, bananas, cruciferous veggies, avocado, and sweet potatoes.

- Wild-caught fish and seafood such as wild salmon, mackerel, sardines, anchovies, and tuna.

Conclusion

In addition to these home remedies, it is also essential to eliminate the factors that may worsen varicose veins, such as standing for prolonged hours, using contraceptive pills, and recurrent constipation to achieve long-term relief from this condition.

Ayurvedic Medications for the Treatment of Cancer

Cancer is a chronic condition due to abnormal cell and tissue growth in any organ or body part. The growth or mass is formed due to the unchecked multiplication of abnormal cells.

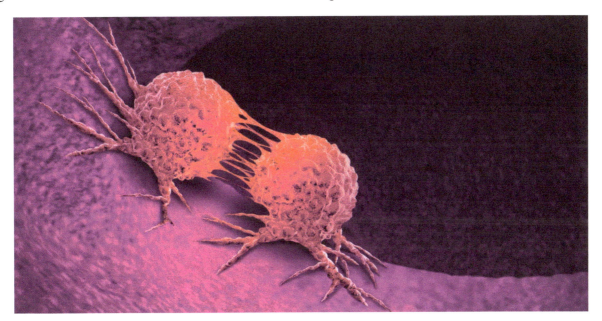

Cancer development is triggered due to the incorrect response of the immune system, which results in the stimulation of the division of unhealthy cells. The conventional treatments for this disease include chemotherapy drugs, radiotherapy, and surgery. The surgery is performed to excise the tumour mass.

Though these treatments are effective to a large extent in ensuring the complete recovery of the patients, they are also known to cause serious side effects. Hence, patients are advised to follow natural therapies, including Ayurvedic medications and conventional treatments, to allow for a faster recovery, ensure destruction of the cancer cells, and minimise the risk of side effects.

What Is Cancer?

Cancer is a disease in which the body's cells and tissues grow uncontrollably and spread to the body's healthy tissues.

Cancer may start almost anywhere in the body. Our body comprises trillions of cells. Usually, the cells grow and multiply to form new cells through the process known as cell division. When these new cells are damaged and become old, they die, and later, new cells take the place of the old cells.

Sometimes, this orderly process breaks down, due to which the abnormal and damaged cells begin to grow and multiply, which they shouldn't. These cells can form tumours that are nothing but the lumps of abnormal tissues. Tumours may be cancerous or non-cancerous.

- The cancerous tumours can invade or spread into the nearby tissues and even travel to the body's distant organs, forming new tumours (through a process known as metastasis). The cancerous tumours are also called malignant tumours. Some cancers grow to form solid tumours, though the blood cancers, like leukaemia, usually do not.

- On the other hand, benign tumours do not invade or spread into the nearby tissues. Once removed, these benign tumours usually do not grow back, while the cancerous tumours may sometimes do so. Benign tumours may, at times, become very large and cause severe symptoms or pose the risk of life-threatening consequences, such as the benign tumour in the brain.

What Is the Difference Between Healthy Cells and Cancer Cells?

Cancer cells are different from normal cells in several ways. For example, cancer cells:

- Tend to grow without any signal telling them to grow or multiply. Normal cells only grow when they receive these signals.

- Ignore the signals that tell the cells to die (a process called apoptosis or the programmed cell death) or stop dividing.

- Invade into the nearby organs and spread to other organs of the body. Normal cells and tissues stop growing once they encounter other cells and usually do not move around in the body.

- Tell the blood vessels to grow towards the tumours. The newly formed blood vessels supply the tumours with essential components like oxygen and nutrients and drain the waste products accumulated.

- Can hide from the immune cells and escape the immune cells' action to eliminate the damaged and abnormal cells.

- Can trick the immune cells into helping the cancer cells grow and stay alive. For example, some cancer cells can convince the immune cells to protect the tumour mass instead of attacking or destroying it.

- Accumulate several changes in their DNA or chromosomes, like deletions and duplications of the parts of the chromosome. Some abnormal cancer cells also have two times the number of chromosomes ordinarily present.

- Can rely on different forms of nutrients than the normal cells. Additionally, some cancer cells can produce energy from nutrients through a different mechanism than most normal cells. This process can allow the cancer cells to grow faster.

Ayurvedic Cancer-Fighting Remedies

Your diet is like a double-edged sword. It can keep you strong and healthy and prevent illnesses or can also worsen your health so much that you easily fall prey to diseases like diabetes, hypertension, and even cancer.

Your diet is a 'do or die' factor for your health. Now, it is in your hands to make it 'do it.' But, unfortunately, much of what we eat is drawn from foods high in saturated or unhealthy fats and refined carbohydrates, which are destructive as well as dangerous for your health. These foods can increase your risk of cancer substantially.

Ditch these fat and carbs-laden foods and switch to the healthy anti-cancer superfoods mentioned below to protect your healthy organs from any form of cancerous activity.

Tomatoes

Thanks to its rich lycopene content, this veggie/fruit is a perfect cancer-fighting superfood. Lycopene is an antioxidant phytochemical, a good source of vitamins A, E, and C, all of which are the worst enemies of cancer-causing toxins and free radicals.

You may stuff your sandwiches with thin slices of tomatoes or use them to top the ready-made pizza dough. In whichever form it is used, tomatoes are sure to help you fight cancer.

Seeds and Nuts

Seeds and nuts provide a rich source of healthy fats and a broad spectrum of nutrients, including minerals, phytosterols, and antioxidants. These nutrients would improve the health of the body's cells and tissues and increase their resistance against cancer-causing toxins.

Chia seeds, flaxseeds, and hemp seeds are rich in omega-3 fatty acids. On the other hand, seeds like sesame seeds are rich in lignans, which produce a strong natural anti-cancer effect.

Women diagnosed with breast cancer are advised to eat these nuts daily to reduce their risk of complications, including mortality associated with this disease. These nuts may also protect against prostate cancer and lung cancer.

Onions

Onion is one of the most potent natural anti-cancer foods. It plays an influential role in fighting the cancerous changes occurring in the body and prevents the progression of the disease.

It would also create a favourable effect on the immune system and identify the abnormal cancer cells among the healthy cells. It would help the immune system selectively aim its destructive action against the cancer cells, thereby ensuring rapid elimination.

Allium vegetables like onion contain organosulfur compounds that release when these vegetables are chopped, chewed, or crushed. These compounds possess natural anti-carcinogenic properties, which would help in reducing the risk of gastric, breast, and prostate cancers.

The organosulfur compounds work by detoxifying the carcinogens (cancer-causing toxins), thus halting the cancer cells' growth and blocking the process of angiogenesis. It should be noted that angiogenesis is a process that stimulates the formation of new blood cells within the tumour mass.

By blocking this mechanism, onions would deprive the tumour mass of the nutrients needed for the survival of the cancer cells, resulting in their death.

Go Greens

'Go green' should be the mantra if you are looking to reduce cancer risks. It is not a mantra to improve the environment's health but to promote your own health. Leafy greens are the best nutrient-dense foods containing substances, protecting the vital organs and reducing your risk of cancer.

These veggies would also protect your body's cells and tissues from the potential damage by the free radicals and toxic additives in foods. Such toxic additives trigger alterations in your DNA structure and initiate mutations that can lead to the increased risk of cancer.

Hence, make sure you eat plenty of green vegetables so that you can reap the benefits of their anti-cancer properties while also basking in their rich nutritional content of proteins and phytochemicals such as folate, omega-3 fatty acids, and calcium.

Berries

All types of berries, including blueberries, blackberries, and strawberries, are superfoods for preventing cancer. These fruits are high in nutrients and low in sugars and provide the vitamins that would promote the health of the normal cells. They may also prevent cell damage caused by high levels of blood sugar.

Berries are full of antioxidants, such as flavonoids, which would prevent the cancerous changes in the DNA of the normal cells. Regular consumption of berries would help prevent breast, colon, rectum, pancreatic, and liver cancers.

Mushrooms

Mushrooms can make up for a delicious addition to any dish. You can simply cook and add them to a salad or use chopped mushroom toppings for a homemade pizza or sandwiches.

The most common forms of mushrooms, including white, Portobello, cremini, oyster, and shiitake, have potent anti-cancer properties. They can also act as an anti-inflammatory agent and prevent damage to the normal cells.

Mushrooms would also stimulate the immune system, slow down cancer cell growth, and prevent DNA damage. Mushrooms also trigger apoptosis, a process that causes programmed cell death and inhibits angiogenesis.

Beans

Beans and other legumes are rich in soluble fibres, which can help lower cholesterol levels. They would also provide a high amount of resistant starch, which the digestive enzymes cannot break down. Hence, they are fermented by the intestinal bacteria into healthy fatty acids that could reduce the risk of colon cancer.

Watermelon

Watermelons offer a rich source of powerful antioxidants that can help prevent cancer by destroying free radicals. Watermelons also contain a high amount of vitamin C and beta-carotene, a form of vitamin A, strengthening the immune system's response against carcinogenic toxins.

Watermelon also contains a popular cancer-fighting substance called lycopene. Eating watermelons at least three times a week would reduce your risk of lung, oral, colon, and oesophageal cancers to a great extent.

Some other anti-cancer superfoods to reduce your risk of cancer:

- Cabbage
- Bell peppers
- Carrots
- Broccoli
- Dried Apricots
- Garlic

- Sunflower Seeds

A nutritionally-deficient, high-carb, and fat-full diet is the perfect recipe for a health disaster. You must avoid eating these foods to prevent diseases like cancer. Instead, you can eat the healthy foods mentioned above, which harness the power of nutrition and prevent cancers. These superfoods will also improve your chances of recovery if you have already been diagnosed with cancer.

Conclusion

Scientific research studies continue to dig deeper into the safe and effective ways to prevent and treat cancer. Given the ever-growing menace it has been, we all need to take necessary precautions to protect ourselves using natural procedures. Being active and eating well are the cornerstones of protecting yourself against this disease. The healthier habits you adopt, the lesser your risk of developing cancer.

What Leukaemia Is and Ayurveda's Role in Managing Leukaemia

Leukaemia is one of the forms of cancer affecting the blood-forming tissues of the body, such as the bone marrow and even the lymphatic system.

There are several forms of leukaemia. This condition is common in young adults and children, while some occur mainly in older people.

Leukaemia usually affects the white blood cells. The white blood cells are the body's infection fighters. These cells typically grow and multiply orderly, as the body needs them.

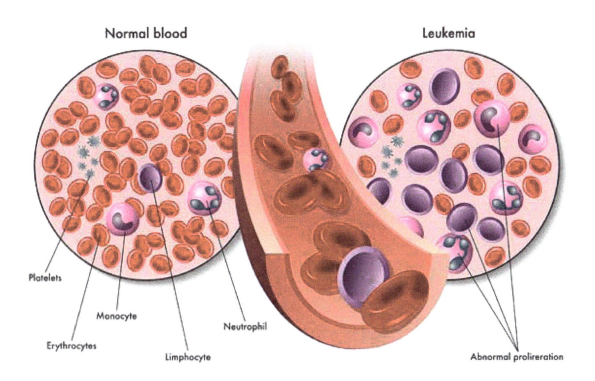

However, in patients with leukaemia, the marrow produces a very high amount of abnormal white blood cells, which do not function properly, due to which the patients develop severe symptoms.

The treatment for leukaemia is often complex. It is based on the specific form of leukaemia and other factors such as the patient's age and symptoms. However, specific strategies and therapies could help make the treatment outcomes more favourable and successful.

What Are the Signs and Symptoms of Leukaemia?

Leukaemia symptoms may vary, depending on the specific form of the patient's disease.

The common signs and symptoms of leukaemia include:

- Fever, usually with chills
- Persistent fatigue and weakness
- Frequent, severe infections
- Swollen lymph nodes
- Losing weight without any apparent reason
- Easy bruising and bleeding
- Enlarged spleen and liver
- Recurrent nosebleeds
- Increased sweating, more at night
- Small red spots on the skin (called petechiae)
- Bone pain
- Bone tenderness

Leukaemia symptoms tend to be vague and non-specific in most patients. You may even overlook the early symptoms of leukaemia as they might resemble symptoms of common infections like the flu and other forms of viral fever.

In some cases, leukaemia is detected during routine blood tests or the tests performed for any other condition.

What Are the Common Causes of Leukaemia?

Scientists have not understood the exact causes responsible for the development of leukaemia. This condition seems to develop due to the combination of environmental and genetic factors.

How Does Leukaemia Form?

Generally, leukaemia is believed to develop when some blood cells undergo changes (or mutations) in their DNA or genetic materials. The DNA of the cells contains a set of instructions that signal the cell what it needs to do. Usually, the DNA also tells the cells to grow at a specific rate and die at a pre-set time. However, in patients with leukaemia, the mutations in the white blood cells tell them to continue to grow and divide.

When this occurs, the production of blood cells gets out of control. Over time, the abnormal cells tend to crowd out the healthy blood cells in the bone marrow, leading to fewer healthy white cells, red cells, and platelets, thus causing the symptoms of leukaemia.

How Is Leukaemia Classified?

This condition is classified based on the speed of cancer progression and the types of cells affected.

The standard classification is based on how fast the condition progresses, as given below:

- In acute leukaemia, abnormal blood cells are immature. These are referred to with the suffix 'blasts'. These cells cannot carry out their normal physiological functions and multiply rapidly. The disease becomes worse quickly in a very brief duration. Acute leukaemia often needs timely and aggressive treatment.

- In chronic leukaemia, the condition tends to persist and progress for a very long duration. There are several different forms of chronic leukaemia. Some of them occur when the bone marrow produces too many cells, while some occur when the marrow produces too few cells.

- Chronic leukaemia may involve the more mature or over-matured blood cells. These cells can replicate and accumulate slowly and normally function for a short period. Some types of chronic leukaemia produce no symptoms initially and may go undiagnosed or unnoticed for several years.

- The second classification of leukaemia is based on the types of white blood cells involved:

- Myelogenous leukaemia: In the type of leukaemia, the myeloid cells are affected. Myeloid cells give rise to red blood cells, white blood cells, and platelet-producing cells.

- Lymphocytic leukaemia: This form of leukaemia affects lymphoid cells (also called the lymphocytes) that form the lymphatic or lymphoid tissue. The lymphatic tissues make up our immune system.

What Are the Different Types of Leukaemia?

- ALL (Acute lymphocytic leukaemia): This is a common form of leukaemia that affects young children. ALL may sometimes affect adults.

- AML (Acute myelogenous leukaemia): It is another common form of leukaemia in adults and children. AML is found to be the most common form of acute leukaemia affecting adults.

- CLL (Chronic lymphocytic leukaemia): CLL is the most common form of chronic leukaemia in adults. Patients with CLL may feel well for several years without undergoing any treatment.

- CML (Chronic myelogenous leukaemia): This form of leukaemia usually affects older adults. A patient with CML might have very few or no signs for several months to years before entering the phase in which the abnormal leukaemia cells start to grow faster.

- Other forms: Some other rarer forms of leukaemia include hairy cell leukaemia, myeloproliferative disorders, and myelodysplastic syndromes.

What Are the Risk Factors for Leukaemia?

The factors that can increase the risk of developing some forms of leukaemia include:

- Genetic disorders: Genetic abnormalities can play a role in the occurrence of leukaemia. Some genetic disorders, like Down syndrome, are linked to a higher risk of this condition.

- History of undergoing cancer treatment: Patients who have had a particular type of radiation therapy or chemotherapy to treat other cancers have a higher risk of developing certain forms of leukaemia.

- Smoking: Smoking cigarettes can increase the risk of some types of cancers, especially acute myelogenous leukaemia.

- Exposure to toxic chemicals: Exposure to some chemicals, like benzene found in gasoline and commonly used in the chemical industries, is linked to increased risk of some forms of leukaemia.

- Family history: If a member of a person's family has been diagnosed with leukaemia, their risk of developing this disease might increase.

Diagnosis of Leukaemia

Chronic leukaemia is often diagnosed during a routine blood test, even before any symptoms have become apparent. When this happens, or if the patient has the signs that point to leukaemia, they may need to undergo some tests and examinations to confirm the diagnosis:

Physical Examination

The doctor would look for the physical signs of leukaemia, such as pale skin due to anaemia, swelling of the lymph nodes, and spleen and liver enlargement.

Blood Tests

Testing a blood sample can help determine if a person has an abnormal level of red blood cells, white blood cells, or platelets that could be suggestive of leukaemia. The blood tests may also reveal the presence of abnormal leukaemia cells, although not all forms of leukaemia cause these abnormal cells to flow through or circulate in the bloodstream. In some cases, the leukaemia cells might continue to stay inside the marrow.

The Bone Marrow Test

Your physician may recommend a procedure for removing a sample of the bone marrow from the hipbone. The marrow is removed with the help of a long and thin needle. The marrow sample is then sent to a laboratory to check for the presence of the leukaemia cells.

Some specialised tests for detecting leukaemia cells might help reveal the specific characteristics used to determine the most suitable treatment options.

Treatment of Leukaemia

The treatment for leukaemia depends on several factors. Doctors would determine the treatment options based on the age and overall health of the patient, the specific form of leukaemia, and whether it has already spread to other parts of the body. The most dangerous areas to look for are the brain or tissues of the central nervous system.

Some common treatments used to treat leukaemia include:

- Chemotherapy
- Radiation therapy
- Targeted therapy
- Engineering immune cells to fight leukaemia
- Immunotherapy
- Bone marrow transplant

Coping and Support

The diagnosis of leukaemia is often devastating. With time, you will find effective ways to cope with the stress and uncertainty of cancer. But, until then, you might find the following ways helpful to cope with the diagnosis:

- Eat a nutritious diet
- Avoid smoking
- Limit your alcohol intake
- Keep friends and family close
- Manage stress with the help of yoga and meditation

Ayurvedic Treatment for Patients with Leukaemia

Alternative and Complementary Therapies

A comprehensive treatment plan for patients with leukaemia may include a broad range of alternative and complementary therapies. Patients are advised to educate themselves and keep their medical providers informed about all of the alternative and complementary therapies they are undergoing. This includes the use of prescribed dietary supplements and drugs.

While herbal therapies and supplements might be the critical components in a comprehensive cancer treatment program, some herbs and supplements might interfere with conventional cancer care.

Hence, it's essential to work with a knowledgeable team of physicians and inform all healthcare providers about the supplements and herbs you are using.

Acupuncture for Leukaemia

Acupuncture might help alleviate the symptoms of leukaemia. Acupuncture would help enhance immune functions, support digestion, and address underlying disease conditions.

Supplements and Nutrition

Following nutritional tips could play a key role in reducing the symptoms of leukaemia:

- Try to eliminate potential food allergens, like dairy (milk, butter, and cheese), wheat (gluten), preservatives, food additives, and corn and soy. Your healthcare provider might need to test for food sensitivities.
- Eat foods rich in antioxidants, such as fruits (like blueberries, tomatoes, and cherries) and vegetables (like kale, bell peppers, and spinach)
- Avoid ready meals and refined foods, like white bread, sugars, and pasta

- Eat healthy proteins favouring organic or free-range sources
- Use healthy unsaturated fatty oils in cooking, like olive oil or coconut oil. Make sure you cook in olive oil only under medium to low heat to prevent the active carcinogens from forming.
- Eliminate or reduce the intake of trans fatty acids found in commercially-baked foods, like cookies, French fries, onion rings, crackers, cakes, doughnuts, margarine, and processed foods
- Avoid coffee and stimulants like alcohol, tobacco, and recreational drugs
- Drink at least eight to ten glasses of clean filtered water every day
- Exercise lightly, if possible. Speak with your physician about the regimen that could be the best for you.

You also need to address the nutritional deficiencies with the use of supplements like:

Probiotic Supplements

Probiotic supplements containing Lactobacillus acidophilus could help maintain immune and gastrointestinal health. The probiotics supplements would strengthen your immunity and boost the body's defence mechanisms against cancer-causing agents.

Omega-3 Fatty Acids

These are healthy fats abundant in olive oil, flaxseeds, chia seeds, avocado, and fish oil. These healthy fats would help reduce inflammation and free radical damage. Healthy oils might also reduce the risk of leukaemia and other forms of cancer.

The Advantages of Herbal Therapies

The Effects of Fruits and Herbs on Leukaemia

In most developing countries, herbal treatment is often the first and the primary form of treatment for several diseases. About 75-80% of the population in the world prefers herbal therapies as one of the treatment options for cancer due to the better adequacy and satisfaction they offer. These therapies enhance the body's symmetry with minimal risk of side effects.

Several fruits and plants have presented as promising natural anti-cancer agents. Some of these plant extracts are being used currently in cancer therapies and prevention.

Some medicinal herbs have symbolised higher safety than modern treatments (like chemotherapy and radiotherapy) that cause severe short-term and long-term side effects. Natural treatments play a vital role in the treatment of cancers.

In patients with leukaemia, the use of alternative and complementary medicines discussed below could be the desirable treatment with a reduced chance of developing side effects compared to modern therapies.

Hibiscus Cannabinus

It contains bioactive components like tannins, saponins, alkaloids, fatty acids, polyphenolics, phospholipids, phytosterols, and tocopherol. The seed oil of this herb also offers a rich and unique source of bioactive compounds having high anti-cancer and anti-oxidative properties.

Ginseng Root

It is a common herbal medication having multi-pharmaceutical functions. Ginsenosides in this herb are considered the active ingredients responsible for its natural and powerful pharmaceutical activities.

Ginsenosides belong to the family of steroidal saponins and contain two significant groups of medicinal compounds, including protopanaxatriol and protopanaxadiol. Several ginsenosides are reported to exert a natural anti-cancer effect and protect you against the risk of leukaemia.

Some other herbs that could be effective for the treatment of leukaemia include:

- Moringa oleifera
- Grape Seeds
- Pomegranate
- Achillea fragrantissima
- Vernonia amygdalina
- Typhonium flagelliforme
- Carrot
- Berberis vulgaris (Barberry)

Conclusion

These alternative therapies and herbal remedies can support the faster recovery of patients with leukaemia and complement the benefits of modern treatments while reducing the side effects caused due to them. Patients are advised to follow a comprehensive treatment plan that includes current conventional cancer treatments like chemotherapy and radiation combined with herbal remedies, nutritional supplements, and healthy dietary and lifestyle strategies to improve the outcomes.

Treatment and Prevention of Skin Cancer through a Comprehensive Plan

Skin cancer occurs due to the abnormal growth of the skin cells. It often develops on parts of the skin exposed to sun rays. However, this common form of cancer may also occur in areas of your skin that are not regularly exposed to sunlight.

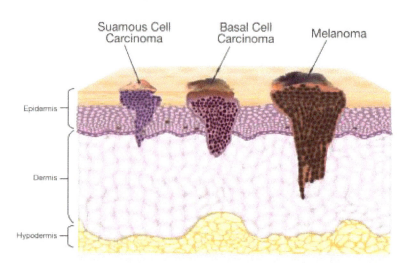

There are three primary forms of skin cancer: Melanoma, Basal Cell Carcinoma, and Squamous Cell Carcinoma.

Cells Commonly Involved in Skin Cancers

Skin cancers begin in the top layer of the skin called the epidermis. It is a thin layer that provides a protective covering for the skin cells that the body continually sheds. The epidermis contains three main types of cells including:

- Squamous cells that lie just beneath the outer surface of the skin and serve as the inner lining for the skin

- Basal cells that produce new cells and sit beneath the layer of the squamous cells

- Melanocytes which produce melanin, a pigment that gives skin its colour. These cells are located in the lower region of the epidermis. Melanocytes can produce more melanin when the person is under the sun to protect the deep layers of the skin.

You can lower your risk of developing skin cancer by avoiding or limiting your ultraviolet (UV) radiation exposure. Checking the skin for any suspicious changes could also help detect skin cancer at its earlier stages. The early detection of cancer would give you the best chance for successful outcomes with the modern and Ayurvedic cancer treatments you follow.

What Are the Symptoms of Skin Cancer?

Skin cancer develops primarily on the areas of sun-exposed skin, including the face, lips, scalp, ears, neck, arms, chest, hands, and legs. However, it can also affect areas, which rarely see the light of day, such as the palms, beneath the fingernails and toenails, and the genital region.

Skin cancers affect people of all skin tones, including those with a lighter and darker complexion. When melanoma occurs in people with a darker skin tone, it is more likely to occur in areas not frequently exposed to the sun, such as the palms and soles.

Signs and Symptoms of Basal Cell Carcinoma

Basal cell carcinoma typically occurs in the sun-exposed body areas, such as the neck and face.

This skin cancer may appear as:

- A flat, brown, flesh-coloured scar-like lesion
- A waxy or pearly bump
- A scabbing and bleeding sore that heals but returns again

Signs and Symptoms of Squamous Cell Carcinoma

Most often, squamous cell carcinoma develops on the sun-exposed areas of the body, such as the face, hands, and ears. People with a darker skin tone are more likely to develop this form of skin carcinoma in areas not often exposed to sunlight.

Squamous cell carcinoma often appears as:

- A flat lesion having a crusted and scaly surface
- A dark red, firm nodule

Signs and Symptoms of Melanoma

Melanoma can develop on any part of the body, even in the otherwise normal skin, and on pre-existing moles that have become cancerous. Melanoma often appears on the face or trunk in affected men. In women, this form of cancer usually develops on the legs. In both men and women, melanoma may also occur on parts of the skin that have not been exposed to sunlight. Melanoma is known to affect people of all skin tones.

The common signs of melanoma include:

- A small lesion having an irregular border and some portions appearing red, pink, blue, white, or bluish-black
- A mole, which changes in size, colour, or feel, and bleeds
- A large brownish spot having dark speckles
- Dark lesions on the palms, soles, fingertips, and toes, or the mucous membrane lining of the mouth, nose, and anus
- A painful lesion that burns and itches

Other, less common forms of skin cancer include:

- Kaposi sarcoma
- Sebaceous gland carcinoma

- Merkel cell carcinoma

Common Causes of Skin Cancers

Skin cancer typically occurs when mutations occur in the DNA of skin cells. The mutations can cause these cells to grow and multiply out of control to form a mass of abnormal cancerous cells.

Potential Causes of Skin Cancer

Much of the damage to the DNA in skin cells occurs due to ultraviolet (UV) radiation in the sunlight and the light used in tanning beds. However, sun exposure does not explain all forms of skin cancers, especially those that tend to develop even on the parts of the skin that are not ordinarily exposed to sunlight. This anomaly suggests that some other factors may also contribute to the risk of developing skin cancer, such as exposure to toxic substances and having a condition that can weaken the immune system.

The common causes and risk factors of skin cancers are discussed below:

Fair Skin

Any person, regardless of their skin tone, can get skin cancer. However, having lesser pigments (melanin) in the skin offers less protection from the damaging UV radiation. Hence, people with red or blond hair and light-coloured eyes and who sunburn or freckle easily are more likely to develop skin cancers than people with a darker skin tone.

Sunburns

Having a history of blistering sunburns as a teenager or child can increase your risk of skin cancers during adulthood. Sunburns in adulthood also are common risk factors.

Excessive Sun Exposure

Any person who spends a considerable amount of time under the sun is likely to develop skin cancers, especially if the skin is not protected by clothing and sunscreen. Tanning, such as exposure to tanning beds and lamps, can also put you at risk of skin cancers. A tan is nothing but the skin's injury response to excessive UV radiation.

Moles

People with multiple moles or any abnormal mole known as the dysplastic nevi are at higher risk of skin cancer. These abnormal moles appear irregular and are usually larger than normal moles.

These types of moles are more likely to become cancerous. Hence, if you tend to develop abnormal moles, it is advisable to watch them regularly for any changes.

Sunny or High-Altitude Climates

Patients who live in warm and sunny climates are exposed to a higher amount of sunlight than those in colder climates. Similarly, living at higher elevations, where sunlight is the strongest, could also expose you to more radiation, thus increasing the risk of skin cancer.

Pre-Cancerous Skin Lesions

Skin lesions like actinic keratoses could increase the risk of skin cancers. These pre-cancerous skin growths usually appear as rough and scaly patches ranging from dark pink to brown. They are common on fair-skinned people's faces, hands, and heads, especially when their skin has become sun-damaged.

A Weak Immune System

People with a weak immune system have a higher risk of developing skin cancers. It includes patients living with HIV or AIDS and those using immunosuppressant medications after organ transplantation.

Family History

If one of the parents or siblings has had any form of skin cancer, they may have a higher risk of developing this disease.

A Personal History of Cancer

Patients who have developed any other form of cancer could be at risk of developing skin cancers.

Exposure to Toxic Substances

Exposure to toxic substances, like arsenic, might increase the risk of skin cancers.

Exposure to Radiation

Patients who have received radiation therapy to manage skin conditions like eczema or acne may have a higher risk of skin cancer, specifically basal cell carcinoma.

Prevention of Skin Cancers

- Avoid sun exposure, especially during the afternoon hours
- Use a broad-spectrum sunscreen having an SPF of at least 30
- Wear protective clothing
- Use sunscreen year-round
- Cover the sun-exposed parts of the skin with dark and tightly woven clothing

- Wear a broad-brimmed hat that provides more protection than the baseball cap
- Avoid tanning beds
- Be aware of the sun-sensitising medications, including antibiotics, as these can make the skin more sensitive to sunlight.
- Check the skin regularly for any new skin growth and a change in the existing moles, birthmarks, bumps, and freckles

The Most Effective Natural Remedies for Preventing Skin Cancer

Pomegranate

The prime reason pomegranate is at the top of the list of anti-cancer foods is the rich content of vitamin C. This fruit is packed with the antioxidant power of vitamin C, which can guard your skin against cancer-causing effects of pollution and sun damage.

Pomegranate seeds contain punicalagin and ellagic acid. Ellagic acid is a polyphenolic compound, which would prevent damage caused due to free radicals, while punicalagin is a super-nutrient that could increase the body's ability to preserve collagen. Collagen helps maintain the health of the skin and prevents skin cancer.

Blueberries

This delicious blue-wonder of nature contains powerful antioxidants that would provide extra protection to your skin against free radicals. It also contains flavonols, and anthocyanins, which reduce cellular degeneration and damage. It also prevents the effect of excessive sun exposure, mental stress, and over-exercising on the skin.

Leafy Greens

Dark leafy greens, like kale and spinach, contain two potent antioxidants: zeaxanthin and lutein, which have been proven to protect the skin. These antioxidants block the adverse effects of UV radiation in sunlight and prevent cancer, sunburns, tanning, and dark spots.

It also supports the body's repair processes and heals the damage caused to the superficial and the deeper layers of skin. It also reduces inflammation and oxidative stress and induces T-cell-mediated immunity suppression, thus reducing age-related degenerative changes and skin cancer.

Avocado

Eating avocados at least twice a week would make your skin as healthy as the fruit itself. It can make your skin vibrant by reducing freckles, wrinkles, age spots, and fine lines. Avocado contains powerful antioxidant properties, which would prevent free radical damage to the skin cells and preserve the skin's health.

This fruit also has essential fatty acids that support the healthy oils in the skin, thus keeping it well moisturised. Biotin and vitamin E in Avocado offer excellent nutritional support to your skin, hair, and nails, thus protecting it against cancer-causing toxins.

Garlic

Garlic is an imperative superfood from the list of natural remedies for enhancing skin health. It is a potent herb that can slow down the ageing process. It also possesses healing properties, which would help reduce acne, acne scars, ulcers, wounds, and warts on the skin.

It would produce a potent antioxidant effect and reduce the impact of advancing age on your skin. It is commonly used to reduce the risk of melanoma, a form of skin cancer caused due to excessive exposure to the sun.

Wild Fish

Wild fish such as sardines, herring, wild salmon, and mackerel offer a rich amount of omega-3 fatty acids, which support the health of the skin and hair. It promotes skin elasticity or firmness by strengthening the skin cell membranes. It would help reduce the risk of skin cancers by boosting immunity.

Some More Foods for Preventing Skin Cancers

- Fibre-rich grains
- Ginger
- Legumes
- Cruciferous vegetables
- Citrus fruits like oranges
- Nuts like almonds and peanuts
- Watermelon

Simple Home Remedies for Relieving the Symptoms of Skin Cancers

Egg White

Egg white provides your skin with excellent astringent substances and works as a natural skin-nourishing formula. It contains hydro-lipids, which would lift the sagging skin and make it healthier and resistant to cancerous changes.

Additionally, egg white can reduce dryness too, a common cause of skin cancers. All these benefits can be availed by simply applying mashed egg white directly on your face.

Massage it gently for a few minutes and wash it off with water. That's all you need to do to regain the natural health and the youthful firmness and radiance of your skin.

Aloe Vera Gel

Aloe vera offers a perfect natural anti-inflammatory solution. You can apply aloe vera gel on your face once or twice a day in a thin layer.

However, the better and more effective way would be to grow the aloe vera plant at home and cut its leaves to obtain a fresh gel-like liquid. Apply this gel on your face twice daily. It would keep your skin well-hydrated and also reduce the sign of sunburns.

Carrots

Carrot contains vitamin A and vitamin E, needed to maintain the skin's health and normal functioning.

Mash one raw carrot to get a paste of creamy consistency and apply it to the face. Wash it off after an hour. Do this once every day. You will observe a marked reduction in the symptoms of skin cancers.

Papaya

The rich antioxidant properties of papayas would offer excellent protection to your skin from its most dangerous enemies like free radicals, UV rays in sunlight, and air pollution.

Papayas would also enhance the skin tone and remove the dead cells from the skin surface. It also rejuvenates the skin from within and makes it appear radiant with its rich vitamin C content.

Apply a face pack prepared with one cup of mashed papaya, half a cup of rice flour, and two tablespoonfuls of honey by spreading it evenly on the face. Rinse it off with tepid water after twenty minutes.

Avocado

Avocado provides a rich nutritional supply to the skin and reduces the signs of skin cancers. Simply spread the avocado pulp on the face. Leave it for ten minutes, then, wash it off with plain water. Do this once or twice a week.

Some more home remedies for reducing the symptoms of skin cancers include:

- Massaging your skin with olive oil
- Applying cucumber juice on the face and under the eyes
- Eating watermelons at least twice a week and rub watermelon chunks on your face
- Mixing a few drops of honey in an equal quantity of lemon juice and a pinch of turmeric and apply it to the face
- Rubbing a raw potato on the face in gentle circular motions
- Applying pineapple extract on the face

Conclusion

You can maintain your skin health and protect it from cancer-causing agents by using nature's treasure of herbs and foods mentioned above. The powerful antioxidant effects of these foods would protect your skin from the impact of sun exposure, pollution, free radical damage, stress, and toxins in the environment. Your skin would be youthful, healthy, and vibrant!

What Is Thyroid Cancer and the Most Effective Natural Remedies to Manage It?

The thyroid is a gland shaped like a butterfly. It is located inside the lower part of the front of the neck. This gland controls body's metabolism. It also releases certain hormones that help several direct functions, including how the cells use energy, how the body produces heat, and how oxygen is consumed.

Different Types of Thyroid Cancer

1. Papillary Cancer

This is the most common type of thyroid cancer, affecting 80% of thyroid cancer patients, though many experience no symptoms.

2. Follicular Cancer

This is the second most common, occurs in a slightly older age group than papillary thyroid cancer, and is less common in children.

3. Medullary Cancer

This thyroid cancer is rare, making up about 3% of all thyroid cancer cases. These tumors may be tender to the touch and painful.

4. Anaplastic Cancer

Anaplastic tumors are the least common and most deadly of all thyroid cancers. Unlike most thyroid cancers, this cancer has a very low cure rate, even with the best treatments.

Thyroid cancer may develop when the cells in this gland change or undergo mutations. The abnormal cells start to multiply in the thyroid, forming a tumour. Thyroid cancer can be treated with better outcomes if this condition is detected early.

What Are the Different Types of Thyroid Cancer?

Papillary Thyroid Cancer

If a person has thyroid cancer, it is likely to be of this form. It is the most familiar form of thyroid cancer, affecting up to 80% of cases. It tends to grow gradually over a period and spreads to the lymph nodes in the neck.

Medullary cancer

This cancer is found in nearly 4% of all cases of thyroid cancer. It is more likely to be found at the early stage as it produces a hormone known as calcitonin, the levels of which need to be evaluated regularly through routine blood tests.

Follicular Thyroid Cancer

This form of cancer makes up nearly 10% to 15% of all the cases of thyroid cancers. It can quickly spread to the lymph nodes and is more likely to spread through the blood vessels.

Anaplastic Thyroid Cancer

This ailment is the most severe type of thyroid cancer as it can become aggressive and quickly spread to other parts of your body. It is a rare form but most complicated to treat.

What Are the Symptoms of Thyroid Cancer?

The primary function of the thyroid gland is to produce hormones that can help the body use energy, avoid the effect of extreme cold weather or stay warm, and control the heart rate and blood pressure. Cancer may happen when the healthy cells in this gland change or grow out of control.

The thyroid gland has two lobes called the left lobe and the right lobe, connected by a thin strip of tissues. When the gland is healthy, each of these lobes is about the size of a quarter; that is why it cannot be easily felt or seen under the skin of the neck.

Thyroid cancer is usually first noticed when one or both these lobes enlarge to form a thyroid nodule that can be easily felt or seen.

This growth may lead to the development of signs and symptoms such as:

- Neck and throat pain

- Difficulty in swallowing

- Lump in the neck (usually seen around the Adam's apple), which seems to be growing quickly

- Painful swollen glands in the neck

- Recurrent cough, which is not due to any infections like a common cold

- Vocal changes such as hoarseness of voice

- Difficulty in breathing, which is sometimes compared to the sucking of the air through a straw

- Pain that begins in the front of the neck and radiates up to the ears

In some cases, thyroid cancer may also cause redness of the face and frequent bowel movements with loose motions. These could be signs of a form of thyroid cancer known as medullary thyroid cancer.

What Are the Causes of Thyroid Cancer?

There are no clear reasons why thyroid cancer develops. However, certain things may raise your risk of developing it, as explained below:

Inherited Genetic Syndrome

Some diseases, especially cancer, develop due to a person's heritage. For example, in about two out of ten patients with medullary thyroid cancer, the underlying factor could result from the abnormal genes the patient has inherited, likely from parents.

So, your chances of developing thyroid cancer are higher if one or both of your parents or your siblings have already developed it.

Also, thyroid cancer could be linked to some other genetic and hereditary problems. In addition, one of these is known to cause extra tissues known as polyps that form in the parts of the intestine and colon. This condition is called familial adenomatous polyposis. Patients who develop these polyps have a higher risk of certain forms of cancer, including thyroid cancer.

Some other genetic problems that are known to increase the chances of developing thyroid cancer include:

- Cowden disease

- Multiple endocrine neoplasia type 2

- Familial medullary thyroid cancer

Iodine Deficiency

If you do not get much of this mineral from your dietary sources, you are likely to be at a higher risk of certain forms of thyroid cancers. This condition is comparatively rare in developed nations like the United States, where iodine is commonly added to salts and other foods.

Iodine is one of the essential minerals found in some food sources. The body needs this mineral to produce thyroid hormones. Some thyroid cancers tend to be more common in parts of the world where iodine intake by people is low. Hence, the healthcare authorities and food manufacturers could add iodine to table salt and some other foods to reduce the incidence of this disease.

Radiation Exposure

Exposure of the head or neck to radiation treatment, especially during childhood, can predispose a person to develop thyroid cancer. So, children who receive radiation therapy to treat some forms of cancers, like lymphoma, have a higher risk of developing thyroid cancer in their adulthood. Compared with children, radiation exposure is less likely to affect adults.

What Are the Risk Factors for Thyroid Cancer?

Thyroid cancer tends to be more common in women than in men. Women are more likely to develop thyroid cancer in their 30s to 50s, while men usually develop it in their 60s to 70s. However, when thyroid cancer develops in men, it grows and spreads faster than in women.

Follicular thyroid cancer occurs more commonly in people with a lighter complexion than those with a darker complexion.

Though the risk of thyroid cancer increases with age, it can affect younger people also. For example, papillary thyroid cancer is more common in young people between 30 and 50 years.

Natural Ways to Control Thyroid Diseases

As discussed earlier, the thyroid is a small gland situated in the neck. It produces hormones, which play a role in regulating the metabolic processes in the body. It can regulate vital body functions, including muscle strength, body temperature, breathing, menstrual cycles, and cholesterol levels.

Any abnormality in this gland can result in higher or lower production of thyroid hormones called Triiodothyronine (T3) and Thyroxine (T4).

The common disorders affecting the thyroid gland include thyroid cancer, hypothyroidism, and hyperthyroidism. Patients diagnosed with hypothyroidism are advised to use drugs like Levothyroxine. However, the use of this drug may lead to a few side effects, including irregular heartbeat, seizures, blurred vision, and double vision.

You can avoid these side effects by following the natural methods given below to improve thyroid functions.

Iodine

Iodine deficiency is a common underlying factor leading to thyroid cancer. It is an essential mineral that works as a building block for metabolism and helps in regulating the production of hormones in the thyroid gland.

You can avoid iodine deficiencies and the resulting thyroid disorders by increasing your intake of high-iodine foods such as kelp or cold-water fish like cod and tuna.

Selenium

Selenium deficiency is a common finding in patients with thyroid cancer and hypothyroidism. This trace mineral is required by the body to convert thyroxine, a thyroid hormone, into triiodothyronine.

Triiodothyronine, in turn, speeds up the body's metabolism and reverses the weight gain. Hence, eating foods rich in selenium is recommended for controlling thyroid cancer and hypothyroidism. The best selenium-rich foods are Brazil nuts, wheat germs, sunflower seeds, and fish, like tuna.

Reduce Stress

Mental stress can affect the balance of hormones in your body and cause thyroid cancer and hypothyroidism. Reducing the stress level through yoga, meditation, and breathing exercises is a great way to reduce your risk of thyroid cancer.

You can also use herbs that possess adaptogenic properties, such as Panax Ginseng, Holy Basil, Ashwagandha, and Rhodiola Rosea. These natural adaptogens would support adrenal functions and increase the production of the feel-good hormones. This effect would increase the ability of your body to cope with stress and prevent thyroid cancer.

Sunlight

Natural sunlight entering the body through the eyes can stimulate the glands in the body, including the pituitary and pineal glands, which play a role in the release of triiodothyronine and thyroxine and prevent the occurrence of thyroid cancer. Hence, make sure your body gets sufficient exposure to the sun for at least half an hour every day.

Coconut Oil

Coconut oil is an incredibly effective natural remedy for thyroid cancer. Thyroid cancer and hypothyroidism occur due to damage or inflammation in the thyroid gland or from autoimmune disorders in which immune cells attack the normal cells of the thyroid gland and damage them.

The effectiveness of coconut oil lies in its ability to decrease inflammation in the body and regulate the immune system. This way, it takes care of the two most essential factors causing thyroid cancer and hypothyroidism.

It produces a favourable effect on the functions of the thyroid gland and significantly reduces the symptoms of thyroid cancer.

Conclusion

These powerful natural remedies would control the symptoms of thyroid cancer and hypothyroidism by correcting the iodine deficiency and hormonal imbalances. In addition to preventing thyroid cancer, these remedies would also help you avoid the side effects of commonly used medications like Levothyroxine.

Management of Colorectal Cancer With Ayurvedic Remedies

Colorectal cancer, also called bowel cancer, rectal cancer, or colon cancer, refers to any cancer that affects the rectum and colon. Colorectal cancer is estimated to be the third most common type of cancer globally, especially in the United States. It is also the second most typical cause of cancer-linked deaths.

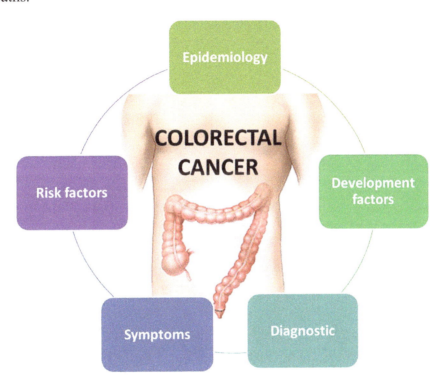

The incidence of this condition varies across the different parts of the world. It is common in countries with a higher economic status, though it will likely affect individuals with a lower income.

What Are the Signs and Symptoms of Colorectal Cancer?

Colorectal cancer usually does not cause any symptoms in the initial stages. If it does, the symptoms may include:

- Changes in the bowel habits
- A feeling as if the bowels do not empty properly
- Frequency of diarrhoea and constipation
- Discharge of bright red blood from the rectum

- Blood in the faeces, making it look black or dark brown
- Fatigue and tiredness
- Abdominal bloating and pain
- Feeling of fullness even when a very long time has passed since the meal
- Anaemia
- Unexplained weight loss

If not appropriately managed, colorectal cancer can spread to the liver. The patient may develop symptoms like jaundice that causes yellowing discolouration of the white of the eyes and nails. If the person has light brown or white skin, the skin may also appear tinged yellowish.

If cancer spreads to the lungs, the patient may have difficulty breathing with or without a cough.

Treatment of Colorectal Cancer

The treatment depends on several factors such as:
- The location and size of tumours,
- Whether the cancer is recurring
- The stage of cancer
- The overall health of the patient

The Most Effective Treatment Options Include:

- Surgery
- Chemotherapy
- Immunotherapy
- Targeted therapy
- Radiation therapy
- Palliative and end-of-life care
- Ablation

What Are the Causes and Risk Factors for Colorectal Cancer?

It is not precisely clear why colorectal cancers occur. Most cases result from a combination of genetic and environmental factors.

Some common associated factors include:
- Advancing age
- Being male
- Eating a diet low in fibres and high in proteins, calories, and saturated fats
- Smoking
- A diet high in processed or red meats
- Consuming alcohol
- A low level of physical activities
- Being overweight
- Inflammatory bowel disease
- History of breast, ovarian, or uterine cancer
- Type 2 diabetes
- Having polyps in the rectum or colon
- History of receiving radiation therapy for any abdominal cancer in the childhood

Diagnosis of Colorectal Cancer

Screening can help detect the polyps linked to colorectal cancer before they can become cancerous. It would also help detect colon cancer in the initial stages, when it can be easier to treat.

Some screening tests recommended for the diagnosis of colorectal cancer include:
- Blood stool test
- Colonoscopy
- Barium enema X-ray
- Stool immunochemistry
- Stool DNA test
- Flexible sigmoidoscopy
- Imaging scans

- CT colonography

Prevention of Colorectal Cancer

Ayurveda and the modern system of medicine recommend the following prevention strategies for inhibiting the development of colorectal cancer:

Regular Screening

Regular screening for colorectal cancer is recommended for people who:

- Have a family or personal history of colorectal cancer
- Have Crohn's disease
- Have adenomatous polyposis or Lynch syndrome
- Are the black Americans above 45 years of age
- Are over 50 years of age and have an average risk

Nutrition

Dietary measures that might help reduce the risk of colorectal cancer include:

- Limiting the intake of processed and red meat
- Eating plenty of fruits, fibres, and vegetables
- Eating complex carbohydrates instead of simple sugars
- Opting for healthy fats, like avocados, fish oils, olive oil, and nuts, instead of unhealthy saturated fats

Exercise and Weight

Regular, moderate exercise could help lower the chances of developing colorectal cancer. Exercises may also help reduce the risk of obesity, which is linked to colorectal cancer.

Conclusion

Colorectal cancer is one of the common types of cancers and a leading cause of cancer-related deaths. The diagnosis and treatment in the earlier stages could help increase the chances of favourable outcomes. Having regular screening could improve the chances of an early diagnosis. Patients are advised to follow the natural methods discussed above to prevent colorectal cancer or recover in a shorter duration if they are already diagnosed with it.

The Safe and Natural Treatment Methods for Cervical Cancer

Cervical cancer is a form of cancer that affects the cells of the cervical tissues in the lower region of the uterus, which connects the uterus and the vagina in women.

Several strains of the Human Papillomavirus (HPV), a common sexually transmitted infection, play a role in causing some forms of cervical cancer.

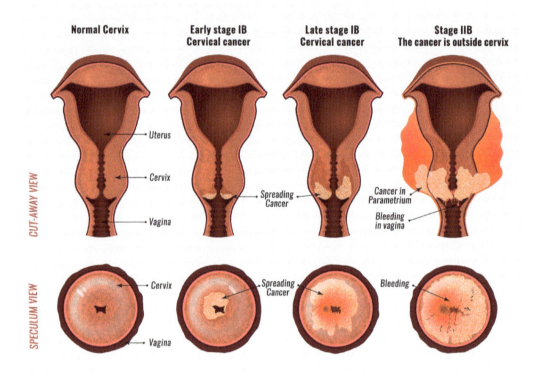

When exposed to the infection by HPV, the immune system of women typically prevents the viruses from causing any serious harm. However, in a tiny percentage of women, the virus may survive for several years, contributing to the processes that cause some of the cervical cells to become cancerous.

You can avoid the risk of developing cervical cancers by having regular screening tests and receiving a vaccination that protects against HPV infection.

What Are the Signs and Symptoms of Cervical Cancer?

The early stages of cervical cancer usually cause no signs or symptoms. The symptoms in the more advanced stages of cervical cancer may include:

- Vaginal bleeding, especially after menopause, after intercourse, or between periods
- Pelvic pain
- Watery or blood-stained abnormal vaginal discharge that is heavy and has a foul odour
- Mild to moderate pain during intercourse

It is vital to watch out for these signs and consult your doctor at the earliest if you notice any of these symptoms.

What Are the Common Causes of Cervical Cancer?

Cervical cancer begins when healthy cells of the cervical tissues develop changes (or undergo mutations) in their cellular DNA. A DNA of cells contains signals or instructions that regulate what and how the cell functions or behaves.

The healthy cells can grow and multiply at a specific rate only; eventually dying once their expected lifespan is over. The mutations can cause the cells to multiply and grow out of control without undergoing programmed death. Afterwards, abnormal cells accumulating in the cervix form a mass, becoming a tumour. These cancer cells can also invade nearby tissues or break off from the tumour to metastasise (spread) to other parts of the body.

It is not clear what exactly causes cervical cancer. However, an infection due to HPV can undoubtedly play a role. The disease due to HPV is prevalent. However, not all women with this virus tend to develop cancer. This exception indicates that other factors like your environment and lifestyle choices can also determine your risk of developing cervical cancer.

What Are the Different Types of Cervical Cancers?

The type of cervical cancer can help determine a patient's prognosis and the best treatment options.

The main forms of cervical cancer include:

Squamous Cell Carcinoma

This form of cervical cancer affects the thin and flat cells called the squamous cells, forming a lining in the outer region of the cervix and projecting into the vagina. Most cases of cervical cancers are squamous cell carcinomas.

Adenocarcinoma

This form of cervical cancer starts in the glandular column-shaped cells that form the lining of the cervical canal.

In some cases, both types of cells may be involved in the development of cervical cancer. In rare cases, it may affect the other cells within the cervix.

Risk Factors of Cervical Cancer

Factors that can increase the risk of cervical cancer include:

- **Having multiple sexual partners:** The more the number of sexual partners a person or her partner has, the higher would be the risk of acquiring HPV and cervical cancer.

- **Early sexual activities:** Having sex at an earlier age could increase the risk of HPV and cervical cancers.

- **Other Sexually Transmitted Infections (STI):** Women who have other STIs like chlamydia, HIV/AIDS, gonorrhoea, or syphilis have an increased risk of HPV and cervical cancer.

- **A weak immune system:** Women are more likely to suffer from cervical cancers if their immune system has become weak due to any other health condition or if she has an HPV infection.

- **Smoking:** active and passive smoking are associated with a higher risk of squamous cell carcinoma of the cervix.

- **Exposure to miscarriage-preventing drugs:** Mothers during their pregnancy in the 1950s would use diethylstilbestrol (DES). This drug had been found to put their children at an increased risk of a specific type of cervical cancer known as clear cell adenocarcinoma.

How to Prevent Cervical Cancer?

Routine Pap Tests

A Pap test can help detect the precancerous state of the cervix. It can be monitored and treated appropriately to prevent worsening and developing into cervical cancer. Some medical organizations also suggest starting the routine Pap tests at 21 years and repeating the test every year.

HPV Vaccination

Receiving the vaccination to prevent HPV infection might reduce the risk of cervical cancer and other cancers related to this virus.

Do Not Smoke

Patients who smoke are advised to quit the habit to reduce the risk of cervical cancer.

Practice Safe Sex

It is possible to reduce the risk of cervical cancers by preventing sexually transmitted infections, like using a condom, avoiding multiple sexual partners, or limiting the number of partners.

Diagnosis of Cervical Cancer

Screening

Regular screening tests could help detect cervical cancers and precancerous cells that might later form into cervical cancer.

The common screening tests for cervical cancer include:

- Pap test: During this test, the doctor scrapes and gently brushes off the cells from the cervix that are later examined in a laboratory for abnormalities like cancerous changes. A Pap test can help detect abnormal cells in the cervical tissues, including cancer cells and cells that have undergone changes, raising the risk of cancers.

- HPV DNA test involves testing the cells obtained from the cervix to detect any infection due to any form of HPV that is more likely to lead to cervical cancer.

- Cone biopsy: If the PAP smear or other tests indicate the possibility of cervical cancer, a cone biopsy may be advised. When cervical cancer is suspected, the doctor is also likely to recommend a complete examination of the cervix. The colposcope, a unique magnifying instrument, is commonly used to detect abnormal cells in the cervix.

- During the colposcopic examination, the doctor is also likely to take a small sample of the cervical cells (biopsy) to be sent for laboratory testing. To obtain the tissue, the doctor might use:

- Endocervical curettage: a tiny, spoon-shaped instrument called the curet or a small brush to scrape the tissues from the cervical region.

- Punch biopsy, involving using a sharp tool for pinching off a small sample of the cervical tissues.

If the endocervical curettage or punch biopsy is worrisome, the doctor may recommend the following tests:

- Conization (or cone biopsy), a procedure that can allow the doctor to obtain the tissues from the deeper layers of the cervix to be sent for laboratory testing, may be performed. A cone biopsy is usually performed under general anaesthesia in a hospital.

- Electrical wire loop using a low-voltage thin, electrified wire to get a small sample of the cervical tissue. This procedure is generally done in the doctor's office under local anaesthesia.

Modern Treatments for Cervical Cancer

- Surgery
- Radiation
- Chemotherapy
- Targeted therapy
- Immunotherapy
- Supportive (palliative) care

Ayurvedic Treatment for Cervical Cancer

There are different methods of treatment available for the treatment of cervical cancer, which involve surgery and are medically intensive. However, some women may not want to undergo surgery, leading to complications in some rare cases. They might like to go in for some natural ways.

The natural ways for the treatment of cervical cancer are as follows:

- Good diet
- Acupuncture
- Castor oil pack

- Exercises

Diet

The first option available to manage cervical cancer and shrink the tumour mass naturally is through diet. The foods you should consume to achieve your goal of defeating the growth and spread of cervical cancer are as follows:

- Fruits: you can eat a lot of different varieties of fruits, especially the fibrous ones like pear and plum. However, control the quantity if you have type 2 diabetes or yeast infections.

- Green leafy vegetables low in starch: You can eat green, leafy vegetables like cabbage, broccoli, and lettuce. These contain a high quantity of vitamins, essential to fight cervical growth. It is good to avoid starchy vegetables like potatoes and sweet potatoes. Cauliflower is another nutritious veggie that you can eat. Raw foods and juices are good under the said condition. You can take a lot of kale and broccoleaf. In fact, as the name implies, broccoleaf is the leaf surrounding the actual broccoli.

- Sprouted beans: Sprouts are a good source of vitamins and can naturally heal cervical cancer. You can sprout your green moong beans to get the sprouts ultra-fresh. Just take a handful of beans and soak them in water overnight. Then carry and drain the water in the morning. Put the beans in a closed container and leave it for 4 to 5 hours. You will see that tiny sprouts have come up. These are a nutritious destroyer of fibroids.

- Rice: you can eat rice, which is whole and organic. Take care to cook it in a slow cooker or crockpot so that it is soft and mushy and easy to digest; adding a little garlic whenever possible will also help.

- Nuts are also a good option as they are full of proteins and minerals. They can be of different varieties like almonds, pistachios, macadamia nuts, and pine nuts. Sunflower seeds are also suitable for shrinking the cervical cancer mass.

Foods to Avoid

You should avoid red meat, alcohol, refined grains, caffeine, and caffeinated drinks like colas at all costs. Not eating all these food items may seem like a big deal at first, but when you see the improvement in the symptoms of cervical cancer, you will find it worthwhile.

Acupuncture

Many women have found relief from pain and other symptoms caused by cervical cancer through acupuncture. Circulation is improved in the pelvic area, and any blockage, which might be there, is also eliminated by undergoing acupuncture.

Moreover, it is a lot less complicated than surgery. The pent-up energy in that 'chakra' is released through the needles. There are also many herbal supplements available to heal fibroids, which complement acupuncture therapy.

Castor Oil Packs

These are very helpful in getting rid of cancerous growths. You can use a castor oil pack one to four times a week. Just soak a square piece of cloth in castor oil and put it on top of the uterus area, and put a hot water bottle on top of it. You can also use an electric warmer for this.

Keep the pack on for five to seven minutes, and then remove it. This treatment is very effective in the case of a growing cancer mass. Many women vouch for the effectiveness of a castor oil pack.

However, there are times when a castor oil pack should not be used. Women should not use it when they are menstruating. It would be best if you did not also use it when pregnant.

Supplements

The next thing you can do is to take iron supplements. You may be anaemic from losing blood during menstruation due to cancer growth, and taking iron supplements would help. They will reduce your exhaustion and help you work better.

Doing Exercise

Exercising is another way of reducing cancer growth. Breathing exercises and pelvic tilts, which increase the blood flow in the pelvic region, are good. All types of relaxation exercises are suitable for shrinking the mass of cervical cancer. Exercise improves blood circulation and thereby helps cut down cancer growth. Yoga is also beneficial in healing abnormal growth.

Avoid Stress

Stress is one of the causes of cervical cancer and should be avoided. For this, you can take up any hobby that relaxes you. Gardening is generally good because it provides much beneficial physical activity as well as mental relaxation. Take adequate rest and do not overwork yourself.

Conclusion

Generally, these non-surgical treatment options would be effective for women who have been advised by their doctor or medical practitioner to not go in for surgery immediately. Summing up, you should eat well, rest well, and relax along with the use of oil packs and supplements to relieve the symptoms of cervical cancer.

Management of Prostate Cancer With Safe and Effective Ayurvedic Remedies

Prostate cancer is the form of cancer that affects the prostate. The prostate is a small gland present in males that is the size of a walnut. It produces seminal fluid, which nourishes the sperm and transports them.

Cancer of the prostate gland is one of the most common forms of cancer affecting men. Most prostate cancers tend to grow slowly and are often confined to the gland itself, where they may or may not cause any severe harm.

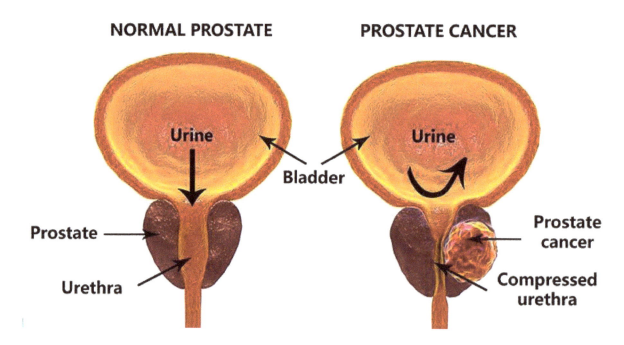

While some forms of prostate cancer grow very slowly and need minimal or no medical treatments, some other types could be aggressive and spread quickly to healthy tissues.

Early prostate cancer detected while still confined to the gland has a better chance of successful treatment outcomes.

What Are the Signs and Symptoms of Prostate Cancer?

Prostate cancer may not cause any signs or symptoms in its initial stages. Prostate cancer that has become more advanced might cause a few signs and symptoms like:

- Trouble in urinating
- Presence of blood in the semen
- Reduced force of the urine stream
- Presence of blood in the urine
- Pain in the bones
- Erectile dysfunction
- Losing weight without any apparent reason

Men who notice any of these symptoms should contact a physician at the earliest to confirm or rule out the diagnosis of prostate cancer. The early diagnosis of prostate cancer can play a vital role in promoting faster recovery and preventing relapse in the future.

What Are the Causes of Prostate Cancer?

It is not clear what exactly causes prostate cancer. Prostate cancer begins when the healthy cells of the cervical tissues develop changes (or undergo mutations) in their cellular DNA. DNA of cells contains signals or instructions that regulate how the cell functions or behaves.

Healthy cells can only grow and multiply at a specific rate, eventually dying after their expected lifespan. Mutations can cause the cells to multiply and grow out of control without undergoing programmed death. That is why abnormal cells accumulating in the prostate form a tumour mass. These cancer cells can also invade the nearby tissues or break off from the tumour to metastasise (spread) to other parts of the body.

What Are the Risk Factors for Prostate Cancer?

Some factors that may increase the risk of men developing prostate cancer include:

Older Age

The risk of prostate cancer tends to increase as a man ages. It is common after the age of 50 years.

Race

For some reasons not entirely determined, people with a darker skin tone have been found to have a higher risk of prostate cancer than those with a lighter skin tone. In Black people, prostate cancer is also likely to be more advanced or aggressive.

Family History

If a close blood relative, like the father, brother, or child, is diagnosed with prostate cancer, your risk of developing this condition might increase. If one has a family history of genes known to increase the risk of other forms of cancers, like breast cancer (of types BRCA1 and BRCA2), and a strong family history of cancer, his risk of developing prostate cancer would be higher.

Obesity

Men who are obese would have a higher risk of developing prostate cancer than those considered to have a normal or healthy weight. In obese men, the cancer is likely to be more severe and aggressive and more likely to relapse after initial treatments have caused complete recovery.

What Are the Complications of Prostate Cancer?

Cancer That Metastasises (Spreads)

Prostate cancer may spread to nearby organs, like the urinary bladder, or travel through the bloodstream or lymphatic tissues to the bones or other healthy organs. Prostate cancer, which spreads to the bones, may cause severe pain and even fractures (broken bones).

Once cancer has spread to other areas of the body, it might still respond to conventional treatments like chemotherapy or radiation treatment. Though it is less likely to be cured entirely, it could be controlled.

Incontinence of Urine

Prostate cancer, as well as its treatment, is known to cause urinary incontinence. Treatment for incontinence is based on symptoms or the type of incontinence you have, the severity of symptoms, and the likelihood of improving over time.

The treatment options often include medications, surgery, or catheters.

Erectile Dysfunction

Erectile dysfunction could result from prostate cancer and its treatments like surgery, hormone treatments, and radiation. Medications, vacuum devices, and surgery are effective treatments to manage these complications.

Screening for Prostate Cancer

Regular testing of healthy men without any symptoms of prostate cancer could be beneficial for the early detection of prostate cancer.

Some of the most sensitive and helpful prostate screening tests include:

- Digital Rectal Exam (DRE)
- Prostate-Specific Antigen (PSA) test

- Ultrasound
- Transrectal biopsy of the prostate
- Collecting a sample of the prostate tissue
- Magnetic resonance imaging

Prevention of Prostate Cancer

Ayurveda recommends healthy dietary and lifestyle strategies to reduce prostate cancer risk. These strategies would also help support the recovery of men who are already diagnosed with this form of cancer. It would help minimise the risk of the spread of cancer and relapse after recovery.

Let us have a look at the best prevention measures for prostate cancer.

Choosing a Healthy and Nutritious Diet Full of Fruits and Vegetables

Consume a variety of fresh fruits, veggies, and whole grains. Most fruits and vegetables have a rich content of several vitamins and minerals that could contribute to your health by strengthening the body's defence mechanisms against cancer-causing agents.

Choosing Healthy Foods and Avoiding Junk Foods

Choosing foods that have a rich content of vitamins and minerals and natural plant compounds that possess medicinal potentials like anti-inflammatory, anti-cancer, and antioxidants properties would help you avoid the risk of prostate cancer.

Exercising Regularly

Exercising regularly for at least five days of the week could improve your overall health and help you maintain a normal weight, thus reducing the risk of prostate cancer. It may also improve your mood and reduce stress.

These benefits could play a role in improving your outlook during cancer treatment and enable you to be more receptive to the benefits, thereby promoting faster recovery.

If you are new to exercises, it is best to start slow and gradually work your way up to exercise for a longer time every day.

Maintaining a Healthy Weight

If your weight is healthy, you can maintain it by choosing healthy foods and exercising at least five days a week. Suppose you are obese and need to lose weight. In that case, it is advisable to add more exercise to your routine and control the number of calories you consume every day.

Creating a plan for weight loss would help you avoid obesity, which is a common risk factor for prostate cancer.

Medications for Prostate Cancer

In case you have a higher risk of prostate cancer due to risk factors like family history, your doctor might consider prescribing medications and other treatments to reduce the risk.

Some research studies have suggested that using drugs like 5-alpha reductase inhibitors, including finasteride and dutasteride, might help reduce the overall risk of prostate cancer. These medications are also used to control the enlargement of the prostate gland and even hair loss.

However, some studies have indicated that people using these medications might also have a higher risk of getting a severe form of prostate cancer, such as high-grade prostate cancer. Hence, it is best to avoid using these drugs unless deemed essential by your physician.

Alternatively, you can choose herbal remedies to protect yourself against this form of cancer. Herbal remedies offer several benefits over modern medications by producing an action that mimics the body's defence mechanisms without causing any severe side effects.

Natural Ayurvedic Remedies for the Management of Prostate Cancer

Cernilton

Some men use herbal remedies made of rye-grass pollens to treat prostate cancer and BPH symptoms. These symptoms might include being unable to pass urine or empty the bladder and the need for frequent urination, especially at nighttime.

This herb may also help reduce the size of the enlarged prostate gland.

Saw Palmetto

This is one of the most effective and popular herbal remedies used to treat prostate cancer. Saw palmetto has been found to reduce the symptoms of this condition. It can inhibit the production of DHT (dihydrotestosterone) and reduce the size of the inner layer of the prostate. Hence, it is also used to treat benign prostate enlargement (BPH).

Pygeum (Or African Plum Extract)

This herb has been shown to possess a wide range of healthy fatty acids, sterols like beta-sitosterol, and alcohols that could produce an anti-inflammatory and antioxidant effect on the urogenital system and reduce the risk of prostate cancer.

A few studies have indicated that consuming about 100 to 200 milligrams of pygeum extract every day or splitting the dosage into two, with each dose of 50 mg to be taken twice daily, could help reduce the symptoms of prostate cancer.

Orbignya speciosa (or Babassu)

It is a species of palm tree native to Brazil. Some indigenous tribes and communities in Brazil use the ground and dried kernels from this tree to treat urogenital symptoms and diseases like prostate cancer and BHP.

The oil from babassu nuts is also effective for inhibiting the production of a male hormone called testosterone. Additionally, other parts of this nut contain potential natural antioxidant and anti-inflammatory compounds.

Cucurbita Pepo (or Pumpkin Seeds)

Pumpkin seeds contain a compound called beta-sitosterol that is similar to cholesterol. Beta-sitosterol might help improve the urine flow and decrease the amount of urine left in the urinary bladder after urination in men with prostate cancer or BHP.

Stinging Nettle

Stinging nettle contains potent anti-inflammatory and antioxidant compounds as those found in saw palmetto and pygeum. Hence, nettle root is often combined with these herbs, especially saw palmetto, to manage prostate diseases.

Lycopene

Lycopene is one of the naturally occurring pigments found in some fruits and vegetables. It might help slow down the progression of prostate cancer and BPH. Tomatoes offer the richest natural source of lycopene available to us. But a few other vegetables and fruits also contain a lower level of this antioxidant.

Generally, it is found that the deeper red or pink the vegetable or fruit is in colour, the higher its lycopene content.

Some other sources of lycopene are:

- Pink grapefruit
- Watermelon
- Carrots
- Guava
- Red bell peppers

- Red cabbage
- Apricots

Zinc

Chronic zinc deficiency has been shown to significantly increase the risk of developing BPH and prostate cancer. Using zinc supplements and increasing the dietary intake of zinc-rich foods might help reduce the urinary symptoms associated with prostate cancer or enlarged prostate.

This mineral is found in higher quantities in several types of nuts and seeds, such as pumpkin and sesame.

Green Tea

Green tea contains natural antioxidants called catechins, which have been shown to improve the functions of the immune system and slow down the progress of prostate cancer.

Conclusion

Complementary or alternative treatments can support men's recovery from prostate cancer, especially when the therapies are combined with conventional measures like radiation or chemotherapy. Complementary and alternative therapies for prostate cancer might also help the patient cope with some of the side effects of the disease and its treatment.

What Is Bone Cancer and How to Manage It With the Help of Natural Treatments?

Bone cancer can affect any bone in our body, though it commonly affects the long bones in the hands and legs, and pelvis. Bone cancer is a comparatively rare form of cancer, making up less than one percent of all cases. Non-cancerous bone tumours in fact tend to be more common than cancerous lesions in the bone tissues.

The term 'bone cancer' does not include the cancers that begin in any other part of the body and then metastasise (spread) to the bone tissues. Instead, those cancers are named based on the organ where they originate, such as the breast cancer that has spread to the bones.

Some forms of bone cancers primarily occur in children, while some commonly affect adults. The surgical removal of the abnormal mass is the most common treatment method for patients with bone cancer. However, chemotherapy and radiation can also be included in the treatment plan.

Also, the decision to use chemotherapy, radiation therapy or surgery is based on the form of the bone cancer to be treated. Moreover, including alternative therapies like Ayurveda is also recommended for hastening patient recovery and minimising the risk of side effects.

Let us have a closer look at the types, risk factors, symptoms, and modern and Ayurvedic treatments for managing bone cancers.

What Are the Common Types of Bone Cancers?

Bone cancers can be categorised into separate forms based on the types of cells where cancer begins.

The common forms of bone cancer include:

Osteosarcoma

It is the most common type of bone cancer. In this form, the cancerous cells can produce bone tissue. This form of bone cancer tends to occur most commonly in young adults and children, especially in the bones of the legs or hands.

In some circumstances, osteosarcomas may arise outside of the bones, in which case it is called the extra-skeletal osteosarcomas.

Chondrosarcoma

It is the second most common type of bone cancer. In this form, the abnormal cancerous cells can produce cartilage. It usually affects the bones in the pelvis, arms, and legs in older and middle-aged adults.

Ewing Sarcoma

This form of bone cancer commonly arises in young adults and children's pelvis, legs, and hands.

What Are the Symptoms of Bone Cancer?

The common signs and symptoms of bone cancer may include:

- Pain in the bone
- Tenderness and swelling in the affected area
- Weakened bone, resulting in a fracture
- Unintended weight loss
- Severe fatigue

It is crucial not to ignore these signs and consult your physician at the earliest if you develop these symptoms. The pain in the bone that comes and goes frequently and becomes worse at night or is not relieved by the commonly used pain relievers should raise a suspicion of a more severe underlying problem such as bone cancer.

What Are the Causes of Bone Cancer?

The cause of bone cancers is not known. Most cases of bone cancers are linked to hereditary factors, while some are connected to previous radiation exposure.

What Are the Risk Factors for Bone Cancers?

It is not clear what causes bone cancer. However, some factors are associated with a higher risk. These factors include:

Inherited Genetic Syndromes

Some rare genetic syndrome may get passed down through the families and increase the risk of developing bone cancer, like hereditary retinoblastoma or Li-Fraumeni syndrome.

Paget's Disease of the Bone

Paget's disease of the bone, most commonly occurring in older adults, has been found to increase the risk of bone cancers in the future.

Radiation Therapy

Exposure to large doses of radiation, like those given at the time of radiation therapy for cancer management, may increase the risk of developing bone cancers in the future.

Diagnosis of Bone Cancers

Some imaging tests could help determine the exact location and the size of bone tumours. These tests can also help check whether the tumour has spread to other organs or tissues of the body.

Imaging tests are recommended depending on the signs and symptoms of patients and bones suspected to be involved.

The tests for the diagnosis of bone cancers may include:

- Computerised tomography
- Bone scan
- Magnetic resonance imaging
- X-ray
- Positron emission tomography
- Needle or surgical biopsies

In some cases, the doctor may advise the patient to undergo a procedure to remove a small sample of affected tissue from the tumour mass for laboratory testing. The testing would tell the doctor whether the tissue is cancerous and the type of cancer you might have.

Ayurvedic Treatments Recommended for the Management of Bone Cancers

Ayurveda recommends making healthy changes in your diet to strengthen the bones and immune system to prevent bone cancer. Ayurvedic treatment also includes foods that can protect the bones against cancerous changes. These treatments can be combined with modern therapies like chemotherapy and radiation to help improve the benefits and support the faster recovery of patients.

Let us have a look at some of the best food sources that can play a role in protecting you against bone cancers.

Best Foods for the Management of Bone Cancers

Dairy products are considered the best to fulfil the body's calcium requirement. It is an essential nutrient needed for maintaining the bones and even the teeth. It also ensures the optimum functioning of your muscles, nerves, and cardiac cells.

Drinking two glasses of milk every day would help prevent calcium deficiency. Additionally, you may eat cheese, yoghurt, or other dairy products to ensure a proper supply of calcium.

However, some people either do not like the taste of milk or may be intolerant of these products. Consuming milk is also contrary to the rules of a vegan diet since it is an animal-based product.

However, it doesn't mean your body will be deprived of calcium if you don't consume dairy products. There are a few fruits and vegetables that can provide a good amount of this mineral. Here is the list of some non-dairy foods rich in calcium:

Bok Choy

Bok choy, also called Chinese cabbage, is a rich source of calcium. Eating one cup of shredded cabbage as a salad could provide 74 mg of calcium. This versatile, nutrient-loaded food also offers a hefty dose of iron, vitamin A, and vitamin C, along with loads of fibres. You can add it to any main dish or stir-fry it with olive oil and garlic for a healthy side dish.

Oranges

Oranges are not just rich in vitamin C, as many people believe. They are also rich in calcium and provide powerful antioxidants. A medium-sized orange contains 65 mg of calcium. You can enjoy this fruit anytime for your mid-meals snack or add it to any dish to enhance the flavour with its citrus tinge.

Blackstrap Molasses

Blackstrap Molasses offers an opportunity to satisfy your sweet tooth while also taking care of your bones. It is richer in flavour and darker in colour than regular molasses and provides a unique flavour and an exciting hue to your desert. It is filled with calcium, along with iron and vitamins.

Bone Broth

Bone broth is a perfect replacement for milk for those who don't like its taste. It also contains several other minerals, including iron, phosphorus, silicon, sulphur, and magnesium.

Broth also provides amino acids called proline and glycine that help improve digestion, skin health, and the nervous system functions and hasten wound healing. These amino acids are also needed to produce glutathione that protects the body from the toxic substances known to cause bone cancers.

Plus, bone broth is easy to make, and hence, you can consume it daily. You can prepare a bone broth from chicken, lamb, beef, bison, and fish bones. All you need to do is boil and simmer the bones for 20 to 30 minutes to allow the calcium and other nutrients to seep into the water.

Even a tiny amount of calcium from bones is absorbed quickly, making this broth one of the best non-dairy sources of calcium.

Dried Figs

Dried figs make up for a tempting dessert. Just eight pieces of dried figs provide 107 mg of calcium. This fruit packs in loads of fibres and antioxidants, which would improve your general health and ease digestion. You can turn the delicious dry figs into a creamy jam or eat them raw for your mid-meal snack.

Fish With Bones

It is agreed that bone broth is easy to make. Yet, some people do not have the patience to wait for that much time to allow it to simmer. If you find making a bone broth too tedious or time-consuming, here's another easier-to-make high-calcium alternative for you using fish bones.

Fish bones are an excellent source of easily absorbable calcium. The recommended way to consume fish bones to get a high amount of calcium lies in canned fish such as sardines and salmon.

Fish bones tend to become soft during the canning process. Hence, they can be chewed easily and consumed with the fish.

One six-ounce serving of sardines and wild salmon would provide about 110 milligrams of absorbable calcium. These foods also contain vitamin D, which can help enhance calcium absorption and increase its availability.

To prepare, you need a tin of sardines or salmon. Sprinkle it with a pinch of salt and add half a tablespoon of lemon juice for a perfect high-calcium dish.

Dark, Leafy Greens

This one's for the vegans; if you avoid dairy products for being a vegan, then the high calcium content of bone broth and fish bones holds no importance to you. It would be best if you turned to the dark leafy greens to ensure your body is not deprived of calcium.

Dark leafy greens provide a rich source of vitamins A, B, C, E, and K and folate. Eat plenty of Collard Greens, Kale, Broccoli, and Turnip Greens, all of which are ranked high in the list of foods containing absorbable sources of calcium.

One cup of cooked Collard greens can provide almost 268 milligrams of calcium. You may also consume spinach and seaweed, which also contain a good amount of calcium; however, the calcium present in these veggies is less absorbable than those in the other greens.

White Beans

These creamy and light legumes provide a great source of calcium. These are also high in other minerals like iron and magnesium.

Just add white beans to a pasta dish with other veggies. You can also skip the chickpeas and make delicious hummus using white beans instead.

Black-Eyed Peas

Half a cup of black beans is filled with 185 mg of calcium, together with a heavy dose of potassium and folate! It is a healthier alternative to the fat-filled mayo. Just whip up some black-eyed pea and spread it on the bread slice for a yummy sandwich.

Some other non-dairy sources of calcium that could reduce your risk of bone cancer include:

- Oysters
- Almonds
- Seaweed
- Oatmeal
- Sesame Seeds
- Soymilk

Conclusion

So, if you are a vegan and suffer from lactose intolerance or simply do not like the taste of milk or other dairy products, you can still have strong bones. All you need to do is replace milk with these calcium-rich foods. The regular intake of these foods would strengthen your bones and minimise your risk of bone cancers. When combined with modern treatments for bone cancers, it would help you recover faster and increase your chances of deriving better outcomes with a reduced risk of relapse.

Ayurvedic Treatments for Patients with Alzheimer's Disease

Alzheimer's disease is a common neurological condition due to brain cells' death resulting in cognitive decline and memory loss. It is one of the most common types of dementia, accounting for nearly 60 to 80% of the cases in the United States.

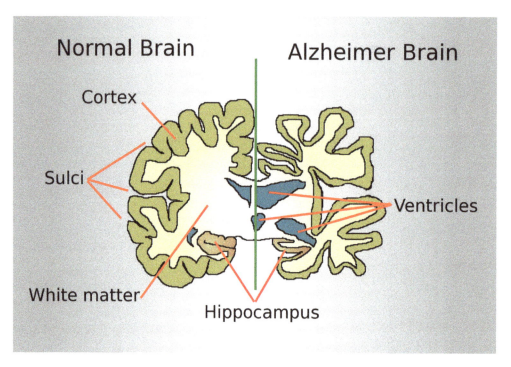

This condition usually affects older people above the age of 65, with only 10% of the cases occurring in younger individuals.

Let us have an overview of Alzheimer's disease and the possible treatment options recommended by Ayurveda to improve memory and prevent the faster decline in the configure functions.

What Is Alzheimer's Disease?

Alzheimer's is a condition that affects the cells in the brain. The symptoms tend to be mild at first and become severe over a period. The common signs and symptoms of Alzheimer's disease are memory loss, impulsive and unpredictable behaviours, and language problems.

One of the critical features of this condition is the formation of plaques or tangles in the brain tissues. Another feature is the loss of connection between nerve cells, called neurons, in the central nervous system.

These abnormal features can prevent the passage of information between the different areas of the brain and between the brain and other organs and muscles. As these symptoms worsen, it can become more challenging for the patient to remember recent names or events, recognise people they already knew, or reason. Eventually, a patient with Alzheimer's disease might need full-time support.

Treatments of Alzheimer's Disease

Currently, there is no cure for most neurodegenerative diseases, including Alzheimer's disease, as it is impossible to reverse the damage or death of the brain cells completely. However, some medications may relieve the symptoms and improve the patients' quality of life.

The following are some crucial elements that must be taken into consideration for effective management of Alzheimer's disease:

- Effective management of other conditions co-existing with Alzheimer's
- Continued support for routine activities
- Day-care programs
- Practising meditation

The practice of meditation can play a role in improving your concentration, memory, and attention span. Let us look at how these alternative therapies would improve the symptoms of Alzheimer's disease.

How to Practice Meditation to Improve Your Concentration, Memory, and Attention Span?

Meditation is an art that allows you to focus your attention on one area. It provides a myriad of health benefits such as increased concentration and memory power, decreased anxiety, better attention span, and an overall feeling of being happy or satisfied with life.

Although a large number of people try this art at some point in their lives, only a small percentage can actually stick to it for the long-term. This predicament is quite unfortunate because it disrobes them of the numerous health benefits they would have achieved by regular meditation practice.

The most common reason for not continuing meditation is that beginners often do not have the mindset required to make the practice more fruitful and sustainable. Many of them do not know the proper ways to meditate. Hence, it is essential to be aware of the practical recommendations for beginners to help them successfully cross the initial hurdles. Only then can they integrate meditation into their daily routine over the long run.

A deeper understanding of meditation and the right ways of practising it would help you derive maximum benefits from this art. You will find an improvement in your memory, concentration, and attention span while reducing the risk of Alzheimer's disease. Keep reading to learn the correct way to practice meditation to prevent Alzheimer's.

- Try to meditate each day, whether first thing in the morning or before your lunch hour. Whichever time you may choose, make it an unshakable part of your routine.

- Meditation is essentially the time for relaxation - the relaxation of your body, your mind, and your inner soul. Hence, it is vital that you practice meditating entirely at your convenience. So, choose a time when you will not be disturbed and feel completely relaxed; hours of the day where nature makes transitions between day and night, the time of sunrise and sunset, are also considered best for the practice.

- Decide the duration of your meditation. While the most seasoned meditators advise people to meditate for at least twenty minutes, twice a day, you can start with just 10 to 15 minutes once a day, and then increase the duration slowly as you gain the ability to focus for a more extended period.

- Choose a peaceful environment. Meditation should always be practised in calm surroundings to enable you to concentrate exclusively on the task at hand. A peaceful environment would ensure that your mind is not disturbed by unpleasant external stimuli. Try to find a place where you will not be interrupted when meditating. The space need not be vast - a walk-in closet is also enough as long as it's comfortable and private.

- Wear comfortable clothes. Keep in mind that the primary goal of meditation is to block out external factors and relax the mind. It might be challenging to achieve this state of mind if you are uncomfortable due to tight or uncomfortable clothing. Wear loose clothing and make sure you remove your shoes. Wear a cardigan or a sweater if you are meditating at a cool place; otherwise, the sensation of coldness might consume your thoughts and tempt you to cut your practice short.

- Avoid any external distractions, especially when you are new to meditation. Turn off the phone, TV sets, and other noisy appliances. If you like to play some music, choose calm, gentle tunes that will not break your concentration.

- Stretch out before each session. Meditation requires you to sit in one place for a certain period. Hence, it's important to avoid cramps, stiffness, or tightness. Doing light stretching for a couple of minutes before each session would also help loosen up your muscles. It would prepare your mind and body for meditation and prevent you from focusing on muscle tension instead of relaxing your mind.

- Sit down at the place you have chosen. Meditation should ideally be practised by sitting on a cushion on the ground. When you are a beginner though, you can choose any comfortable posture that allows you to remain balanced. You may sit down on a mat in a lotus position or sit without crossing your legs on a chair or bench. Tilt your pelvis forwards so that the spine is centred over the bony bits in the butt. These spots will bear your weight.

- Traditional meditation practices involve placing your hands on your laps with your palms facing upward and your right hand on the top of the left.

- Close your eyes. Though meditation can also be performed with your eyes open, it is best to meditate with your eyes closed, especially if you are a beginner. This step would help you block out the external visual stimuli and prevent getting distracted.

- Follow your breathing. Focus your mind on the spot above your navel. Concentrate on the rising and falling of your abdomen while breathing in and out. Breathe normally and focus entirely on it. Avoid making any conscious efforts to change your breathing pattern.

- Repeat a mantra. Chanting a mantra is a common form of meditation that involves repeating a word, sound, or phrase until your mind is silenced. It would allow you to enter a deep and serene meditative state. The mantra may be anything as long as you can remember it easily. A good mantra includes words like peace, calm, one, or silence. If you want to use the traditional mantras, use the word 'Om' that symbolises an omnipresent consciousness, or the phrases like 'Chit, Sat and Ananda', which means 'Consciousness, Existence, and Bliss'. Whisper the word through your mind. As you enter a deeper level of consciousness or awareness, it would not be necessary for you to continue repeating the mantra.

Continue with this for the duration of your meditation. Then, open your eyes and relax for some time, after which you can get back to your routine. After the session, you will feel much difference in your attitude, energy, mental and emotional status, and senses. The effect will last for the entire day.

Meditation will allow you to enjoy several health benefits and improve your physical and mental well-being. It would boost your memory and concentration power and reduce your risk of Alzheimer's disease. It may also improve your attention span allowing you to focus on your work or study for a longer time without feeling fatigued. It would help you seek joy, peace of mind, calmness, vibrant health, more incredible energy, positive relationships, and fulfilment in life. It would also freshen up your mind and maintain its delicacy and beauty while bringing about emotional stability and harmony that will nourish you from within. With regular practice, you will notice an improvement in your memory and other cognitive functions. Your sharper mind would also be able to face the challenges with renewed confidence and focus. It would become easier to achieve the goals you have set while avoiding neurodegenerative diseases like Alzheimer's.

Natural Remedies for Improving Your Memory and Reducing Anxiety Associated With Alzheimer's Disease

Anxiety is a feeling that all of us have experienced several times in our life. It is a sense of some unknown fear or something terrible will happen, making us feel uneasy. Though this feeling of fear or anxiety passes off on its own in most cases, sometimes, it can continue to bother you for long and repeatedly. This happens especially if you are suffering from a chronic disease like Alzheimer's.

Prolonged anxiety or a tendency to get anxious over trifles can lead to significant psychological, neurodegenerative, and physical disorders, including Alzheimer's disease, depression, obsessive-compulsive disorder, hypertension, and even heart attacks. Hence, it is essential to get rid of this feeling with some effective natural remedies as given below:

Chamomile

A cup of chamomile tea is what you need when having a jittery moment. It would act as a great stress-buster and help you calm down. Chamomile contains compounds that would reduce negative emotions by binding to the brain receptors, similar to the most commonly used antipsychotic drugs like Valium.

Patients who have Alzheimer's or generalised anxiety disorder (GAD), a psychological condition characterised by unnecessary or excessive anxiety over several aspects of life, are advised to drink chamomile tea. At least 3 to 4 times a day for several weeks will help achieve desired results.

You could control the imbalances in the nervous system and avoid experiencing counterproductive emotions that affect your personal and professional life and hinder your ability to make sound decisions.

Valerian

Valerian is a potent medicinal herb specifically used to counter the effect of imbalanced levels of hormones and neurotransmitters in the central nervous system. It would produce a soothing effect on the nerves and prevent anxiety.

It would also act as a sedative agent and promote sound sleep. Lack of sleep can make a person feel weary and give rise to stress and anxiety. Lack of sleep can also reduce the ability of a person to work productively during the daytime resulting in mistakes that trigger anxiety.

By acting as a sedative, Valerian would help you sleep well and thus, prevent anxiety. However, since Valerian can make you feel sleepy and reduce your level of alertness, you must avoid using it during the daytime to reduce the risk of injuries.

The advantage of using Valerian over the common anti-anxiety drugs is that Valerian is non-sedative, which does not cause intentional sleepiness. This effect makes it a safer remedy to use even during the daytime when performing several functions that require focus and alertness.

Green Tea

Green tea contains an amino acid called L-theanine, which could produce a calming effect on the mind by curbing the blood pressure and heart rate and protecting the brain against degenerative changes that can trigger the development of Alzheimer's disease.

Regularly consuming green tea could also help ensure a balance of chemical substances in the brain called neurotransmitters. These neurotransmitters play an essential role in triggering anxiety and Alzheimer's disease.

It may also boost the production of feel-good hormones like serotonin and dopamine, thus promoting a positive attitude in patients with Alzheimer's disease.

Lavender

Lavender can create an intoxicating yet safe aroma that is highly soothing for your mind. It would relax the mind and reduce anxiety. It would help you calm down by lowering stress levels. It may also work by correcting the imbalance of hormones in the nervous system.

It would also act as an anti-inflammatory agent and reduce the negative effect of environmental toxins like pollution on the brain, thus correcting the malfunctioning of the nervous system responsible for the development of Alzheimer's disease.

Interestingly, spreading the aroma of lavender oil into the waiting room is commonly followed by many dentists to reduce patients' anxiety.

Inhaling the aroma of lavender oil just before meeting your doctor or an examination could positively impact your emotional status. It would reduce your anxiety and help you focus better, thus improving your efficacy.

Lavender is also used to reduce anxiety in patients with Alzheimer's disease and Generalised Anxiety Disorder. It is found to be as effective as lorazepam, a commonly used anti-anxiety medication.

Some more tips for controlling the symptoms and reducing the risk of Alzheimer's disease include:
- Applying lemon balm

- Laughter therapy
- Practising yoga
- Avoiding the consumption of alcohol
- Minimising the intake of regular tea and caffeine
- Exercising regularly
- Quit smoking

Though several anti-depressant medications can help relieve anxiety in patients with Alzheimer's disease, those drugs are known to cause serious side effects, primarily when used over several weeks or months. Simply using the natural remedies given above would help you get rid of anxiety and allow you to feel calm and relaxed without causing any side effects.

Conclusion

Alzheimer's disease is one of the common neurodegenerative conditions. A build-up of tangles and plaques in the brain, along with cell death, can cause cognitive decline and memory loss.

Currently, there is no cure for this disease. However, medications and other treatments could help slow down or ease the emotional, cognitive, and behavioural symptoms and even improve the person's quality of life. Complementing these treatments with the use of Ayurvedic herbs and other alternative therapies is recommended for improving the results and enabling the patient to lead a healthier and more independent life.

What Is a Headache or Migraine, and How to Manage It?

A migraine is a stronger form of a headache concerning its intensity and the frequency of recurrence. It often comes with other symptoms like nausea, vomiting, and increased sensitivity to light. It may last for a few hours to even several days.

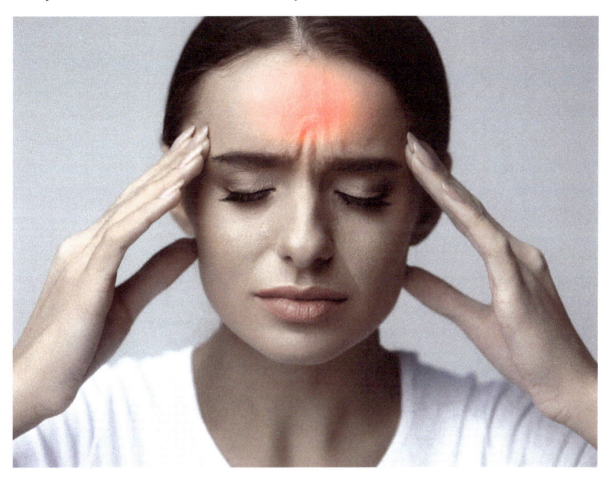

What Are the Risk Factors for Migraines or Recurring Headaches?

Sex

Women tend to have migraines three times more often compared to men.

Age

It is observed that most people start having migraine attacks between the ages of 10 and 40 years. But, most women find that their attacks get better or even go away after 50 years.

Other Medical Conditions

Some medical conditions like depression, anxiety, sleep disorders, bipolar disorder, and epilepsy could raise your chances of recurring headaches.

Family History

Nearly 4 out of 5 people with migraines have their other family members suffering the same issue. If one of the parents has a history of developing these forms of headaches, the child would have a nearly 50 percent chance of getting them. Also, if both the parents have a history of migraine, the risk may jump to as high as 75 percent.

Migraine Triggers

Some of the most common triggers for migraine attacks include:

Hormonal Changes

Most women notice that they develop headaches when they get their menstrual periods while pregnant and ovulating. The symptoms could also be tied to hormonal changes occurring during menopause, birth control pills that include hormones, and hormone replacement therapy.

Foods

Certain foods and drinks like alcohol, aged cheese, food additives such as nitrates (in hot dogs, pepperoni, and lunchmeats), and monosodium glutamate (MSG) could be responsible for migraines in some patients.

Stress

When you are stressed, the brain releases some chemicals, which can cause specific changes in the blood vessels that might lead to a migraine attack.

Skipping Meals

Skipping a meal can result in fluctuations in the blood sugar level and a dip in energy supply to the body, thus triggering a migraine attack.

Caffeine

Getting too much caffeine or not getting as much caffeine as you are used to could cause headaches. Also, caffeine itself is one of the effective treatments for acute migraine attacks.

Change in Weather

Sometimes, storm fronts, a change in barometric pressure, changes in altitude, and strong winds could also trigger an attack.

Senses

Bright lights, loud noises, and strong smells may set off migraine attacks.

Medications

Medications like vasodilators that widen the blood vessels may trigger an attack.

Physical Activities

These include intense workouts and exercises. Such activities trigger migraine attacks, primarily if the person is not used to extreme physical activities.

Tobacco

Excessive use of tobacco or smoking cigarettes may result in a severe migraine attack.

Change in Your Sleep Schedule

You might get a headache when you sleep for long hours or do not get enough sleep.

Natural Ayurvedic Remedies to Get Rid of Migraines Quickly

Popping pain killers seems to be the easiest way to get rid of migraines. Patients who use these pills frequently and for too long may develop dependency!

If you are taking migraine medicines frequently, you are at risk of some severe side effects. Also, some of them are not suitable to be used by pregnant and breastfeeding women.

If taking these pills comes with just one advantage of relieving the pain but too many disadvantages, wouldn't it be wise to find a safer and equally effective alternative?

If you agree, read on to find the list of safe and effective ways to get rid of migraines, as recommended by Ayurveda.

Drink Water

Migraine is often triggered by dehydration. Hence, it is a good idea to drink sips of water as soon as you start getting a headache. You can also make it a habit to drink 8 to 10 glasses of water every day to stay hydrated and prevent a migraine attack.

But, if the attack has already flared up and is causing considerable discomfort, refrain from drinking chilled or ice-cold water as it can exacerbate the pain.

Cold Compresses and Ice Packs

Cold compresses and ice packs can help treat migraine headaches by reducing the pressure in the blood vessels in the head.

Ice also works as a natural anti-inflammatory agent, which is helpful against migraine headaches. Ice packs work by constricting the blood vessels, which leads to reduced blood flow into the head.

To get quick relief from migraines, take a cloth and soak it in ice-cold water; get rid of the excess water by wringing it slightly and placing it on your forehead. Refresh the fabric every 15 minutes.

If you want to avoid soaking the cloth again and again, seal it in a sandwich bag and keep it in the freezer for 30 minutes. Place it on the forehead without taking the fabric out of the bag.

Hot Water Treatment

Water has a fantastic quality of relieving headaches from inside and outside. Drinking it abundantly can ease migraines by improving your hydration and help when used externally to soak your feet.

If you are at home when the attack strikes, soak your hands, feet, or both in a tub of hot water.

This method will increase blood flow into the legs and hands by drawing blood away from the head, thus reducing pressure inside it. Applying a hot water bag on the back and the neck can also work similarly.

Muscle Relaxation

Muscle relaxation can reduce tension in the head and regulate the blood flow, which helps ease the pressure in the cranium and reduces the headache.

You can lie down comfortably and allow for complete relaxation of the body. Take deep breaths.

The ideal way to relax your muscles is to let a particular part of your body tense for a few seconds and then loosen those muscles. Focus on the feeling of relaxation while relaxing the muscles.

Caffeine

A caffeinated beverage like coffee, green tea, or black tea, when used carefully, would help relieve migraine symptoms.

The level of adenosine in the blood increases during a migraine attack. Since caffeine blocks the adenosine receptors, the nervous system could fail to detect the pain, thus relieving a migraine.

However, you should avoid an over-indulgence in caffeinated beverages, especially if you suffer from more than two migraine attacks per week.

Massage

Gentle massage of different parts of the face, scalp, forehead, and neck can significantly relieve migraine attacks.

You may begin with the temple region, which lies between the corner of the eye and the top of the ear. Then, massage the part in circular motions starting from the temple, moving towards the forehead.

You can also massage the bridge of your nose with the tip of your index finger. Massaging the scalp would ease headaches by relaxing the blood vessels and regulating the blood circulation in the head.

Ginger

Ginger is widely hailed as a potent decongestant and anti-inflammatory agent, making it an ideal natural remedy for treating migraine headaches. Ginger would also reduce nausea, which usually accompanies a migraine attack.

It also reduces the production of neurotransmitters called prostaglandins, which cause pain, thus easing the symptoms of migraines. Ginger would also regulate blood flow and reduce the pressure in the blood vessels in the head.

You can grate or crush a small piece of fresh ginger and add it to boiling water. Let it steep for a few minutes. Strain this ginger tea into a cup, add one teaspoon of honey, and drink it!

Aerobic Exercise

Aerobic exercise may not cure an acute migraine attack but is an effective preventive measure. It has been found that people who exercise regularly tend to have a much lower frequency of migraine attacks than those who never exercise.

Regular exercise is especially recommended for people leading a sedentary lifestyle. They can take brisk walking, biking, or swimming to lead a healthy life and prevent recurrent migraine attacks.

Lavender Oil

Aromatherapy with lavender oil would provide quick relief from the disturbing symptoms of migraine. Simply add four drops of lavender oil in two cups of boiling water and take deep inhalations of the resulting vapours.

You may also use lavender oil to massage the temples and forehead. Alternatively, you can open a bottle of lavender oil and smell its fragrance with a deep inhalation. This action is the most convenient way to get rid of migraine headaches when travelling.

Some more essential oils and herbs you can use to keep migraine attacks at bay:

- Feverfew (Tanacetum parthenium)
- Butterbur (Petasites hybridus)
- Turmeric
- Peppermint oil

- Holy basil

Conclusion

Armed with these natural remedies, you would not have to worry about a migraine attack popping up, spoiling your moods, and reducing your effectiveness at home or the workplace. With these simple home remedies, the migraine attacks would be relieved within just a few minutes.

Depression and Its Management Using Natural Methods

Everyone feels a little sad, annoyed, or disappointed with life at some point in life. However, if this feeling of despair or stress does not go away with time and seems to have taken hold of your life, you could be suffering from depression.

Depression is a common but serious illness, which can interfere with the normal functioning of our day-to-day life. It is a state of low mood or a particular dislike towards activities that affect our feelings, behaviours, and thoughts. It is an actual illness, which can also make people feel sad, anxious, helpless, worthless, or hopeless.

Depression is a little different from normal sadness and can impact your ability to work, eat, sleep, study, and lead a normal life.

Let us examine some of the common causes and symptoms associated with depression. In addition, we will also see why it is essential to recognise and identify the hidden signs of depression and treat the condition properly.

What Are the Causes of Depression?

Depression is caused by several and sometimes a combination of psychological, environmental, genetic, and biological factors. Some of the major causes are explained below:

- **Life events:** Bullying, loss of loved ones, mental abuse, neglect, troubled relationships, grief, jealousy, separation, and natural calamities can significantly increase the likelihood of experiencing depression.

- **Chronic medical illness and treatment:** Depression can sometimes arise from non-psychiatric diseases such as chronic pain, cancer, multiple sclerosis, diabetes, certain neurological conditions, and nutritional deficiencies. In addition, certain medications can also exacerbate the depressive mood, including the ones for hypertension, anxiety, hepatitis C and hormonal treatments.

- **Genetic factors:** Some forms of depression are purely genetic and tend to run in families. Researchers are currently studying whether some genes can put people at a greater risk of depression.

Some studies have revealed that depression may result from a complex interaction between genes and environmental factors.

- **Psychiatric disorders:** Depression is one of the main symptoms of several psychiatric disorders, including bipolar disorder, obsessive-compulsive disorder, posttraumatic stress disorder, and anxiety disorder.

What Are the Signs and Symptoms of Depression?

Some of the common symptoms experienced by patients with depression include:

- Persistent feeling of sadness or anxiousness
- Reckless behaviour
- The feeling of being hollow or a sense of emptiness
- The feeling of worthlessness and guilt
- Increased fatigue and decreased energy levels
- Increased irritability and restlessness
- Decreased interest in any activity and core hobbies
- Loss of appetite or a tendency to overeat
- Insomnia or excessive sleepiness
- Decreased interest in maintaining a sexual relationship
- Difficulty in paying attention to details and an inability to remember things correctly

- Suicidal thoughts or suicide attempts
- Digestive disorders, headaches, or cramps that do not go away with treatment

Not all individuals with depression show the same symptoms. In addition, they might not even exhibit any of the symptoms above.

The frequency, severity, and duration of symptoms experienced by an individual may differ according to their particular illness.

Hence, close friends and family members need to be aware of the hidden signs of depression. Any change in the person's usual behaviour should also raise the alarm.

What Are the Hidden Signs and Symptoms of Depression?

Depression is not only about the feeling of sadness, melancholy, or crying. There can be certain subtle mental clues in hidden symptoms that might also depict the person's state of depression. Some of these invisible symptoms include:

- Having a workaholic behaviour or becoming too busy in some other activities to cope with or stay away from their buried emotions
- **Practising less optimism than usual**
- Wearing a constant 'forced' happy face and frequently making excuses to get away from the crowd
- Getting angry at small things
- **Talking more philosophically than any other average individual**
- **An exaggerated response to trifles**

Importance of Timely Diagnosis and Treatment of Depression

It is of utmost importance to identify the symptoms associated with depression and treat them. Depression is one of the significant risk factors for suicide. The feeling of emptiness and worthlessness makes the depressed individual believe that suicide is the only way to escape their unfavourable situation, which is never the case.

Therefore, it is important to recognise such suicidal behaviours and other warning signs to prompt medical intervention for timely treatment and faster patient recovery.

Some of the warning signs of suicidal tendencies associated with untreated depression include:

- Calling to say goodbye

- Saying things like, "Everyone would be better off without me…"
- Talking about killing oneself
- Trying to get the life affairs in order
- Talking about making a will

Untreated depression may also result in risky behaviours such as excessive alcohol consumption and drug addiction. It may also affect the patient's professional life and ruin their relationships.

In the case of extreme depression, you might feel that your problems are permanent. However, if proper treatment and professional help are taken, the issues would seem to fade away. You would feel better and more confident to face the challenges in life.

Remember that it is just a temporary feeling, which can easily be tackled with proper medical intervention and by following the right diet.

Food and Mood: How Diet Relates to Your Mental Health and Depression

You must be aware of how the deficiency of certain nutrients can result in some physical illnesses. But, do you know that your nutritional status is linked to your moods and can cause depression too?

Let us look at how nutrition is related to your mental status.

Diet not only creates havoc on your body in terms of weight gain, blood pressure, and cholesterol, but it also affects your mental health in a big way.

Nutrition plays an essential role in causing the onset of mental disorders such as depression. In addition, nutrition also impacts the duration and severity of depression. Apart from depression, food plays a vital role in developing and managing several other mental health problems, including attention deficit hyperactivity disorder (ADHD), obsessive-compulsive disorder (OCD), schizophrenia, and Alzheimer's disease.

Daily intake of food items that have balanced and adequate amounts of amino acids, carbohydrates, vitamins, minerals, and essential fats ensures sound mental well-being. Let us examine the role each of these dietary nutrients play in maintaining perfect mental health and the positive effects they can have on your mood, as recommended by the Ayurvedic system of medicine.

Depression and Nutrition

What could be a more exciting way to keep depression at bay by eating? Several scientific studies conducted in the past have revealed that the diet of depressed people often lacks multiple nutrients, including essential vitamins, omega-3 fatty acids, and some minerals.

Researchers have also found that supplying amino acids in supplements can also help alleviate the symptoms associated with depression to a large extent.

These amino acids are converted into neurotransmitters that help reduce depression and other mental health problems inside the body. Research has linked the low serotonin levels, a neurotransmitter, with an increased risk of suicide.

This relatively new therapeutic intervention called nutritional treatment, already recognised by Ayurveda, is also being explored by modern medicine for its effectiveness in managing depression and mood disorders by researchers worldwide.

Consider yourself to be a person who suffers from deep depression and primarily relies on prescription drugs. You must be aware that these drugs can result in a few side effects, some of which can be very harmful, forcing you to stop taking them. Would that help with your condition? No. Instead, you may start to develop suicidal tendencies.

But, there is nothing to be scared of as yet. When these medications do not work, nutritional therapy may come to your rescue. The key lies in identifying what nutrients would help you get a hold of your feeling of sadness, anxiety, or dullness in life.

Positive Role of Specific Nutrients in Managing Depression

The most common nutritional deficiencies seen in patients with mental disorders are vitamins, minerals, amino acids, and omega–3 fatty acids. More specifically, depletion of neurotransmitters such as noradrenaline, serotonin, and dopamine is also associated with major depression.

Here is the account of some nutrients that might play an essential role in keeping the mental disorders, including depression, away:

Proteins

Proteins are made up of amino acids, which, in turn, can act as the building blocks for a majority of neurotransmitters in the brain. Since depression may result from the deficiency of one or more kinds of neurotransmitters, consuming proteins can be a boon for your mental status.

Serotonin is synthesised from an amino acid, tryptophan, and the neurotransmitter dopamine, synthesised from the amino acid tyrosine. Deficiency of both these neurotransmitters results in aggression and low mood.

Therefore, consuming food items that contain these amino acids, such as beans, grains, peas, milk, and eggs, is recommended by Ayurveda to help alleviate the symptoms of depression.

Carbohydrates

Have you ever wondered why you crave carbohydrate-rich foods when feeling depressed or under stress? That's because carbohydrates can increase the production of serotonin, which has a calming effect on the brain.

It is believed that the intake of a diet low in carbs tends to precipitate depression since the carb-rich food triggers the production of mood-enhancing serotonin and tryptophan.

It is known that food items containing 'good' carbs like fruits, vegetables, fish oil, and whole grains help alleviate the depression symptoms. On the other hand, refined carbs present in pasta, bread, and red meat may increase the risk of depression. Hence, make sure you stick to the healthy carbs and limit your intake of refined carbs.

Omega-3 Fatty Acids

Research suggests that consuming food products rich in omega-3 polyunsaturated fatty acids can help protect us against depression and reduce its severity. These food items may include flax seeds, chia seeds, fatty fish, and walnuts.

The key to keeping depression away is having a balanced diet and not skipping any meal of the day, especially

A good breakfast keeps you energetic throughout the day while maintaining a sense of calmness. Eating your meals every day is also essential as you may feel irritated because of the fluctuating blood sugar levels in the absence of a meal.

Remember the saying, "You are what you eat"? Choose your food wisely. A meal can make you feel energetic, strong, and comfortable, depending on how wisely you choose your foods.

Know the Effect of Junk Food on Depression

According to the World Health Organization (WHO), depression is one of the most common forms of modern disorders that exist in the world today.

We already discussed that "you are what you eat!"

A study published in the American Journal of Clinical Nutrition has claimed that what we eat contributes to depression.

A more specific study the researchers at the University of Las Palmas de Gran Canaria and the University of Granada conducted has found that 51% of people who consume junk food are at a higher risk of developing depression than those who consume little or no junk foods.

Participants for this study were those who had never been diagnosed with depression or taken anti-depressants at any point in their lives.

Junk food includes fast foods such as hot dogs, pizza, hamburgers, and commercially baked goods such as cakes and croissants. These strikingly similar study results would definitely make you question your choice of foods.

While a bit of junk food may not have such a significant impact on your health, consuming too much of it could affect your entire body system.

Whatever you eat gets into your limbic system, and when it's junk food, it can make you feel less active and lethargic. On the other hand, the minimally-processed foods such as canned tuna, roasted nuts, bagged salads, and frozen fruit do not seem to have the same harmful impact.

Let us take a closer look at how junk foods can trigger the symptoms associated with depression. In addition, we will also explore certain food items that must be avoided to improve your mental health and prevent depression.

How Does Junk Food Trigger Depression?

Foods rich in carbs and sugar, two of the most common ingredients in junk foods, rank higher on the glycaemic index (GI) scale.

A GI scale measures the level of blood sugar after eating any food. An increased blood sugar level triggers a hormonal response to reduce sugar levels. The same hormonal response may also trigger a biological reaction in the body that triggers or worsens symptoms of depression, including fatigue, irritability, and mood changes.

As you already know, nutrition plays a vital role in maintaining good mental health, especially the essential fatty acids, including omega-6 and omega-3. A majority of fast food items are rich in trans fats, which replace the crucial fatty acids in the brain. This change, in turn, could harm your mental health.

Consuming fat-rich junk food may also trigger specific chemical changes in the brain resulting in anxiety and depression.

Also, regular consumption of fast foods makes you less likely to eat nutritional foods, such as fresh fruits and vegetables. This habit, in turn, would deprive your body of the minerals and nutrients that are essential for maintaining sound mental health.

Junk foods also result in weight gain, which perpetuates a sense of depression, stress, and anxiety. So, why put your mental and physical health at stake for the five minutes of pleasure for your taste buds? About time you give this a serious thought. Don't you think so?

Foods to Avoid to Prevent and Treat Depression More Effectively

When you are depressed, your eating habits also suffer with you. Therefore, it is essential to note what, when, and how much you are eating to minimise the effect of depression on your overall health.

Overeating junk food can make you overweight. And believe me; life is too beautiful to waste your efforts for losing those extra pounds gained during a temporary phase of depression.

Eating junk foods rich in sugar, fats, or carbs may have a temporary soothing effect on your anxious nerves. However, long-term consumption of such 'comfort' foods could increase the risk of other health problems, including diabetes, heart diseases, and weight gain.

Some of the food items that you must avoid include:

- Refined sugar
- Salty food – potato chips, salted peanuts
- Artificial sweeteners
- Alcohol & soda
- Processes carbs such as cereal, pasta, snack foods, bagels, doughnuts, white bread
- Caffeine
- Saturated fats such as butter, margarine, high-fat dairy, deli meat
- Hydrogenated oils such as French fries, fried calamari, fried cheese sticks, fried chicken

It is recommended that you seek prompt treatment for depression as soon as you notice a change in your eating habits. This should be especially when junk foods slowly become your closest friend.

Remember, any change in your eating pattern could be a symptom of depression too. Making healthy dietary choices would help you stay healthy and avoid mental health disorders.

How Can a Nutritional Imbalance Lead to Depression?

Ayurveda suggests that good nutrition is necessary for your mental health. A nutritious diet can cut down the risk of mental disorders like depression. Food has a crucial role in developing and preventing depression, attention deficit hyperactivity syndrome (ADHD), and schizophrenia. A balanced diet can protect a balanced positive mood with adequate amounts of carbohydrates, amino acids, minerals, vitamins, essential fats, and water.

Popular Nutritional Supplements for Depression

Fish oil rich in omega-3 fatty acids, vitamin B of various forms, vitamin D, amino acids, and thiamine is among the most popular nutritional supplements for patients suffering from depression.

Although there is no direct evidence to demonstrate the link between these nutrients and depression, various studies have established that a significant majority of patients with depression benefit from these supplements.

'Good' Nutrients for the Brain

Many nutrients are known to directly affect the body and create some specific moods.

For example:

- Omega-3 fatty acids would reduce inflammation and boost memory, thus maintaining a good mood.

- Amino acids build proteins and promote brain functions. Furthermore, its deficiency could make a person sluggish, depressed, and unfocused. The best natural sources are eggs, nuts, fish, beans, seeds, and beef.

- Vitamin D deficiency is associated with dementia. Its daily need is 5,000 to 10,000 international units a day.

- Iron deficiency can lead to anaemia resulting in the symptoms like depression and fatigue. The right dose for adults is about 12 mg daily. The natural sources are poultry, red meat, and fish.

- Magnesium is a strong relaxant. Available in beans, seaweed, and green vegetables, around 400 mg of this mineral is required every day for men and 310 mg for women.

- Vitamin B Complex would cut down the risk of strokes. Its deficiency can affect mental health. It is available in poultry, seafood, leafy vegetables, and bananas. The daily intake needed for men is 1.7 mg, and for women, it is 1.5 mg.

- Folate improves the response of the body to anti-depressant medications. The daily need of the adults is 400 mcg. It is available in citrus fruits, leafy greens, legumes, and beans.

- Tryptophan would help the body produce serotonin. People with depression have lower levels of serotonin. It is available in soy, red meat, dairy products, and turkey.

- Zinc activates the digestive enzymes and helps break down the food. It promotes DNA repair and protein production and curbs inflammation. A daily intake of 11 mg is suitable for adult men and 8 mg for adult women.

- Iodine affects thyroid functions. It controls energy levels, metabolism, body temperature, growth, immune functions, and brain performance. It is available in iodine-enriched salt and dried seaweed, shrimp, and cod.

- Magnesium helps the body produce energy and promotes the proper functioning of the muscles, arteries, and heart. Magnesium may also help in a quick recovery from depression. It is available in leafy vegetables, nuts, and avocados.

- Selenium is an important antioxidant. Hence, adults need 55 mcg of this nutrient per day. The best food source is Brazil nuts.

It is clear that fresh ingredients nourish the body better than processed and packed food, fast foods, sweets, and other junk foods. Fresh food turns into protein-building blocks, enzymes, brain tissues, and neurotransmitters. These foods can help a great deal in controlling your moods and thus, act as natural anti-depressants.

Many nutrients can increase the transmission of impulses between the brain cells, thus improving brain functions.

Hence, it is crucial to go for foods that have multiple nutrients. Good nutrients tend to boost your emotional well-being. A balanced diet full of nutrients can do much good for your body and mental health.

Ayurvedic Herbs You Must Include in Your Diet to Protect Yourself From Depression

A diet full of vegetables, beans, nuts, fruits, olive oil, and fish has been found to keep depression away. Colourful berries, leafy greens, apples, melons, broccoli, oats, almonds, bananas, tomatoes, and walnuts are very effective in the fight against depression.

Dietary changes do alter the brain chemistry and help control your moods. Raw foods provide natural hydration, extra nutrients, and enzymes.

Other than these, many herbs can be included in your diet to reduce anxiety and depression.

Here are some of the best herbs you can include in your regular diet. These herbs act as natural remedies for stress and depression.

Anti-Depression Herbs

- Add nutmeg powder to the juice of fresh gooseberries and drink it three times a day to treat the symptoms of depression.

- Consume one or two grams of powder of dried roots of Asparagus or Shatavari at least once a day.

- Ginseng has natural anti-depressant properties. Two tablespoons of its powdered form with a glass of water can help overcome melancholy.

- Ginger and turmeric have excellent anti-inflammatory and mood-elevating properties. Use them in your regular cooking.

- Eat five grams of Brahmi powder with a glass of milk regularly to improve your mood. A head massage with Brahmi oil would also reduce the symptoms of depression.

- Add sage and basil leaves while preparing your tea and take it twice a day to reduce depression.

- Chamomile flowers could improve digestion. It has calming properties. The fragrant flowers would help calm down the nerves and reduce stress gently.

- Black cohosh root is used to combat nervous irritability in women during the menopausal period. It can also be used as a tonic for reducing stress. It is used to calm the nervous system as it works as a mild sedative.

- The aromatic catnip herb calms the nerves, helps you unwind, and promotes sleep. It can be consumed as a soothing brew.

- A lavender infusion at bedtime calms the nerves and keeps insomnia away. Lavender aromatherapy is also effective against anxiety.

- Hops give most beers their bitter-aromatic flavour. It is used to promote mental relaxation and overcome sleeplessness and nervous tension. It has a soothing effect on the nerves.

- Kava calms and relaxes the mind. Moreover, kava is soothing for the nerves and relieves tension. This pepper plant root acts as a mild anti-depressant and has no side effects.

- Lemon balm tea comforts the mind, calms the nerves, and eases tension. This tasty tea is usually taken after lunch or dinner.

- Passionflower is being used for mental relaxation and relieving sleeplessness. It is recommended for people experiencing internal chatter or hearing 'voices in their head'. It also promotes tranquillity.

- St. John's Wort is a natural anti-depressant. It relieves mild to moderate depression. It would restore your energy levels and lift your spirits. It is accepted as a standard herbal aid for emotional wellness.

- The extract of rhizome and roots of nardostachys, spikenard, or jatamansi could have a tranquilising effect on the brain. These herbs can control aggression by being mild sedatives.

- When sandalwood powder is applied daily on the forehead, it could soothe the mind and promote sound sleep.

- One to three cups of licorice could prove to be soothing for patients with depression. Its powder can be taken with milk.

Some Other Natural Remedies for the Management of Depression

Some other natural remedies for the management of depression include apples, cashew nuts, cardamom, rose essential oil, avocados, cabbage, walnuts, and saffron.

Aromatherapy for Depression

Aromatherapy is another method recommended for treating depression by using natural products like the fragrant oils of lavender, ylang-ylang, sandalwood, basil, angelica, geranium, clary sage, juniper, mint, chamomile, and rosemary. They can be used to lighten the mood in your room, for massage, or bath. It is also effective against insomnia and mental fatigue.

While it has been established that diet has a critical role in making the brain stress-free, how exactly it works is not known. But, more and more natural foods and their nutrients prove helpful in combating stress and depression. It's time to include these herbs in your regular diet to root out stress from your life.

Happiness: A Key to Unlocking and Getting Rid of Negative Thoughts

Negative thinking can dominate the human mind, possibly because survival is our most vital concern. It is the root cause of much of the tension and stress we suffer. This instinct leads to depression and unhappiness.

Many techniques can be followed to get rid of these negative thoughts. The most accessible and influential are meditation, pranayama, and yoga, which form a closely-related group of remedies for saying 'goodbye' to negative thoughts.

Let us look at the beliefs on which these therapies are based. Inculcating these methods will help you get rid of stress and depression.

Slaves of Ideas

We usually are the slaves of our thoughts. We always know that we should not be doing certain things. But, there comes a moment when our mind begins to think in its set groove and set patterns, and so, we overeat, smoke, waste time, and money and keep away from the things we should be doing.

Thought Is an Electrical Pattern

Our thoughts form an electrical pattern in the brain. The brain finds it easy to repeat the same thinking process over and over again. It is difficult and complex to think of a new idea or concept. The brain keeps traversing the world of ideas without direction or goal, like in a dream of our own making.

It is chaotic. We keep thinking, almost unconsciously, about whatever we have come across and remember.

How Do Meditation, Pranayama, and Yoga Help You Control Your Thought Process and Overcome Depression?

Monitoring and Controlling the Body

Meditation, yoga postures, and pranayama are the means that can monitor and then regulate the thinking process effectively to lead our thinking on the chosen lines and in the desired direction.

We can eliminate unwanted ideas collected by our minds about the past when we start thinking about the same particular point or thing.

Disciplined Training

Prolonged and disciplined training in yoga postures, pranayama, and meditation techniques can help discipline our thought processes. We can train our minds to choose a point for consideration at the moment.

We can also train ourselves to ignore some unrelated issues. We can train our brains to ignore many things and concentrate only on the points we have chosen. We can begin to focus on the subject of our choice with the help of these techniques.

Detached Considerations

We can have a better ability to analyse the issue or a problem that has been haunting us. We can consider various aspects of the issue, the factors leading to it, and the ramifications of choosing one of the many paths available for us, all in our thoughts. Then, we can reach an idea that could benefit us in the long run.

Blissful Experience

When we attain this level of concentration and thinking by detaching ourselves from all other influences, we experience something close to bliss.

Even normal human beings experience this state of mind on rare occasions while doing something we love. It releases stress, and we feel at peace with the world.

The Path to Bliss

Meditation boosts the purity and virtues of the mind. It makes us wise and promotes relaxation, peace, and health. Meditation takes us to a positive frame of mind.

Anuloma-viloma, a breathing technique of pranayama, too, can lead you to the experience of serene peace.

Ayurvedic experts suggest specific postures and steps for the practice of meditation and pranayama.

They have different degrees of physical difficulties, but the essence is: sit in a comfortable posture in a quiet place. Let your body and muscles relax and soften. Concentrate on something you like. Become more and more aware of your inner world. Keep breathing deeply. Just follow these steps, and you will begin experiencing peace inside you.

Getting to the Positive Frame

When you start meditating, you begin thinking positively, realise that nothing is entirely negative, and search for positivity even in problems. You can begin blocking the negative thoughts.

So, whenever you start feeling stressed out or tense, just close your eyes, breathe deeply, concentrate on the breath, and push the disturbing thoughts out of your mind. With practice, this should become fairly easy.

Helpful Yoga Postures

Many yoga postures can help relieve depression and reduce high blood pressure. The suryanamskara exercise rids you of stress. In a series of 12 postures, suryanamskara increases oxygen flow in the body and relieves depression. Other postures like shashangasana, sarvangasana, vipareet karani asana, bhujangasana, garbhasana, shavasana, and halasana too can relieve depression.

Yoga and meditation are proven self-improvement and relaxation techniques. They can help you live in harmony with the surroundings without being burdened by the influence of external attractions. They turn the mind towards your authentic self and help the body free from stress and tension.

Conclusion

We examined the intricacies associated with one of the most common mental disorders in the world – depression. The condition is considered more common than diabetes, cancer, and AIDS combined. Estimates claim that 9 million American adults are living with depression today. You may take a sigh of relief, for you are not alone!

There are several treatment methods available today in the form of medications and psychotherapy to help you beat your temporary state of sadness and come out feeling energetic, hopeful, and kicking. However, nothing beats a relatively effective therapeutic intervention called nutritional therapy, especially when combined with Ayurveda.

Your mental health and nutrition go hand in hand. The deficiency of certain nutrients in the body, including vitamins, minerals, amino acids, and omega-3 fatty acids, has been associated with an increased risk of depression. In addition, excess and regular consumption of junk food can do nothing good for you and your condition. However, eating the correct type of food at the right time and in the right way would help you keep the depression symptoms at bay.

The best part is that you don't necessarily need to visit a therapist to get started with it. Instead, you can begin your nutritional therapy all by yourself at home. Remember that certain types of dietary imbalances can lead to depression. Ensure that you eat the right foods that incorporate all the essential vitamins and minerals to put yourself at ease.

We also explored a few herbs that you must include in your diet to ward off depression. Make sure that you start to incorporate these herbs into your daily meals.

And last but not least, you need to create room for happiness in your life, help yourself come out of the condition, and fill yourself with positive vibes by eating nutritious foods.

Several methods can help relax your body and mind, including yoga and meditation. It would be best if you made an effort to steal some time out of your busy lives and incorporate these relaxing techniques into your schedule so that your mind feels calm and relaxed.

Follow the tips given in this chapter and eat a diet containing all the essential nutrients to ultimately come out of depression and never fall back into that state of darkness.

Treatment of Chronic Fatigue Syndrome Using Natural Methods

The self-explanatory Chronic Fatigue Syndrome is a condition that causes a person to feel weak and tired daily for several years.

Most patients with Chronic Fatigue Syndrome wake up in the morning with severe pain all over the body that persists throughout the day and night. They can neither do any routine activities properly nor get enough rest at night. The patients often get up in the morning because they have to rush to school or work. But, they feel too drowsy due to the lack of sleep. Sometimes, they have to take a sedative at night to sleep well without any muscle pains.

This disease can make them dependent on others for their routine activities. It is also called Myalgic encephalomyelitis. 'Myalgic' means pain in the muscles, and 'Encephalomyelitis' means inflammation in the brain and spinal cord. So, in short, patients with Chronic Fatigue Syndrome have muscle pains because of inflammation in the nervous system.

They feel as if every part of the body is throbbing with pain, including their muscles, joints, back, and head. They find it very difficult to get up from bed, brush their teeth, take baths, and travel to and from the office. Even a small task like getting up from sitting unnerves them due to the high intensity of pain!

Most physicians advise patients with Chronic Fatigue Syndrome to make some changes in their diet. They counsel patients to eat plenty of green vegetables and fresh fruits. It is essential to ensure the body is not deficient in iron and other essential minerals and vitamins.

Ayurvedic physicians also recommend limiting their intake of dairy products even if they never had any problems with consuming milk. Following this advice could help energy levels to soar up.

Another change in the diet that could help reduce weakness and pain is avoiding coffee. Most patients with Chronic Fatigue Syndrome are used to drinking several cups of coffee every day because they think it is a good stimulant and would help them feel fresh and energetic. However, this is wrong. The caffeine in coffee can have long-term adverse effects and make the person feel weaker in the long run.

Also, instead of three large meals, they are advised to eat small meals every 3 to 4 hours. They should also include starchy foods in their diet to keep up their energy levels.

Treatment of Chronic Fatigue Syndrome

It is often disheartening for the patient to know that there is no cure for Chronic Fatigue Syndrome. They can only take medications and supplements to relieve the symptoms and prevent deficiencies. They have to use painkillers to ease muscle and joint movements.

Some patients also have to take antidepressants for a variable period. The constant pain and restricted movements caused due to this disease may engulf their emotional state, drawing them into depression. Luckily, the timely help and support from the family and the doctor could protect them from mental health diseases like depression.

Ayurvedic doctors often propose that it is not the medications but how patients manage their lifestyle and routine that can help them control the disease. It may help if they try to get frequent short naps interspaced throughout the day. It is rest and not the actual sleep that is beneficial.

So, patients with Chronic Fatigue Syndrome are advised to take frequent breaks during their working hours, with each break not lasting more than 20 minutes. This rest period could help them regain their strength and allow them to concentrate on their work for another few hours.

Prevention of Complications

With severe joint pains, muscle pains, and weakness, it can become challenging for patients with Chronic Fatigue Syndrome to concentrate on any activity. Whether at home or the office, the pain does not let them perform or enjoy any activity. But, taking proper precautions to prevent pain and other symptoms could prevent the disease from progressing and causing complications like depression.

They can also adopt natural relaxation therapies like yoga and breathing exercises. They should avoid exerting themselves too much while performing these activities. These techniques can help improve their pain, as well as sleep problems. It may also reduce their stress and anxiety.

Patients with Chronic Fatigue Syndrome should also eat a balanced diet so that the body gets all the nutrients. They are also advised to undergo graded exercise therapy and cognitive-behavioural therapy. These therapies can also help control the progress of the disease to some extent.

Daily Limitations and Fears of Patients with Chronic Fatigue Syndrome

Not being active enough could be a significant problem that Chronic Fatigue Syndrome can cause. Patients with this condition also deal with the fear of recurring infections due to weakness and lowered immunity. Even a minor disease can worsen their feeling of tiredness by several folds. They have to take proper hygienic precautions to ensure they are safe and protected from bacteria and viruses.

What Are the Psychological Effects of Chronic Fatigue Syndrome?

Chronic Fatigue Syndrome can affect the patients physically as much as it can affect them emotionally. They often feel as if they are racing against time to do in just a few years what could have quickly been done in 15 to 20 years if they were not suffering from this condition.

They also have to secure their future before the disease could leave them disabled. Additionally, there is also the fear of increasing joint pains and the inability to do simple tasks.

Hence, it is advisable to adopt natural and healthier strategies to improve energy levels and relieve pain to avoid the fears and other consequences of Chronic Fatigue Syndrome.

Keep reading to learn some of the best foods patients with Chronic Fatigue Syndrome should eat and food to avoid to relieve the symptoms and slow down the progress of this condition.

Foods that Can Worsen the Symptoms of Chronic Fatigue Syndrome

For most patients suffering from a disorder like Chronic Fatigue Syndrome, which is often caused due to chronic inflammation, a diet high in carbohydrates and low in proteins can be detrimental.

It has been proven that consistent consumption of a low protein and high carb diet is often at the root of chronic inflammation.

However, a predominantly plant-based diet has been found to reduce chronic inflammation and relieve the symptoms of this condition.

This finding implies that you must reduce your intake of refined sugars to reduce your risk of disorders caused due to chronic inflammation.

Various other foods can produce a similar harmful effect. Let us look at the foods you must avoid to keep inflammation responsible for triggering Chronic Fatigue Syndrome in check:

Sugar

An excessive intake of sugar is linked to obesity and a higher risk of inflammation that causes diseases such as Chronic Fatigue Syndrome and type 2 diabetes.

Refined sugars and foods with a high glycemic index can put more pressure on the pancreas to secrete a higher amount of insulin. This compound can prompt the immune system to initiate an abnormal response that is detrimental to the healthy functioning of the organs.

Refined sugar also slows down the process of detoxification in your body and weakens the immune system. As a result, your body's ability to fight infections is reduced. Eventually, each time your body is exposed to any organism, it gains an advantage over the weak immune system and infects the healthy tissues and organs.

Chronic Fatigue Syndrome is also a chronic inflammation-induced disease that originates from consuming a high amount of sugars. The inflammation triggered by refined sugars can cause significant damage to the muscles and joints, resulting in severe pain and restriction of movement.

Dairy Products

Since childhood, we have believed in the benefits of drinking milk and consuming dairy products every day. Dairy products offer complete nutrition in the form of several vitamins and minerals.

However, non-organic dairy products have been linked to inflammation, especially in women. This issue is genuine of the dairy products obtained from the industrially-raised livestock; I mean those not fed on grass but fatty by-products.

These products contain common allergens that can trigger an inflammatory response and are considered pro-inflammatory.

Vegetables Cooking Oils

Oils that contain a very high level of omega-6 fatty acids and a low level of omega-3 fatty acids can promote inflammation. Consuming vegetable oils containing the wrong combination of omega-3 and omega-6 fatty acids could harm your body by contributing to inflammation.

Using these oils in cooking can negatively impact your body, especially the liver and gallbladder. Omega-6 fatty acids can also trigger inflammation in these organs and reduce their metabolising fats and cholesterol.

This effect can invite severe disorders such as Chronic Fatigue Syndrome, hypertension, heart attacks, atherosclerosis, and stroke.

Though the immense anti-inflammatory potential of omega-3 fatty acids is indisputable, the higher amount of omega-6 fatty acids in vegetable oils is dangerous for your body. So, if you are trying to counter inflammation-induced Chronic Fatigue Syndrome, avoid using vegetable oils in cooking.

Instead, it would be advisable to rely on the supplements that provide the right combination of omega-3 and omega-6 fatty acids so that you can derive the benefits of both and stay in good health.

Meat

Meat, especially red and processed meat, is linked to an abnormal immune response. It can trigger chronic inflammation and worsen the symptoms of Chronic Fatigue Syndrome. Meat contains a form of animal protein, which can increase your risk of inflammation-induced disorders.

When you consume meat, it is metabolised into arachidonic acid, a precursor to pro-inflammatory prostaglandins. Prostaglandins are substances that play a role in the process of inflammation. Hence, it is best to limit your meat consumption to minimise inflammation.

Wheat

Wheat and most gluten-containing foods are responsible for causing allergies. These foods can trigger an abnormal response of the immune system and cause chronic inflammation.

Wheat is a staple diet in several parts of the world. People continue to consume this food over several years without realising the damage it is causing slowly and progressively to their organs.

It is commonly consumed in the form of whole-grain bread and pasta. Several other food sources containing refined flour and gluten invoke a similar response. Consumption of wheat and whole grain products can also cause joint inflammation and increase your risk of Chronic Fatigue Syndrome and arthritis.

Hence, it is crucial to choose your foods carefully to minimise inflammation in the muscles and joints and protect yourself against the symptoms of Chronic Fatigue Syndrome.

The Best Foods to Eat for Relieving Symptoms of Chronic Fatigue Syndrome

Oatmeal

Oatmeal is a perfect breakfast to begin your day. It provides a host of nutrients, especially fibres, which could keep you from binge eating or having a dip in energy level later in the day.

It has been shown that eating oatmeal for breakfast at least three times a week can reduce the symptoms of Chronic Fatigue Syndrome and help you lose at least two pounds a week. It would also lower your cholesterol levels and keep your heart and brain vigorous.

Oats also contain omega-3 fatty acids, potassium, and folate. Potassium and folate are essential nutrients needed for the body's healthy functioning, while omega-3 fatty acids are great as far as maintaining a high energy level is concerned.

If you suffer from severe symptoms of Chronic Fatigue Syndrome, avoid the flavoured oatmeal products as they are packed with sugars, which can neutralise the beneficial effects of oats. Instead, add a bit of honey, chopped fruit, or nuts to sweeten your bowl.

Bananas

Bananas would definitely help you stay energetic so that you can jump from one job to another effortlessly. They are packed with nutrients and keep your mid-morning slump at bay.

This yellow fruit provides the best source of resistant starch, a form of healthy carbohydrate, which can prevent a dip in your energy level. You can eat a banana as it is or slice it up and add it to your oatmeal or cereal.

Eggs

Eggs are incredibly edible and are embraced as a healthy source of nutrients and proteins. It is rich in vitamin D, which is essential for maintaining the health of bones.

You can eat eggs for breakfast, lunch, and dinner practically every day without feeling bored because they can be used in various ways. You can boil them, cut them into halves and sprinkle them with salt and pepper or make a filling omelette.

Almond Butter

If you are a vegetarian or don't eat eggs, you can turn to almond butter as an alternate source of proteins. It is also filled with monounsaturated fats and several nutrients. It can be paired with an apple or a banana or used as a delicious spread on slices of whole-grain bread.

Alternatively, you can also use peanut butter, as both are comparable in terms of calorie content. A tablespoon of both peanut butter and almond butter contains about 100 calories.

Why almond butter is considered healthier is because it contains a slightly less amount of saturated fat than peanut butter. Another definite point favouring almond butter is that it is safe even for those with an allergy to peanuts.

Watermelon

As the name suggests, watermelon is a storehouse of water. It is an excellent food to hydrate your body in the morning. It will help you feel fresh and energetic throughout the day and prevent fatigue.

Another advantage of eating watermelon is that it is the best source of lycopene, a nutrient essential for your muscle health, vision, cancer prevention, and heart health.

Above all, watermelon gives you just 40 to 50 calories per cup, making it one of the most relished negative-calorie foods. It burns more calories during digestion than it adds in. So, if you are looking to avoid obesity, which can worsen inflammation and accelerate muscle damage, make the most out of this juiciest fruit.

Blueberries and Strawberries

Fresh blueberries and strawberries are tiny superfruits that pack a flurry of healthy punches. Eating blueberries for your breakfast or with any meal has several advantages. It could improve your memory, enhance your stamina, boost your metabolism, and regulate your blood pressure and blood sugar levels.

The higher metabolism means your body would be able to burn calories faster, allowing you to feel energetic all day long. Strawberries are high in antioxidants and low in calories. One cup of strawberries contains the total daily recommended allowance for vitamin C, along with high amounts of fibres and folic acid.

Conclusion

Including these foods in your meals would satisfy your appetite, give you energy, and help you perform your regular activities with better ease. Including nutritious foods in your diet would also enable you to slow down the progress of Chronic Fatigue Syndrome and reduce pain and inflammation in the muscles and joints. This lifestyle change is expected to improve the overall quality of your life and help you achieve your goals with improved efficiency.

What Is Insomnia and How to Avoid Its Consequences on Your Health?

How often has it happened that you get up feeling like you haven't slept at all? And when this happens, you already know how your day's going to be like, right? All drowsy, dull, and sleepy!

If you are facing this problem frequently, the result could be disastrous! Not getting enough sleep can affect your routine. It can also cause mental stress and increase your risk of depression.

But, these are the apparent after-effects of sleep deprivation. There is more to it than you are aware of.

If you want to know what other health problems you are putting yourself at risk by not paying attention to your sleep, read on to find why sleep deprivation could be the worst concern for your health.

Common Consequences of Sleep Deprivation for Your Health and Future Life

Weight Gain

When you don't sleep well and stay awake, you end up thinking of things like what's in your fridge. That piece of cake you kept in the refrigerator would keep disturbing you until you decide to get up and have a bite! The result? Weight gain and lots of belly fat! This relation means that the less you sleep, the more you will be weighty, literally.

Troubles With the Digestive System

Sometimes constipation, sometimes loose motions! If you are experiencing these symptoms, you can blame it on your sleep, or rather the lack of it. Improper sleep can trigger inflammatory changes in your body, including your intestine.

Due to this, you may develop digestive diseases like irritable bowel syndrome and ulcerative colitis resulting in alternate diarrhoea and constipation. So, if you want your bowel movements to be smooth and regular, make sure you get a sound sleep of 8 hours every night.

Poor Heart Health

Sound sleep is essential to keep your heart healthy and work at its highest efficiency. A research study has linked the lack of proper sleep to a higher risk of heart attacks. It means that by chucking out sleep to accommodate your busy schedule, you might be putting your heart health at stake!

Allergies

Lack of sleep can cause dysregulation in the way your immune system functions. It might put you at risk of allergic diseases like dermatitis, rhinitis, and even asthma.

Hallucinations

If not detected and appropriately treated, insomnia may result in mental health issues that cause hallucinations. You might end up seeing giant lizards crawling on the walls if you do not sleep well. It has been proved that when sleep deprivation continues for long enough, you may start hearing or seeing things that aren't there. This issue might also occur because of the altered chemical balance in your brain due to sleep deprivation and resulting stress. It affects your ability for rational thinking and disturbs your judgment causing you to hallucinate!

Dark Circles

Nobody loves to have those ugly dark circles under their eyes, which we all know results from lack of sleep. But if you think that that's all sleep deprivation can do, then you are in for a rude shock! It turns out that sleep loss can even lead to lacklustre skin, wrinkles, and fine lines.

Improper sleep can cause your body to release a stress hormone called cortisol. This 'bad' hormone can break down the collagen in your skin. This reaction can reduce the skin elasticity and make it appear wrinkly, dull, lusterless, and all that you don't want to happen to your youthful skin!

Frequent Infections

Most people complain that they are falling sick more frequently than they did in their child hood. Something as trivial as the common cold starts disturbing them too often. They usually blame pollution for the increased frequency of the common cold.

But, they do not know that it could be the result of sleep deprivation. As strange as it may sound, it is a fact that not getting sound sleep can make you prone to catch a cold too frequently by reducing your immunity.

Sleep deprivation can lower your body's ability to fight infections, thus resulting in repeated attacks of cold and other diseases!

Affects Intellectual Skills

"If you want to come out laughing after yearly appraisals, stay awake and complete all your work and even take up extra responsibilities to please you know whom."

If this is what your boss tells you, it's time to let your work do all the talking. And making sure you sleep well every day is actually the best way to come out laughing after an appraisal.

If you listen to your boss and overwork yourself, you have to compromise on your sleep schedule and even go without sleep at times. This response can only reduce your work productivity and pull you away from promotions!

Affects Academic Performance

If you want to score well in exams, never make the mistake of compromising your sleep to study more. It will only affect your academic performance adversely. The right way to do better in academics is to ensure you sleep well to work to the best of your abilities during the daytime.

Reduces Memory

This effect might happen if you do not ensure you get sound sleep every day. One research study has shown that the lack of sleep can affect the brain events known as the 'sharp-wave ripples', which are responsible for consolidating your memory.

These ripples serve as a transport mechanism to carry the memory of learned information in the hippocampus to the brain cortex, where long-term memories and information are stored.

These sharp-wave ripples usually occur during the deepest level of your sleep. Hence, if you are not sleeping well, you are likely to disturb this mechanism and face memory issues frequently.

Increases Diabetes Risk

Chronic sleep deprivation can affect the hormonal balance in your body, in which your pancreas might stop producing adequate insulin. Insulin plays a role in lowering blood sugar levels. Low insulin production can increase your blood sugar levels resulting in diabetes.

Risk of Accidents

Ignoring the importance of sound sleep may cost you your own and others' lives as it can increase the risk of accidents.

A survey conducted by the National Sleep Foundation has revealed that most road accidents occur due to a drowsy driver behind the wheels. Need I say any more?

Triggers Cancerous Changes

Yes! Sleep deprivation can cause cancer too. A clinical study has revealed that women with irregular work schedules are more likely to develop breast cancer.

It was found that the incidence of breast cancer was significantly higher in women who worked in shifts. Similarly, even men are at a higher risk of prostate cancer due to chronic sleep deprivation.

The risk has been linked to the disrupted circadian rhythm due to the lack of sound sleep. Your body's internal clock regulates several biological functions. Manipulation of the sleep-wake cycle can affect these functions and reduce the body's defences and repair mechanisms, thus triggering cancerous changes in the healthy tissues.

Suicidal Tendency

Never make the mistake of taking your sleep lightly because it can increase the risk of suicidal tendencies. Sleep deprivation can affect your fighting spirit and even cause immense mental stress and depression. These consequences have been linked to a suicidal tendency.

Believe me, life is beautiful. Never take such a drastic step no matter what challenges life gives you. Sleep well, and you will find that the next day brings you hope and joy!

I understand that our modern society's expectations and ever-rising demands have placed us under significant time constraints. And this is why we are making the mistake of cutting back on sleep to meet such expectations.

However, research studies and our clinical experience have made it increasingly clear that the cost of sleep deprivation is much higher than we tend to believe! If you do not want to develop the complications we discussed above, listen to the expectations of your tired mind and body. Do gift yourself a comfy mattress to get a sound and undisturbed sleep of at least 8 hours every night!

Moreover, sleeping well has its benefits. Some people simply sleep because it's a part of their daily routine! Some people sleep because they don't want dark circles under their eyes and ugly wrinkles on their skin! That's what they call a beauty sleep!

However, there are several other benefits of sound sleep. It is essential to be aware of these benefits to encourage you to adopt healthier strategies to fight insomnia and improve your sleep-wake cycle.

What Are the Health Benefits of Sleep?

Sleep is not a luxury but a necessity! You should get a sound sleep every day because it is essential to keep your body in good health.

Not getting enough sleep can lead to a state of disorganisation within your body and lead to several diseases. On the contrary, getting enough sleep brings in loads of benefits. Take a look at the list given below to know what you are losing by not getting enough sleep:

Improves Heart Health

Lack of sleep is associated with worsening cholesterol levels and blood pressure, the most common risk factor for heart diseases. So, when you don't get good sleep, you are putting yourself at risk of heart attacks and cardiac failure. Your heart can be healthier when you get seven to nine hours of sleep every night.

Allows the Body to Repair Itself

Sleep is a time when the body is allowed to relax and repair itself. The workload of the body is less when you are sleeping. So, it can devote this time to the processes it could not perform during the daytime when it was busy working on other activities.

When you are sleeping, your body gets time to repair the damages caused by ultraviolet rays, stress, and other forms of harmful exposure. It is also when the cells produce more proteins, which form the building blocks of our body.

That is why it is crucial to get enough sleep daily so that the body gets enough time to work on these critical functions.

Prevents Cancer

It has been found that people who do not get enough sleep have a higher risk of developing colon and breast cancer. The link between lack of sleep and cancer risk is caused by fluctuating levels of a hormone called melatonin due to staying awake at night and the resulting exposure to light.

Light exposure reduces the levels of melatonin that regulates the sleep-wake cycle. This hormone is also believed to protect against cancer by suppressing the growth of tumours. Hence, it is essential to get sound sleep at night to avoid exposure to light and reduce your risk of cancer.

Improves Alertness

A good night's sleep not just makes you feel fresh and energised the next day but also helps you stay extra alert. It improves your focus and increases your productivity. Being alert and engaged in the activities at hand, in turn, helps you feel great and also increases your chances of getting a good night's sleep the next day as well.

Enhances Memory

Do you know that your mind stays surprisingly busy while you are asleep? Your memories are strengthened, and you can "practise" the skills you learned while awake during sleep. This process is called consolidation.

When you are learning something new, whether intellectually or physically, you can to a certain point learn it with practice; however, something happens when you are sleeping that helps you understand things better. If you sleep well, the memories of what you have learned tend to get consolidated in a part of the brain. It can also improve your ability to recall. This phenomenon is surprising but true!

Reduces Stress

Our lives are full of stress arising from expectations to succeed in a career, academics, and the fundamental need to stick to a routine. It is sleep that allows the body to come out of stressful thoughts and relax.

The relaxation applies to the body as well as the mind. But, when the body is deprived of sleep, stressful thoughts linger in the mind. And as is known, high-stress levels could worsen your health and lead to diseases including hypertension, cancer, and stroke. This trouble highlights the importance of sleep in maintaining your health and preventing infections.

Combats Obesity

It has been found that sleeping less than seven hours at night could increase your risk of being overweight. The lack of sleep can affect the balance of hormones like ghrelin and leptin in the brain that regulate your appetite.

Apart from this, when you stay awake at night, you are more likely to help yourself with some high-calorie snacks. So, if you are trying to lose weight, make sure you are getting adequate sleep.

Reduces Your Risk of Depression

Sleep could affect the production and release of some chemicals in the body, such as serotonin. A serotonin deficiency could increase your risk of developing psychological diseases like depression. Making sure you get the right amount of sleep every night can protect you from this illness.

Improves Quality of Life

Sleep can affect the things that we take for granted. When we sleep better, we can live better not just in terms of years but also in terms of quality, satisfaction, and happiness.

We know that going without sleep even for a day could make us feel terrible, while getting a good night's sleep could help us feel fresh and ready to take up the challenges in the world. This routine allows us to achieve better outcomes with our efforts.

Helps Live Longer

Not getting enough sleep is linked to a shorter lifespan. It's not clear whether it's the effect or the cause. But, it has been proven that the people who sleep for less than five hours a day have a shorter lifespan than those who get a sound sleep of six or more hours per night.

Sleep also plays a role in metabolism, immune functions, learning, and memory. All of these, when combined, improve the quality of our life.

Some more benefits of sound sleep:

- Allow you to be a safer driver
- Builds muscles
- Helps you stay fit
- Better moods and less risk of anxiety disorders
- Reduces the risk of diabetes

- Prevents migraines
- Healthier skin
- Reduces your likelihood to abuse alcohol
- Minimises the risk of taking impromptu financial decisions
- Prevents you from making dangerous mistakes
- Improves your reflex actions
- Better vision
- Stronger immune system
- Reduces the risk of allergies

If you want to get all these benefits and keep yourself healthy, go ahead and snooze! Sound sleep every day will make you feel fresh throughout the day, improve your performance, and lead you toward success!

Seven Best Yoga Poses You Should Practice to Fight Insomnia and Get a Sound Sleep

Nothing can beat the healing power of sleep. In case you are not getting enough sleep, you could only be depriving your body of its natural ability to repair itself and restore health.

A lack of sleep could mean a loss of eight precious hours that your body needs to repair itself. That is why if you have insomnia, you are likely to develop several chronic disorders that arise due to continued inflammation and damage to the body.

These diseases may include diabetes, Alzheimer's disease, Parkinson's, or even cancer.

The most effective way to let your body repair itself is to add a touch of healing power, which can derive from none other than yoga poses.

Some yoga poses' restorative and calming powers would help your mind and body enter a phase of serenity and induce sleep. Above all, once you can beat insomnia with these yoga poses and get sound sleep, your body's natural healing powers will only get complemented by those of yoga.

If you want to enjoy this dual benefit of yoga, read on to learn the best yoga poses that are then best when it comes to sleeping well.

Supta Jaṭhara Parivartānāsana

Supta Jaṭhara Parivartānāsana is recommended for men and women who experience immense mental stress throughout the day or suffer from muscle stiffness. This pose would relax the muscles and lessen the strings of stressful thoughts crowding your mind, thus allowing you to sleep well.

To practise, lie on your back and bring both knees close to your chest. Then, rock back and forth for a few minutes. Then, spread your arms apart and bend your knees. Turn your body from below the waist to one side so that the knees fall to the other.

Stay in the position for a few seconds. Repeat the same to the other side. Do this five to ten times before you get up to go to bed.

Ananda Balasana

If you have seen happy babies playing with themselves by holding their toes, you will understand why babies get much better sleep than us. What they are actually doing is practising Ananda Balasana.

You, too, can try this pose to beat insomnia. It's effortless. Just lie on your back and bring both knees close to your chest. Then, grasp the big toes of both feet with your middle and index fingers. Then, pull your heels to face the ceiling while keeping your tailbone touching the ground.

Now is the time to get some enjoyment and laughs with your knees pulling into your underarm area, rocking back and forth. This routine will cause a gentle spine massage and also relieve abdominal discomfort.

Do this for four to five minutes and release. Now you can go to sleep feeling relaxed and happier. As you may have guessed correctly, this pose is recommended for those who suffer from digestive troubles and back pains, which prevent them from sleeping well.

Balasana

Joint pains caused due to mild to moderate arthritis are what older people often have to bear while struggling to get some sleep. If these pains are not letting you get restful sleep, you may try this pose.

According to a research study, this pose would help you enjoy restorative sleep and allow you to derive the benefits of a night of sound sleep.

Start in a seated pose by resting your gluteus on the heels. The tops of your feet should be touching the floor. This pose would cause a gentle stretching of the knees and ankles and ease the pain.

Then, sink your hips back to the heels, raise your hands, and bend forward to bring your chest close to your knees. Maintain this position for a few seconds and then rise again. Repeat this 10 to 15 times, with two to three sessions per day. This routine would ease joint pains and minimise the sleepless period of your nights considerably.

Savasana

Research studies have proven that Savasana could be a great sleep aid for patients with chronic insomnia.

It is a straightforward yoga pose, which perhaps most of us have been doing to some extent without knowing that it is somewhat like a yoga pose.

To practise Savasana or the Corpse pose, all you need to do is simply lie down on your back with your legs slightly apart. Place your arms along the sides of your body but not touch it.

But do you know how to improve the benefits of this pose specifically to help you sleep well? The key lies in your focus and breathing! Perhaps you have been trying Savasana so far while watching television or simply lazing about on the bed while browsing on your smartphone; if you want to practise it correctly to get refreshing sleep, keep aside your smartphone and switch off that television too.

Just lie down in the recommended pose and let your body relax completely. Breathe in deeply and slowly. Concentrate on how every muscle of your body loosens up. Keep up the focus on the movement of air within your body as you inhale and exhale. Do this for 10 minutes before bedtime to get an undisturbed sound sleep of eight hours.

Viparita Karani

If you are a chronic insomniac, Viparita Karani is the yoga pose you need to practise every night before going to bed. It is a classic restorative yoga pose that may take you not more than five minutes and help you sleep well for as long as seven to eight hours.

To practise, place a blanket parallel close to a wall. Sit sideways on the blanket such that your hip is against the wall. Then, swing both legs up the wall and lie on your back. Alternatively, you may place the blanket about 10 cm from the wall so that when you lie on your back, the blanket is extended only till the lower back and your buttocks fall on the floor between the wall and the blanket. This variation is particularly recommended when you have stiff or tight hamstrings.

The next step is to keep yourself relaxed as much as possible. You may push yourself slightly away from the wall in case you feel uncomfortable.

Then, close your eyes and breathe slowly. Focus on how air enters and leaves your lungs as you inhale and exhale. After about five minutes, get up and go to bed. The relaxation induced by this pose will help you sleep better.

Supta Baddha Konasana

This pose is meant explicitly for women who experience pain in the lower back or pelvic region.

To practise, lie down on a mat and bring the soles of your feet close to and facing each other. Let your knees fall apart, and then pull your heels toward your pelvis as tight as possible but without causing any discomfort.

This pose would cause a gentle stretching of the pelvic, lower abdominal, and back regions and relieve the stiffness and tension in these regions that are causing discomfort while sleeping.

Now, place your left hand on your heart region and your right hand on your belly. Breathe slowly and evenly. Close your eyes, relax your face, and maintain the pose for five minutes. Release and go to sleep.

You may practise this pose at any other time to relieve back pain and pelvic discomfort that causes disturbed sleep.

Research has proven that yoga poses can help women overcome the psychiatric morbidity associated with menstrual irregularities and help them sleep well.

Siddhasana (Perfect Pose)

Siddhasana, also called the Perfect Pose, is your insomnia aide if you are one of those who tend to get up even when a person residing two floors above sneezes. Then once you get up, getting back to sleep becomes impossible.

But you can turn the tables against insomnia in such cases and get your deprived dose of sleep back by practising Siddhasana.

To practise, sit straight with your eyes closed and allow your breaths to become slow and soft. There is no need to lift or stretch your back or hold your shoulders backwards at this stage. I would instead recommend you to keep the spine comfortable.

Then, attempt to sit in a cross-legged position keeping your ankles parallel to each other. Maintain the posture and focus on breathing. Within a few minutes, you will find a feeling of relaxation emanating throughout your body. It would calm your main and remove all thoughts preventing you from sleeping while relaxing all the muscles. This routine would gradually put you back into sleep mode again.

Note: Avoid this pose if you suffer from severe sciatica.

Sleeplessness and insomnia would trouble you no longer if you inculcate these yoga poses into your routine. Please choose the best yoga poses, alone or in combination, depending on your specific sleep-linked problems. Follow the steps to practise them at the recommended time and duration.

These poses are how you will be able to beat insomnia and enjoy a comfortable, undisturbed sleep of eight hours every night on your soft mattress.

Foods That Can Keep You Awake and Prevent a Good Night's Sleep

What you eat for dinner can profoundly affect your ability to sleep well. It is astonishing to know that, in most cases, the dinner habits and the foods a person has included in his meals could keep him from sleeping well.

Want to know which foods I am talking about? Check out the list of foods that you should never have for your dinner or after-dinner treats if you wish to prevent wakefulness and get a sound sleep of wish hours.

Spicy Foods

Spicy foods have a unique ability to keep you awake by causing heartburn and pain in the abdomen.

They irritate the stomach mucosa resulting in a sensation of burning and pain. These symptoms can only intensify if you suffer from Gastro-oesophageal Reflux Disorder GERD.

Research studies have shown that spicy foods can increase the acid secretion in the stomach. And when you lie down to sleep, these acidic contents get an opportunity to change their route from the intestine towards the oesophagus.

This problem is called GERD.

So, instead of going forward, the stomach contents go back into the oesophagus, thus causing heartburn or a burning sensation in the throat. And this sensation is enough to keep you awake.

Burgers

Nowadays, most people, including kids, have started having burgers for their dinner!

This custom is a serious trend. In the first place, burgers, from no angle, can be considered a wholesome meal. Yet, some people prefer to replace their dinner with a burger.

Besides being highly unhealthy, burgers are also counterproductive to the quality of your sleep. The problem here is their high-fat content and more fats mean a higher production of acid in your stomach, which, in turn, means more heartburn and pain.

The backward flow or regurgitation of acidic stomach contents into your oesophagus would keep you awake the whole night. Hence, make sure this high-fat food doesn't find a place in your dinner.

Coffee

Having coffee at night is equivalent to taking a loan when interest rates are at their peak. If you take a loan when the interest rates are high, you only have to repay much more. This pattern can be disastrous for your financial stability.

Similarly, if you have a mug of coffee after dinner or close to bedtime, you will stay alert when it is the time to sleep. This effect could be disastrous for the quality of your sleep.

In short, the stimulant effect of caffeine in coffee will set up a perfect stage for a wakeful night.

Cheese

If you love your pizza or sandwich to be loaded with some extra cheese, you are keeping yourself from sleeping well. The cheese in your dinner won't let you get up, saying 'Cheese' with a broad smile because it won't let you sleep well to be able to feel fresh in the morning.

Research studies have shown that cheese contains tyramine, increasing alertness and even triggering a migraine attack. These effects of tyramine in cheese can keep you awake at night.

Yoghurt, Flavoured Ones

If you prefer to have your yoghurts be flavoured, you might lose the soothing flavours of the night. The high carbohydrate content of the flavoured yoghurt would boost your energy levels, which is not what you want to happen when it is time to sleep, right?

Broccoli

Broccoli is also one of the foods that can cause sleeplessness. This veggie is loaded with so many nutrients that we are often advised to consume broccoli regularly. However, it would be best to exclude it from your dinner menu because it contains many fibres.

Fibres are undoubtedly good for your health. They help lower cholesterol levels, are suitable for the heart, prevent constipation, and even improve digestion. However, you can enjoy these benefits by eating broccoli in the daytime.

If you eat it for your dinner, the high fibre content would stimulate digestion and make your gut active enough to keep you awake, thus preventing you from getting any sleep.

Chocolates

Munching on chocolates for your post-dinner desserts or a midnight treat would take you back by an hour or two from your expected sleeping time.

Chocolates, especially dark chocolate, contain caffeine, which has stimulant properties. Research has shown that caffeine can increase your alertness level and help you feel fresh when you would instead want to get some sleep.

Hence, avoid eating chocolate bars after your dinner so that your body can continue with the sleep process uninhabited.

Fluid Intake

Water, or any fluid, is not suitable for you at bedtime if you do not want your sleep disturbed by frequent bathroom visits.

Drinking too many fluids shortly before bedtime can, in all probability, force you to get up several times in the night to pass urine. Hence, you must restrict your water intake and other fluids to the minimum after the evening hours.

Alcohol

Most people believe that a glass of wine before bedtime would help them sleep well. However, the fact is that a glass of wine, that too at bedtime, could do more harm than good during the evening hours.

It is not to recommend having a glass of wine in the evening but to compare the harm caused by it when consumed at different times. When you have alcohol at night, it creates an instant sedative effect followed by a long-lasting opposite effect. And this opposite effect can cause you to feel more alert, preventing you from sleeping well.

Also, since your body can process alcohol more quickly, the sedative effect wears off pretty soon.

It means that the rest of the night, your sleep will be fragmented with frequent awakening.

That is why it is best to avoid alcohol before bedtime. But again, having it in the evening doesn't make it any less harmful. We all know the dangerous consequences of alcohol consumption.

Keeping these foods out of your dinner and post-dinner eating habits will take you a step closer to fighting insomnia and getting a sound sleep without any pain, discomfort, or unnecessary alertness.

How to Put Your Sleep Schedule Back in Sync

Here are some easy strategies that would put your sleep schedule back on track so that you can sleep on time every night and get up on time every morning!

Rethink Your Expected Sleep Schedule

Any action or activity you practise for sleeping well and maintaining a scheduled sleep pattern won't provide the desired results until you set the expectations.

So, ask yourself, when is the relaxing time you would like to go to sleep and at what time you need to get up. Keep in mind your other responsibilities like your working hours and the time you reach home. Also, keep in mind the time you have to leave for the office and when you need to get up to finish off all the chores before leaving.

However, makes sure you get a sleep of at least eight hours every day, but not more than ten hours. This practice will give you a rough idea of when you can go to sleep and when you need to get up. Once you have set your expectations, you can move on to the next step that will help you stick to this schedule.

Set the Alarm

Now, the next step is to go to bed at the time you have decided. Also, set the alarm half an hour before your intended bedtime, ten minutes prior, and another at bedtime.

When the first alarm goes off, it's time to check that you are done with all the preparations for the next day. You have some breathing space here to finish the chores that have missed your attention.

Now, when the second alarm goes off, there are still ten more minutes to bedtime. Use this time to brush your teeth, which is a must and without fail, visit your restroom once. This routine will help you avoid getting up in the night to pass urine.

And then, when the third alarm rings, you can go to bed and lie down with your eyes closed.

Do this regularly, even if you don't sleep for longer durations after going to bed. With time, your body will recognise your routine and adjust itself accordingly, thus falling asleep at the same time every day.

Set Time to Wake Up

It's going to be similar to what you did to set a fixed schedule for going to sleep. Set the alarm. But, this time, not three, but just one!

Setting up multiple alarms for getting up in the morning is not recommended. If you already have this habit, it's good to change it now! Because if you don't get up after the first alarm and go to sleep again, your brain won't get enough time to enter the deeper REM phase of sleep. And by the time the successive alarm rings and you finally get up, you will have to bear with a feeling as if you haven't slept well.

This disruption will not only reduce the quality of your sleep but even hamper your efforts to create and maintain a healthy sleep schedule.

Avoid Noise

Any form of disturbance is not good for your sleep-wake cycle. And noise disturbances are on top of it.

Anything that can create noise while sleeping or trying to sleep must be dealt with strictly. It may be your pet dog jumping in your bed at 4 am or your neighbour turning in the ignition of his truck too early in the morning.

Shut off all these noises to enjoy undisturbed sleep. Something as tiny as earplugs could help you do this trick and ensure you can sleep well so that your efforts to reset your body's cycle are successful.

Modify Lighting

Light can enter your eyes even when you have closed them! Another problem is that the skin of our eyelids is thin. So, what happens due to these two problems is, in case, you keep the lights switched on at night, even if it's a dim light, the rays will enter your eyes through the lids.

And once your eyes receive light signals, they pass them on to the brain. The light signifies daytime for the brain and sends signals that keep you awake. These signals are received by various body parts, telling them it's the morning already. This constant transmission of signals is what could keep you awake!

Switching off the lights at night when you sleep would make the brain believe it's nighttime. It would help you fall asleep faster and enjoy a deep restorative sleep so that you can get up feeling fresh once the morning alarm rings.

Have Dinner Early

What happens when you have an early dinner is that your stomach has already processed the food and have pushed it to the next part of the digestive tract by the time you go to sleep.

This process means there will be less chance of food your stomach might regurgitate into your oesophagus once you lie down. This process would prevent heartburn, a common symptom in patients with Gastro-oesophageal Reflux Disorder (GERD) that prevents them from sleeping peacefully by causing discomfort and burning pain in the abdomen and chest.

Research has proven that having an early dinner can promote sleep quality in patients with GERD by preventing the reflux of acidic stomach contents into the throat.

Conclusion

Now that you have learned some of the most effective strategies to reset your internal biological clock, make sure you incorporate them into your routine to avoid sleeplessness and reduce your risk of complications of insomnia.

What Is Multiple Sclerosis and the Most Effective Ways to Manage It

Multiple sclerosis (or MS) is a potentially disabling disease that affects the brain and the spinal cord.

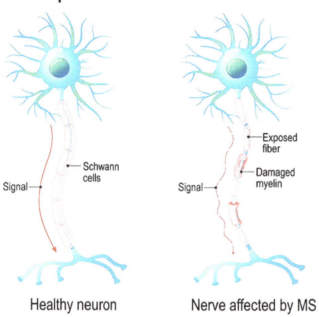

MS occurs when immune cells attack the central nervous system, specifically the protective sheath (called myelin), which covers the nerve fibres resulting in problems with communication between the brain and the rest of the body.

Eventually, this disease may cause permanent damage to and deterioration in nerve functions.

This disease's signs and symptoms often vary widely depending on the extent of nerve damage and exact nerves affected. Some patients with severe MS might lose their ability to walk independently or entirely. Others may experience prolonged periods of remissions without developing any new symptoms.

There is no cure or treatment for reversing the nerve damage caused due to multiple sclerosis. However, some treatments may help speed up recovery from recurring attacks, slow down the course of this disease, and relieve its symptoms.

Here is a brief discussion about the causes and symptoms of multiple sclerosis and the treatment options.

What Are the Signs and Symptoms of Multiple Sclerosis?

The signs and symptoms of multiple sclerosis may differ significantly from one person to another and throughout this disease, depending on the exact location of the affected nerve fibres.

The symptoms that can affect the movements of the patient include:

- Numbness and weakness in one or both hands and legs that typically occur on only one side of the body at a time
- Electric shock-like sensations occurring with some neck movements, especially while bending the neck forward. This symptom is called the Lhermitte sign.
- Tremors
- Unsteady gait
- Lack of coordination
- Vision problems
- Complete or partial loss of vision, usually in one eye at a time, often accompanied by pain during eye movements
- Blurring of vision
- Prolonged double vision

Multiple sclerosis symptoms sometimes also include:

- Dizziness
- Extreme fatigue
- Pain and tingling in different parts of the body
- Slurring of speech
- Problems with bowel or bladder functions

Disease Course or Pathogenesis of Multiple Sclerosis

Most patients with MS have a relapsing-remitting course of the disease. They often experience recurring periods of new symptoms and relapses that develop over a few days to weeks and worsen entirely or partially. These relapses are usually followed by quiet periods of remission that may last for a few months to even years.

Also, a slight increase in body temperature may temporarily worsen the signs and symptoms of this disease. However, these are not considered true relapses.

At least 50% of patients with relapsing-remitting forms of MS develop a steady progression in symptoms, with or without periods of remission, within about 10 to 20 years from the onset of the disease. This status is called secondary-progressive multiple sclerosis.

The worsening of symptoms usually includes difficulties with gait and mobility. This disease's progress rate varies greatly among patients with secondary-progressive multiple sclerosis.

Some patients with MS may experience a gradual onset with a steady progression of the signs and symptoms without developing any relapse. This status is called primary-progressive multiple sclerosis.

What Are the Causes of Multiple Sclerosis?

The causes of multiple sclerosis are not known. It is considered an autoimmune disorder in which the body's immune system attacks its healthy tissues.

In MS, the immune system malfunction destroys fatty cells and tissues that coat and protect the nerve fibres in the spinal cord and brain called the myelin sheath.

Myelin may be compared to the insulation covering or coating on electrical wires. When this protective sheath of myelin is damaged, the nerve fibres are exposed. As a result, Messages travelling along the nerve fibres may be slowed down or even blocked.

It is unclear why multiple sclerosis develops in some patients and not in others. A combination of environmental and genetic factors appears to be responsible for triggering this condition.

What Are the Risk Factors for Multiple Sclerosis?

Some factors that may increase the risk of developing multiple sclerosis include:

Age

MS can occur in patients of any age, though the onset of this disease usually occurs between 20 and 40 years. However, younger and older people may be affected by the condition.

Sex

Women are two to three times more likely to have the relapsing-remitting form of MS than men.

Race

White people, especially those of Northern European descent, have been found to be at the highest risk of developing this condition. People of African, Asian, and Native American descent have a comparatively lower risk.

Family History

If one of the parents or siblings of a person has had MS, they are at a higher risk of developing this disease.

Certain Infections

Infections due to some viruses have been linked to a higher risk of MS, including Epstein-Barr, a virus known to cause infectious mononucleosis.

Climate

The prevalence of MS is more in countries having a temperate climate, including Canada, New Zealand, the northern United States, Europe, and south-eastern Australia.

Autoimmune Diseases

Patients with other autoimmune disorders like thyroid disease, psoriasis, pernicious anaemia, type 1 diabetes, and inflammatory bowel disease have a slightly higher risk of MS.

Vitamin D

Having a low level of vitamin D in the body and lower exposure to sunlight could be associated with a higher risk of MS.

Smoking

Smokers who experience the initial event of symptoms that might signal MS are more prone to develop the second event that confirms the relapsing-remitting form of MS than non-smokers.

What Are the Complications of Multiple Sclerosis?

Patients with multiple sclerosis may develop a few complications such as:

- Paralysis, usually in the legs
- Muscle stiffness and spasms
- Mental changes, like forgetfulness and mood swings
- Problems with bladder and bowel functions
- Epilepsy
- Depression

Diagnosis of Multiple Sclerosis

Tests that can help in diagnosing multiple sclerosis include:

- Neurological examination of the patients
- Blood tests for ruling out the other diseases having symptoms that are similar to those of MS
- Tests to check for specific biomarkers that are associated with MS
- A lumbar puncture (or spinal tap) that involves withdrawing a small sample of cerebrospinal fluid from the spinal canal to be sent for further analysis in a laboratory
- An evoked potential test that records electrical impulses created by the nervous system or neurons in response to any stimulus
- MRI to detect areas of MS-induced lesions in the brain or the spinal cord

Treatment of Multiple Sclerosis

Currently, there is no cure for multiple sclerosis. The treatment typically focuses on speeding up the recovery from acute attacks, slowing down the progress of the disease, and relieving MS symptoms. Usually, patients who have mild symptoms do not need any active treatment.

Some treatments recommended for the management of MS include the following:

- Corticosteroids, like oral prednisone or intravenous methylprednisolone prescribed for reducing nerve inflammation. Some side effects of these drugs may include increased blood pressure, insomnia, increased blood glucose levels, fluid retention, and mood swings.

- Plasma exchange (or plasmapheresis) in which the liquid portion of a part of the blood (plasma) is withdrawn and separated from blood cells to obtain plasma. The blood cells are later mixed with the protein solution (called albumin) and re-infused back into the body. Plasma exchange is usually recommended for patients with new and severe symptoms that have not responded to other treatments like steroids.

Treatments for Modifying the Progression

For patients with primary-progressive MS, medications like ocrelizumab may be used as a disease-modifying therapy (DMT). It is the only FDA-approved medication that may be prescribed to some patients to slow down the progress of the disease.

For the relapsing-remitting form of MS, there are several disease-modifying therapies available.

Abnormal immune responses associated with the development of multiple sclerosis occur during the early stage of the disease. Hence, aggressive treatments with these drugs as early as possible could lower the risk of relapse, slow down the development of new lesions, and significantly reduce the risk of disability and brain atrophy.

Most of the disease-modifying treatments used to manage MS carry significant risks. Selecting the best therapy for any patient would depend on carefully considering multiple factors, including the severity and duration of the disease, effectiveness of previous MS treatments, other pre-existing health issues, and the child-bearing status.

Treatment options for relapsing-remitting forms of MS include oral and injectable medications. Injectable treatments include interferon-beta medications and glatiramer acetate.

Physical therapy by an occupational or physical therapist could be included in the treatment protocol to teach the patients some strengthening or stretching exercises. In addition, showing them how to use devices could make it easier for them to perform routine tasks to live an independent life.

Physical therapy coupled with the use of mobility aids, when necessary, could also help manage leg weakness and similar gait problems often associated with multiple sclerosis.

Muscle relaxants are recommended for patients with uncontrollable or painful muscle stiffness and spasms, particularly in the legs. Muscle relaxants might help in some cases.

Medications to reduce fatigue and increase walking speed are also recommended in some cases.

Ayurvedic Treatments for the Management of Multiple Sclerosis

Most modern drugs commonly used to treat MS are known to cause serious long-term side effects. Hence, patients often prefer to use ayurvedic medications or adopt healthy dietary and lifestyle strategies to relieve their symptoms and minimise their dependency on modern drugs.

Lifestyle and home remedies recommended by Ayurveda for deriving relief from symptoms of multiple sclerosis are explained below.

Getting Plenty of Rest

Looking at your sleep habits and making sure you are getting adequate rest and sleep is essential to relieving your symptoms of MS. To ensure you are getting enough sleep, you might have to evaluate yourself for possible sleep disorders like obstructive sleep apnoea.

Meditation and yoga are also effective for regulating sleep patterns and enabling yourself to enjoy deep restorative sleep.

Exercising

If you suffer from mild to moderate MS, regular yoga and some physical activities and exercises could help improve your muscle tone, strength, balance, and muscle coordination.

Swimming and other water exercises are also good options if you are bothered by symptoms linked to the rise in body temperature. Other forms of mild to moderate physical activities recommended for patients with MS include stretching, walking, low-impact aerobics, tai chi, and stationary bicycling.

Cooling Down

MS symptoms often become worse when the body temperature increases. Avoiding exposure to excessive heat and using devices like cooling scarves and vests could be helpful in this regard.

Eating a Balanced Diet

There is no evidence supporting the benefits of a particular diet for managing MS. However, experts recommend eating a healthy and nutritious diet to slow down damage to the nerves and improve the brain's activities. It would also help you avoid complications linked to MS. Some research suggests that eating foods rich in vitamin D could potentially benefit patients with MS.

Avoiding Stress

Stress can trigger or worsen the signs and symptoms of MS. Yoga, massage, tai chi, meditation, aromatherapy, and deep breathing might help reduce stress and relieve symptoms of MS.

Conclusion

Patients with MS are advised to follow a combination of alternative and complementary treatments in combination with the use of modern drugs to manage their symptoms, like fatigue or muscle pain.

Activities like exercises, meditation, eating a healthier diet, yoga, massage, relaxation techniques, and acupuncture can also help boost their overall physical and emotional well-being and improve their quality of life.

What Are the Symptoms, Root Causes, and Treatments for Dementia?

Dementia, sometimes referred to as senility, refers to the age-related deterioration in a person's mental health. It is characterised by the loss of intellectual abilities associated with old age.

There are two major forms of dementia identified as Alzheimer's-type dementia and those related to vascular problems. Dementia linked to Alzheimer's disease occurs due to the generalised "atrophy" of the brain, in which the patient develops loss of memory and other symptoms related to cognitive deterioration. The term senile dementia is generally used to refer to Alzheimer's disease.

Vascular problems associated with dementia may include a cerebrovascular stroke.

What Are the Symptoms of Senile Dementia?

Dementia is characterised by a decline in a patient's cognitive functions such as memory, attention span, and problem-solving skills. It may also cause a mental decline in which the patient experiences an inability to focus, recall information, and judge a situation.

Senile dementia linked to Parkinson's or Alzheimer's disease may also present a few physical symptoms related to ageing, such as:

- Stooped posture
- Loss of muscle strength
- Stiffness of the joints
- Loss of or reduced vision
- The appearance of wrinkles and fines lines on the skin
- Brittleness of the bones
- Atherosclerosis or hardening of the arteries

These physical symptoms are referred to as senility and can be differentiated from senile dementia by their physical nature, though the underlying factor responsible for both is ageing.

What Are the Causes of Dementia?

Actual psychological changes caused by dementia are caused by cortical cell's degeneration in the brain.

Alzheimer's disease is one of the most common causes of dementia. This condition begins with difficulty in learning and remembering past and recent events.

The risk of dementia is higher in patients suffering from major depression.

Degenerative brain disorders can also lead to senile dementia. A variety of cerebral conditions, including Parkinson's disease, Pick's disease, vascular dementia, Creutzfeldt-Jakob disease, and Huntington's disease, are known to contribute to the development of dementia. These facts indicate that patients diagnosed with an autoimmune disorder are more likely to develop dementia.

Pre-existing autoimmune conditions such as Huntington's disease can trigger the development of dementia at a relatively younger age. Hence, patients diagnosed with autoimmune disorders should consult a doctor to assess their risk of dementia and seek proper treatment.

Treatment of Dementia

The treatment of dementia involves the identification of the primary cause, such as Huntington's disease, stroke, or Alzheimer's disease. The treatment can be administered to improve the symptoms by supporting brain functions and minimising the speed of degeneration of the brain.

Preventing damage to the brain cells due to autoantibodies also forms a part of dementia treatment when symptoms have occurred due to an autoimmune disorder.

Patients can also choose natural herbs that can boost brain functions like memory and attention span.

Conclusion

Early identification of the root cause of dementia and correcting the underlying abnormalities with the help of natural herbs can slow down the progress of this condition to a great extent and allow patients to live an active and healthy life.

The Adverse Effects of Nicotine Consumption on Your Body and How to Get Rid of the Addiction

Nicotine is a chemical containing nitrogen made by some types of plants, such as the tobacco plant. It can also be produced synthetically.

Nicotine addiction cycle

Cigarette smoking → Nicotine absorption → Arousal, Mood modulation, Pleasure → Tolerance and physical dependence → Drug abstinence produces withdrawal symptoms → Craving for nicotine to self-medicate withdrawal symptoms → Cigarette smoking

Nicotiana tabacum, a form of nicotine found in tobacco plants, is derived from the nightshade family of plants. Red peppers, tomatoes, eggplant, and potatoes are some examples of the nightshade family.

Though not excessively harmful or cancer-causing on its own, nicotine is highly addictive and can expose you to hazardous effects such as tobacco dependency.

Smoking is one of the most common preventable causes of death linked to nicotine addiction.

Some Facts About Nicotine

- Chewing and snorting tobacco and tobacco products usually results in more nicotine in the body than smoking.
- The common side effects of nicotine could affect your heart, hormonal balance, and gastrointestinal system.
- Nicotine is nearly as tricky as heroin to give up.

Adverse Effects of Nicotine Intake

Nicotine can produce a range of effects on our body, as explained below:

- It is both a stimulant and a sedative.
- When the body is exposed to nicotine, the person may experience a 'kick'. It is partly caused due to nicotine's stimulatory effects on the adrenal glands, resulting in the release of feel-good hormones like adrenaline.
- The surge in adrenaline levels stimulates the body. There is also an immediate release of carbs represented by glucose, along with an increase in heart rate, blood pressure, and breathing activity.
- Nicotine can also make the pancreas produce less insulin, causing a mild increase in blood sugar levels.
- Nicotine also indirectly causes a release of dopamine in our brain's motivation and pleasure areas. A similar effect may occur when people use recreational drugs like heroin and cocaine. The drug user often experiences a kick or a pleasurable sensation.
- As the user becomes more tolerant to the effect of nicotine, they tend to need a higher dose to enjoy the same kind of kick or effect.

Dopamine is a chemical that can affect our emotions, sensations of pain and pleasure, and movements. Feelings of contentment or pleasure are intensified if dopamine levels in the brain rise.

Depending on the dosage of nicotine used and the nervous system arousal of the person, nicotine may also act as a sedative.

Pharmacologic Effect of Nicotine

When the body is exposed to nicotine, it will increase heart rate, oxygen consumption rate by the heart muscles, and cardiac stroke volume. These are called the pharmacologic effects of nicotine.

Psychodynamic Effects

Nicotine is linked to a raised level of alertness, a sensation of being happy and relaxed, and euphoria.

Reduced Anxiety

Nicotine can also increase beta-endorphin levels that reduce anxiety.

Addictive Effective

People who consume nicotine regularly and then stop using it suddenly experience withdrawal symptoms, like:

- Difficulty focusing or paying attention
- Extreme cravings
- Depression
- A sense of emptiness
- Anxiety
- Irritability
- Moodiness

Side Effects of Nicotine

Nicotine can cause a wide range of side effects affecting vital organs and systems of the body, some of which are explained below.

The blood circulation may be involved in several ways, causing:

- An increased tendency for abnormal clotting, leading to a higher risk of blood clots
- Enlargement of the aorta
- Atherosclerosis, in which cholesterol plaques form on the arterial walls

Side effects of nicotine in the brain include:
- Dizziness

- Irregular or disturbed sleep
- Light-headedness
- Nightmares
- Bad dreams
- Possible restriction of blood flow to the brain

In the digestive system, nicotine may have the following effects:

- Nausea and vomiting
- Dry mouth (xerostomia)
- Peptic ulcers
- Indigestion
- Heartburn
- Diarrhoea

The heart may experience the following side effects after using nicotine:

- An increase in blood pressure
- Changes in heart rhythm and rate
- An increased risk of stroke
- Constrictions and diseases of the coronary artery

Women who smoke during pregnancy have the following risks for themselves or with the development of the baby:

- Infertility
- High blood pressure
- Obesity
- Respiratory difficulties
- Type 2 diabetes
- Behavioural issues
- Problems with brain development

What Are the Effects of Smoking on the Skin?

Nicotine is hazardous for your lungs, heart, and brain. These are undoubtedly the reasons enough to stop this unhealthy habit. But now you have even more reasons to quit smoking. Smoking can also affect your appearance. It can damage your skin and make your face look much older and unattractive.

Here are some basic mechanisms by which smoking can ruin your appearance:

Acne

Acne has mainly been associated with puberty and hormonal imbalances. It is known that incidences of acne are highest in adolescents at puberty due to changes in levels of hormones in the body occurring during this period.

However, smoking is another common factor responsible for acne. It can affect the functions of your immune system. As a result, your skin cannot fight infections using the sebaceous glands that produce an oily substance called sebum.

Smoking can also increase the risk of flaring up the infections in these glands, thus increasing the acne on your face.

Puffy Bags Under Eyes

Puffiness under the eyes is a sign of a lack of sleep. Most of us hate it when it shows on our faces. Luckily, these puffy bags disappear as the day passes, provided you are a non-smoker. But, you cannot escape these ugly signs if you are a smoker.

In fact, smokers are four times more likely to develop puffy bags under their eyes than non-smokers. And when these signs do occur, they tend to persist for longer, which means you cannot expect them to disappear even by evening!

Premature Wrinkles

Wrinkles can make you look anything but wise or mature if they show up at a younger age. Getting trapped into a smoking addiction can accelerate skin ageing and cause premature wrinkling.

A smoker looks almost two years older than non-smokers of the same age. These wrinkles appear because smoking reduces blood supply to the skin of the face, thus depriving it of its supply of nutrients.

As a result, the skin cells do not receive enough vitamin A, vitamin C, and proteins that increase collagen production, promote wound healing and maintain skin health.

Tobacco smoke can also damage elastin fibres and collagen that provide elasticity and strength to your skin. As a result, the skin tends to sag, and wrinkles appear prematurely.

Loss of Natural Glow

Smoking can rob the natural glow off your face. Cigarette smoke contains a high amount of carbon monoxide that displaces the oxygen in the skin. Additionally, the nicotine present could reduce blood flow, thus leaving your skin dry and lustreless.

It would also deplete several nutrients, including vitamin A and C, which help protect and repair your skin. The cumulative result of these effects of smoking can become evident in the form of the loss of natural glow on your face.

Uneven Skin Tone

Smoking can trigger telangiectasia, a condition caused due to widened blood vessels on the skin. Moreover, it can result in the appearance of thread-like red lines or patterns on the face. This effect could lead to an uneven skin tone and the loss of smooth texture.

Ugly Scarring

Nicotine in cigarettes can cause constriction of blood vessels. This effect could limit blood flow to the face, thus reducing oxygen supply and other nutrients needed for wound healing.

It means any wound on your face would take a longer time to heal. The delayed wound healing can result in the formation of scars that are redder and bigger than if you were a non-smoker.

Psoriasis

If you have heard of psoriasis, you must be aware that it is an autoimmune disease, and so, it can crop up even if you have not smoked a cigarette ever. However, it has been found that smokers have a higher risk of developing psoriasis than non-smokers. Your risk of developing this scaly skin condition could go up by almost 20 to 60% if you have been puffing one pack a day for 10 to 20 years.

This disease can cause white scales to appear on your skin with tiny bleeding spots beneath them. The worst part is that there is no cure for psoriasis!

Stains on Your Teeth

Your teeth are an essential part of your overall health and personality. Sparkling white teeth are considered a sign of good health and hygiene. That is why all of us love to have dazzling white teeth.

But, if you smoke, you can bid goodbye to white teeth because the nicotine in cigarettes could leave ugly stains on your teeth.

Skin Cancer

And finally, smoking may increase your risk of some forms of skin cancers. Smokers have a three times higher risk of developing squamous cell carcinoma than non-smokers. The earlier you quit smoking, the safer you would be from this form of skin cancer.

These effects of nicotine on the skin are just signs of how dangerously it can affect your health. You can take the step today and minimise damage caused due to nicotine. The earlier you quit this habit, the lesser its impact on your face, skin, and general health.

It will not just help your lungs breathe easily but also preserve the youthful and vibrant glow of your skin. Also, quitting the habit earlier will undo the damage already done to some extent.

Treatment of Nicotine Addiction

Treatment for nicotine dependency is called smoking cessation therapy. It aims to reduce the urge to consume nicotine and prevent the associated risks or health problems.

Medications for Nicotine Addiction

Nicotine replacement therapy is the most common therapy recommended for patients with nicotine addiction.

Psychological Support and Counselling

Reviews have suggested that nicotine replacement therapy and other medications commonly used to treat nicotine addiction are most effective when supported by psychiatric care and counselling.

This supervision could range from counselling advice by a primary care physician to quitting smoking or even individual, family, and group therapy.

These interventions could help patients with nicotine dependency to overcome the psychological aspect of withdrawal, like low moods and irritability. Furthermore, medication therapy would help tackle the physical or chemical side effects of dependency.

Conclusion

Ayurveda strongly recommends taking steps at the earliest to prevent adverse effects linked to nicotine intake. The results of nicotine on the skin are highlighted in the Ayurvedic system of medicine to give you an overview of just how harmful this habit can be.

Undergoing regular treatment and counselling could help you overcome nicotine dependency and protect against complications linked to this dangerous habit.

Alcohol Hangover and the Best Detox Mechanisms to Overcome It

Hangovers are usually due to various factors, such as the direct effects of alcohol intake on the different systems and organs of the body, or factors associated with the drinking behaviours.

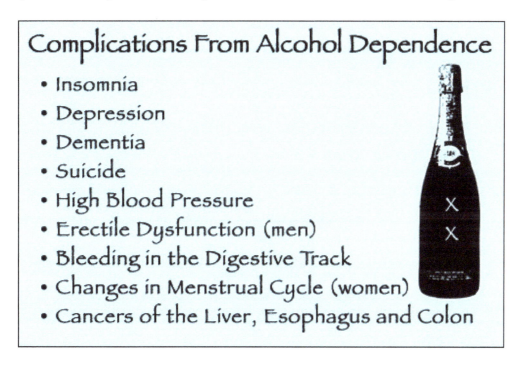

Although the direct effects of excessive alcohol intake on the organs result in the most unpleasantness, some other symptoms may also result from the withdrawal of alcohol from your body and the effect of metabolites produced when alcoholic beverages are consumed.

The chemicals in alcoholic beverages, the behaviours associated with alcohol drinking, and the person's characteristics might influence the severity of the symptoms and the toxicity resulting from it.

Direct Effects of Alcohol Intake

There are several ways by which alcohol contributes to hangover symptoms:

An alcoholic hangover refers to a group of unpleasant symptoms like nausea, heartburn, and dehydration that occur after consuming too much alcohol. Frequent hangovers may also be associated with poor liver health, inefficient physical performance, strained personal relations, and conflicts at work.

Generally, the severity of symptoms of a hangover depends on the amount of alcohol consumed. Yet, no specific amount indicates how much alcohol you can safely consume to avoid the hangover.

It is because every person's body reacts to alcohol in different manners.

Here is a brief discussion about what exactly happens when you consume alcohol and the biochemical processes occurring in your body during its metabolism.

Biochemical Processes Responsible for Symptoms of Alcoholic Hangover

The Role of Ethanol

Hangover symptoms occur primarily due to the presence of ethanol (CH_3CH_2OH) in most alcoholic beverages, including beers and wines.

Ethanol produces a wide range of effects on our bodies, causing sleep deprivation and dehydration. Again, ethanol could be responsible for the changes in cardiac functions and hormonal imbalances that occur due to alcohol consumption.

Let us find out more about the role of ethanol in alcohol hangover symptoms.

Ethanol is broken down and then metabolised in the liver in the presence of an enzyme called alcohol dehydrogenase. This process is supported by a coenzyme called nicotinamide adenine dinucleotide (NAD), resulting in acetaldehyde (CH_3CHO), also known as ethanal.

Since the metabolism utilizes NAD, its levels tend to reduce after alcohol consumption.

Acetaldehyde, thus produced, is highly toxic. It could be responsible for the short-term and long-term damage to the liver and other symptoms of a hangover caused due to alcohol consumption.

This compound is a reactive compound that can mediate oxidative stress. It not only contributes to an alcoholic hangover but also increases the risk of alcoholic hepatitis, cirrhosis, and liver cancer.

How Do Your Body's Organs React to the Increased Level of Acetaldehyde?

Your body attempts to neutralize the damage caused by acetaldehyde by producing an enzyme called aldehyde dehydrogenase (ALDH). ALDH can oxidise acetaldehyde, restoring the normal mitochondrial functions of cells and protecting you against toxicity.

ALDH works by converting acetaldehyde into a relatively innocuous compound called acetate.

Effect of Acetaldehyde

As far as the alcoholic hangover is concerned, acetaldehyde is not the only substance it should worry about.

Alcoholic beverages contain a low concentration of other complex organic compounds called congeners that can exert toxic effects. Congeners include acetone, furfural, and tannins, potentially harming the liver and overall health.

Now that we have learned how alcohol is metabolised in the body, let us look at the common symptoms of a hangover.

What Are the Common Signs and Symptoms of an Alcoholic Hangover?

- Alcohol may irritate the mucosa of the stomach and increase gastric acid production. As a result, you might experience sour eructation, heartburn, nausea, and vomiting.
- Alcohol possesses diuretic properties. It means it could increase the production of urine, causing dehydration.
- Alcohol intake can limit glucose production in the body, in which you might develop extremely low blood sugar levels. This deficiency may result in severe fatigue and dizziness.
- Alcohol intake can create electrolyte imbalances and contribute to irritability, fatigue, headaches, and weakness.

Detoxification for Reducing Alcohol Hangover Symptoms

Different organs like the liver, kidneys, lungs, lymphatic system, intestines, skin, and blood have to work together to transform the toxins into less harmful compounds, which are later excreted from the body.

What Is a Detox Diet?

The initial part of a detox diet involves fasting, during which you have to go without food for two days. This practice is followed by a diet that includes a few specific foods that promote the elimination of toxins.

Most detox diets encourage a form of 'cleansing' by using an enema or colonic irrigation. Some detox plans also include laxatives and some supplements that assist the purification processes.

What Are Toxins, and How Does a Detox Diet Help Get Rid of Them?

Toxins are chemicals that can have an unfavourable effect on the body. They enter the body by ingesting foods and beverages like alcohol and substances used in growing crops like pesticides and insecticides. Some toxins can also enter the body through the intake of polluted water and the air we breathe. These toxins are processed through the liver and kidneys and then eliminated from the body through urination, perspiration, and bowel movements.

However, natural elimination processes of the body are not completely capable of eliminating these toxins. As a result, they tend to accumulate in the digestive and lymphatic systems and cause harmful effects like fatigue and headaches.

Over a period, these toxins may cause considerable damage to normal tissues resulting in chronic disorders like cancer, peptic ulcers, fibroids, menstrual irregularities, and much more.

A detox diet involves supplying the body with specific substances, boosting the processes that eliminate the toxins. A detox diet also contains foods low in fats and rich in fibres. It includes natural, healthy foods that could improve nutrition and enhance overall health and well-being.

Foods to Avoid During a Detox Diet

- Eggs, milk, cream, and cheese
- Chicken, red meat, turkey, and other meat products like burgers and sausages
- Processed foods, ready-made sauces, ready meals, and takeaways
- Wheat products include bread, cereals, croissants, cakes, pies, pastry, and biscuits
- Chocolate, jam, sweets, and sugar
- Margarine and butter
- Fizzy drinks and squashes
- Alcohol
- Tea and coffee

Conclusion

Being aware of how your body reacts to alcohol and the biochemical reactions involved in its metabolism is essential for making conscious efforts to quit drinking.

If you experience severe hangover symptoms, you can try a detox diet to overcome them. It is also advisable to quit drinking to minimise damage to your vital organs and restore health.

Natural Ayurvedic Therapies for Improving Memory and Cognitive Functions

Memory refers to the group of processes performed by the brain to acquire, retain, and store information for later retrieval. There are three primary forms of procedures involved in the processing of memory, which include encoding, followed by storage, and retrieval.

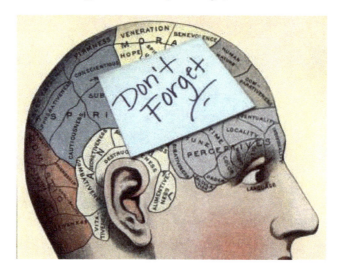

The human memory can preserve and recover information a person has learnt and experienced. However, this process is not flawless. Sometimes, we misremember things or forget things. Also, sometimes, things may not be encoded in memory properly, by which their storage and retrieval may fail to occur efficiently.

The problems with memory could range from mild annoyances, such as forgetting where you left your home keys, to some major diseases, such as Alzheimer's and dementia. Such conditions affect the patient's quality of life by reducing their ability to remember names, tasks, vital information, or skills.

The research on human memory and other brain cognitive functions has revealed that the lack of sleep could be one of the major factors responsible for a decline in these functions.

Let us look at the role of sleep in the formation and storage of memory.

The Role of Sound Sleep in Memory

Memories are of several types; some memories are based on facts such as the names of capitals of states, while some are episodic memories based on specific events or circumstances in life.

Instructional (or procedural) memories can help you learn and retain information about performing activities, including writing computer programs or playing the piano.

Any information you learn could become a memory through three vital functions: acquisition, consolidation, and recall.

The stage of acquisition involves learning anything new. In contrast, stages of consolidation and recall help the memory become more stable in the brain and provide an ability to access them.

The consolidation of any form of memory predominantly occurs while you are asleep. Without proper consolidation, any newly acquired skill or information could be lost from your brain's memory storage. So, it would not be available for recall and use in the future when you try.

Thus, without adequate sleep, the brain could have difficulty retaining and recalling memories.

These basic physiological processes also suggest why it is essential to ensure you get a sound sleep of eight hours every night to improve your memory and cognitive performance.

Effect of Lack of Sleep on Memory and Other Cognitive Functions of the Brain

Scientists believe that the hippocampus and neocortex regions of the brain are where the long-term memories get consolidated and stored.

During sleep, the hippocampus gets activated. It replays the events or the information that has been learnt during the daytime. This information is later reviewed by the neocortex and processed to form long-lasting memories to make them last longer.

Specific memories tend to become more stable during the rapid eye movement (REM) phase of our sleep. REM sleep is the deeper sleep phase when the mind and body are fully relaxed.

People who have insomnia or disturbed sleep with frequent awakening due to mental stress, restless leg syndrome, and sleep apnoea cannot enter REM sleep. As a result, the memory consolidation processes in the hippocampus and neocortex fail to occur.

Additionally, the lack of sleep might also interfere with their learning processes by affecting the ability of the brain to secure the memories or make them more stable.

This circumstance indicates why people who cannot sleep well usually suffer from poor memory and reduced efficiency and productivity.

Let us have a deeper understanding of how insomnia could affect different aspects of your cognitive functions.

How Does Lack of Sleep Affect Cognitive Functions?

Recall Memories

Sleep could improve your ability to recall the information you have learned. Insomnia, on the other hand, might adversely affect your memory recall, thus causing fogginess, confusion, and disorientation while working on important tasks.

Motor Memories

Procedural memory, sometimes referred to as motor memories, comprises your ability to learn and adopt some physical skills like riding a bike or playing instruments.

Lack of sleep could affect your motor memory and prevent you from learning new physical skills. On the other hand, sound sleep can positively influence your procedural memory.

Declarative Memory

Insomnia might also affect your declarative memory, which refers to recalling facts, including the events, dates, and places you need to memorise for examination. This factor can result in poor academic performance of students.

Memories related to facts learned recently can also become more robust when the quality and the duration of your REM sleep are improved.

Focus or Concentration

Sleep deprivation could reduce a person's attention span, focus, and concentration. This status may negatively influence the academic performance of students and the workplace efficiency of executives.

It might also reduce your working memory and increase reaction time. As a result, you might experience difficulties responding efficiently and promptly at the time of emergencies.

Rational Thinking

Sleep deprivation could alter the functional neurons connecting the prefrontal cortex and the emotion or reward-processing centres located in the brain. This status might impair the brain's executive functions, including rational thinking and problem-solving skills.

As a result, you could become hypersensitive to the rewarding stimuli, thus heightening your emotional response leading to illogical thinking and irrational behaviours.

Dementia

People with chronic insomnia are more vulnerable to developing degenerative brain disorders, including dementia and Alzheimer's disease.

Sleep deprivation could encourage the deposition of amyloid-beta plaques in the brain, thereby triggering the development of these diseases.

Insomnia could accelerate the decline in memory and attention span in patients with Alzheimer's disease and may cause disorientation of the time and space at a much younger age.

Ayurveda offers effective therapies for improving memory and cognitive functions of the brain. It also recommends taking steps to improve your sleep to enhance your brain functions.

Meditation has profoundly positively impacted memory by improving sleep, reducing stress, and promoting brain functions. Let us look at how to practice meditation to improve your memory.

Herbal Remedies for Improving Memory and Attention Span

- Holy basil
- Brahmi
- Mucuna pruriens
- Sage
- Ginseng
- Guarana
- Peppermint
- Rhodiola Rosea
- Rosemary
- Ashwagandha

Conclusion

Meditation and using Ayurvedic herbs would boost your memory and concentration power. They may also improve your attention span, allowing you to focus on your tasks or study for a longer time without feeling tired or fatigued.

They would help you seek joy, peace of mind, calmness, vibrant health, more incredible energy, positive relationships, satisfaction, and fulfilment in life. Your mind would be fresher and maintain its delicacy and beauty. The changes may also bring about emotional stability and harmony that would nourish you from within. It can calm you whenever you feel overwhelmed or distressed.

Regular practice will help you remember things more efficiently and recall them promptly and with better ease. This routine would not just improve your academic or workplace performance but also help you avoid the risk of diseases like dementia and Alzheimer's disease.

Learning to Cope With the Challenges Posed by ADHD to Lead a Normal Social, Personal and Academic Life

Introduction: What Is ADHD?

Children who have trouble paying attention or find it hard to control their behaviour might have Attention Deficit Hyperactivity Disorder or ADHD.

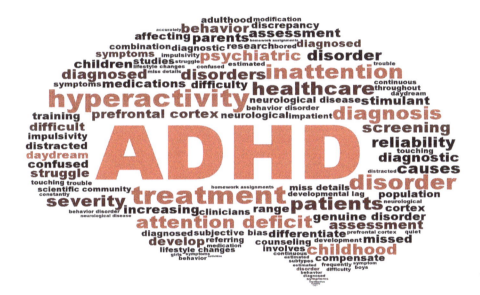

ADHD is a common form of mental disorder that can affect children and may continue into adulthood. A person with ADHD may find it hard to focus, concentrate, stay still, and talk without a break.

A child with ADHD shows increased inattention, impulsive behaviours, and hyperactivity than other children of the same age. This condition affects their school performance and behaviour at home. Fortunately, with the guidance of an experienced doctor and other specialists, this condition can be controlled to a large extent.

What Are the Common Causes of ADHD?

Unfortunately, there are no known factors that can cause ADHD. However, most researchers believe it occurs because of the complex interaction between genes and non-genetic or environmental factors.

Genetics is thought to play the most critical role in causing ADHD. The disorder is believed to run in families with different genes playing a small part in the condition. Despite several theories, a genetic test is not yet available for diagnosing the disorder.

Some of the non-genetic factors that may cause ADHD in children include:

- Low birth weight
- Birth complications
- Smoking or alcohol consumption during pregnancy
- Exposure to toxic substances such as lead
- Social deprivation
- Neglect and abuse
- Food additives and dyes that worsen hyperactivity

What Are the Early Warning Symptoms of ADHD?

ADHD has numerous symptoms. Some of these symptoms may seem like normal behaviour in the child at first, but those symptoms worsen over time. A child with ADHD shows at least six of the following symptoms related to inattention, hyperactivity, and impulsiveness during the first 12 years of their life.

Inattention:

- Does not seem to listen when spoken to
- Has a habit of daydreaming and gets confused easily
- Becomes quickly bored with a task until something interesting is given to them
- Gets distracted easily and misses out on important details
- Cannot focus on more than one thing simultaneously
- Finds it hard to organise or complete a task
- Not able to learn anything new
- Not able to follow instructions
- Processes information slowly and less accurately as compared to others

Hyperactivity

- Talks non-stop
- Is not able to sit still in school or at home
- Constantly remains in motion
- Touches or plays with anything that comes into sight
- Wriggles or twists their body in their seat
- Feels difficulty in quietly doing any task

Impulsivity

- Feels impatient
- Finds it difficult to wait for the things they want
- Spontaneous blur of words and emotions
- Acts without thinking about consequences
- Interrupts others' conversations and activities

Sometimes, it is difficult for a parent to identify the ADHD symptoms in children that need immediate attention. The symptoms may look like other behavioural problems common in kids at this age, like lack of interest in studies, unwillingness to listen to parents or anger issues.

For example, when a child sits quietly in a corner, you may think that they are doing homework, though it could be a sign of anxiety due to the inability to follow the instructions. Or you might mistake hyperactivity or destructive behaviour at school with disciplinary or emotional problems.

Suppose you observe your child having trouble adjusting with others or following the usual daily activities at home or school for a long time. In that case, you should immediately consult a doctor as these symptoms could be due to ADHD.

The Types of ADHD

ADHD can be categorized into three subtypes as described below:

1. Predominantly hyperactive-impulsive type: The symptoms of this type mainly belong to the hyperactivity-impulsivity categories. Inattention might be present despite the presence of fewer than six symptoms.

2. Predominantly inattentive type: A majority of symptoms belong to the inattention category. Hyperactivity-impulsivity may still be present despite showing fewer than six symptoms. A child suffering from the predominantly inattentive type of ADHD gets along well with other children. They may sit quietly and not pay attention to anything; thus, there are chances that you might overlook them and not notice ADHD.

3. Combined inattentive and hyperactive-impulsive types: Such children show six or more symptoms from all categories. A majority of children have this type of ADHD.

Challenges Associated with ADHD

Children and teens with ADHD can have a tough time managing their school and personal life. Even though hyperactivity gets better as the child becomes a teen, problems like disorganisation, inattention, and poor impulse control may continue.

Such children may find it difficult to concentrate in school, and hyperactivity may cause an increase in behaviour-related complaints from the school. As the child reaches teenage, risky behaviour and not following rules and regulations may majorly hinder achieving their educational and career goals.

Most adults with ADHD do not know that they suffer from it. A typical adult with ADHD may have a history of failure at home or problems at work. It is difficult for them to stick to a single job, arrive on time at work, and be productive.

Effective Methods for Minimising the Effect of ADHD on a Child's Daily Activities

Attention Deficit Hyperactivity Disorder (ADHD) affects the nervous system, usually caused by genetic or biological reasons. A common childhood disease may continue into adulthood.

Children find it difficult to focus on the task at hand or pay attention to something. They fail to control their behaviour and become overactive. Adults cannot manage their time and fail to organise themselves, set goals, or retain their job. Relationships, self-esteem, and addiction too can become a problem for them. ADHD does affect performance in school or at work.

Parents and teachers have a significant role in managing ADHD in children. They should watch against committing the following acts that make up the strict Don'ts for ADHD patients.

- Don't stop ADHD patients from exercising: It reduces stress and spends the restless energy in children and adults. Exercise improves blood flow to the brain, changes the mood better, and makes you more alert and focused.

- Don't interfere with their sleep: Sleep problems can aggravate ADHD symptoms. So, don't do anything that will interfere with their sleep.

- Do nothing that will induce stress, which exacerbates ADHD. Go for relaxation techniques like yoga and deep breathing instead.

- Do not try to manage the daily activities of your ADHD-affected child yourself. Let them learn to govern themselves. Evolve a system they can run.

- Do not impose your ideas about life, career, and achievements on the child. The affected will have some skills. Try to identify those. Let them pursue those rather than insisting on what you think would be good. Let the child take as much control of their life as possible.

Here are some more Dos to follow for controlling the ADHD symptoms in yourself or your child:

- Do set a routine

Routine makes daily activities comfortable for ADHD-affected persons. Many patients have no fundamental understanding of a structured life.

They cannot set goals, do not know what they will need to do for themselves or others, and have no idea when a particular process will occur. They cannot organise much. Everything is chaos for them.

But a realistic and reliable routine can do them well. Begin with small, manageable goals. Keep modifying their existing pattern in a small way. When one such step is accepted, go for the next. Let the person know the detailed schedule and how much time each task will need so that they can decide their own pace to achieve their target.

- Do use visual cues

Keep using visual cues because ADHD patients respond to them well. They will like and understand it better if the school time, playing hours, work period, and commuting time are shown in different colours. Cultivate in them the habit of using a checklist all the time.

- Do use a schedule planner

Many devices are now available to plan your day. These include a voice recorder, paper planner, talking watch, or computer reminders. Use the method that an ADHD person is most comfortable with but never overdo the routine exercise. The affected person often does not like f their sense of freedom curtailed. The routine should be used as a support, not a restraining framework.

- Do avoid stress and the urge to hurry up

ADHD affected patients should try not to hasten while performing any task. They should slow themselves down. They should stop work at the scheduled hour because they need more frequent breaks than others. They should allow some time for unstructured entertainment and recoup after every focused effort over a pre-determined period. They should be able to relax after their strenuous effort to concentrate. Let them cultivate the habit of meditating regularly.

Some Dos to Be Followed by Parents and Teachers

Parents and teachers have a challenging and trying role to play in dealing with an ADHD child. They have to overcome the problems at every step, and should adopt the following strategies to keep doing their job well for as long as necessary.

Do Learn to Stay Calm and Control Your Emotions

They must stay calm. Losing a temper will prove counter-productive and make the patient angrier. Don't argue with the child, as it will not produce the desired result. Be conciliatory rather than combative. They should support the person without making the person dependent on them. Theirs should only be a guiding, and protective hand extended only in times of difficulties.

Do Allow Some Amount of Freedom to the Child

Parents and teachers should set the limits within which the ADHD child should be free to act. Don't put pressure on them. Allow them to do things in their own way. Let them have some choices too. Don't be harsh on them when they break the rules. Ask them what should be the consequences now. Let them know what they are doing and what they will face if they do certain things.

Do Teach to Avoid Procrastination

ADHD patients tend to put off all their problems for the next day. They find it difficult to start work on a new task or problem. They are afraid that they will not be able to do it. Even when they begin work on a particular thing, they get involved in umpteen other activities on the way. Only some are motivated to finish their work quickly when they realise that the deadline is close by. But, many of them panic and are overwhelmed by the sudden closeness of the deadline.

The right approach is to help these people understand why they are tempted to put things off. If it is a considerable task, teach them to divide it into smaller ones. Simplify the tasks. Encourage them to ask others how to do it. Find ways to make the job more interesting and let the affected person set the deadline. And convince them about the importance of avoiding distractions while working on a task with a deadline.

Do Give Undivided Attention to the Child

It is always better to avoid the stimuli that tend to distract the ADHD patients from focusing on the activity at hand. Parents and teachers should keep the television set off and not check their emails or messages or pick a newspaper/magazine with the ADHD patient. They should always try to follow a consistent timing in their routine activities.

These tips will help the child or adult suffering from ADHD manage their routine activities with better ease. Over a period, these habits will be taught, and slowly, an effort can be made to guide the patient to the comparatively more complex tasks or routines.

Strategies at Workplace or School for Overcoming ADHD Challenges

Employers want employees who can focus on their work and have a meticulous and systematic approach with a capacity for speedy work. These qualities are conspicuous by their absence in adults with ADHD. They are restless, fearful, and unsure of themselves and can get easily distracted. They have no correctly structured sense of time or various activities. So, it is difficult for them to retain their job. But, that doesn't mean patients with ADHD cannot excel in studies and their careers. It may be difficult for them, but surely not impossible. Here are a few ways to help you improve your effectiveness at school or work and boost your performance.

Improving Competency

Medication therapy, guidance from experts, meditation, relaxation techniques, a job that you will be interested in, a job that does not physically and mentally demand too much from you, flexible working hours, quiet working conditions and helpful colleagues; All of these would make up a perfect combination that can make it possible for adults with ADHD to reach the competency levels acceptable to their employer. But, not all adults affected by ADHD will find such positions. They can think of taking up independent services that they can handle confidently and comfortably.

Steps That Help Retain a Job

ADHD adults can discuss the needs of their condition and get help from their boss. Keep a planner and refer to it constantly; write down the points discussed with colleagues, plan regular breaks for you to recoup, set achievable goals and be happy with what you achieve. These tips will surely help you retain your job and slowly climb the ladder of success towards a higher position.

Improvement in School Performance

ADHD children will have many difficulties in their school. They fare better when they set a daily classroom routine, have all the rules mentioned on a classroom wall, and refer to the lessons displayed on the blackboard. They can be given the sense of a structured life by providing them with a timetable, lists, deadlines, and frequent and regular reminders.

Development of Executive Functions

Executive functions need good memory, reasoning out things, and flexibility in approach, planning, execution, and solving problems. ADHD children have to be trained to master these to some degree with the help of experts. They have to be prepared to analyse problems, evolve a workable plan to solve them with the help of a coach, learn to organise everything necessary to put the plan into action, develop different solutions for the same problems, learn to adjust and modify their solution to a changing problem, and complete the task with single-minded determination without allowing anything to distract them. The development of these management capacities will help the child and the adult affected by ADHD.

Time Management

Time management does not come easily to the persons affected by ADHD. They have to be put through regular practice sessions to estimate broadly the time needed for a small number of elementary tasks like drawing a simple sketch, writing a few paragraphs, finishing lunch or walking from the classroom to the workshop. They should be persuaded to use a clock as often as they can. They should be given a few minutes to perform an activity, and the alarm should be set for that time so that they get an idea of how time flows.

A Quick Start

ADHD-affected persons have to be trained to start a job as soon as they have it. This step is one of the most challenging tasks for them, and they should be prepared every day to begin their work quickly on any given activity. They should also be encouraged to look back at what they have done in the previous hour and record it to have some clarity about the task, time, and organisation needed to do it.

Accept Children as They Are

Parents of an ADHD child have first to accept the child's limitations. They have to recognise the child's other hidden skills or capacities, learn to respect them and help them develop their skills and use them fully. Each child has some strengths. Parents have to try and focus on them and motivate the child to achieve the best with them.

Love and Understanding

Often, the child may not be able to use these capabilities and perform some elementary tasks. The parents must not lose heart and patience at such times. They have to display understanding, love, and empathy for the child in such difficult phases and urge them to perform even simpler tasks to gain confidence and learn and perform more complex jobs in the future.

Curb Impulsiveness

ADHD persons are hyperactive and impulsive. These symptoms can take many forms, from reasonable to dangerous or offensive behaviour. They tend to let out some remarks they will be sorry about immediately afterwards. Adults with ADHD are usually able to curb their impulsive traits. However, the child must cultivate the habit by explaining the consequences of such actions with great patience and empathy.

Counter-Measures

The best way to control impulsiveness involves regular treatment and medication, understanding ADHD and its effects in one's own practical life, being attentive to everything that is happening in the present. Additionally, noting down the impact of their actions and remembering them, countering the negative thoughts with something positive as soon as they occur to you, taking steps that will make it difficult for you to act impulsively and learning to relax with a calming activity at the first sign of impulsive behaviour will prove fruitful.

Life cannot be easy for persons affected by ADHD. It is equally difficult for the parents of ADHD-affected children. It is highly recommended for parents to learn everything about ADHD and handle the child or the grown-up person with love, trust and understanding so that the child responds by doing his best, realises his true potential and excels in something he is interested in.

Effective Conventional Treatment Options and Counselling methods to Prevent Your ADHD Traits from Decreasing Your Effectiveness

A child affected by attention deficit hyperactivity disorder (ADHD) often becomes a target of fun and even ridicule in a classroom full of average students. Their physical imperfections set them at a disadvantage. The general reaction of their peers scares them and puts more pressure on them. They need much more than a helping hand from the teachers and the school.

Medicines

Medicines are prescribed to curb symptoms of ADHD. Symptoms include hyperactivity, inattention and impulsivity. Medication and behavioural therapies complement each other in the treatment of ADHD children. It is necessary to observe the children when they start on medication. The dose has to be correct, as there is a possibility of side effects in some patients. In most cases, the severity of the side effects decreases within a few weeks of taking the medicines. The dosage can be modified if necessary.

Types of Medicines

The usual medicines used in treating ADHD are stimulants, atomoxetine, clonidine, guanfacine and antidepressants. Stimulants are instrumental in cutting down hyperactivity and impulsivity and improving focus. Clonidine and guanfacine treat aggression, inattention and impulsive characteristics.

These medicines must be taken on a continuous basis. The medication effects have to be carefully observed and meticulously recorded. In fact, close observation and an extensive recording of the behaviours of an ADHD child form the basis of treatment of an ADHD patient.

ADHD Counselling

Counselling for ADHD includes talking therapies. These encourage the affected children to talk about their problems. These can be useful for children and also parents. Discussions give a vent to pent-up feelings and have a bit of a cathartic effect. They also do much good to the parents. Behavioural therapies usually have a reward system that tempts ADHD children to curb their symptoms. These back specific actions by promising a small reward for performing that action.

Behavioural Therapies

Cognitive-behavioural therapy tries to change the thinking and subsequent actions. Training in social skills puts the child in various roles. Role-play helps them understand how to behave with others and how their ways affect them. Counsellors can also be involved in individual, small group or extensive group guidance sessions. They can guide the parents as well as teachers.

Parental Response

Parents have to accept the child as they are. They have to realise that the medicines can only help control the symptoms, not cure them. When they tackle the child, they must understand the difference between discipline and punishment. They must not punish the child because of the failure to curb some behaviour. Parents should not cultivate a habit of rejecting every idea of their child. They should respond positively to the excellent conduct of their child. They should also anticipate some potentially dangerous situations and act early to defuse them.

Family Education

Family education programs are for parents of ADHD children. They are taught how to speak with the affected child, spend time with the children by playing with them, and speak or not to speak to them. Specific training programs help the parents learn ways to improve the child's behaviour and attention span. Sometimes, these courses can be organised for the child and their parents.

Behavioural Training

Children with ADHD have to develop specific skills to be able to listen to something for long. They have to learn to be attentive and to follow directions. They need to be trained in various social competencies. If they are trained in these basic skills, they can be more successful in their social and academic life.

Group Discussions

Group discussions among parents of ADHD children can produce ideas that can be very helpful in individual cases. Such gatherings keep coming up with good new ideas and strategies.

Some of the ideas are innovative. Each parent can assess these for use at home and devise a way to better control their child. Such groups prove to be an invaluable support in the long. It is not easy for the parents of ADHD children to connect with parents of normal children. They are often frustrated and experience loneliness. Parent support groups play a very positive role in such situations. Most parents are the victims of such a feeling, at least in the initial stage after confirming the ADHD diagnosis in their child.

The life of ADHD children is not easy. They cannot sit still in a classroom. They cannot concentrate for long. They cannot perform most academic exercises. They find it challenging to complete homework. This circumstance leads to their having a tough time in class with other students and teachers. They need a helping hand, much special attention and regular coaching with patience. They need to be allowed to work at their own pace. Parents, teachers and the school have a special and a more personal role to play in the life of all ADHD children.

Holistic Approach to ADHD Management

The purpose of yoga and meditation is to bring our body, mind and soul into harmony with the help of breathing exercises and some physical poses. The practice of yoga can help ADHD patients achieve a balance necessary for their physical, emotional, and spiritual health. Patients diagnosed with ADHD are usually distracted, stressed out, and unable to focus. They can benefit from yoga as it ensures excellent stress relief, self-awareness and increased focus.

The Benefits of Yoga for ADHD Patients:

- Yoga teaches the patient to concentrate and pay attention to specific small movements and processes in the body, such as breathing. These muscle movements can be the ones you have been unaware of previously.

- When you begin to master movements and control the muscles in the body, it allows you to unlock the hidden powers of the mind.

- Yoga creates a relaxed and focused mind. The constant assault on our senses worsens symptoms of ADHD due to technology, and mental stress or frustration can be countered by practising yoga.

- To get into a yoga posture, you have to slow down to gain control over your actions. Patients with ADHD often have an untamed mind that diverts their attention and pulls them in several directions all at once.

- Balancing the body required for practising yoga postures helps balance the mind and control the thought process.

- Yoga offers a drug-free way to gain more control over your body and mind. It is a safe and effective means of improving concentration and relaxation without fearing side effects and drug interactions.

The Role of Meditation and Breathing Exercises in Managing ADHD

Patients with ADHD can have a peaceful and skilled mind by regularly practising meditation and deep breathing exercises. Here's how you can practice these therapies to achieve the benefit of this unique therapy:

1) Find a comfortable position or your comfort zone to eliminate additional distractions in any form of physical discomfort. Remember, you are the best judge of the most comfortable position for you.

2) Take slow and deep breaths. As you relax, your breathing will slow down naturally.

3) Choose a focus for yourself, like something to listen to. You can pay attention to your breathing or even repeat a phrase or word in your mind. You can also opt for a visual focus like a candle flame. Continue for 5 minutes initially and gradually increase to 15 minutes a day.

4) Most patients with ADHD get unbearably restless when they are required to be still for an extended period. Hence, it is crucial to work with your weaknesses rather than forcing yourself to be still when you have a higher need for activity. Experts recommend a moving form of meditation as an effective variety for sitting meditation for ADHD patients. I would recommend you to choose a simple and repetitive activity for meditation, like walking.

5) It's time to meditate. Yet, you may have some thoughts still clamouring for your attention. When you feel your attention drifting apart, gently disengage your attention to bring your mind back to focus. Keep taking deep breaths while doing the same.

6) Once you have gotten into a meditation groove, you will attain a state of relaxation more quickly. A few deep breaths would be enough to do the trick once you get used to the routine. Regularly practising this will help you increase your attention span and improve your focus and concentration. It will also control your impulsive and hyperactive behaviours.

Exercises to Sharpen Your Mental Skill and Reduce Your Anxiety and Impulsiveness

Exercise 1

Take a book, open any page and count the words in any paragraph. Then, measure the words again to check whether you have counted them correctly.

Once this becomes easy, you can try counting the words from the whole page. Upon mastering this, do the counting mentally with your eyes, without using your finger to point at each word.

Exercise 2

In your mind, count the numbers backwards, from 100 to 1.

Exercise 3

Count the number from 100 to 1 in your mind, skipping every two or three numbers, like 100, 98, 96, and so on.

Exercise 4

Recollect the names of all the children in your class. Try to remember their full names and possibly, in the order of their roll numbers.

Exercise 5

Take a bowl, add into it different types of grains and mix. Then, separate all the grains. This routine will help improve your focus and attention span.

These exercises may seem too simple, but they can be difficult for a child with ADHD. But, remember, constant practice is the secret to achieving success. The more time your child devotes to these exercises, the faster they will be able to progress. However, it would help if you allowed them to do it gradually. Start with the easier ones and then move progressively to exercises that take more time or need more focus.

How to Improve Your Child's Self-Confidence and Prepare Them to Be a Capable Adult

ADHD parents have to spend a lot of time, energy, and money managing and helping the child through school and college years. The skills and knowledge learned during these years may not ensure the child an entry into the workforce. The child has to be able to manage his life independently, tackle and overcome the obstacles coming in the way in his everyday life, and take failures in his stride so that they can face life with renewed zest.

The First Step

The ADHD child must first gain a reasonably clear idea of their capacities and limitations. Can they take care of themselves independently as far as the ADHD medications and other Dos and Don'ts are concerned? The answers to this will decide if the child has a chance to lead a reasonably independent life.

Healthy Self-Esteem

One major contributor to such a happy state is to help the child develop self-esteem. Children with high self-esteem can demonstrate their independence through their actions. They will not shy away from assuming the jobs of responsibility. They will take the right amount of pride in their achievements and will be able to take frustration in their stride. Self-esteem will also allow them to be ready to take upon themselves new and newer tasks, have excellent control over themselves, be prepared even to help others and accept help from others. They will feel that they are wanted and cared for by all the persons around them.

Let the Child Struggle a Bit

Parents have to allow the child to handle as many aspects of their life as possible. They should not jump in to help them all the time. Let them struggle a bit. Let them work hard and gradually learn to work enough to handle themselves without the help of parents all the time.

Let the children adapt themselves to the challenges they face. Parents will always be there as solid support, but they will have to let ADHD children manage their life to the greatest extent possible. They should be able to handle minor problems that prop up time and again in this context.

Support Independence in Everyday Life

ADHD children should be trained to get up by themselves at the right time in the morning, complete morning chores, prepare to go to school/workplace, walk up to the bus stop, travel by bus, get down at the right stop, handle money matters and then, work through office hours – all these without being overcome by fatigue, disinterest or boredom. They should also be able to concentrate on the work at hand, tackle people in their work, analyse problems and find their solutions. The parents and the child have to work together to make all these things possible so that everybody's life becomes much more meaningful, satisfying, and filled with happiness.

Social Skills

An ADHD child has to be trained in social skills. Furthermore, they have to practise learning to address someone after making eye contact. They have to be told repeatedly not to interrupt anyone while talking. They must realise that they must speak in turns. They have to be trained to react to teasing, which they often have to face in school life.

The Biggest Influence

It is for the parents to cultivate such an attitude in their children by treating them correctly all the time, being supportive and encouraging, and being frank and firm. Parents should realise that they have the most significant influence over their child and every act of theirs has to be positive and full of love. They should praise the child, not be critical all the time and should develop a positive outlook about their child.

Financial Transactions

ADHD persons need to be able to handle their finances competently. However, this can create different types of practical problems and much stress for them. Hence, they have to be trained assiduously in each financial process they cannot avoid. They should be able to drive the fear of such transactions from their mind. They should be taught in using technology to ease the pressure of financial processes. They also have to be helped to develop the habit of not spending impulsively.

Discussion and Reenactment

It is always good for everybody to talk things over. A discussion helps define a problem. Role models can be found during such talks. Venting out anger and openly admitting that some development hurt you can continuously improve the situation. Discussions and reenactments of the situations help to show ADHD children that every issue can be seen from a different angle by different people. They are then ready to modify their responses and become more willing to consider the viewpoints of others.

ADHD kids and adults will need their parents all the time. But, it will be in the interest of their own life to make them as independent as possible in as many spheres of life as possible. You are advised to follow the tips given here one by one so that the process of being independent becomes less complex for the children and they can become capable adults.

Conclusion

Attention Deficit Hyperactivity Disorder (ADHD) was considered a disease affecting only children. It was thought that it could persist in adulthood only in a few rare cases. Now, it is known that a large percentage of children who have ADHD continue to suffer from at least some of its effects in adulthood.

There is no standard or universal method for diagnosing and treating ADHD in children and adults. The diagnosis is usually based on the information gathered from parents and the affected person's school assessments, complete physical check-ups, and the evaluation of their speech and language.

Parents and teachers have a significant role in the development of ADHD children along the right lines. They should strictly avoid criticizing the children. They have to be patient and cannot expect these children to do the things like the other regular students. ADHD children tend to lose concentration quickly, have problems beginning some activity, cannot sustain their interest in anything for long and have almost no structured idea about time. These cases must be considered while setting goals for the ADHD child.

Parents and teachers have to be supportive and encouraging. However, they must let the ADHD children struggle on their own to reach their levels of competencies in various spheres. They have to coax and cajole them into becoming independent in as many fields as they possibly can. The parents and the teachers have to ensure that the ADHD kid can manage their medications, prepare themselves for school, and catch the bus or the right mode of transport to reach school and back home, and handle their money well.

Impulsive activity is another of the traits of persons affected by ADHD. Its incidence is low in adults compared to that in children. The problem-solving strategies, skills training and self-monitoring usually succeed remarkably in improving self-control for preventing impulsiveness.

Neither diagnosis nor treatment of ADHD is straightforward. Both are complex and debatable. There can be no consensus on making an accurate diagnosis and what treatment is to be prescribed to ensure long-term progress. It usually boils down to the best the parents and teachers can do for the child and what best ADHD adults can do for themselves. Each case is treated in a unique way that sounds best for that individual. There has to be a thorough review when a child becomes an adult. The approach and treatment during this transition have to change regularly per the changes in the affected person.

Learning everything that you can about ADHD and evaluating your child's strengths and weaknesses will help you understand work on their weaknesses to turn them into their strengths. Encourage him to improve on his skills and look for ways to help your child use these skills as a means for earning a livelihood. Make sure your child gets the primary education at least, and make them a capable adult who is financially independent.

Symptoms, Causes, and Treatment for Duchenne Muscular Dystrophy

Duchenne Muscular Dystrophy or DMD refers to a rapidly progressive form of muscular dystrophy that is caused due to the mutations in the DMD gene. Ayurveda offers effective treatment for controlling the symptoms of this condition.

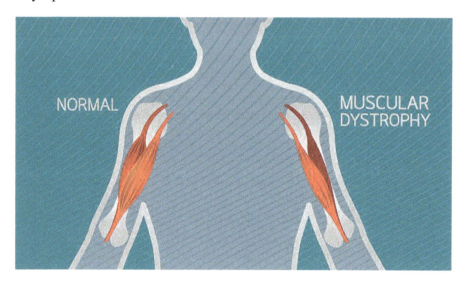

Here is a brief discussion about the causes and risk factors of DMD and natural Ayurvedic treatments to relieve the symptoms of this condition.

What Is Duchenne Muscular Dystrophy?

DMD refers to a rapidly progressive type of muscular dystrophy, which primarily affects boys. This disorder is caused due to alterations (mutations) in a gene, known as a DMD gene, inherited in families in the X-linked recessive manner.

The DMD gene is the second largest gene that can encode the muscle protein known as dystrophin. Boys diagnosed with Duchenne muscular dystrophy have defects that prevent the formation of the dystrophin protein in the muscles. As a result, they develop a progressive loss of muscle functions and weakness. These symptoms often begin in the legs.

Duchenne muscular dystrophy has been found to affect nearly 1 in 3500 male births across the world. Since it is an inherited disorder, the common risk factors include having a family history of DMD. However, it can also occur in patients who have no known family history of this condition.

What Are the Symptoms of DMD?

The symptoms of DMD usually appear before the age of six years and sometimes as early as during infancy. Typically, the initial noticeable sign is the delay of motor milestones, such as sitting or standing independently. The average age for walking in boys diagnosed with DMD is approximately 18 months. There is also progressive muscle weakness in the legs and pelvic muscles.

These symptoms are associated with losing muscle mass (or wasting). The muscle weakness, thus caused, can also lead to a waddling gait and difficulty in climbing stairs.

Muscle weakness may also occur in the neck, arms, and other body areas. However, it may not be as severe or occur as early as in the lower part of the body.

The progress of DMD may continue to occur over time, causing several other symptoms. For example, the calf muscles initially become more prominent in size. Enlarged muscle tissues are eventually replaced by fats and connective tissues resulting in pseudohypertrophy. Muscle contractures begin to occur in the legs, making the muscle tissues unusable.

These changes occur due to the shortening of muscle fibres. Fibrosis occurring in the connective tissues can also be responsible for these symptoms in boys with DMD.

Occasionally, there may be pain in the calf muscles.

This disease's symptoms usually appear in boys aged one to six years. There is a steady decline in muscle strength between the ages of six and 11 years. By the age of 10 years, braces might be required for walking, and by the age of 12, most boys with DMD are wheelchair users.

Moreover, bones grow abnormally, resulting in skeletal deformities in different body parts, especially the spine.

Skeletal deformities and muscular weakness frequently contribute to the risk of breathing disorders in these boys. Cardiomyopathy (enlargement of the heart) can also occur in nearly all cases of DMD. These complications may develop in the early teenage in some boys and all boys after 18 years of age.

Intellectual impairment may also occur, though it is not inevitable and not known to become worse as the condition progresses.

Unfortunately, very few boys with DMD can live beyond 30 years. Breathing complications and cardiomyopathy are the common causes that contribute to the risk of mortality.

How Is DMD Diagnosed?

The clinical diagnosis of DMD is often made when a boy develops progressive and symmetrical weakness of muscles. The symptoms presenting before the age of five years and the highly elevated levels of creatine kinase in the blood could point to the diagnosis of DMD in these patients.

Genetic testing for assessing the genetic instructions in the body could be performed on a blood sample to determine the changes in the DMD gene to establish its diagnosis, often with or without a muscle biopsy.

In most cases, a combination of the clinical findings, changes in creatine kinase levels in the blood, family history, muscle biopsy, and dystrophin studies are performed to confirm the diagnosis.

If left untreated, the affected boys may become wheelchair-dependent before turning 13.

Treatment of Duchenne Muscular Dystrophy

The treatment of DMD is aimed at relieving the symptoms. The aggressive management of complications such as dilated cardiomyopathy with the help of anti-congestive drugs is often recommended. In some cases, cardiac transplantation may be needed to treat dilated cardiomyopathy.

Assistive devices for managing respiratory complications are recommended, especially at night, to prevent breathing difficulties.

Medications like prednisone, a steroid, are given to improve functions and strength of the muscles in boys with DMD. Prednisone might help by prolonging the ability of the patient to walk by nearly two to five years. However, this drug is known to cause severe side effects, including weight gain, behavioural changes, high blood pressure, and delayed growth.

Physical therapy may help improve mobility and prevent the risk of developing contractures. Surgery might be needed for treating scoliosis and severe contractures.

Ayurvedic Treatment of Muscular Dystrophy

Ayurveda can offer effective treatment for muscular dystrophy. The therapy aims to support muscle growth to improve the patient's quality of life. As this condition is inherited, the chances of complete cure to this disease are too less. However, regular treatment could improve the range of movements in the body's joints.

The Ayurvedic treatment plan includes a combination of different programs that could bring about muscle empowerment.

Some of these treatments include:

- Panchakarma therapy
- Elakizzhi
- Abhyangam
- Til-Masha
- Pinda Swedam
- Navarakizhi
- Kashaya Vasti
- Anuvasana Vasti

These Ayurvedic treatments are believed to work by removing harmful toxins from the body, balancing the doshas, and rejuvenating the body's cells, including muscles, thus improving muscle strength and flexibility.

Besides these therapies, Ayurveda also recommends including yoga and meditation sessions in the treatment protocol. Yoga and meditation are incorporated for improving blood circulation to all the body organs, including the muscles and joints. This practice would help minimise the risk of developing other medical conditions by improving breathing and other vital functions of the body.

The proper diet plan is also one of the most effective ways to control the symptoms of DMD. It would ensure that appropriate nutritional support is provided to the body such that it can aid in muscle development and other organs and tissues of the body.

A nutritious and balanced diet would also help pacify the imbalanced doshas and restore the normal functions of the body's vital systems and hormonal levels.

A herbal decoction may also be included in the treatment plan to improve the results further. The internal consumption of herbal decoction would provide relief from symptoms while also reducing inflammation and oxidative stress at the cellular level, thereby slowing down the progress of the disease.

Conclusion

Ayurveda provides safe and effective treatments for boys with DMD. It would reduce the disabilities experienced due to the lack of muscle tone and coordination. The Ayurvedic therapies may also reduce muscle strain, relieve pain and stiffness, and slow down muscular dystrophy.

It may also support the build-up of new muscle mass and thus, improve the quality of life of boys affected with DMD.

A customized treatment plan for boys with DMD based on their symptoms and the imbalances in the doshas could help them recover from muscle weakness. The treatment would also promote recovery from the symptoms by rejuvenating the mind and soul, allowing them to feel better.

What Is Down Syndrome and Can It be Treated?

Down syndrome is a genetic disorder caused by abnormal cell division resulting in an extra partial or complete copy of chromosome 21. The additional genetic material causes abnormal changes during development resulting in the typical physical features of this syndrome.

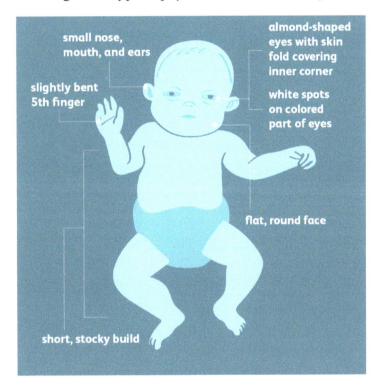

The symptoms of Down syndrome vary in severity among different individuals, causing developmental delay and lifelong intellectual disability. It is one of the most common genetic chromosomal disorders known to cause severe learning disabilities in children. It can also cause other medical abnormalities, such as cardiac and digestive disorders.

A better understanding of why Down syndrome occurs and early interventions could significantly improve the quality of life of children and adults affected with this disorder and help them live a fulfilling life.

What Are the Symptoms of Down Syndrome?

Patients with Down syndrome often experience intellectual or developmental problems that could be too mild, moderate, or intense. Some patients are healthy, while some develop significant health problems like heart defects.

Adults and children with Down syndrome often have distinct facial features. As also indicated by the image above, some of the typical features of this condition include:

- Small head
- Flattened face
- Protruding tongue
- Short neck
- Upward slanting of the eyelids
- Unusually shaped or small ears
- Poor muscle tone
- Short height
- Broad and short hands with just one crease on the palm
- Excessive flexibility
- Relatively shorter fingers and smaller hands and feet
- Small white spots on the iris of the eye known as the Brushfield's spots

However, it should be noted that not all patients with this condition have the same facial or other physical features.

Intellectual Disabilities in Patients With Down Syndrome

Most patients with Down syndrome have moderate to severe cognitive impairment. The language learning is delayed, and their short and long-term memory may be impaired.

What Are the Causes of Down Syndrome?

Human cells contain 23 pairs of chromosomes, and one chromosome for each pair comes from the father and the other from the child's mother.

Down syndrome occurs due to the abnormal cell division in chromosome 21. The abnormalities in the process of cell division can result in the extra full or partial chromosome 21. This additional genetic material is responsible for valuing the specific characteristic features and the developmental problems in children with Down syndrome.

One of the three genetic variations given below can lead to Down syndrome:

Trisomy 21

In nearly 95% of cases, Down syndrome is caused by trisomy 21, in which the patient has three copies of chromosome 21, instead of the regular two copies, in all the cells of the body. This case is caused by abnormalities in cell division that occurred during the development of an egg cell or a sperm cell.

Translocation Down Syndrome

Down syndrome may occur when the part of chromosome 21 gets translocated or attached to another chromosome before or during conception. Children who have this abnormality have the usual two copies of chromosome 21. However, they also have some additional genetic material from chromosome 21 attached or translocated to another chromosome.

Mosaic Down Syndrome

Mosaic Down syndrome is a rare form of Down syndrome in which a patient has only a few cells with extra genetic material or an extra copy of chromosome 21. The mosaic of abnormal and normal cells is caused due to the abnormal cell division occurring after fertilisation.

Is Down Syndrome Inherited?

In most cases, Down syndrome is not inherited. It is caused due to mistakes occurring during the process of cell division during the early phase of the fetus development.

However, translocation of Down syndrome may be passed from parent to child. Only about three to 4% of patients with Down syndrome have translocation, and a very few of them have inherited it from one of their parents.

When a balanced translocation is inherited, the father or mother has some form of rearranged genetic material from chromosome 21 on the other chromosome, but without any extra genetic material. This case suggests they may not have any signs of Down syndrome but may still pass on the unbalanced translocation to the child causing Down syndrome in them.

What Are the Risk Factors of Down Syndrome?

There are no known environmental and behavioural factors that can cause Down syndrome.

Some parents have a higher risk of having a child with Down syndrome. The common risk factors for this condition include:

- A woman's age. The risk of giving birth to a baby with Down syndrome increases with the mother's age as older eggs have a higher risk of abnormal chromosome division. The risk of women conceiving a child with Down syndrome rises after 35 years of age. But, children with Down syndrome are also born to women under 35 years.

- Being carriers of abnormal genetic translocation responsible for causing Down syndrome can cause the mother or father to pass on the genetic translocation for Down syndrome to the child.

- Parents who have one child diagnosed with Down syndrome or parents who have the translocation themselves have a higher risk of having another child with this syndrome.

Genetic counsellors could help parents assess their risk of having a child with Down syndrome.

What Are the Complications Linked to Down Syndrome?

- Heart defects are common in children with Down syndrome. These defects may occur due to abnormalities in the division of cells.

- Gastrointestinal defects can occur in some patients with Down syndrome. It may include the structural abnormalities affecting the intestines, trachea, oesophagus, and anus. The chances of developing digestive conditions like heartburn (gastroesophageal reflux), GI blockage, and celiac disease may be higher in patients with this condition.

- Immune disorders may occur due to abnormalities in the development of the immune system. Patients with Down syndrome often have an increased risk of developing autoimmune conditions, infectious diseases like pneumonia, and some forms of cancer.

- Sleep apnea may occur in patients with Down syndrome due to the changes in the throat's soft tissues and skeletal structures. These changes could lead to an airways obstruction, putting the children and adults with this syndrome at risk of obstructive sleep apnea.

- Patients with Down syndrome have a higher tendency to become obese compared to the general population.

- Some patients with Down syndrome may develop a misalignment of the top two vertebrae in the neck resulting in atlantoaxial instability. It can put them at risk of severe injuries to the spinal cord due to the overextension of the neck.

- Young children with Down syndrome tend to have an increased risk of developing leukaemia.

- Patients with Down syndrome have a higher risk of dementia. The signs and symptoms of dementia may begin around 50 years. Having Down syndrome can also increase their risk of developing neurodegenerative disorders like Alzheimer's disease.

Prevention and Treatment of Down Syndrome

There are no known ways to prevent Down syndrome development in a child. People, who are at a high risk of having a child with this syndrome or those who already have one child diagnosed with Down syndrome, should consult a genetic counsellor before planning pregnancy.

A genetic counsellor would help them understand their chances of having a child with Down syndrome.

Ayurvedic Treatment for Down Syndrome

Ayurveda recommends several herbal formulations for the effective management of Down's syndrome.

Ayurvedic treatments and herbal formulas would help improve the brain's functions and reduce symptoms of this condition, such as the bulging of the tongue, slanting of the eyes, and loss of muscle tone. It can also help facilitate improved mobility in the lives of patients with Down's syndrome.

Down Syndrome Concepts in Ayurveda

The disease referred to as Down syndrome in Western medicine has been classified as the Adhyatmika disease in Ayurveda. These diseases tend to have symptoms that are caused due to poor mental health or spiritual factors.

The diseases included under the category of Adhyatmika often comprise conditions that are genetic or congenital. The term commonly used to refer to genetic conditions is Anuvamshika Roga.

According to Ayurveda, the disturbances caused due to an Anuvamshika Roga could affect a child's intellectual, emotional, and social abilities. It may also hamper their learning ability while reducing their motivation, determination, and memory.

Ayurvedic medicines could help patients suffering from this syndrome by improving memory, physical abilities, hearing, vision, cognitive functions, muscle tone, and coordination, thereby relieving various functional deficits. Ayurvedic treatments would also help improve the patient's quality of life and promote social realisation.

Ayurveda applies several yogic techniques, including some asanas and exercises, to help children overcome the symptoms of Down syndrome. This natural system of healing also offers numerous medications and methods for the improvement of symptoms, some of which are aimed at:

- Relieving the effects of physiological or genetic damage

- Restoring the normal development of speech abilities, and motor and cognitive functions
- Improving the memory
- Enhancing the development of independent life skills for better adaptation of the patient to social life

Conclusion

The use of herbs such as Brahmi could help support the brain's functions in these patients. Ayurveda advises patients to adopt healthy lifestyle systems like meditation to improve the symptoms of Down syndrome and promote their intellectual and physical abilities.

Can Ayurveda Provide Relief From the Symptoms of Parkinson's Disease?

Parkinson's disease is a neurodegenerative disorder that affects the functions of the nervous system in which a person's movements are affected. The symptoms of this disease occur due to reduced dopamine levels in the brain.

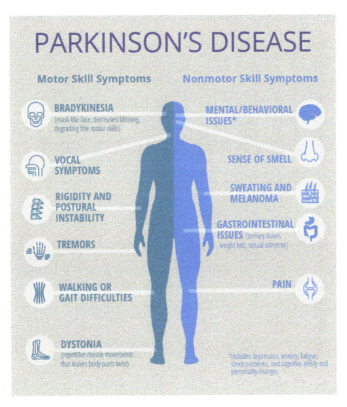

It is believed that genetic changes and exposure to environmental factors, like toxins, might play a vital role in developing this disease.

Given below are the early symptoms of Parkinson's disease and its causes.

Early Signs of Parkinson's Disease

The symptoms of this disease usually develop gradually. They often begin with slight tremors in one hand and the feeling of stiffness. Over a period, other symptoms develop. Some patients may also experience dementia.

The common early signs of Parkinson's disease include:

- Balance and coordination impairments that could cause the person to fall over or drop things
- Movement changes, like tremors
- Fixed facial expressions due to changes in the nerves controlling facial muscles
- The loss of sense of smell
- Changes in gait, such that the person leans slightly forward and shuffles while walking
- More cramped or smaller handwriting
- A voice tremor and a softer voice
- Rapid eye movement sleep disorder
- Sleep problems that might result from restless legs

These movement symptoms often start on one side of the body and affect the other sides gradually.

Some other common symptoms of this condition include:

- Fatigue
- Mood changes and depression
- Dementia
- Constipation
- Difficulty in swallowing and chewing
- Delusions and hallucinations

What Are the Causes of Parkinson's Disease?

Parkinson's disease is a neurological disorder, which develops when abnormal changes occur in the brain. It may occur due to a combination of factors such as:

Low Dopamine Levels

The symptoms of Parkinson's disease mainly result from low levels of a neurotransmitter called dopamine in the brain. It may occur when cells that secrete dopamine in the brain die.

Dopamine plays a crucial role in sending messages to parts of the brain, which control coordination and movements. Hence, low dopamine levels make it harder for the person to control actions.

Low Norepinephrine Levels

This disease may also involve long-term damage to nerve endings, which may halt the production of another neurotransmitter called norepinephrine that contributes to automatic body functions like blood circulation.

The low level of norepinephrine may increase the risk of the motor as well as non-motor symptoms, such as:

- Postural instability
- Stiffness and rigidity
- Difficulty focusing
- Tremors
- Anxiety
- Depression
- Dementia

This deficiency explains why patients with Parkinson's commonly have orthostatic hypotension. Orthostatic hypotension refers to the change in blood pressure when a person stands up, which leads to lightheadedness and increased risk of falling.

Lewy Bodies

Patients with Parkinson's disease often have clumps of a protein called Lewy bodies or alpha-synuclein in their brain.

The accumulation of these Lewy bodies can lead to the loss of nerve cells, resulting in changes in movements, behaviours, thinking, and moods. It may also lead to dementia.

Genetic Link

Experts have identified that some changes in specific genes could have links with the risk of Parkinson's disease.

Prevention of Parkinson's Disease

While it is not possible to prevent the development of Parkinson's disease, some lifelong healthy habits could help reduce the risk of this condition. Ayurveda recommends several healthy strategies to protect yourself against the risk of this condition as discussed beneath:

Avoiding Toxins

It would be best if you took precautions while using potentially toxic chemicals, like herbicides, solvents, and pesticides.

If possible, you should take the following steps to avoid toxic damage caused by exposure to harmful substances:

- Avoiding unnecessary usage of herbicides and pesticides
- Using alternatives to products containing known toxins, like paraquat
- Taking precautions like wearing protective clothing

Avoid Head Trauma

For protection against a traumatic brain injury that could lead to Parkinson's disease, consider taking the following steps:

- Wearing a helmet while cycling or biking
- Using protective headgear while playing contact sports
- Seeking medical attention for a concussion
- Using a safety belt while travelling by car

Exercise

Regular physical activities might help prevent or reduce the symptoms of Parkinson's disease. Physical activities might help maintain the dopamine level in the brain.

Dietary Choices

Some dietary choices could also help reduce the risk of developing Parkinson's. Ayurveda recommends the use of the following herbs and nutritional tips to prevent or relieve symptoms of Parkinson's disease:

- Turmeric: This mild spice is commonly added to curries, teas, soups, and other dishes. It contains an antioxidant ingredient we have been talking about called curcumin. It would help reduce the risk of developing Parkinson's disease by preventing inflammation and oxidative stress and inhibiting the clumping of the alpha-synuclein proteins.
- Flavonoids: It is a natural antioxidant that may lower the risk of Parkinson's disease. Apples, berries, some vegetables, green tea, and red grapes are rich in flavonoids.
- Avoiding aldehydes: The heating and reusing of some cooking oils, like sunflower oil,

might cause aldehydes to form. Aldehydes are toxic chemicals that could increase the risk of Parkinson's disease. For example, potatoes fried in the previously used cooking oils can have a high level of aldehydes.

Conclusion

Parkinson's disease is a chronic condition that involves neurological changes in the brain.

Though experts do not know why this disease occurs, genetic and environmental factors are believed to play a role. Experts have explicitly found strong links between past traumatic brain injuries or exposure to toxins that can increase this condition's risk.

Regular exercise, avoiding toxins, and a healthy diet might help prevent Parkinson's disease and relieve its symptoms to some extent.

What Is Indigestion and Acid Reflux? Ayurvedic Treatments for Improving Digestion

Acid reflux refers to the burning sensation in the lower chest. It occurs when acidic contents of the stomach flow back into the food pipe or the oesophagus. It is called gastro-oesophageal reflux disease (GERD) if it happens too frequently.

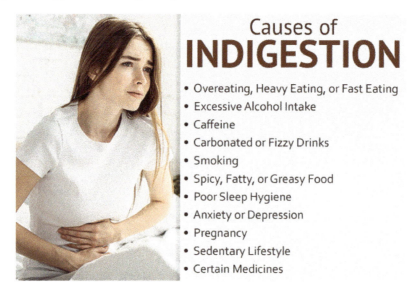

Acid reflux is also called heartburn or acid indigestion. It usually occurs after a heavy meal.

The strong and corrosive hydrochloric acid produced by your stomach lining promotes food digestion and eliminates harmful bacteria. The lining can also protect the stomach from the effects of acid.

The oesophagus though does not have such a protective lining. It is protected only by the gastro-oesophageal sphincter, a ring of muscles, which acts as a one-way valve allowing the food to pass into the stomach while blocking anything that tries to come back into the oesophagus.

This mechanism may fail to operate correctly. When it does so, the acidic content of the stomach could go back into your oesophagus, resulting in the burning sensation.

What Are the Common Symptoms of Acid Reflux?

- Heartburn is an uncomfortable burning sensation in the oesophagus usually felt behind the breastbone. It often originates in the abdomen and spreads to the neck or the throat. It may aggravate when you lie down or bend. It usually lasts for two hours and gets worse after eating

- Sore throat or trouble in swallowing
- Regurgitation of the bitter, acidic fluid into the mouth leaving a bitter taste and an unpleasant burning sensation in the mouth
- Wheezing and nausea
- Persistent dry cough
- Hoarseness in the morning
- Bad breath
- Children and infants may have vomiting, cough, or respiratory problems

People of all ages can get affected by recurring acid reflux. Various factors could contribute to the development of this condition.

A physical abnormality affecting the stomach and diaphragm called a hiatus hernia occurs due to a hole in the diaphragm that allows a part of the stomach to enter the chest cavity, causing GERD.

Pregnancy can lead to acid reflux as there can be additional pressure on the internal organs.

Some other factors that can cause acid reflux and indigestion include lifestyle or dietary issues.

Although all the reasons for the occurrence of acid reflux cannot be known, it can be blamed on some lifestyle aspects such as:

- Obesity
- High salt intake
- Low intake of dietary fibre
- Absence of sufficient exercise
- Active or passive smoking
- Intake of drugs for asthma, painkillers, antidepressants, sedatives, and antihistamines

It is better not to leave acid reflux or GERD untreated for long. It may lead to several complications, some of which could be serious.

Complications of Indigestion and Acid Reflux

- The acid damage can produce a scar that makes swallowing difficult.

- An increased risk of stomach or oesophageal cancer. Frequent heartburn can be a precursor to cancer of the oesophagus, stomach, or vocal cords.

- Repeated ulceration of the oesophagal tissues could lead to the formation of a scar, which has no elasticity. As a result, a stricture is formed that cannot expand and relax to facilitate the passage of food through the oesophagus.

- Due to this, the food tends to get stuck at different places in the oesophagus as it moves down into the stomach.

- Inflammation of the oesophagus lining causes irritation, bleeding, or even ulcer formation.

- In Barrett's oesophagus, the tissues lining it change into the cells in the lower gastrointestinal tract. These cells have a higher tendency to turn malignant.

Some simple ways could help the symptoms of indigestion and acid reflux to subside. These include eating smaller meals, avoidance of foods, drinks, and medicines linked to your heartburns, not lying down for two to three hours after meals, avoiding increased pressure on your abdomen, losing weight if you are obese, and stopping smoking.

A patient affected by acid reflux should note the circumstances that led to attacks of symptoms in detail, such as foods eaten, smoking, medications, or stress.

This information can be analysed to find the correlation between heartburn and the possible triggers. Avoidance of the stimuli could decrease the frequency of indigestion and acid reflux symptoms.

Appropriate lifestyle changes can appreciably relieve the symptoms and their frequency. Patients can also obtain substantial relief by following a proper diet and making some simple changes in their lifestyle.

Diet Recommendations for Patients with Indigestion and Acid Reflux Disease

The lower end of the oesophagus has a ring of muscles that acts as a one-way gate for food to pass to the stomach but stops anything from returning from the stomach into the food pipe.

As discussed earlier, when its operation becomes faulty, the stomach's acidic contents tend to splash back into the oesophagus, creating heartburn.

Hoarseness, cough, and shortness of breath may also occur when the stomach contents seep into the breathing passages.

Some foods can contribute to the relaxation of the lower oesophageal muscle, thus causing GERD.

Cereals, vegetables, dairy products, fruits, and meats are usually safe and do not lead to GERD. A vitamin C supplement might be necessary if you cannot tolerate oranges or tomatoes due to their acidic nature.

Here are some foods that can aggravate GERD symptoms and have to be kept out of your diet.

- Fatty or fried foods
- Foods or soups with cream
- Whole milk
- Fast foods
- Oils
- Chocolate
- Peppermint and spearmint
- Onions
- Tobacco in all forms because nicotine can weaken the oesophagal muscles
- Alcohols
- Chewing gum and hard candy could lead to the swallowing of more air and worsen belching and reflux

Some foods can cause irritation and inflammation of the lower oesophagus, and hence, their intake must be curtailed or avoided altogether.

Here is the list of such foods:

- Citrus fruits like orange, pineapple, grapefruit, tomato, and their juices
- Caffeinated soft drinks
- Coffee
- Spicy or acidic foods
- Tea

An essential aspect of a GERD diet is that some foods in some groups can be eaten, while others in the same group need to be avoided.

For example, low-fat milk may be consumed, while whole milk and chocolate milk should be avoided. While some vegetables can be consumed, fried and creamy vegetables and tomatoes have to be kept out. Similarly, while apples, pears, melons, peaches, bananas, and berries could be included in your diet safely, oranges, pineapples, and grapefruit should not be. Bread and grains with low-fat content are also okay, provided they are not prepared with whole milk and high-fat ingredients.

Sweets prepared with low-fat milk are often allowed. Chocolate and desserts made with oils and fats are not suitable for these patients. Soups, too, should be fat-free or low-fat.

Below are some GERD-friendly foods that could help patients susceptible to GERD reduce their symptoms.

- Complex carbohydrates like oatmeal, rice, whole grain bread, and couscous should ideally form a large chunk of your regular diet.

- Potatoes and other root vegetables can provide good healthy carbs and fibres sources.

- Probiotics like yoghurt have good bacteria. They can promote digestion and offer some protection against harmful bacteria. Probiotics could be helpful for most people suffering from GERD.

- An increased fibre intake from fruits and vegetables can be helpful against GERD.

- Choose grilled, poached, baked, or broiled lean meats.

- Lean proteins are recommended for GERD patients.

- Consume unsaturated fats from peanut butter and plants like olive, canola, sesame, sunflower, avocados, and peanuts. Polyunsaturated fats like safflower, corn, or soybean and fatty fish like trout and salmon are excellent choices.

However, individuals differ significantly in their response to various types of foods. Some of them may not be affected at all by the foods listed here, though they are known to aggravate the GERD symptoms, while some would be badly affected by the healthy and safe ones listed above.

GERD patients need to modify these lists for themselves and manage their diet to bring out the best results.

Maintaining a diary of what you eat, how much you eat, when you eat, and the results can help achieve the desired results.

Suppose there is any doubt about a specific food. In that case, you can initially try it in less quantity and then gradually increase consumption until you reach the amount an average person would check if you develop any symptoms. This step will help you create a list of safe, healthy, and balanced foods for you.

Effective Natural Herbs and Home Remedies for Treating Acid Reflux

Several chemical-based medications claim to offer immediate relief to people suffering from heartburn and acid reflux. However, the relief provided by the over-the-counter and prescription medicines is often temporary.

On the other hand, some people prefer adopting lifestyle changes that help them overcome the burning sensation caused by acid reflux and indigestion. One such change includes herbal remedies, which can be easily prepared at home.

Let us look at some of the best herbs and simple home remedies for treating acid reflux. We will also examine some lifestyle changes that can help treat and avoid acid reflux.

Aloe Juice

Aloe juice is known to provide relief in severe burns, sunburns, and inflammation. The soothing property of aloe vera is not restricted just to the external parts of the body; it may also help ease and soothe the digestive tract.

The anti-inflammatory action of aloe vera juice would help treat heartburn and indigestion. When you feel that your stomach or oesophagus is irritated or inflamed due to acid reflux, try consuming a glass of fresh aloe vera juice to instantly get rid of the condition.

Regular consumption of this juice would prevent inflammation around the lower oesophageal region and reduce the risk of ulcers and cancer.

Apple Cider Vinegar

One of the common misconceptions associated with acid reflux and indigestion is that it is caused only by an excessive amount of acid in the stomach. This myth has stemmed thanks to the presence of "acid blockers" in the commonly available over-the-counter medicines for heartburn.

However, a lower quantity of acid in the stomach may also result in acid reflux.

The higher amount of acid in the stomach secreted in response to the food you have eaten tells the lower oesophageal sphincter (LOS) to close off so that there is no acid movement from the stomach to the oesophagus. In the absence of an adequate amount of acid in the stomach, the LOS loosens up a bit, resulting in acid reflux.

Therefore, sometimes consuming more acid could help curb acid reflux. Apple cider vinegar is one such remedy that can help in this regard.

To obtain quick relief from the symptoms, you can try consuming one tablespoon of apple cider vinegar diluted in six to eight ounces of water.

Banana/Apple

Bananas contain antacids that could help balance the acid. The most straightforward herbal remedy to treat heartburn, acid reflux, and indigestion is to consume one fully-ripened banana every day. You may even try slicing up an apple every day and consuming it a few hours before hitting the bed at night.

Sodium Bicarbonate

Sodium bicarbonate, commonly known as baking soda, also acts as an excellent home remedy for relieving the burning sensation caused by acid reflux.

Sodium bicarbonate is basic. Therefore, it would help neutralise the acid present in the stomach.

It would neutralise the acid reaching up into your throat, thereby sparing you of the burning sensation.

Chewing Gum

Chewing gum could sometimes provide relief to people with chronic heartburn and GERD.

Chewing a piece of gum triggers the salivary glands to produce more saliva. The excessive amount of saliva dilutes the acid that reaches up the throat and thus, neutralises and washes it away. This effect could help provide relief from the GERD and indigestion symptoms.

Other than the remedies mentioned above, you can also try consuming a cup of mint, fenugreek, or chamomile tea. Health experts advise people prone to heartburn to eat three to four raw almonds after every meal to eliminate the risk of burning sensation caused due to acid reflux. Almonds can help balance the pH in the stomach.

Natural Ways to Treat Chronic Acid Reflux

Acid reflux may be a significant problem for many of you. You must have experienced severe heartburn at one point or the other. What's more, some people complain about acid reflux and indigestion at least once a month. It is neither possible nor safe to use antacids every time you get a bout.

But, untreated and continuous acid reflux and indigestion could lead to severe consequences like oesophageal cancer. This ailment is because heartburn or acid reflux results from the stomach acids streaming back into the oesophagus. It can corrode and damage the delicate oesophageal mucosa. Hence, there is a need to adopt healthy strategies to overcome acid reflux and indigestion.

Here are some great tips and remedies to help kick off chronic acid reflux and indigestion to protect yourself against these complications.

Get Rid of Acid Reflux

Midnight acid reflux and indigestion can create a high level of discomfort. The resulting bitter taste in the mouth could not only disturb your sleep but even make it elusive.

If you are looking for a way to permanently treat acid reflux and indigestion, you are advised to change your lifestyle besides making some dietary changes.

Some helpful tips for relieving these symptoms are listed below:

Maintain Healthy Weight

Even the slightest increase in your weight can worsen the heartburn symptoms. Maintaining a healthy body weight would help you reduce acid reflux and indigestion symptoms.

Avoid Trigger Foods

Make a note of the foods that trigger acid reflux and indigestion. These foods can be different for every person.

Common foods that cause exacerbations include garlic, onions, caffeinated drinks, peppermint, chocolate, high-fat foods, and fried foods. Besides, citrus fruits like oranges can also cause acid reflux and indigestion.

Relax While You Eat

Stressful eating or eating in a hurry can cause a higher production of the acids by the stomach. Relax after the meals to avoid these consequences. However, avoid lying down. Go for the relaxation techniques like meditation, yoga, or deep breathing.

Stay Upright After Eating

Sitting upright after a meal reduces the chances of the stomach acid flowing back into the oesophagus. Also, avoid bending over or straining to lift heavy objects.

Wear Loose-Fitting Clothes

Tight clothes, specifically around the waist, can put pressure on the stomach. It can result in an aggravation of acid reflux symptoms. Therefore, make sure you wear loose-fitting clothes, especially around the waist and when going to bed.

Quit Smoking

Smoking can worsen the symptoms of heartburn. It not only irritates the gastrointestinal (GI) tract but also relaxes the muscles in the oesophagus that play a role in keeping the stomach acid in its actual place and preventing its regurgitation.

Avoid Heavy Meals at Night or Late-Night Eating

Make sure you have your last meal of the day at least two to three hours before bedtime. It would reduce the stomach acid while allowing the stomach to empty its contents before sleeping.

Large meals can put pressure on the stomach. Therefore, try to take five to six small meals a day rather than three big meals. Also, avoid heavy meals post evening.

Wait Before Exercise

Exercise and regular workouts are the best ways to deal with any health issues. However, when you are suffering from acid reflux or heartburn, it is crucial to maintain a gap of at least half an hour between the meals and the exercise.

Reduce Your Intake of Caffeine

It has been found that many people complain of acid reflux and indigestion after drinking coffee. Most patients report having obtained substantial relief after they reduced their intake of coffee.

Hence, it is advisable to limit your intake of coffee to avoid the symptoms of acid reflux and indigestion.

Sleep Position

When you lie down in your bed, your throat and stomach come to stay at the same level. This position makes it easier for the acid to flow back into the oesophagus, thus leading to heartburn and indigestion. It is, therefore, advisable to elevate your upper body while sleeping.

This position can be done in two ways:

- Put the head-side of the bed on five to six-inch blocks.

- Try to sleep on a wedge-shaped pillow. The pillow should at least be six to eight inches thick on one side. However, avoid substituting with regular pillows as they raise the head and not the entire upper body.

If, in any case, you don't find these lifestyle changes helpful and effective for reducing symptoms of heartburn and indigestion, see a doctor and start taking the medications.

Indications for consulting a doctor might include severe symptoms like continuous eructations, difficulty in swallowing, vomiting due to heartburn, and persistent heartburn even after using antacids for more than two weeks.

How Can Ayurveda Help Improve Your Gut Health and Reduce Indigestion?

Slight discomfort in the stomach can prevent us from concentrating on our work. It can affect our productivity and even make us grumpy and agitated. And THIS is the effect a single episode of digestive problems could have on our day-to-day activities! Can you imagine the difficulties you might have to face if you experience recurring digestive troubles?

Your gut health is of prime importance if you want to feel at ease and avoid indigestion. Most of us experience symptoms due to problems with gut health such as bloating, cramps in the stomach, constipation, loose motions, and heartburn.

Ayurveda recommends simple lifestyle changes and dietary habits that could improve your gut health and help you avoid the discomfort caused due to indigestion.

The Concept of Gut Health in Ayurveda

The Ayurvedic concept of digestion is based on the principles of Agni, a Sanskrit word for fire. Ayurveda considers Agni or fire as a source of life. It believes that an impaired Agni is often at the root of imbalances in the gut. Hence, the importance of Agni for your gut health can not be understated.

Agni refers to the digestive fire that must be stimulated before eating to ensure proper food digestion. A weak digestive fire could often result in fatigue after eating. Ayurvedic experts recommend eating a small piece of ginger before meals to ignite the digestive fire. You can also add half to one tablespoon of lemon juice and sprinkle a pinch of salt on a piece of ginger. This combination of ginger, lemon, and salt would activate the secretion of enzymes by the digestive glands and promote assimilation and absorption of food.

Eat In a Calm Environment

The human body needs an uplifting and peaceful environment to digest and absorb the nutrients from foods. Hence, Ayurveda recommends eating your meals at a place where you can focus on the meal without any disturbance.

You can select a calm and soothing surrounding to eat your meals. If this is not possible, you may eat the food sitting down and not while walking, standing, and driving.

When you sit down to eat, your stomach will be in a relaxed posture. This state can improve its ability to accommodate and digest the foods and prevent uneasiness, heaviness, or discomfort after eating.

Setting Up Your Meal Times

Ayurveda is based on the principles of nature. Hence, it recommends scheduling your meals by following nature's prescribed times and the body's natural processes. Since Agni is associated with fire and heat, Ayurveda recommends timing the largest meal of your day, lunch, based on the amount of sun rays your body receives.

Ayurvedic physicians believe that the digestive fire is the strongest between 12:00 noon and 2:00 pm when the sun rays are directly overhead. During this phase, the digestive fire is at its maximum. It lowers in intensity later as the sun goes down.

Hence, you should have a heavy lunch between 12:00 noon and 2:00 pm and have a light dinner before 8:00 pm. You should also avoid late-night meals as your body begins to burn off toxins after 10:00 pm. Eating after 10:00 pm could cause toxins to accumulate into your system and even weaken digestion.

Meditation for Gut Health

Regular meditation would restore digestive functions and relieve the discomfort associated with most digestive diseases. You can meditate for about 20 to 25 minutes every day.

It is a simple practice that involves closing your eyes and focusing your thoughts on breathing to stimulate the sources of positive energies within your body. This practice would ignite the digestive fire and promote the digestion, assimilation, and absorption of food.

Practise Yoga

Ayurveda advises patients suffering from poor gut health to practice yoga regularly. Furthermore, yoga asanas would restore the normal motility of your gut. You would find relief in symptoms of indigestion, irritable bowel syndrome, gastritis, peptic ulcers, and ulcerative colitis.

The most effective yoga poses for improving gut health include Ardha Matsyendrasana (a half-seated spinal twist), Parighasana (the gate pose), and Jathara Parivritti (an abdominal twist).

Consume High-Fibre Foods

Ayurveda recommends eating a high-fibre diet for supporting your gut health. Moreover, it would increase stool output and inhibit constipation. A high-fibre diet can also help movements of foods through the gut. It would also ease abdominal discomfort, flatulence, bloating, and constipation by holding more water within its cellular structure.

Some foods that could relieve constipation and improve gut health with their high-fibre content include citrus fruits, bananas, berries, papayas, and fresh vegetables like broccoli, peas, and beans.

Whole grains also have a high content of dietary fibres. Include these foods in your regular diet to enhance gut health.

Drink Plenty of Water

Ayurveda believes in improving gut health by flushing out toxins from the body. Hence, it advises drinking water first thing in the morning. It would eliminate the toxic build-up from the body and enhance digestive functions. This routine would provide relief from the symptoms of digestive disturbances such as constipation, flatulence, bloating, and nausea.

Conclusion

Your gut plays a vital role in maintaining your body's overall functioning. All organs in your body, including your brain and heart, obtain energy to perform their functions from foods digested in the stomach and intestine.

Hence, it is essential to ensure your digestive system is working at its best to improve your overall wellness.

Managing gut health by following lifestyle and dietary recommendations of Ayurveda would provide relief from the symptoms of digestive issues like acid reflux and indigestion. They would also reduce the risk of gastrointestinal diseases such as peptic ulcers, ulcerative colitis, irritable bowel syndrome, leaky gut syndrome, and hepatic dysfunctions.

Common Signs, Causes, and Treatments for Gluten Intolerance

Gluten intolerance is a common concern characterised by adverse reactions to a protein called gluten found in wheat, rye, and barley.

There are several gluten intolerance causes, such as celiac disease, wheat allergy, and non-celiac gluten sensitivity. All three forms of gluten intolerance cause widespread symptoms – most of which have no direct link with digestion.

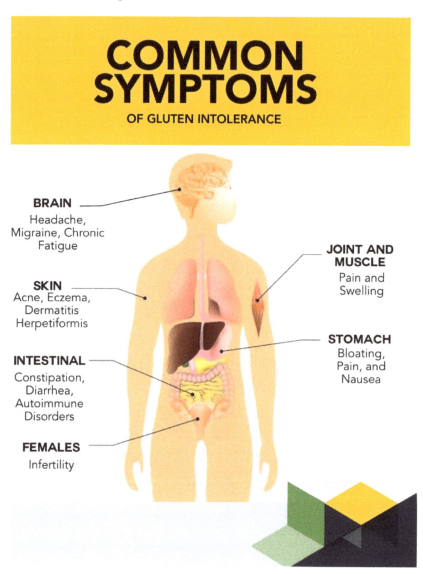

What follows is a brief discussion about gluten intolerance and the right way to manage it.

What Is Gluten Intolerance?

The sensitivity to wheat primarily occurs due to the presence of a protein known as gluten. It is called gluten sensitivity. Gluten intolerance can trigger a complex autoimmune response, in which you may develop long-term complications like leaky gut syndrome.

Some other gluten-containing foods that trigger food sensitivities are barley and rye.

You might develop symptoms of food sensitivities and intolerance from consuming foods containing one or more of these ingredients. These include most bread, pasta, cakes, biscuits made of wheat, and several other foods that we may eat daily without even realising that they could be causing inflammation and damage to the gut.

Hence, it is advisable to check the label of any food you buy and check that it does not contain any foods you have sensitivity to. You can also try gluten-free cooking and baking at home, using gluten-free grains, like amaranth.

What Is Food Intolerance?

Food intolerance refers to the inability of the directive system to tolerate certain foods like gluten, resulting in the lack of efficient breakdown, absorption, and assimilation. As this condition involves the digestive tract, the symptoms are often limited to the same.

It means you may develop digestive troubles like pain and discomfort in the stomach and indigestion. You might also get loose motions after consuming gluten-free foods to which you are intolerant.

The other common forms of food intolerance include:

- Lactose intolerance caused due to the absence of an enzyme needed for the digestion of lactose-containing foods such as milk and other dairy products
- Irritable bowel syndrome, which causes abdominal cramping with alternative diarrhoea and constipation
- Sensitivity to food additives such as sulphites that are used as preservatives in most dried fruits, and canned foods

What Are the Symptoms of Food Sensitivities?

Food sensitivities are a form of digestive trouble caused by consuming food you are intolerant to. It can occur when certain foods make you feel bloated and cause constipation and headaches.

Celiac disease is the most familiar and most severe form of gluten intolerance.

It is an autoimmune disease known to affect nearly 1% of the population. Celiac disease may lead to severe long-term damage to the digestive system. It may cause a wide range of symptoms, such as skin problems, mood changes, gastrointestinal issues, and more.

Here are a few of the most common symptoms of celiac disease.

- Diarrhoea or constipation
- Fatigue
- Skin reactions
- Increased risk of psoriasis, alopecia areata, and chronic urticaria
- Depression and anxiety
- Unexplained weight loss
- Iron-deficiency anaemia
- Increased risk of other autoimmune disorders
- Frequent joint and muscle pain
- Leg and arm numbness

The common signs and symptoms of non-celiac gluten sensitivity include:

- Bloating
- diarrhoea and constipation
- Stomach pain
- Headaches
- Fatigue
- Depression and anxiety
- Pain in the joints and muscles
- Brain fog

What Causes Gluten Intolerance and Why Is Gluten so Harmful to Your Health?

Gluten refers to a group of proteins that contains peptides like glutenin and gliadin. Gluten is commonly found in wheat, semolina, rye, spelt, Kamut, and barley.

Medical researchers have increasingly recognised that some of the common dietary factors such as gluten could be the key contributors to the risk of autoimmune diseases. Some of these are namely celiac disease, rheumatoid arthritis, multiple sclerosis, dermatitis herpetiformis, and bullous pemphigoid.

Most patients with gluten intolerance and celiac disease can significantly relieve the symptoms by eliminating gluten-containing foods from their diet.

Gluten is one of the most common dietary triggers that could erode into the tissues and lining of the gut, stomach, joints, skin, and muscles, thus making them less efficient at performing their physiological functions.

Also, some gluten-containing grains may be problematic for patients who suffer from inflammation and autoimmune diseases as these foods could directly affect the lining or the gut barrier. This reaction may lead to the loss of intestinal permeability, thus putting the person at risk of the leaky gut syndrome and inflammatory bowel diseases.

Gluten may also trigger the immune system to form antibodies against gluten peptides, which may worsen the symptoms of autoimmune disorders further. This response is why it is crucial to eliminate gluten from the diet to relieve symptoms of gluten intolerance.

Some common foods containing gluten include:

- Wheat, barley, or rye in any form such as bread, cakes, crackers, cereals, and cookies
- Additives and preservatives in some packaged and processed foods
- Gluten cross-reactive grains and foods such as oats, potatoes, corn, quinoa, rice, millet, and sorghum

Avoiding these foods is the key to preventing gluten intolerance symptoms and complications.

A gluten-free diet could help people who are sensitive or intolerant to gluten. However, if you are buying gluten-free products, check if they are fortified with essential nutrients.

Conclusion

Avoiding gluten often takes some effort as it is present in most foods we eat daily. Gluten-containing grains, such as wheat, are also commonly found in processed foods and packaged foods.

Moreover, some foods not considered 'processed' might also contain gluten.

Hence, avoiding gluten can be a difficult task. Still, making the right choices while buying groceries, reading the ingredient labels of foods you purchase, and finding a healthier replacement to gluten could help control symptoms of this condition and protect you against severe complications like leaky gut syndrome and autoimmune disorders.

Ayurvedic Treatment for Diarrhoea and the Common Causes of Loose Motions

Diarrhoea is one of the most common symptoms affecting the digestive system in which the person has to evacuate the bowels repeatedly. The characteristic symptoms of this disease are watery or liquid stools, gas, bloating, and cramping.

If the frequency of stools does not reduce or bowel movements do not become regular in a few days, you may face severe complications like dehydration.

Here are some common causes and symptoms of diarrhoea and the right way to treat this condition.

What Are the Common Signs and Symptoms of Diarrhoea?

The symptoms typically begin with crampy pain in the abdominal region, followed by loose motions that usually last no more than three to four days.

- Inflammation of the intestines
- Loose motions
- Watery or liquid stool
- Fever
- Weight loss
- Loss of appetite

- Reduced urination
- Coldness of the skin
- Dehydration leading to dryness of the skin, parched lips, increased thirst, lethargy, and sunken eyes
- Blood in stool
- Severe fatigue
- Vomiting or nausea

What Are the Causes of Diarrhoea?

In most cases, diarrhoea is caused by gastrointestinal infections. Microorganisms responsible for causing these infections include bacteria, viruses, and parasites.

Diarrhoea is often highly contagious as the infection may spread rapidly from one person to another through contact or ingestion of contaminated foods or drinks.

Infections can also spread rapidly through contaminated water, pets, dirty hands, and contact with faecal matter (for example, from dirty diapers and toilets). Children exposed to the infections may spread the condition to others through contaminated objects like toys or changing desks at school.

In infants, common viral causes of this condition include Rotavirus, coxsackievirus, and enteroviruses. Common bacterial and parasitic causes of diarrhoea include E. coli, Campylobacter bacteria, Salmonella enteritidis, Giardia parasite, Shigella, and Cryptosporidium parasite.

Ayurvedic Treatments for Children with Diarrhoea

Most infectious diseases, including diarrhoea, are self-limiting. It means they tend to resolve independently within a few days, provided the person's immune system is functioning efficiently. Prevention is the key to managing diarrhoea.

Some of the treatment and preventive measures include:

- Hand-washing before eating, before cooking, and after using the restroom. Hand-washing is considered the most effective way to avoid diarrhoeal infections, which may be passed from an infected person to others.
- Replenishing the water and electrolytes lost due to loose motions. Diarrhoea, mainly when caused due to viruses, can be managed well by using oral rehydration solution (also called ORS).

Ayurveda recommends following a simple diet and some lifestyle strategies and using a few herbs to strengthen your digestion, boost the body's defence mechanisms against pathogens, and regulate bowel movements.

Dietary Advance for the Prevention of Diarrhoea

- Eat nutritious, well balanced, and smaller meals
- Drink warm liquids to treat and prevent dehydration
- Drink Oral Rehydration Solution (ORS) to prevent dehydration
- Breast milk, light pulses and daal, and tender coconut water may be given to infants and children
- Avoid the intake of tea, soda, gelatin desserts, fruit juices, sports drinks, or chicken broth
- Include foods like ginger, Indian gooseberry (amla), yoghurt, mashed banana, and buttermilk in the diet

Lifestyle Habits Recommended by Ayurveda for the Prevention of Diarrhoea

- Wash vegetables and fruits before cooking and eating
- Develop the habit of washing hands, kitchen counters, and utensils
- Wash raw meat and poultry to prevent the risk of diarrhoea
- Drink clean water

Treatment of Diarrhoea

In most cases, it is possible to manage diarrhoea at home. In some cases, when the patient has developed severe loss of water due to loose motions, it could be essential to seek immediate medical intervention.

In mild cases of diarrhoea, when the person has had four to five bouts of loose motions, they may be given water or electrolytes. Simple electrolytes can be prepared at home by mixing a pinch of salt and one teaspoon sugar in a glass of clean, boiled, cooled, and filtered water.

Depending on the extent of dehydration, the patient might need an intravenous infusion of electrolytes in a clinic or hospital setting.

Home Remedies for Diarrhoea Management

- Yoghurt: Eat yoghurt with rice. You may add a little honey or sugar to sweeten it.

- Ginger and Honey: Add a pinch of ginger (finely grated) with honey and eat. Avoid drinking water or any other liquid immediately afterwards.

- Fenugreek seeds: Chew one teaspoon of fenugreek seeds and eat a tablespoon of curd. This combination would help control diarrhoea.

- A concoction of cumin seeds: Make a powder of roasted cumin seeds by grinding them. Mix the powder in a glass of water. Add a tablespoon of honey. Drink this to avoid nausea, vomiting, bloating, flatulence, and other symptoms linked to diarrhoea.

- Coconut water: Coconut water provides a rich source of nutrients, including vitamins. It also has a cooling potency that could be helpful in diarrhoea management.

- Wood Apple Candy: Take one tablespoon of wood apple candy once or twice to overcome nausea and vomiting.

Conclusion

Dehydration is the most significant cause of concern in patients with diarrhoea. If you suffer from loose motions, make sure you stay well hydrated. Follow the home remedies discussed above to relieve symptoms and allow your bowel movements to return to normal within a shorter duration.

Ayurvedic Treatment for Vomiting

Vomiting, which is often accompanied by nausea, is one of the most common symptoms of an underlying condition rather than a disease itself. The medical term used to refer to vomiting is emesis.

Vomiting can be defined as the forcible emptying of the stomach's contents wherein the stomach needs to overcome the pressure generally in place to keep foods and gastric secretions within itself.

The causes of vomiting often vary. They include food-borne diseases (or food poisoning), central nervous system or brain problems, infections, and systemic diseases. Some diseases can also cause nausea and vomiting, even when no actual stomach and gastrointestinal tract is involved. Some examples include pneumonia, sepsis, and heart attack.

Vomiting may also be a side effect of some medications, like drugs used in chemotherapy and radiation therapy used to manage cancer.

Here is a brief discussion about vomiting, its causes, and the most effective home remedies to treat it safely.

What Is Vomiting?

More commonly referred to as throwing up, vomiting is the forceful discharge of the stomach's contents. It may be a one-time event linked to something that does not settle in the stomach. In some cases, recurrent vomiting may occur due to an underlying medical condition.

Frequent vomiting can also result in dehydration that could be life-threatening when not treated appropriately.

What Are the Causes of Vomiting?

Nausea and vomiting are common symptoms of digestive diseases. Overeating or drinking too much alcohol often makes a person throw up. This reaction is usually not a significant cause of concern. Also, vomiting itself is not a disorder. As said earlier, it is more of a symptom of some other condition.

These conditions include indigestion, food poisoning, infections (associated with viral and bacterial illnesses), pregnancy-linked morning sickness, motion sickness, prescription medications, chemotherapy, headaches, anaesthesia, and Crohn's disease.

Recurrent vomiting not related to these factors could be a symptom of cyclic vomiting syndrome. This condition is marked by vomiting for more than ten days. It is often coupled with nausea and a severe lack of energy. It usually occurs during childhood.

The cyclic vomiting syndrome can affect children between the ages of three and seven years. It affects approximately 3 out of 100000 children.

This condition may cause frequent episodes of vomiting several times throughout the year, especially if left untreated. It may also cause serious complications, including tooth decay, dehydration, esophagitis, and a tear in the oesophagus.

Vomiting Emergencies

Though vomiting is a common symptom, it may sometimes require immediate medical attention.

Patients should immediately visit the doctor if they:

- Suspect food poisoning
- Have vomiting for more than a day
- Have severe headaches accompanied by stiffness in the neck
- Have intense abdominal pain

They should seek emergency services if there is blood in the vomitus, called Haematemesis.

The symptoms of Haematemesis include:

- Vomiting of a large amount of bright red blood
- Coughing up of a substance that resembles coffee grounds

- Spitting up dark blood

Vomiting of blood is usually caused due to ulcers in the stomach and oesophagus, ruptured blood vessels, and stomach bleeding. It may also be caused due to some forms of cancer. This disease is often accompanied by mild to moderate dizziness. If you have blood vomiting, seek medical attention immediately or visit the nearest emergency care centre.

What Are the Complications of Vomiting?

Dehydration is one of the most common complications of vomiting. Vomiting can cause your stomach to expel not just food but also fluids. Dehydration can cause dryness of the mouth, severe fatigue, dark urine, headache, and confusion.

Dehydration is usually severe in young children and infants who have frequent vomiting. Younger children have a smaller body mass and have less fluid in their bodies to sustain themselves.

Parents of children who show signs of dehydration should consult the paediatrician immediately to seek timely treatment and prevent complications linked to dehydration.

Malnutrition is another common complication of vomiting. The failure to keep solid foods down into the stomach can cause the body to lose most nutrients. This issue can lead to malnutrition.

Treatment of Vomiting

The treatment for vomiting is aimed at identifying and addressing the underlying cause.

Treatment may not be necessary for patients who have had just a single bout of vomiting. However, it should be noted that dehydration can occur even if the person has vomited only once. Drinking plenty of clear liquids is highly recommended as the first line of treatment to avoid dehydration in patients who have had one or more bouts of vomiting. Clear fluids or water containing electrolytes would help provide the essential nutrients lost due to vomiting.

Solid foods often irritate the sensitive stomach and increase your risk of throwing up. Hence, it might be beneficial to avoid solid foods until the liquids are well-tolerated.

Alternative remedies such as the use of ginger, lemongrass oil, or bergamot can also help. Dietary changes are also helpful for controlling frequent vomiting. These are specifically helpful for women who suffer from morning sickness during pregnancy. Foods that might help alleviate vomiting include non-fat foods, saltine crackers, and ginger products such as ginger ale.

You may also try eating frequent smaller meals instead of eating three large meals throughout the day.

Prevention of Vomiting

Vomiting triggers often vary between people. These may include excessive alcohol consumption, migraine, overeating food, exercising after eating, hot or spicy foods, stress, and the lack of sleep.

Changing your dietary habits and adopting healthier lifestyle habits may help prevent episodes of vomiting.

It may be difficult to avoid the viruses that can cause vomiting entirely. However, you can reduce your risk of contracting a viral infection by following good hygiene, such as washing your hands before eating and cooking.

Being aware of how to treat the recurrent episodes of vomiting can help avoid further complications.

Ayurvedic Treatment for the Management of Vomiting

Nausea and vomiting are usually the initial signs of the high pitta dosha in the stomach. The increased acidic secretions in the gut can irritate and inflame the gastric mucous membranes, resulting in a sickly feeling.

Hence, it would be good to steer clear of overly hot, spicy, and fermented foods.

Here are some of the most effective home remedies recommended by Ayurveda for the treatment and prevention of vomiting.

- Chew one or two cardamom seeds. The change in the taste would help soothe the sensation of vomiting.

- Add about ten drops of lime juice and half a teaspoon of sugar to one cup of water. Then, mix half a teaspoon of baking soda into it and stir. Drink immediately. This effective home remedy would stop nausea and vomiting within a shorter period.

- A tea made of one teaspoon of cumin seeds with a pinch of nutmeg steeped and brewed in a cup of hot water would also prove to be effective.

- Ginger is a highly effective remedy that can help relieve several digestive and stomach-related issues. If vomiting is caused due to indigestion, or food poisoning, mixing one teaspoon of ginger juice or ginger pulp (freshly grated) and one teaspoon of onion juice would also help you get past the queasy feeling safely and effectively.

- A mixture of equal parts of honey and lemon juice can provide quick relief from the uneasy feeling induced by nausea and vomiting. You can dip your finger into this mixture and lick it as and when you feel nauseated.

Conclusion

Adopting healthy lifestyle habits could help prevent episodes of vomiting. It may be challenging to avoid viruses that can cause vomiting entirely. But, you can reduce the risk of getting the viruses by practising good hygiene.

Knowing how to treat the recurrent episodes of vomiting would also help you avoid future complications.

What Is Inflammatory Bowel Disease and How to Manage It Naturally?

Inflammatory Bowel Disease (IBD) is an idiopathic disorder that involves an immune system reaction of the body to the tissues of its digestive system. IBD comprises two major diseases that include ulcerative colitis and Crohn's disease. These disorders have a few distinct and overlapping clinical and pathologic characteristics.

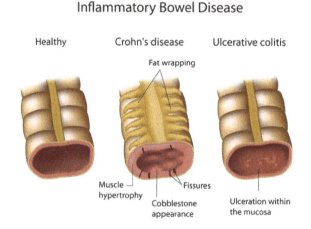

What Is Inflammatory Bowel Disease?

It represents a group of disorders that can cause prolonged inflammation in the digestive tract.

The digestive system comprises different organs, including the following:

- Mouth
- Oesophagus
- Stomach
- Small intestine
- Large intestine

It is responsible for breaking down the foods we eat, extracting essential nutrients, and removing unusable material like waste products.

Inflammation in any organs or tissues along the digestive tract can interfere with these normal processes. IBD is often very painful and disruptive to patients' routine life. In rare cases, it can even be life-threatening.

What Are the Types of Inflammatory Bowel Diseases?

Several diseases are included under the term IBD. The two most common ones include ulcerative colitis and Crohn's disease.

Ulcerative colitis occurs due to inflammation in the large intestine. Crohn's disease may cause inflammation in any part or tissue of the digestive tract. However, it usually affects the tissues at the end of the small intestine.

Ulcerative colitis is a condition caused by the development of ulcers along the lining of the colon and rectum. Ulcers are formed at sites where the immune system's inflammatory response has led to the destruction of the cells lining the colon. The disease may extend proximally from the anus and even involve all or a part of the colon.

As the colon's lining becomes ulcerated and inflamed, it loses its ability to adequately process foods and waste or absorb water, resulting in diarrhoea (loose stools). In severe cases, it may lead to rapid weight loss.

Most patients with ulcerative colitis or Crohn's disease experience an urgency for bowel movements and abdominal cramps. Inflammation may cause small sores (or ulcers) to form in the rectum and colon. These ulcers can join together, developing larger ulcers that can bleed and cause bloody stools. Blood loss may eventually lead to anaemia when left untreated.

The common symptoms of ulcerative colitis are diarrhoea and rectal bleeding. Variability of symptoms reflects vast differences in the extent of the disease and tissues of the colon and possibly inflamed rectum.

Usually, patients with inflammation confined only to the rectum or a short segment of the colon adjacent to the rectum have mild symptoms with a better prognosis than patients with more widespread colon inflammation.

Based on the area affected due to inflammation, there are some primary types of ulcerative colitic called ulcerative proctitis, left-sided colitis, procto-sigmoiditis, pan-colitis, and fulminant colitis.

IBD is among the top 3 high-risk factors for colorectal cancers with the colon's involvement. Colorectal cancer accounts for nearly 10 to 15% of all deaths in IBD patients. Also, patients with IBD colitis are six times more likely to suffer from colorectal cancer than the general population and have a higher risk of developing multiple synchronous colorectal cancers.

What Are the Causes of Inflammatory Bowel Disease?

The exact causes of IBD are not known. However, some of the most significant risk factors for developing ulcerative colitis or Crohn's disease include:

Genetics and Family History

People who have parents, siblings, or a child with IBD are more likely to develop these conditions themselves. This factor is why researchers believe that IBD might have a genetic component.

Age

IBD can affect people of all ages. However, it begins before the age of 30 to 35 years in most cases.

Ethnicity

IBD can affect people belonging to all populations. However, certain ethnic groups, such as the Ashkenazi Jews and white people, have a greater risk of developing this condition.

Gender

IBD is found to affect men and women equally. Ulcerative colitis is generally more common in men above 45 years of age than in women of the same age group.

On the other hand, Crohn's disease is more prevalent in girls and women above 14 years of age.

Environmental Factors

People living in industrialised countries and urban areas have a much higher risk of developing IBD.

Residents of industrialised countries tend to eat more fatty and processed food. This factor is likely to be the cause of the higher incidence of this disease among these people.

IBD is common in people living in the northern climates, where the weather is frigid all year round.

The assessment of the impact of environmental factors on the risk of developing IBD has revealed that people living a sedentary lifestyle or having a sedentary job have a higher risk of IBD.

On the other hand, physical activities in the pre-illness period could help reduce the risk of the onset of IBD. This reduction has been more substantial and effective for Crohn's disease than ulcerative colitis.

Immune System

The immune system might also play a role in the development of IBD. The immune system defends the body against pathogens known to cause infections and diseases.

A viral or bacterial infection in the digestive tract could trigger an abnormal immune response. Organs of the digestive tract may become inflamed as the body attempts to create a robust immune response against these invaders.

The inflammation resolves or goes away in patients with a healthy immune response once the infection clears out.

However, in patients with IBD, the inflammation in the digestive tract tends to occur and persist for longer, even when there is no infection. It occurs when the immune cells attack bodily tissues. This reaction is known as the autoimmune response.

IBD may also occur when the inflammation does not disappear even after the infection is cleared. The inflammation can continue for several months to even years in these cases.

Smoking

Smoking is one of the common risk factors for Crohn's disease. Smoking can also aggravate pain and other signs associated with this disease. It can increase the risk of serious complications too.

However, ulcerative colitis can more commonly affect non-smokers and even ex-smokers than smokers.

What Are the Signs and Symptoms of Inflammatory Bowel Disease?

The symptoms of IBD often vary depending on the severity and location of the inflammation.

Some of the initial symptoms of this condition may include:

- Diarrhoea that occurs when the affected part of the bowel is unable to reabsorb water
- Bleeding ulcers that can cause blood to show up in stools (a condition called hematochezia)
- Pain in the stomach with cramping or bloating due to obstruction in the bowels
- Anaemia and weight loss that can cause a delay in physical growth and development in young children
- Patients with Crohn's disease can also get canker sores in the mouth. Sometimes, fissures and ulcers also appear around the anus or genital area.

IBD may also be associated with problems outside of the digestive tract, such as:

- Arthritis
- Skin disorders

- Eye inflammation

What Are the Complications of Inflammatory Bowel Disease?

The possible complications of IBD are malnutrition, weight loss, colorectal cancer, and fistulas or tunnels, which go through the bowel walls, creating holes in different parts of the digestive tract.

It may also cause intestinal rupture, also known as perforation, and bowel obstruction.

In some cases, a severe episode of IBD may make the person go into shock. This response could be life-threatening. The shock is caused by severe blood loss due to prolonged or sudden blood-stained loose motions.

Ayurvedic Concepts for IBD Management

In Ayurveda literature, Rakta, Vatika grahani, and Pithathisara are linked to this condition.

The cause of all these diseases lies in digestion, wherein the digestive system is working optimally and is supported by correct lifestyle habits and correct quality and quantity of the food as per the Prakruti of the individual.

The food ingested is later broken down into its constituents that can nourish the tissues and support the everyday functions of the body's organs.

The seat of Agni is called Grahani. The link between Agni and Grahani is similar to the relation between functions and structure. When the digestive fire that burns in the stomach is affected due to a person's incorrect eating and lifestyle habits, it can lead to food toxins called Ama Visha.

Ama tends to get stuck in the intestine's villi, forming a thick coating. The Ama and the increased heat in the digestive tract can cause the vitiation of Kapha, leading to loss of the intestine's snigdhatha (mucous secretions and oiliness).

Mucous, being eliminated, would then be passed in the stool. Usually, the loss of properties of kapha dosha leads to the aggravation of Pitta. This effect initiates inflammatory changes in the intestine and ulcerations. These changes can also result in mucus or bloody diarrhoea.

The long-term progress of these conditions can cause structural changes in the intestinal walls failing the absorption mechanisms. This failure of absorption and impaired intestinal movements can cause severe weakness, tiredness, diarrhoea, weight loss, and anaemia in patients with IBD.

Ayurvedic treatment for this condition aims to heal the ulcers, digest the Ama, remove the toxins, balance the doshas, and boost the immune system to control the symptoms and prevent its progress.

Ayurvedic Approach to IBD Management

In chronic conditions like IBD, structural changes in the intestinal lining can make the patient weak. In such situations, efforts should be made to restore normal health.

Here are some herbal medications recommended for the long-term management of IBD:

Internal medicines (or Oushadha Prayoga) of the following qualities in the forms of various kinds of churnas (or powders), Lavanas (or salts), ksharas (or alkalis), sura, asava, and different varieties of probiotics like buttermilk are usually used.

- Digestive Pachana Oushadha to digest Ama
- Agni Deepana for appetite stimulation
- Vrana Ropana for ulcer healing
- Grahani, the digestive formulation, for reducing diarrhoea and the lack of appetite
- Stambhana that stops the movements and elimination of blood and mucus and restores normal appetite

Ayurvedic therapies that could be beneficial for patients with IBD include:

- Mrudu Virechana (induced purgation) that is aimed at Vathanulomana (helping to calm Vatha) and relieve pain
- Vasthi (or medicated enema) when the lower digestive tract is affected

When no ulcerations have developed in the initial stage of the disease, the therapies aim to remove residual morbid matters from the intestine through Poorva Asthapana, Sneha Sweda, and Vasthi (Swedana and Abhyanga followed by the medicated decoction enema). Medicated oil enemas like Anuvasana Vasthi may follow this process.

Along with these treatments, lifestyle modifications such as getting sound sleep at night, having appropriate physical activities, and reducing stress can also be beneficial.

A calm and peaceful mind and healthy food habits like eating wholesome foods at the right time, in the right quantities, and the right place when feeling hungry are often recommended.

Herbal remedies like aloe vera, coconut water, drumsticks, and honey are also effective for managing IBD. Patients should also avoid dairy products and include omega-3 fatty acids in their diet to reduce inflammation.

Conclusion

With the help of natural home remedies and lifestyle modifications, the treatment of IBD can help patients derive long-term benefits and protect them against risks of complications.

Management of Intestinal Parasites Using Ayurvedic Remedies

Parasites are organisms that can infect the bodies of other living beings and live off their hosts for their survival. Some parasites do not create any symptoms in the hosts, while some may cause severe symptoms.

Parasitic infections can occur when the parasites grow and reproduce or invade the organs making the hosts ill.

Some of the most common parasitic infections affecting humans include the following:

- Toxoplasmosis
- Giardiasis
- Cryptosporidiosis
- Trichomoniasis

What Are the Symptoms of Parasitic Infections?

Most parasitic infections occur due to the consumption of water and food that have been contaminated. Travelling to places where more prevalent parasitic infections occur can also expose you to risks of infections caused by parasites, mainly tropical parasites.

Depending on the parasite you have and the body system it has affected, the symptoms of infection may include the following:

- Vomiting
- Pain in the stomach
- Nausea
- Cramps in the stomach
- Bloating and flatulence
- Dehydration
- Weight loss
- Fever
- Constipation
- Diarrhoea
- Upset stomach
- Flu-like symptoms
- Irritation
- Swollen lymph nodes
- Itching
- Aches and pains
- Redness

Diagnosis of Parasitic Infections

A parasitic infection is often diagnosed by testing a stool sample. The stool sample is tested in a laboratory to detect the presence of parasites or their eggs or remnants.

Treatment of Parasitic Infections

Once you know the type of parasitic infection you have, treatment may be started accordingly. Some parasitic infections tend to disappear on their own, mainly when the patient eats a balanced diet and their immune system is strong and healthy.

Parasites that do not go away on their own can be treated using oral anti-parasitic medications.

The treatment is generally adequate for eliminating the infectious organisms from the body and restoring health.

You can also choose natural Ayurvedic remedies to rid the body of parasites. Some of the best home remedies for managing parasitic intestinal infections are discussed below:

Home Remedies for Parasitic Cleanse

It is estimated that a large percentage of the population across the world has parasitic infections, most of which tend to go undetected due to the absence of symptoms. However, everyone needs to undergo regular parasitic cleanse to eliminate these parasites from the body since these organisms may continue to erode the body's tissues and cause damage slowly over time.

The parasitic cleanse is usually performed once every year. However, the frequency of the cleanse could be modified depending on various factors. These include the person's overall health, history of parasitic infections, and presence of risk factors such as living in an area where these infections are prevalent.

Cleansing and detoxifying the body to eliminate parasitic infections can be performed with the help of herbal remedies such as anise, berberine, clove oil, black walnut, curled mint, goldthread, barberry, and goldenseal. Some other natural remedies like propolis, oregano oil, grapefruit seed extract, wormwood, and Oregon grape have also been effective for performing parasitic cleanse.

Other natural plant-derived therapies could help cleanse the parasites from various organs and body systems, including the liver and intestines.

You can also choose gentle herbs for the detox. Some herbal detox programs tend to last up to two weeks. This procedure is followed by a period of two weeks, during which the patient follows their routine. After two weeks, another two-week protocol for parasitic cleanse is administered. The same mode of therapy with alternating periods of treatment and rest are followed for up to one or two months to ensure the body is thoroughly cleansed of parasites.

Parasitic Cleanse Diet

It is essential to follow a healthy and balanced diet high in nutrients but low in refined carbs and processed foods during the parasite cleanse. This combo would help you derive optimum benefits while avoiding symptoms like fatigue.

Eating foods rich in fibres is also particularly important, as it can keep bowel movements regular while undergoing parasitic cleanse.

A nutrient-rich diet would help strengthen the immune system while the parasites are flushed out of the body. This therapy, combined with a healthy dose of probiotics, would help protect the body against other infestations.

Honey, garlic, pumpkin seeds, or papaya seeds can be included in the diet to support the cleansing. These foods possess natural anti-parasitic properties. Including these foods in your diet would help you derive faster and better results.

Some Ayurvedic practitioners also recommend a sugar-free and grain-free diet to avoid the symptoms linked to sensitivity, intolerances, and allergies. A sugar-free diet would also cause parasites to starve off, resulting in their destruction. Limiting fruit intake to reduce the consumption of dietary sugars further can also be beneficial for supporting a faster cleanse.

Ayurvedic experts recommend that you avoid eating raw and undercooked seafood and meat, to prevent parasitic infections in the future after cleansing. While travelling internationally, you should avoid drinking water that is not bottled or purified, ice, fruits that you cannot peel, and bathing or swimming in freshwater.

Ayurvedic Home Remedies for Parasitic Infection Management

- Mix Vidanga powder (Embelia Ribes) with warm water or honey and drink it once every day, preferably in the morning.

- Take a concoction of dry adrak (ginger), kali mirch (black pepper), piper longum (pippali), and honey for 10 to 15 days to prevent these infections.

- Consume Tulsi leaf juice with peach juice and honey.

- Always drink clean and boiled water. You may drink coconut water or water medicated with vidang or ajwain.

- Include foods like ajwain, black pepper, asafoetida, black salt, garlic, dry ginger, and turmeric in your diet. These are natural deworming foods that can protect you against parasitic infections.

- You can also take ajwain with a pinch of salt on an empty stomach in the morning for about one week to eliminate parasites.

- A decoction of daruharidra, nagarmotha, and drumstick bark with the powder of vidanga and piper longum can also help remove parasites.

- For children up to four to five years: soak a cotton ball in groundnut oil or sesame oil and place it close to the anus to relieve itching.

Ayurvedic management of parasitic infections primarily involves making changes in the diet and using these herbal medications. Ayurveda also advises avoiding factors that can cause krimi.

Precautions should be taken to ensure the complete removal of parasites from the body. On full recovery, care must be taken to restore functions of the digestive system by improving Agni or digestive fire.

Dietary Recommendations for Parasitic Infection Management

- Avoid foods rich in carbohydrates like refined flour and packed fruit juices
- Increase your intake of pomegranates, beets, raw garlic, pumpkin seeds, or carrots
- Eat more fibre rich foods as it might help get rid of parasites

Lifestyle Modifications for Parasitic Infection Management

- Avoid holding the urge to pass stools or urine for too long
- Follow cleanliness and good hygiene habits

Conclusion

Natural parasitic cleanses are often effective for preventing and treating these conditions. Patients who suffer from frequent infections can try a parasitic cleanse and adopt the dietary and lifestyle changes Ayurveda recommends to avoid episodes.

Management of Peptic Ulcers Using Natural Ayurvedic Remedies

A peptic ulcer refers to a sore formed when the acidic gastric juices wear off the stomach lining or the intestine's initial part. Peptic ulcers may occur in the stomach lining, the lower part of the oesophagus, or the upper part of the duodenum.

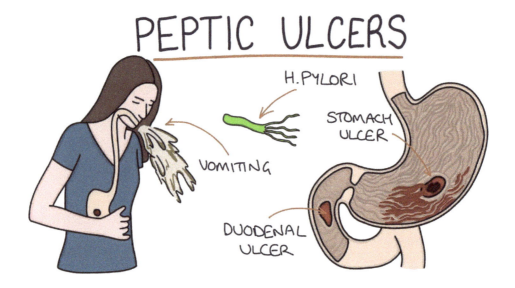

Here is a brief discussion about what peptic ulcers mean, why they occur, and whether Ayurveda can help manage them.

What Are Peptic Ulcers?

Peptic ulcers can occur anywhere in the digestive system. However, the stomach, duodenum, and oesophagus are the most typical affection sites for this condition.

What Are the Symptoms of Peptic Ulcers?

- Intense abdominal pain right after meals or when the stomach is empty
- Abdominal pain that is worse during sleep
- Feeling unwell after eating
- Food eaten regurgitates back
- Difficulty in swallowing food
- Nausea and vomiting
- Weight loss
- Loss of appetite
- Vomiting of blood
- Stools with dark red blood
- Black and tarry stools

What Are the Causes of Peptic Ulcers?

- Stomach infections due to H. Pylori bacteria
- Genetics or family history of peptic ulcers
- Smoking
- Alcohol consumption
- Long term use of corticosteroids or painkillers like non-steroidal anti-inflammatory drugs (NSAIDs)
- Mental stress

What Are the Common Complications of Peptic Ulcers?

The risk of complications linked to peptic ulcers increases if the condition is left untreated.

The common complications may include:

- Peritonitis
- Internal bleeding
- Pyloric stenosis
- Hemodynamic instability
- Scar tissue

Treatment of Peptic Ulcers

Ayurveda recommends certain dietary changes for the treatment and prevention of peptic ulcers.

- It is essential to avoid fried foods or foods and flavourings that can cause the stomach to produce more acids, such as garlic, chilli powder, black pepper, ginger, and caffeine. Alcohol can have the same effect on the stomach and hence, must also be avoided.
- Your diet should contain foods that provide vitamin A and fibres, such as oats, carrots, apples, oranges, flax seeds, psyllium husk, legumes, nuts, and barley.
- The best natural sources of vitamin A include liver, spinach, sweet potatoes, broccoli, kale, and collard greens.
- Foods high in antioxidants, like berries and snap peas, are also recommended.
- Green tea has demonstrated a restrictive and preventive effect on the growth of bacteria

called H. pylori, responsible for triggering the development of peptic ulcers.

- A balanced diet filled with fresh fruits and vegetables and devoid of intense spices and flavouring agents could be perfect for minimising the symptoms of peptic ulcers and promoting the healing of damaged tissues.

- Also, H. pylori infection is known to upset the balance of bacteria and other pathogens in the gut. The use of probiotics like Lactobacillus naturally present in the gut would help restore the natural gut flora.

- Some studies have also suggested that taking probiotic supplements containing certain strains of microorganisms could help relieve antibiotic treatment-linked side effects and improve the balance of gut bacteria.

- Fermented foods can also play a role in maintaining the balance of microbes in your gut. Fermented foods are rich in healthy microbes, like bacteria and yeasts. Eating foods containing these microbes could restore the balance of the gut microbiome and promote healing of the stomach lining. Some of the best-fermented foods to include in your diet to relieve peptic ulcer symptoms are yoghurt, sauerkraut, kimchi, and kefir.

Conclusion

Some evidence suggests that dietary interventions may help prevent and treat stomach ulcers. Following a balanced and nutritious diet is essential for those with stomach ulcers. Making appropriate nutritional changes as recommended by Ayurveda could help alleviate symptoms, keep the body healthy, and reduce the risk of developing stomach ulcers.

The prognosis for patients with peptic ulcers is generally excellent when appropriate dietary changes are adopted.

However, if left untreated, it may progress to cause stomach carcinoma. Hence, it is crucial to avoid factors that can cause or worsen peptic ulcers and adopt healthy dietary and lifestyle habits to relieve the symptoms and protect yourself against complications.

Weight Loss Strategies Recommended by Ayurveda

'How to lose weight' is perhaps the most searched phrase on any search engine. Men and women of all ages want to lose excess fats in the body in hopes of having the perfect figure they see celebrities flaunting on screen. But is there something more to just 'looking good' for the desperation to lose weight?

Yes, weight gain or obesity is a highly complex medical condition. Let's look at this problem from a multifaceted view.

What Is Obesity?

Obesity is a medical condition associated with having excess fat in the body. The state is defined by environmental and genetic factors difficult to control by simple dieting.

How Is Obesity Measured?

A person is considered obese when their Body Mass Index (BMI) is 30 or greater. However, it doesn't mean that people having BMI between 20 and 30 or less than 20 are healthy.

The scope of the term obesity goes beyond just BMI. The need for weight loss for any person doesn't only arise when they cross this 30 mark.

Here are a few other criteria that should be considered for deciding whether or not a person needs to lose weight.

- Family history of obesity: A person with a BMI of more than ten may need to be conscious of their weight if they have a family history of obesity and related illnesses like hypertension and diabetes.

  Positive family history is an indication that a person is more likely to develop obesity and resulting complications in the future. Hence, they need not wait for the BMI to cross 30 before taking steps for losing weight.

- A misleading BMI: Though BMI is considered the best estimate for healthy body weight, one should not ignore that it is just a statistical measurement derived from the height and weight of a person. It does not measure the percentage of body fat, thereby misleading the scale of weight gain.

  For example, the BMI of a muscleman or an athlete may be higher even if he has less fat compared to an unfit person with a lower BMI.

- Unequal distribution of fats: Unequal distribution of fats results from irregular dietary habits and an incorrect proportion of fats, carbohydrates, and proteins in the diet. It is also common in women after pregnancy.

The common parts of the body where unequal distribution of fats is prominent are the belly, arms, thighs, and chest. A protruding tummy or bulging thighs could make a person look quite unattractive.

Strategies for losing weight from these parts of the body are different from the strategies advocated for people who are obese from all over.

Hence, the need to lose weight for any person can be determined only after considering all of these factors.

Why Is It Important to Lose Weight?

An obese person has accumulated so much fat in the body that it can harm their health.

The health risks associated with obesity are given below:

- Bone and cartilage degeneration
- Gallstones
- Asthma
- High blood pressure

- High total cholesterol
- Sleep apnea
- Coronary heart disease
- Stroke
- Type 2 diabetes

Economic Consequences of Abnormal Weight Gain

Being overweight can cause a significant adverse impact on the economic well-being of a person. Healthcare costs associated with obesity and related complications are enormous. It can also have a few indirect costs related to loss of income from decreased productivity, absenteeism, restricted activities, and premature death.

These reasons are enough for anyone to understand why it is essential to maintain a healthy weight.

Before we learn how to lose weight, it's crucial to know why a person gains weight in the first place.

Common Mistakes Made by People While Trying to Lose Weight

Crash Dieting

Dieting or reducing your calorie intake is imperative for losing weight. However, people often tend to do it in the wrong way. One fine day, they decide they want to lose weight and stop eating altogether! They do it well on day-1 and day-2 and may continue till maximum day-3 only to return to their old eating habits.

Too Much Exercise

Just like dieting, exercising, too, is something we often start overenthusiastically. But, starting with one hour of rigorous exercise on the first day itself can result in nothing but severe body aches the next day.

This effect would put an immediate halt on your exercise routine and, consequently, on your weight loss program. And by the time the muscle pains are gone, the desire to lose weight, too, would have disappeared.

Checking the Weight Too Often

Most people buy a new weighing scale and check their weights several times a day to know if their weight loss efforts are yielding any results. They don't realise that the body cannot lose weight overnight.

The effect of dieting and exercising can take at least a week to reflect on the weighing scale. Most often, this habit results in disappointment, in which they give up their efforts thinking they will never be able to lose any weight.

Why Do Most People Gain Back the Weight They Have Lost?

Losing weight is difficult, but maintaining weight is even more complicated!

After all, when your clothes stops shrinking in size and the compliments start pouring frequently, just one more cookie doesn't seem like a big deal. After the success of your attempt at losing weight, you start thinking it's not all that difficult, and you can do it anytime at your will. You start feeling overconfident about your weight loss strategy. Losing weight doesn't seem like a great challenge as it used to be, and that's where the journey of faltering with your weight loss program begins.

Here are some essential habits that could make you gain back the lost weight:

Yo-Yo Dieting

There exists a typical yo-yo pattern of dieting in people trying to lose weight. It simply means alternate periods of overeating and crash dieting that keep following each other turn by turn. It is often a result of a diet that's too restrictive. It can also arise from the desperation for quick results.

However, it can put you back to your regular high-calorie diet sooner than expected as the body is not used to eating so little and would send desperate signals to the brain, compelling you to overeat.

People, who follow a very low-calorie diet, tend to regain significantly more weight than those who opt for a more forgiving plan. Hence, experts advise people to start with a sensible diet program that is not too low in calories to give your body some time to adjust to the lower quota of daily calories.

Avoiding the Scale

After the initial success of your weight loss efforts, you may not find it very important to keep a regular check on your weight. You should thus give a miss to the weighing scale too often.

And as you avoid keeping tabs on how your body is changing, it would become easier for those extra pounds to creep into your body and get out of control before you realise that it's happening!

So, never avoid stepping on the scale! Slip in on your skinny jeans once in a while, or run a measuring tape around your waist to keep a check on your weight. Browsing through your selfies from time to time would also help you get alarmed about the weight you have regained.

Skipping the Gym

Our body gains or loses muscles depending on how much and what kind of physical activities we perform. So, hitting your weight-loss target is not an excuse to forgo your exercise routine.

Regular exercising can regulate the hormones that control your appetite making it easier to resist impulsive bingeing. Regular exercises would boost the metabolism of the body. This effect would improve the rate at which calories are burnt, thereby stabilising your weight.

Overeating

Emotional eating is common to all. Once you have lost a few pounds, it would be hard to ignore the temptation to binge eat.

Initially, it may happen less often and then go on to become a daily routine. And the faster it happens, the faster you would gain back the weight you had lost. This outcome is bound to put you back to the same point on the weighing scale from where you started!

Shedding pounds is necessary, but it should not become just your favourite pastime, something that you start doing as and when you like and then stop doing when you think it's no longer needed.

Make it a continued effort and imbibe it as a habit or a part of your daily routine so that you can keep your weight stable.

The Right Attitude for Weight Loss

Ask any diet trainer or weight loss professional what the most crucial factor that determines the success of the weight loss regimen is, and most of them would surely say it is the attitude of a person.

Having a positive attitude is undoubtedly the first thing you need to achieve and maintain a healthy weight. Without this, you don't stand a chance of achieving your weight loss goals.

What Is Meant by the 'Right' Attitude?

Attitude means your preparedness to take the right action. It is your approach to your situation, in this case, you being overweight, based on your:

- Feelings
- Values
- Beliefs
- Behaviour

Attitude could be positive or negative. It can determine how you choose to view the world. Where weight loss is concerned, the degree to which you maintain a positive attitude about yourself, the people around you, and the circumstances will determine your likelihood of achieving your target weight.

The Wrong Attitude

A wrong attitude could be a significant roadblock for success in your efforts.

Here are a few specific signs of negative attitude to weight loss:

- You believe that eating only healthy foods can stop you from having fun in life
- You tend to place greater value on relaxing than on being active
- You feel that exercise is a punishment for eating well
- You fail to make proper lifestyle changes because you think, "It's all too hard"

These are just a few examples of a wrong attitude. To find out if you have a negative mindset to healthy eating, exercising, and weight loss, listen carefully to what that inner voice says when you think about making positive changes in your life.

Developing The Right Attitude

Developing a positive attitude is the first thing you need to achieve your weight loss goals successfully.

Most obese people believe that they were born to be fat. However, several studies have found that people who 'think' their gene pool regulates their waist size are more likely to be heavier than those who do not blame their genes.

Though genes do indeed have some impact on your weight to some extent, it is, after all, the lifestyle choices you make that determine how shapely or large you become. You must correct this attitude and accept the responsibility that your shape and weight are determined by your lifestyle and food choices.

"I'll never lose this weight!" This remark is the common statement of overweight individuals who have given up after several unsuccessful attempts. This attitude only shows that the person may have set their expectations too high.

If you think you can get back to your high school weight, you are bound to feel overwhelmed! Research has shown that people with moderate obesity can improve their overall health and drastically decrease their risk for heart diseases and diabetes by reducing just 7 to 10% of their weight.

Attitude adjustment for this kind of thought process involves setting challenging but reasonable goals that can lead to long-term weight loss success.

Here are some effective ways to develop the right attitude for weight loss:

- Make positive lifestyle changes. Don't think you're 'on a diet'; instead, believe you are 'getting healthy'. These phrases are affirming and more positive and would not bring a feeling of restriction and deprivation to mind.

- Get clear about why you want to lose weight. What exactly do you want to gain by being slim and healthy? When you finally achieve that slim figure, what will be you most thrilled about? Write these reasons down and read them daily so that you stay motivated.

- Build yourself up. Never talk down to yourself. Avoid berating yourself when you eat something you should not have. Do not engage in defeatist thinking like, "I'll never lose this weight."

- Do not try to 'hurry up to lose weight'. The faster you want to lose weight, the more you will constantly call attention to things moving seemingly slower than you had expected. All this could make you feel frustrated and more likely to give up because you are not getting the results you expected. So, keep affirming that you have plenty of time. Adhere to a patient attitude. This mindset would relieve the pressure in getting results faster and allow you to feel good about the results you are achieving – rather than feeling obsessed about the results you haven't.

- Ditch the negatives and focus on the positives. Spend a few minutes every day tuning in a vision of yourself being healthier and slender. Try to bring the feeling into your body. Focus on this feeling at least once a day. This attitude would make achieving your goal seem more realistic.

- Becoming an optimist will bring you many benefits. This mentality would lead to success and improve your ability to cope with stressors. By developing the right attitude, you would be able to attain a healthy weight, have more energy, feel greater inner strength, develop the ability to motivate yourself and be happier.

The Critical Role Nutrition Plays in Losing Weight

A nutritious diet is the key to the success of any weight management program. The benefits of good nutrition include a rise in overall energy, control of blood sugar levels, reduction of blood pressure, and improvement in cholesterol levels.

Many of you must have tried one or other popular diet programs and experienced the vicious unhealthy weight loss/weight regain cycle.

Some diets suggest eliminating specific food groups, while others suggest taking mega-doses of vitamins and supplements. But, the fact is that this 'yo-yo' cycle eventually gets you no closer to your weight loss target. All you are left with is feeling discouraged.

A healthy weight management program recommended by Ayurveda incorporates a nutritious diet. Here are the answers to common questions that would help you understand why eating a nutritious diet is critical to a healthy weight loss.

What Is a Nutritious Diet?

The three basic principles of good nutrition are balance, moderation, and variety. Adding a variety of food to your diet is critical to ensuring you eat from the five major food groups. This is important because there is no single food that can supply all the required minerals and nutrients our body needs. A balanced diet supplies the calories and nutrients the body requires when eaten in appropriate amounts.

The exact serving size may differ among individuals based on their age, gender, and activity level. Some people believe they must deprive themselves of their favourite foods to lose weight, but eating these foods in moderation could be a key to long-term weight loss.

What Is Meant by "Eating the Rainbow"?

"Eating the rainbow" is just a simple phrase that makes eating veggies and fruits more pleasurable! While making your plate full of fruits and veggies, choose foods packed with essential minerals and vitamins and have vibrant colours that appeal to your senses.

For example:

- Red: Bell peppers, onions, strawberries, red beets, cranberries, cherries, tomatoes, and watermelon

- Green: Dark lettuce, cabbage, broccoli, cucumber, kiwi, spinach, grapes, avocado, honeydew, and kale

- Orange and Yellow: Carrots, bananas, oranges, sweet potatoes, mangoes, apricots, peaches, and squash

- Blue and purple: Grapes, blackberries, plums, blueberries, purple carrots, purple cabbage, and purple potatoes

Does the Term 'Fat-Free' Mean No Calories?

The term 'fat-free' only means the food has fewer calories than the full-fat version of the same product. Besides, most processed fat-free foods contain as many calories as the full-fat versions of the same food. These foods may also have added refined sugars, starch, and salt to improve the texture and flavours after fats are removed. Eating these foods only adds plenty of calories to your diet.

Tips to Make Sure You Eat a Nutritious Diet:

- Eat small portions
- Make sure half of your plate for each meal contains fruits and veggies
- Choose fresh fruit items or yoghurt for dessert
- Use a smaller plate when eating your favourite foods. Keep track of how much and how often you eat your favourite food. This practice will help you analyse the success or failure of your weight loss efforts.
- Eat proteins like whole grains, eggs, beans, nuts, and poultry
- Limit added sugars and salt (sodium) in your food
- Limit the use of toppings that are high in calories like cheese, mayonnaise, bacon, tartar sauce, and salad dressings
- Sip on cold water instead of soda
- Pick baked or steamed items over fried ones

Understanding the importance of nutrition for your health and weight loss efforts and making sure you eat a balanced diet are the keys to shedding those extra pounds and keeping them at bay. Incorporating proper nutrition is essential for achieving sustained weight loss.

Conclusion

Weight loss is tough to get through! It requires a lot of patience, determination, and a positive attitude to succeed. Start with accepting that your weight gain results from the bad habits you have developed for yourself over the years. It does not mean you have to blame yourself; it is just about taking responsibility for your actions. This approach would help you understand that the solution also lies within you if you created the problem.

Only you can take steps to lose weight. Once you realise this, the rest will be easier.

What Is Metabolic Syndrome and the Best Natural Ways to Manage It

Metabolic syndrome refers to a cluster of conditions that occur together, increasing the risk of heart diseases, stroke, and diabetes. These diseases range from increased blood pressure, excess fat depositions around the waist, high blood sugar, and abnormal cholesterol and triglyceride levels.

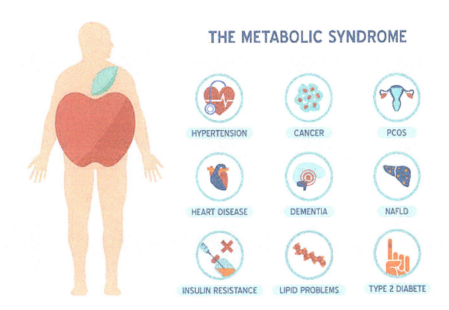

Having just one of these conditions does not necessarily mean you suffer from metabolic syndrome. However, it does mean that you have a higher risk of other serious diseases. If you develop more of these disorders, your chance of severe complications, like type 2 diabetes and cardiac diseases, becomes more likely.

What Are the Symptoms of Metabolic Syndrome?

Most diseases linked to metabolic syndrome do not have apparent signs and symptoms. One sign that could be visible is a larger waist circumference. Also, if your blood sugar level is high, you would notice some signs and symptoms of diabetes like increased thirst or urination, severe fatigue, and blurred vision.

What Are the Causes of Metabolic Syndrome?

Metabolic syndrome is linked to obesity and physical inactivity.

It is also associated with a condition known as insulin resistance. The digestive system breaks down the foods you eat into sugar in normal individuals. A hormone called insulin secreted by the pancreas helps sugars enter the cells to be used as fuel.

However, in patients with insulin resistance, the cells do not respond to insulin normally, resulting in glucose not entering the cells efficiently. Due to this, the blood sugar levels tend to rise even when the body produces more insulin to reduce blood sugar levels.

What Are the Risk Factors for Metabolic Syndrome?

The following factors can increase the risk of developing metabolic syndrome:

- Age: the risk of metabolic syndrome rises with age.
- Ethnicity: Hispanics, particularly Hispanic women, appear to have the greatest risk of developing metabolic syndrome.
- Diabetes: You are more likely to develop metabolic syndrome if you have diabetes or a family history of diabetes.
- Obesity: Too much body weight, especially in the abdomen, can increase the risk of metabolic syndrome.
- Other diseases: The risk of metabolic syndrome is more in patients with polycystic ovary syndrome, non-alcoholic fatty liver disease, and sleep apnoea.

Ayurvedic Treatment for Metabolic Syndrome Prevention

Eat Enough

It would be best if you ate enough to speed up your metabolism. Though it is crucial to cut down your calorie intake to lose weight, a drastic reduction in your food consumption can slow down your metabolism.

When you starve yourself or eat too little, your body would slow down its metabolic functions and begin to break down the muscle tissues for its fuel requirement.

As a result, you would not lose any weight despite eating less. So, the best way would be to reduce your calorie intake by avoiding fatty and high-carb foods while maintaining the quantity of food you eat the same.

Never Skip Breakfast

It is natural for people to skip their breakfast to prevent diseases linked to abnormal metabolisms such as obesity and diabetes.

But, this could prove to be counterproductive to your overall health, putting you at risk of metabolic syndrome. Eating breakfast can jump-start your metabolism and keep the energy level high all day long and reduce your risk of diabetes and metabolic syndrome.

So, make sure you never skip your breakfast. You can eat a cup of yoghurt, an apple, oatmeal, or any low-calorie food in the morning to keep your metabolism working at its best.

Eat Plenty of Whole Grains

Whole grains like brown rice, quinoa, oats, barley, and millet are packed with fibres. They can fill you up more than other foods with the same calories. This effect would leave you with hardly any room for a second helping and allow you to burn more calories by stimulating the digestive system to work harder.

Eat High-Fibre Foods

High-fibre foods can be the best foods to eat when fighting against obesity and body fats. If you want to increase your metabolic rate and burn the fats stored in the body, you should eat fruits and veggies high in fibre, like oranges, melons, pumpkin, and papaya.

These foods are difficult to digest and demand more effort from your digestive tract. This response would result in the flaming up of your body's metabolic functions and reduce your risk of metabolic syndrome.

Drink Cold Water

Drinking cold water could help boost your metabolism. When your drink cold water - the more chilled it is, the better - the body has to spend more calories to bring it to the body temperature. This reaction would help increase the body's metabolic rate.

Organic Foods

It has been found that the people who eat foods containing organochlorines experience a more significant dip in their metabolic rate.

Organochlorines are pollutants present in food that has been sprayed with pesticides during their cultivation. Organochlorines are stored in the body in fat cells, causing you to gain weight. These toxins can interfere with your metabolism and energy-burning processes.

The non-organic versions of foods contain the highest levels of pesticides. Hence, make sure you choose organic foods when buying apples, peaches, bell peppers, nectarines, celery, strawberries, grapes, cherries, lettuce, and pears.

Exercise

Exercises of any form, including cardio, would help increase your metabolic rate or burn calories more effectively if you follow a strict workout schedule. Regular exercise is what you need to boost your metabolism and keep it at its peak.

Regular exercises would not just help you burn more calories but also modify your DNA, thus increasing your metabolism.

Cardio

Cardio is the best workout to rave up your metabolism. It would boost the metabolic rate and keep your metabolic functions running smoothly. Doing cardio for 45 minutes two to three times a week is enough to ensure an enhanced metabolism. When combined with a healthy diet, it would help you lose one or two pounds in just two to three weeks.

De-Stress Yourself

Mental stress can significantly influence the metabolic functions of your body. It can not just drive you crazy and make you prone to depression but also slow down your metabolism. This effect of stress could be attributed to the stress hormone called cortisol.

Long periods of mental stress would increase the level of this hormone, which, in turn, would inhibit the ability of your body to burn fat. Hence, the best way to increase your metabolism is to de-stress yourself.

Take a few moments out from your busy routine to perform stress-busting exercises like yoga and meditation to keep your metabolism in check.

Do a Mini-Workout

A mini-workout of 10 minutes can effectively maintain your metabolic rate. When you are pressed for time, you can still manage to remain fit in enough exercises to burn almost 200 calories a day.

Skipping your exercise routine on busy days could reduce the benefits you have achieved so far with your hard work of several weeks or months. So, even when you do not have the time for a full workout, sweat out for a few minutes to avoid losing the benefits of your long-drawn efforts!

Foods You Should Eat to Prevent Metabolic Syndrome:

- Citrus fruits
- Cayenne pepper
- Broccoli

- Dark Chocolate
- Green tea
- Cinnamon

Conclusion

Making simple changes in your diet would allow your body to burn more calories and restore a healthy metabolism. Adopting these habits would speed up weight loss, protect you against obesity and diabetes, and reduce your risk of developing metabolic syndrome.

Ayurvedic Treatment and Prevention for Gallbladder Stones

Gallstones are the hardened deposits of digestive juices formed in the gallbladder. The gallbladder is a pear-shaped, tiny organ present below the liver at the right side of our abdomen. It holds digestive juices called the bile released into the small intestine.

Gallstones often range in size, from as small as the grain of sand or even as large as a tennis ball.

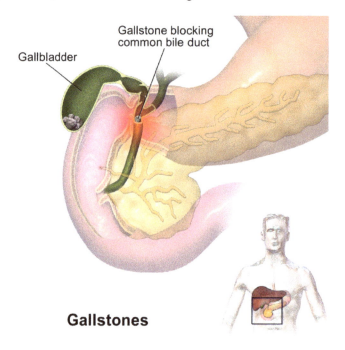

Gallstones

Some patients develop just one gallstone, while others simultaneously develop multiple stones in the gallbladder.

What Are the Causes of Gallstones?

It is not clear what causes gallstones to form. Some of the possible factors responsible for causing gallstones include:

- Bile contains too much cholesterol and enough chemicals to dissolve the cholesterol excreted by the liver in typical cases. However, if the liver releases more cholesterol than the bile can dissolve, the extra cholesterol may form crystals that eventually turn into stones.

- Bile contains too much bilirubin. Bilirubin is a chemical produced when the body breaks down or disintegrates the red blood cells. Some conditions can cause the liver to release too much bilirubin. These conditions include liver cirrhosis, certain blood disorders, and biliary tract infections. The excess of bilirubin can contribute to the formation of gallstones.

- The gallbladder fails to empty correctly. When the gallbladder does not empty often enough or entirely, the bile may become highly concentrated, contributing to the development of gallstones.

What Are the Different Types of Gallstones?

The types of gallstones that may form in the gallbladder include:

- Pigment gallstones are the black or dark brown stones formed when the bile contains too much bilirubin.
- Cholesterol gallstones: These are the most common forms of gallstones. The cholesterol gallstone usually appears yellowish in colour. These stones are mainly composed of undissolved cholesterol but may also contain other components.

What Are the Risk Factors for Gallstones?

The factors that could increase your risk of developing gallstones include:

- Being over 40 years of age
- Being female
- Being of Mexican or Hispanic origin
- Being a Native American
- Being pregnant
- Eating a diet rich in foods containing cholesterol
- Eating a low-fibre diet
- Having a family history of liver diseases or gallstones
- Being sedentary
- Eating a high-fat diet
- Pre-existing blood disorders, such as leukaemia or sickle cell anaemia
- Being obese or overweight
- Losing weight too quickly
- Pre-existing diabetes

- Taking drugs that contain oestrogens, like oral contraceptives and hormone replacement therapy medications
- Pre-existing liver disease

What Are the Symptoms of Gallstones?

Gallstones may not cause any signs or symptoms. The resulting signs and symptoms only develop when a gallstone lodges in a duct and causes an obstruction.

Some of the common signs of gallstones include:

- Nausea and vomiting
- Sharp, rapidly intensifying, and sudden pain in the upper right part of the abdomen
- Back pain between the shoulder blades
- Rapidly intensifying, sudden pain in the centre of the abdomen, just below the breastbone
- Pain in the right shoulder

Pain caused due to gallstones usually lasts several minutes to a few hours.

It is advisable to seek immediate medical care in case you develop signs and symptoms of severe gallstone complications, such as:

- Abdominal pain that is so severe that you can not even sit still and find any comfortable position
- High fever with shivering or chills
- Jaundice (yellowish discolouration of the skin, nails, and the white of your eyes)

What Are the Possible Complications of Gallstones?

The complications of gallstones include the following:

Inflammation of the Gallbladder

A gallstone may become lodged at the neck of the organ, causing cholecystitis (inflammation of the gallbladder). Cholecystitis may cause severe pain with fever.

Blockage in the Common Bile Duct

Gallstones can sometimes block the ducts (or tubes) through which the bile flows from the gallbladder or the liver to the small intestine. Severe jaundice, pain, or bile duct infection may result.

Obstruction in the Pancreatic Duct

The pancreatic duct is the tube running from the pancreas and connecting to the common bile duct (CBD) before entering the duodenum. Pancreatic juices that support the process of digestion flow through this duct.

Gallstones may obstruct the pancreatic duct causing inflammation in the pancreas (pancreatitis). This condition may cause severe, constant pain in the abdomen and usually requires immediate hospitalisation.

Gallbladder Cancer

Patients with a history of gallstones often have a higher risk of gallbladder cancer. However, gallbladder cancer is extremely rare.

Diagnosis of Gallstones

- Blood tests to detect infections, pancreatitis, jaundice, and other complications caused by gallstones.
- Abdominal ultrasound
- Endoscopic retrograde cholangiopancreatography
- Endoscopic ultrasound (EUS)
- Other imaging tests

Ayurvedic Recommendations for Gallstone Prevention

You can reduce your risk of gallbladder stones if you:

- Avoid skipping meals. Ayurveda recommends sticking to strict mealtimes every day. Skipping your meals and fasting could increase your risk of developing gallstones.
- Lose weight slowly. When you are trying to lose weight, go slower. Rapid weight loss may increase your risk of gallstones. Aim to lose about 1 or 2 pounds (or 0.5 to 1 kilogram) of weight per week.
- Eat high-fibre foods. Including fibre-rich foods in your diet, like fresh fruits, whole grains, and vegetables, could lower the risk of gallstones.
- Maintain a healthy weight. Being overweight or obese could increase your risk of gallstones. Working to achieve a healthy weight based on your height by controlling your intake of high-calorie, high-fat, and high-carb foods and increasing the number of your

physical activities could help you maintain an average weight and avoid gallstones.

Once you achieve an average weight, you can work towards maintaining that weight by sticking to your healthy dietary habits and continuing to exercise.

Herbal Remedies for Gallstone Treatment

- Garlic
- Allium Cepa
- Asafoetida
- Holy basil

Conclusion

Regular use of herbal remedies and adopting preventive strategies to improve your diet and physical activities are the keys to avoiding your risk of gallstones.

The Best Ayurvedic Herbal Remedies for Liver Health

There is an alarming rise in the incidence of diseases affecting the liver worldwide. Many patients around the globe live with conditions involving the functions and structure of the liver, such as cirrhosis, alcoholic liver disease, non-alcoholic fatty liver disease (NAFLD), liver cancer, hepatic failure, and hepatitis.

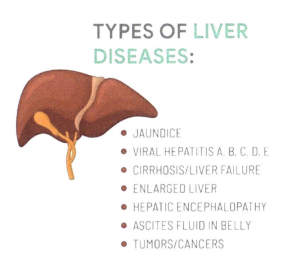

The common risk factors for these liver diseases include increased alcohol intake, obesity, high blood sugar level, high blood pressure, elevated cholesterol and triglyceride level, and viruses.

Liver diseases can be treated in several ways, including medications, nutritional therapies, lifestyle changes, and immunotherapy.

In addition to these standard treatments, alternative therapies, including herbal remedies, could also help in improving and protecting liver functions.

Here are some of the best herbs that have been shown immense promise in managing liver diseases.

Turmeric

Turmeric and its active component curcumin are linked to various impressive medicinal benefits.

Turmeric has potent antioxidant, anti-inflammatory, and anticancer properties that make it an effective herb for patients with liver disease.

A study in patients with NAFLD has demonstrated that the daily treatment with about 500 mg of curcumin for eight weeks could significantly reduce the liver fat content. It would also help control the levels of ALT and AST while improving liver functions.

Green Tea

Green tea and its primary polyphenol compound called epigallocatechin-3-gallate (EGCG) could effectively treat liver conditions.

Some studies have revealed that supplementing with the extracts of green tea could help treat patients with liver diseases safely and effectively.

It has been found to reduce the markers for liver damage such as alanine aminotransferase (ALT) and aspartate aminotransferase (AST) and cause a marked improvement in the symptoms of liver conditions.

Liquorice

Liquorice root has been shown to possess antiviral, anti-inflammatory, and hepato-protective properties.

The primary active component of this herb is a saponin compound called glycyrrhizin, commonly used in traditional Japanese and Chinese medicine to treat liver ailments.

Liquorice extract can be effective in the management of fatty liver diseases. It would also significantly reduce the markers for liver damage, including gamma-glutamyl transferase (GGT), ALT, and AST.

Milk Thistle

Silymarin, also called milk thistle, comprises a group of compounds extracted from the seeds of milk thistle plants (Silybum marianum). The compounds include silybin, silydianin, and silychristin.

Milk thistle can be effective in treating liver and bile duct conditions. Research shows that this herb may have powerful liver-protective properties.

It is suggested that silymarin can produce a strong antioxidant effect that might help promote cell regeneration in the liver, reduce inflammation, and thus, alleviate patients with liver diseases.

Silymarin may help protect against the progression of liver diseases and prolong the life of patients with alcoholic cirrhosis. It could also enhance patients' overall quality of life with chronic liver diseases.

Ginseng

Ginseng is one of the most effective herbal remedies known for its powerful antioxidant and anti-inflammatory properties.

Several studies have demonstrated that this herb could produce antioxidant effects and protect against liver injuries caused due to viruses, alcohol, and toxins. Moreover, it may also boost liver cell regeneration, especially after surgeries.

Ginger

Ginger root is another culinary ingredient commonly used to treat several health conditions, including hepatic diseases.

It would reduce ALT levels and total and bad cholesterol (LDL). It may also help control the fasting blood sugar and level of an inflammatory marker called C-reactive protein (CRP).

Danshen

Danshen is commonly used in traditional Chinese medicine. It is a dried root of Salvia miltiorrhiza Bunge. Several studies have shown that this herb may have a positive effect on the functions of the liver.

Danshen may help protect the liver tissues against alcohol-related damage and promote regeneration of the liver tissues. Danshen may also help reduce liver fibrosis and hepatic carcinoma symptoms with other herbal remedies like ginger and garlic.

Garlic

Botanically, garlic is considered a vegetable. However, it is one of the most popular components of most herbal remedies. It is packed with powerful antioxidant, anticancer, and anti-inflammatory plant compounds, like allicin, ajoene, and alliin, that could help support liver health.

One study has found that patients who took 800 mg of a garlic supplement per day for at least 15 weeks have experienced a significant reduction in the levels of hepatic damage markers such as ALT, AST, and LDL (bad) cholesterol, compared with a placebo group.

Garlic can also help in improving the severity of liver fat accumulation.

Astragalus

Astragalus is commonly used in Ayurvedic and traditional Chinese medicine. Potent natural medicinal compounds, such as saponins, polysaccharides, and isoflavonoids characterise this medicine. It has powerful therapeutic and preventive properties.

Astragalus is generally considered safer than most commonly used drugs to manage liver diseases. It has not been associated with any form of liver damage.

This medicine may also help protect against liver cirrhosis and fibrosis. The high-fat diet-induced hepatic diseases such as fatty liver could also be prevented by regular use of this herb.

Ginkgo biloba

Ginkgo biloba is one of the most popular herbal remedies that have been linked to improved liver functions. It may help reduce liver fibrosis symptoms and enhance liver functions while slowing down the prognosis of chronic hepatic diseases.

Conclusion

These herbs have been associated with improved liver functions. These are effective natural herbal remedies for patients with liver conditions and those at a higher risk of developing liver diseases due to risk factors like a high-fat diet, alcohol intake, and family history.

However, it is essential to make appropriate changes in your diet and lifestyle, such as limiting your intake of unhealthy fats like trans fats and saturated fats. You should also ideally avoid alcohol intake to protect yourself from the severe complications of liver diseases.

The Natural Remedies for the Treatment and Prevention of Liver Cirrhosis

Liver cirrhosis is a chronic, end-stage liver disease primarily caused by portal hypertension. Over time, it leads to fluid collection in the peritoneal cavity or ascites.

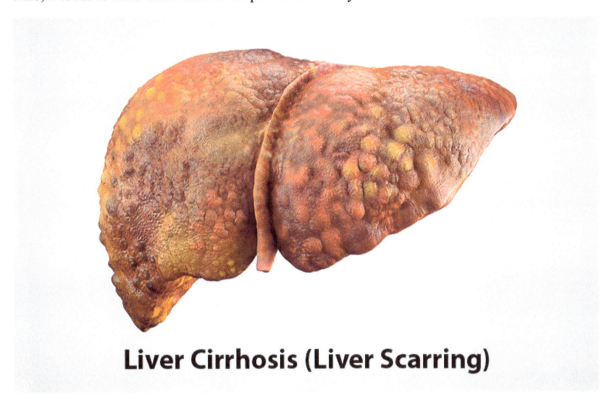

The liver is one of the most vital organs that help perform many metabolic processes. It also helps maintain the process of digestion. It must be taken good care of.

It is usually people who consume excessive alcohol and live a sedentary lifestyle without exercise or healthy habits like yoga and meditation are likely to develop liver dysfunctions that eventually lead to liver cirrhosis.

In some advanced cases, liver transplantation is the only possible mode of treatment for patients with cirrhosis. Here is a brief discussion about what liver cirrhosis means, why it occurs, and the natural remedies to manage this condition.

What Is Liver Cirrhosis?

Cirrhosis is a chronic disease affecting the liver. It occurs when healthy cells in the liver are replaced by unhealthy, damaged or scarred cells, in which the liver functions are disturbed.

These changes are often linked to long-term damage and occur due to unhealthy dietary and lifestyle habits.

Cirrhosis develops due to the excessive collection of toxins and reduced metabolic functions, leading to insufficient nutrition available to cells and tissues.

It is a slowly progressive condition that develops over several years. If the disease is allowed to progress, the build-up of scar tissues could eventually completely inhibit liver functions.

Cirrhosis develops when continuous and long-term damage to the liver occurs. When healthy liver tissues are destroyed and replaced by scar tissues, the condition becomes more serious. The result can be blood supply blockage to the hepatic tissues.

What Are the Causes of Cirrhosis?

The common causes of cirrhosis of the liver are:

- Fatty liver disease
- Long-term alcohol abuse
- Infections due to hepatitis B or C virus
- Genetic diseases
- Exposure to toxic metals

What Are the Symptoms of Cirrhosis?

One of the primary methods to help diagnose this condition is through laboratory blood tests.

Symptoms are not very common during the early stage of this disease.

However, as the scar tissues accumulate, the ability of the hepatic cells to function correctly is severely affected.

Once these changes develop, patients may develop the following signs and symptoms:

- Dilation of blood capillaries that become visible under the skin of the wall of the upper abdomen.
- Itching of the skin
- Insomnia

- Loss of appetite
- Fatigue
- Loss of weight
- Pain and tenderness in the area the liver is situated
- Nausea
- Intense weakness
- Red and blotchy palms

The following signs and symptoms may develop as liver cirrhosis progresses:

- Faster heartbeat
- Bleeding gums
- **Difficulty in digesting drugs**
- Loss of mass in the body, especially in the upper arms
- Dizziness
- Confusion
- Fluid build-up on ankles, feet, and legs, known as oedema
- Increased susceptibility to bruising
- Hair loss
- Reduced memory
- Jaundice or yellowing discolouration of the skin, white of the eyes, and tongue
- Frequent fevers
- Muscle cramps
- Increased risk of infections
- Breathlessness
- Nosebleeds
- Problems with walking

In some cases, as the fibrous scar tissues completely replace the liver tissue, regenerative nodules begin to form. These small lumps appear as the hepatic tissues try to repair the damage.

Treatment of Cirrhosis

Treatment for Alcohol Dependency

It is imperative to treat the patient for alcohol dependency to ensure a faster recovery. Patients must be educated about the need to stop drinking alcohol as cirrhosis is likely to worsen faster due to the long-term or regular and heavy consumption of alcohol. In most cases, a treatment program for managing alcohol dependency is essential.

Medications

The patients have often been prescribed drugs that help control liver cell damage caused due to factors like hepatitis B and C.

Reducing Pressure in the Portal Vein

Blood flow may 'back up' into the portal vein that supplies blood to the liver, causing an increase in the pressure in this vein. Medications or herbs may be prescribed to regulate pressure in the portal vein and other blood vessels in the body.

These medications aim to prevent the risk of severe bleeding. The signs of bleeding could be detected with the help of endoscopy.

If the patient passes bloody stools or vomits blood, he probably has developed severe complications like oesophageal varices from the increased portal pressure. Immediate therapy must be administered to the patient to prevent life-threatening complications linked to oesophageal varices.

Ayurvedic Herbs for the Treatment of Cirrhosis

There are numerous benefits of using Ayurvedic herbs for managing cirrhosis. Ayurvedic herbs can help slow down the progress of cirrhosis by working through a variety of mechanisms, as explained below:

- Detoxification of the liver and other body organs is considered essential for keeping the liver healthy. Natural herbs possess an abundance of powerful antioxidants. These herbs could help eliminate hazardous toxins and chemicals from the body and thus, improve liver functions, thereby preventing tissue scarring.

- Proper digestion is known to play a significant role in improving the health and functions of the liver. Natural herbal remedies could help enhance the process of digestion and prevent cellular damage to the liver.

- Ayurvedic herbs could boost your immunity against bacteria and viruses and protect the liver against chronic hepatitis caused due to infections.

- Herbal remedies contain nutrients that can support tissue repair and cellular growth, thus enabling faster recovery of patients.

- Natural herbs could help maintain optimum blood circulation and eliminate excess toxins and fats from the body. This effect would help you maintain a healthy body weight and reduce the risk of cirrhosis.

According to the Ayurveda guidelines, it is possible to protect yourself against the risk of cirrhosis by adopting the following habits:

- Eat fresh fruits and vegetables

- Avoid alcohol consumption

- Do meditation and yoga to keep the body and mind healthy and active

- Detoxify your body regularly to keep your liver cells healthy and functional

- Do fasting for two days a week to support natural cleansing and keep the body free of toxins

- Increase your intake of antioxidant-rich foods

- Keep your body well-hydrated by drinking at least 2 to 2.5 litres of water every day

- Eat a low-salt diet

Some of the best herbs that could help reduce the risk of cirrhosis or slow down the progress of this disease. As mentioned in this chapter, these herbs include Liquorice, Turmeric, Flax Seeds, Amala, Green Tea, Giloy, Triphala, Guggul, Long Pepper, Brahmi, and Neem.

Conclusion

The chances of a patient surviving cirrhosis depend on the severity and extent of the scarring.

Continued alcohol consumption and advanced age are linked to higher mortality risk in people with cirrhosis. On the other hand, those who adopt healthier dietary and lifestyle habits such as limiting alcohol intake and eating a nutritious diet can improve the prognosis.

Best Ayurvedic Remedies for the Management of Arthritis and Other Bone Diseases

Most people think that arthritis and most other bone diseases can only affect the knee and hip joints. This is one of the reasons they believe it will not impact their life; even if they are leading a sedentary life that involves spending a significant part of the day sitting at one place and with minimum mobility.

However, some forms of arthritis, such as rheumatoid arthritis and osteoarthritis, could affect the hands and other joints. The smaller joints in your fingers become progressively challenging to move, which severely impacts the quality of your life.

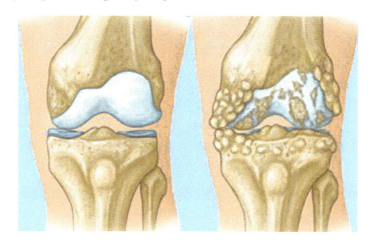

Imagine not being able to hold a cup of coffee in your hands, write properly, cut vegetables, or even brush your teeth. Over a period, your life becomes dependent on painkillers, which only worsen your overall health by causing severe long-term side effects.

Luckily, you could avoid all of this by simply using the natural Ayurvedic remedies that work effectively in treating arthritis and other bone diseases shown below:

Before that, let's look at the common causes of bone diseases and the most effective natural ways to relieve them.

What Causes Arthritis and Back Pain?

Strain and Sprain

Strain and sprain is the most common cause of acute or short-lasting arthritis and back pain. It usually stems from a sudden or excessive strain on your back, resulting in tension and injuries. The common causes of arthritis and back pain related to strain and sprain include:

- Strained ligaments and muscles
- Injuries, fractures, and falls
- An increased muscle tension
- Damaged intervertebral disks
- Muscle spasms

Some of the activities that could be responsible for causing strains and spasms in the back muscles and ligaments include:

- Lifting something improperly
- Making an abrupt and awkward movement
- Lifting something too heavy

Structural Problems

Structural problems in the back could also cause excessive strain on back muscles and bones, resulting in back pain.

Some of these include:

- Bulging disks: When the discs bulge backwards, they impose pressure on the nerves passing through the two vertebrae spaces. This stance could result in more pressure on the nerves and cause pain in the back and legs.
- Ruptured disks: All the vertebrae in your spine are cushioned by disks to protect them against shocks and jerks. The rupture of these disks may deprive your back of protective mechanisms resulting in more pressure on the muscles and nerves, resulting in back pain.
- Sciatica: Sciatica refers to a sharp, shooting pain that radiates to the lower back through the buttock along the back of the leg. The pain often runs to the ankles or heels and causes severe discomfort and irritation. This cause of back pain is linked to the herniated or bulging disc pressing on the sciatic nerve.
- Abnormal curvatures of the spine: The spinal column of a human body is designed to have a unique curvature that helps us maintain balance and avoid falling. An abnormal spine curvature could increase your risk of back pain as it can create more pressure and strain on

your muscles while maintaining balance.

- Arthritis: Osteoarthritis is a significant cause of back pain in obese individuals. It occurs from inflammation at the ends of bones that worsens when they rub against each other during movements.

- It usually affects the thighs and knees as these are the weight-bearing bones of your body. Hence, they are likely to suffer damage due to the entire body weight exerted on them.

- If not appropriately managed, osteoarthritis can worsen over a period resulting in severe loss of mobility and even disability. When osteoarthritis affects the vertebral column, the space around the spinal cord narrows due to the inflammatory changes like swelling. This condition is called spinal stenosis.

Besides these, a few factors can cause or worsen back pain. These factors are usually related to your lifestyle, and hence, easily modifiable.

Let us learn more about such causes of back pain that you can easily avoid by making healthy changes to your lifestyle.

Modifiable Causes of Arthritis and Back Pain

Living a Tech-Dependent Life

You are more likely to suffer from back pain if you are a screen-king. Whether it is your television, laptop, or smartphone, the longer you spend with these gadgets, the higher your risk of developing arthritis and back pain.

Your Movements and Posture

The most common modifiable cause of back pain results from your everyday activities and incorrect or poor posture. These activities strain the muscles in the back more and cause arthritis and backache.

Some of the examples include:

- Severe coughing and sneezing
- Sitting in a hunched position while working on computers
- Over-stretching to reach out to something
- Sleeping on a mattress, which does not support your body or keep your spine straight
- Bending forward, backward and sideward awkwardly

- Lifting, pushing, pulling, and carrying a heavy load
- Bending for long periods
- Sitting or standing for long periods
- Straining your neck forward while driving

Choosing Inappropriate Footwear

Sky-high stilettos are surely a no-no if you want to protect the joints in your knees, hips, and back. However, it turns out that even flats can cause trouble. However, flip-flops and sandals do provide a little arch support.

Hence, you are advised to choose your footwear wisely and avoid these forms to keep back pain at bay.

Sleeping on Your Stomach

Sleeping on your back or the sides could keep your spine neutral and elongated. But, if you have a habit of snoozing on your tummy, the strain on the back muscles tends to increase, making you prone to developing arthritis and backache.

Ignoring the Core Muscles

Your core is composed of much more than just the 6-pack abs. It also includes muscles in the back, hips, and sides. These muscles allow you to stand upright, twist, bend and rotate easily with your abs.

If you only work out your abs and ignore other muscles in your core, they would still stay weak and less developed, causing arthritis and back pain.

Smoking

Cigarettes are dangerous not just for your lungs and heart but also for your back. It has been observed that the incidence of arthritis and backache is higher in smokers.

This conclusion could be attributed to the nicotine present in cigarettes that restricts blood flow to the vertebrae and disks, thus depriving them of vital nutrients. This effect may cause these structures to age prematurely and grow prone to breakage.

Now that you have learned the different causes of back pain, you can surely take steps to avoid most of them. Here are some simple exercises that you can perform to strengthen your leg and back muscles and prevent arthritis and backache.

Simple Exercises to Prevent Arthritis and Back Pain

Exercises offer a great way to relieve arthritis and back pain – the exercises mentioned below aim to improve back support and strengthen the muscles in the region.

Let us have a look at them one by one.

Though these exercises also involve the neck and shoulder regions, they are aimed at strengthening your core and the balance of entire body to ensure less pressure is exerted eventually on your knees, hips, and back.

Spine Extension Exercise

Lie down on your stomach and prop the upper body up on the elbows. Allow the pelvis to sag down while extending the neck backwards.

Then, breathe in as you maintain the same position. Exhale slowly and come back to the initial position. Remember not to lift hips.

Pelvic Rolling

Lie down on your back on a hard surface. Then, bend your knees comfortably and close them together.

Roll the knees to one side followed by your pelvis and hold for 5 seconds. Then, bring it to the initial position. Repeat the same on the other side.

Make sure your head rotates on the opposite side of the movement of the pelvis and knees. Also, your chin should be tucked in and the upper body relaxed.

Pelvic Bridging

Lie down on a flat and hard surface on your back. Bend your knees only as much as you feel comfortable.

Let the arms rest flat on the sides. Slowly lift your pelvis upward and hold for 4 to 5 seconds and then relax and come down to the initial position.

While lifting upwards, breathe in deeply, and while coming down, breathe out slowly. Repeat 10 to 15 times.

Knee to Chest

Lie down on a flat and hard surface on your back. Then, bring one knee closer to the chest. Grasp the lower part of your thigh and bend until you feel comfortable.

Hold this position for about five seconds and release. Then, repeat on the other leg. Perform this exercise ten times with each leg. Remember that you must completely lower the legs while relaxing.

Coccyx Exercise

Squeeze the buttocks together to bring them close to each other. Then, hold the position for 5 seconds. Repeat ten times.

Prone Leg Raise

Lie down on your stomach. Keep both hands under your forehead such that the head rests on your forearms.

Then, lift one leg off the ground and extend it as much as you can without feeling any discomfort.

Make sure your pelvis is not lifted or tilted while doing so. Hold the position for 4 to 5 seconds and then relax. Repeat the same with the other leg. Perform this exercise ten times with each leg.

Elbow Planks

Lie on your stomach and lift the body on your elbow. Keep the shoulders at the top of the elbows.

Then, keeping the knees straight, point your toes downward. Squeeze the buttocks in and slowly breathe in. Maintain this position for about 10 to 15 seconds and relax.

Side Planks

Lie down on one side with one foot resting on the other. Your elbow should be under the shoulder.

Now, lift the hips so that they form a straight line between your groin and legs through the middle of your neck. Hold this position for 15 to 20 seconds. Repeat ten times.

Wall Push-Ups

Hold your palms against the wall at shoulder level. Keep them about shoulder-width apart. Now, try to push the wall by bending the elbow. Hold the position for 5 to 10 seconds.

Repeat ten times.

Resistance Exercises

Clasp your fingers and place them on your forehead. Try to push the forehead in the front without moving your head or hand.

Repeat the same by keeping your hand at the back of your head.

Then, keep the palm of the left hand at the left side of the head and exert pressure on the head with the hand without moving both. Repeat on the other side.

While applying pressure, hold the position for about 5 seconds. Then, relax for 2 seconds.

Repeat the activity ten times on each side.

Shoulder Shrugs

Slowly bring the shoulders upwards and hold the position for 5 to 10 seconds. Repeat ten times.

Reverse Planks

Lie on the back, keeping the palms under your shoulder. Your heels should be touching the ground.

Now, lift the body by pressing your palms and heels against the ground. At the same time, drive the hips up towards the ceiling such that the body takes a linear shape from the ankles to shoulders.

Hold this position for a few seconds or till you feel comfortable. Repeat ten times.

Practice these exercises regularly to relieve arthritis and back pain naturally. However, do not go overboard with any of them. The idea is to begin slowly and develop over a period.

Stop the activities if you feel even the slightest discomfort. Only practice until you feel comfortable. Over a few days or weeks, you would be able to follow these exercises with better ease and obtain considerable relief from joint pains and backache.

Ayurvedic Remedies for the Treatment of Arthritis and Backache

Ginger and Turmeric Tea

Ginger and turmeric possess anti-inflammatory properties, which could help in reducing pain, inflammation, and swelling in the fingers and hand joints.

Plus, turmeric can modulate the body's immune response and prevent the development of rheumatoid arthritis, which is an autoimmune disorder caused by a faulty immune system.

Grate a small piece of ginger and add it to a glass of water along with half a spoon of turmeric. Allow it to boil and let it simmer for 10 to 15 minutes. Strain the liquid, and enjoy this healthy drink twice daily. You can add a spoonful of honey for better taste.

Pectin and Grape Juice

The combination of pectin and grape juice is highly effective. It helps restore the health and strength of the synovial tissues of the knee, hip, finger, and hand joints to a more lubricated and elastic state, which would help reduce pains and discomfort associated with arthritis.

Mix half a glass of grape juice in one tablespoon of liquid pectin and drink it 1 or 2 times daily. You would achieve a remarkable improvement in the symptoms within a month of using this remedy.

Golden Raisins

Sulfides added to the processing of Golden raisins to give them their peculiar colour is rich in glucosamine and chondroitin. Both these components are highly beneficial for your sore joints. They would improve collagen production and protect the joints against degenerative changes caused due to advancing age, rheumatoid arthritis, and osteoarthritis.

Place 1 cup of golden raisins in a dish, and pour in gin just enough to cover them. Cover the dish with a towel and store it in a dark place for about two weeks so that the gin can evaporate. Eat nine of these raisins every day.

Epsom Salt Soak

Magnesium sulfate in Epsom salt would work as an excellent natural antioxidant and anti-inflammatory agent. Regular use of Epsom salt could prevent the progress of rheumatoid arthritis and osteoarthritis and relieve the symptoms.

To use, fill a bowl with warm water. Then, add to it half a cup of Epsom salt. Stir well, and submerge your fingers in the liquid.

Capsaicin Ointment

Capsaicin, a common component in hot bell peppers, is found to inhibit the action of prostaglandins, the substances involved in the transmission of pain signals to the brain.

Capsaicin may interfere with this process by blocking prostaglandins production, thus minimising the joints' pain and discomfort. Just include bell peppers in your regular diet to manage arthritis in the joints safely and naturally.

Peppermint and Eucalyptus Oil

A blend of peppermint and eucalyptus oil would help ease the stiffness and pain in the joints of the knees, hips, fingers, and hands. They can act as a local anaesthetic agent and reduce the pain.

The blend may also create a cooling effect that could override your discomfort and produce a soothing sensation in the joints.

Mix 5 to 10 drops of peppermint and eucalyptus oil in 1 or 2 tablespoons of carrier oil. The carrier oil is used to dilute the essential oils to prevent any skin irritation. You can use olive oil or grapeseed oil as a carrier oil.

Store this oil blend in a glass bottle away from direct sunlight. Use it to massage the affected joints in your legs, back, and hands once every day to relieve the pain.

Boswellia

The gum resin extracted from the Boswellia plant works as a potent anti-inflammatory and analgesic agent. It would work by 'disabling' the white blood cells that cause swelling and shrink the already inflamed tissues.

Take 2 to 9 grams of dried Boswellia resins every day for effective results.

Exercise Your Joints

Most people think that giving rest to the joints is the best way to treat arthritis. They make minimal movements and avoid doing work that involves the affected joints.

Though taking rest and restricting the movements are necessary for patients with some bone and joint disorders such as fractures and severe osteoporosis, these precautions could be detrimental for rheumatoid arthritis and osteoarthritis patients.

In fact, not moving the joints could increase the joints' stiffness, soreness, and pain.

Exercising can strengthen the muscles supporting the joint and improve lubrication, thus making the movements more manageable and friction-free.

The best exercise for relieving arthritis in the knees and hands is to use a sponge ball or any other soft ball small enough to be held comfortably in your hands and keep pressing on it. You can do this as many times as possible in a day.

Some more tips for relieving arthritis:

- Apply ice packs or cold compresses on the joints
- Use diluted Apple Cider Vinegar to soak the affected joints
- Mix half a teaspoon of cinnamon powder and one tablespoon of honey and eat this mixture once every day
- Massage with olive oil

Conclusion

We use our knees, hips, back, fingers, and hands while performing almost all the activities throughout the day. Swollen joints, stiffness, inflammation, and pain caused due to arthritis or other bone diseases can hinder your routine life to a great extent.

Using the natural remedies given above could provide significant relief from these symptoms and allow you to enjoy your life to the fullest!

Benefits of Ayurvedic Herbs for Maintaining Dental Health

Brushing and flossing your teeth once or twice a day is essential for maintaining optimum oral hygiene. Ayurveda believes in the importance of cleaning the teeth properly every day to reduce the risk of dental caries and cavities and even enhance digestion and general health.

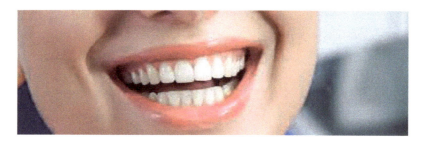

In ancient times, people used to clean their teeth with twigs of some specific plants. The tradition is followed even today in many countries.

While modern medicine also recommends maintaining oral hygiene as an effective way to improve general health and digestion, there is a vast difference between the dental and oral hygiene of people who use Ayurvedic methods and those who follow the modern methods of brushing.

It has been found that people using Ayurvedic methods are less likely to suffer from tooth decay and other issues linked to oral health.

Let us learn more about the Ayurvedic methods of maintaining oral and dental health. We will also discuss natural herbs you can use to keep your teeth clean and sparkling white.

Ayurvedic Methods of Maintaining Oral and Dental Health

It was common for people to use twigs of plants, especially bitter plants such as Neem, to clean the teeth in ancient times. The antimicrobial and antibacterial properties of these bitter-tasting twigs could help keep the mouth and teeth germ-free.

Herbs with a pungent taste are also suitable for maintaining oral hygiene. They are likely to help flush out the toxins and fight bad breath.

The twigs of Neem, Peepal, and Mango are most commonly used for maintaining oral hygiene.

How to Use a Twig?

The twig should approximately be 20 to 25 cm long. It should be as thick as a finger so that you can hold it comfortably. To use the twig as a toothbrush, start by chewing its tip and then stroke your teeth gently with it.

Effective Home Remedies to Whiten Your Teeth

Hydrogen Peroxide

Hydrogen peroxide produces a mild bleaching effect, which can make your yellow teeth white again.

You can use hydrogen peroxide as a mouthwash to rinse and gargle with. But, make sure you do not swallow it. Alternatively, you can also make a thick baking soda and hydrogen peroxide paste and brush your teeth with it.

However, you must use hydrogen peroxide with extra caution as it may cause gum irritation and increase teeth sensitivity, causing pain.

Lemon

Lemons work as a strong bleach. But, it can also irritate the gums and make your teeth sensitive. Hence, it is best to reserve this remedy for emergencies. Lemons should not be used for teeth whitening regularly. You can use it occasionally as and when needed.

The bleaching property of lemons would help you get rid of the yellow discolouration, and its acidic nature would help dissolve the plaques.

You can use lemon water for gargling. You may also scrub your teeth with a lemon peel. You can also mix a few drops of lemon juice and a pinch of salt and apply this mixture to the stained teeth. Rub it gently over the teeth and leave it on for 5 minutes. Then, rinse it off thoroughly with water.

Baking Soda

The best way to whiten your teeth lies in baking soda. It gives faster results and is very easy to use.

Mix one-fourth teaspoon of baking soda in a small amount of toothpaste. Use this gritty mixture to brush your teeth for three minutes. Then, rinse with warm water. Do this once or twice a week. It would remove the plaques and help the pearly whites shine again.

Alternatively, you may add half a teaspoon of baking soda in a few drops of lemon juice and white vinegar and brush your teeth with this mixture.

Orange Peel

Orange peel offers an effective way to keep your teeth sparkling white. You can clean your teeth with a fresh orange peel every day for two to three weeks to see noticeable results. It would reduce that yellow tinge on your teeth.

You can also rub the orange peel over the teeth just before going to sleep. The calcium and vitamin C in the peel would fight the microorganisms throughout the night and reduce the appearance of plaques.

Apples

Eating one apple every day would keep you away from doctors as well as dentists. It would help you eliminate the yellowish stains accumulated on your teeth.

Eating a crunchy apple works like a scrub and cleans the plaques accumulated on your teeth. The scrub may also work like a toothbrush and make your teeth whiter.

Make sure you chew it well so that the rough fibre-rich flesh and the acidic nature of apples get enough time to work on your teeth.

Strawberries

Strawberries are also rich in vitamin C, which could make your teeth whiter. Take 4 to 5 strawberries and grind them to make a fine paste. Rub this paste gently on your teeth. Do this twice every day for one month. It would help lighten that yellow tinge on your teeth.

Another option is to add the pulp of one strawberry in half a teaspoon of baking soda and a few drops of lemon juice and spread this mixture onto your teeth. Let it sit for a few minutes before rinsing it out.

Charcoal

Charcoal contains a powerful crystal-based substance that could whiten your teeth. Just mix the charcoal powder in your regular toothpaste and brush your teeth with it. Do this twice every day to keep your teeth sparkling white.

You can also use the ashes of burnt rosemary or burnt bread similarly if you do not have charcoal powder.

Holy Basil

Holy Basil is one of the most revered herbs known to possess strong medicinal properties. The leaves of Holy Basil contain natural teeth whitening properties. They can also protect the teeth from pyorrhea, a periodontal disease, which causes inflammation and infection of the gums and the bones that hold the teeth.

To use Holy basil for better oral health and whitening your teeth, put a few leaves in the sun for at least two hours to let them dry. Then, grind the dried leaves to make a powder. Mix this powder in your regular toothpaste and use it to brush your teeth.

Salt

Salt is the fundamental dental cleansing agent used for ages for cleaning teeth. It could help replenish the lost mineral content of the teeth and revive their white colour.

Instead of toothpaste, you may use salt as a tooth powder to brush your teeth, though only occasionally. Another way of using salt to whiten your teeth is to mix common salt in charcoal powder and use this mixture to brush your teeth.

What Else Can You Do?

- Quit smoking as it can cause significant tooth decay and discolouration and damage your teeth significantly
- Avoid drinking too much tea or coffee as they can cause stains on the teeth
- Avoid sugary drinks as the carbohydrates in these drinks would feed the bacteria in the oral cavity and help them grow faster
- Replace your toothbrush every three months
- Make it a habit to brush right after eating
- Don't forget to clean your tongue after brushing

Conclusion

Clean and sparkling white teeth would help you appear more attractive, younger, and healthier. You may try the home remedies mentioned above and spread the joy of life with an infectious smile. These remedies would also help keep your oral cavity free of germs and protect you against caries and holes in the teeth.

Ayurvedic Remedies for Fighting Bad Breath

Bad breath, sometimes called halitosis, is a prevalent problem that often indicates poor oral and dental hygiene. It may occur due to an infection in the mouth, tooth cavity, and the build-up of plaques or tartar on your teeth.

Eating foods having a strong odour, dryness of the mouth, excessive smoking, and some gum diseases are also known to contribute to halitosis or bad breath.

Some of the rare causes of this condition include stomach problems, including gastritis and respiratory problems like common cold or sinusitis.

Let us look at some of the most effective home remedies for reducing bad breath and how they would help avoid the causative factors of foul mouth odour. These remedies would also ensure your breaths feel fresh.

Neem

You must have heard that Neem twigs were commonly used as a toothbrush in ancient times to avoid bad breath and maintain oral and dental health.

According to one research study, Neem has been regarded as the herbal panacea in the field of dentistry for its potent antibacterial and antimicrobial properties.

Neem can help maintain dental and oral hygiene by acting as an antibacterial and anti-candidal agent and producing antiplaque activities. It may reduce your risk of tooth cavities, bacterial and fungal infections in the teeth and other tissues of the oral cavity. It may also inhibit the deposition of plaques on your teeth.

You can chew on a Neem twig for about 2 to 3 minutes every day. If you find this a bit difficult, you may gargle your mouth using a solution of one tablespoon of Neem oil and a cup of water.

Apple Cider Vinegar

Gargling with a solution of apple cider vinegar once every day could effectively avoid bad breath.

Apple cider vinegar is loaded with potent medicinal properties that could help you avoid the common causes of halitosis, such as infections, gum disorders, and gastric conditions.

Stomach diseases like GERD (Gastro-Oesophageal Reflux Disorder) and hyperacidity are known to affect the pH balance in the stomach. It can trigger the regurgitation of the stomach's contents like food and digestive juices back into the oesophagus. This form of reflux of partially digested foods can cause severe bad breath.

According to one research study, apple cider vinegar could help reduce bad breath by maintaining the pH balance in your stomach. It would prevent hyperacidity. It may also inhibit the regurgitation of foods by improving the peristaltic movement of the digestive tract.

It is also an effective and simple home remedy you can use to fight bad breath, especially if you are prone to develop cavities in your teeth. The antibacterial property of apple cider vinegar would prevent infections in the oral tissues caused due to the decaying of the tooth. This action would help you avoid bad breath.

To use, make a solution of the apple cider vinegar by adding about half a tablespoon of it to one cup of slightly warm water. Use this to gargle your mouth or as a mouthwash. Gargle for at least 30 seconds every day to avoid moderate to severe halitosis.

Fennel Seeds

Fennel seeds can provide a quick-fix solution for those in dire need to hide their bad breath. It is a very simple-to-use home remedy that also offers quick results.

You simply need to chew on one teaspoon of fennel seeds and swallow them to mask the odour. You may use it regularly if you are prone to oral infections and cavities.

According to one research study, fennel seeds can produce an anti-inflammatory, antimicrobial, and antibacterial effect. It would kill the pathogens that could cause bad breath and cavities and ensure your breaths feel and smell fresh.

Gum inflammation caused due to a condition known as gingivitis may also be managed effectively by using fennel seeds.

Ginger

Ginger often works wonders for those suffering from a common cold or sinusitis-induced bad breath. Sinusitis is one of the rare and lesser-known factors causing bad breath.

The infections, bacteria and foul-smelling secretions in the sinuses and nasal passages could give off a severe noxious odour. It is possible to avoid bad breath caused due to this condition by simply using ginger.

It has been found that ginger could relieve the signs and symptoms of sinusitis. These incluse nose blocks, headaches, mucus secretions, and congestion, and thus, help reduce bad breath.

To use, you can grate about a half-inch piece of fresh ginger and squeeze it to extract its juice. Then, add the liquid to a cup of lukewarm water and use the solution to rinse the mouth.

You should do this at least two to three times a week if you suffer from chronic sinusitis. You may increase the frequency of rinsing with the ginger solution during acute sinusitis attacks based on the severity of the symptoms like bad breath.

Cardamom

Cardamom is often revered as the king of spices for its delightful aroma. It has been used since ancient times to mask or reduce bad breath. Besides its pleasant and soothing fragrance, this wonder spice could also offer several other benefits for avoiding bad breath.

It has been found that the oil extracted from cardamom pods possesses a rich amount of flavonoids, terpene, and cineole. These compounds can produce an antiseptic action to help inhibit bacterial infections in the tooth and oral cavity.

The antimicrobial and anti-inflammatory effects of cardamom may also be effective against the common oral pathogens such as Streptococcus mutans and Candida albicans that are known to trigger or worsen bad breath.

You may chew a cardamom pod as a whole once every day to overcome this annoying symptom. You can swallow the pod once you have chewed it well. You may also peel the pod and only chew the seeds inside it.

Eucalyptus Oil

Gargling the mouth with Eucalyptus oil is another safe and effective way to fight bad breath. Eucalyptus oil has been shown to produce a natural fungicidal and bactericidal effect on a wide range of fungi and bacteria.

It would also produce an antioxidant, anti-inflammatory, and analgesic effect. It may alleviate ulcerations, swelling, and pain in the oral cavity, thereby lessening the foul odour.

To use, you need to add 2 or 3 drops of eucalyptus oil to half a cup of warm water. Gargle with this solution for 2 minutes, once every day. Rinse the mouth well after gargling with plain water.

Mint and Tulsi Leaves

Slow chewing of herbal leaves like Mint and Tulsi could provide instant benefits for avoiding bad breath. These herbs possess a strong aroma that could mask the foul odour.

Also, these herbs' beneficial effects are not only limited to masking the foul odour. They would also help eliminate the underlying cause of this condition and provide long-lasting relief.

Mint and Tulsi would also improve dental and oral hygiene by enhancing and maintaining the balance of the salivary pH. Moreover, these herbs may also produce a natural antibacterial effect, preventing cavities and infections in the oral cavity.

These properties of Mint and Tulsi, coupled with their pleasant and soothing fragrance, would provide an instant yet long-lasting solution to bad breath.

All you need to do is chew a few leaves of Mint or Tulsi once or twice every day to improve your breaths and oral health.

Lemon Juice

If you relish the fresh and soothing fragrance of lemons and lime, you have a pleasant surprise. Lemons and lime possess potent medicinal properties that could help you avoid bad breath.

Citrus concentrates such as lime or lemon juice could help in reducing and preventing foul odour. This remedy is believed to work by producing antimicrobial, anti-inflammatory, antioxidant, and antibacterial effects.

It would prevent plaque formation on your teeth and maintain the oral cavity's natural and healthy microbial flora. It would also reduce your risk of cavities in the tooth, thereby reducing the chances of foul odour.

To use, you can add 1 or 2 teaspoons of freshly squeezed lemon or lime juice to about two tablespoons of yoghurt. Apply this mixture to your teeth and leave it for about 3 to 5 minutes. Then, rinse the mouth properly. Use this remedy twice or thrice a week to manage bad breath safely and naturally.

Conclusion

Bad breath could be highly embarrassing. It may severely affect your self-esteem and self-confidence, especially when you find your colleagues, acquaintances, and friends turning their faces away from you while talking. It is possible to avoid such an embarrassing situation by using the Ayurvedic remedies mentioned above.

Using these natural home remedies would prevent bad breath and help you avoid loss of self-confidence and self-esteem caused due to it.

What Is Sinusitis and How Can It Be Treated With Ayurvedic Remedies?

Sinusitis is a common respiratory condition defined as inflammation in the paranasal sinuses. Furthermore, the sinus cavities produce mucus needed by the nasal passages to work effectively. Inflammation in these sinus cavities results in sinusitis.

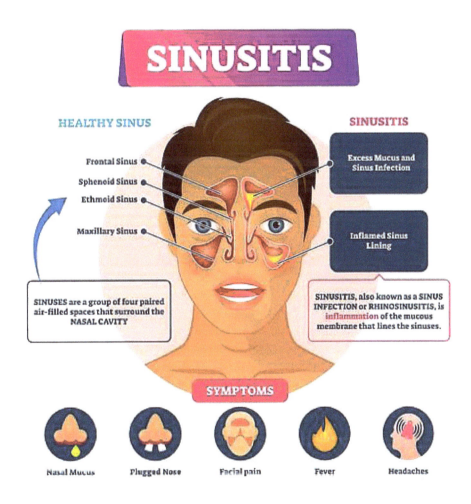

Sinusitis may be acute or chronic. Common causes of sinus inflammation are infections due to viruses, fungi, bacteria, allergies, and autoimmune reactions.

Although painful and highly uncomfortable, sinusitis usually disappears without any active medical intervention. However, if the symptoms are severe or persistent and occur repeatedly, you may need to seek long-term treatment.

Here is a brief discussion about what sinusitis means and the best way to manage this condition with the help of Ayurvedic remedies.

What Is Sinusitis?

A sinus refers to any hollow space in our body. There are several types of sinuses in the body, though the term sinusitis refers to the cavities near the nose called the paranasal sinuses. These are the spaces behind the cheekbone and forehead and on either side of the face, leading to the nasal cavities.

The inner mucosal lining of these sinuses has a similar composition as that of the nose lining. The sinuses produce mucus secretions that help keep the nasal passages moist and trap germs and dirt particles in the air we breathe.

Sinusitis occurs when the mucus secretions accumulate, and the sinuses become inflamed and irritated.

What are the Signs and Symptoms of Sinusitis?

The symptoms of sinusitis vary depending on how long the condition persists and the severity of the inflammation.

The common symptoms of this condition include:

- Nasal discharge that may be yellow or green
- Facial pain and pressure
- A postnasal drip, wherein the mucus secretions run down the back of the throat
- Cough
- Blocked or running nose
- Bad breath
- Fever
- Sore throat
- Reduced sense of taste and smell
- Headaches
- Toothache
- Tenderness and swelling around the nose, cheeks, eyes, and forehead

What Are the Causes of Sinusitis?

Sinusitis often stems from a combination of factors. However, in most cases, it results from the accumulation of fluid in the sinuses, allowing germs to grow and multiply.

The most common cause of this condition is an infection due to viruses or bacteria. Triggers may include asthma and allergies, and exposure to pollutants in the air, like chemicals or irritants.

Mould and fungal infections may trigger fungal sinusitis in some patients, especially those using steroidal drugs for a prolonged duration.

What Are the Risk Factors for Sinusitis?

- Sensitivity to substances like dust, pollen, or animal dander
- Having a pre-existing respiratory tract infection, like a common cold
- Having a weak or compromised immune system due to a chronic health condition or the use of medications
- Seasonal allergies
- Nasal polyps that are tiny benign growths in the nasal passages, which can lead to inflammation and obstruction
- Having a deviated nasal septum

Home Remedies for Managing Sinusitis

In more than 70% of cases, symptoms of acute sinusitis resolve without any active treatment or use of any prescription drugs. Here are some home remedies that can relieve the symptoms in a shorter duration.

- Nasal irrigation: You can rinse and clear your nasal passages with a saline solution or saltwater. A neti pot could be one way to try this. However, make sure you use sterile equipment and clean water for nasal irrigation.
- Warm compresses: Apply warm compresses gently to the affected parts of the face to relieve pain, discomfort, and swelling.
- Rest: Make sure you get adequate rest and sleep. You can rest with your head and shoulders slightly raised on a pillow. You can also sleep on the painless side of the face, if possible.
- Pain relief: Steam inhalation can often help drain the mucus secretions away and relieve pain. You can inhale steam from a pot of hot water or place a warm, moist towel on your

face.

- Essential oils: Aromatherapy can be highly effective for reducing symptoms of sinusitis. Add a few drops of eucalyptus oil or menthol to the hot water or a handkerchief, and, placing it close to your nose, breathe in deeply.

Treatment of Acute and Chronic Sinusitis

The treatment options for sinusitis depend on how long the symptoms persist.

Acute and Subacute Sinusitis

If the symptoms persist for longer than a few weeks or are severe, you may continue aromatherapy and steam inhalation.

Suppose a bacterial or viral infection is present. In that case, you may use natural herbs like holy basil, turmeric, and ginger which possess potent antibacterial and antiviral properties. To derive instant relief from the symptoms, you can drink warm milk brewed with a tablespoon of turmeric.

Chronic Sinusitis

Ayurveda recommends reducing your exposure to triggers like dust mites, pollen, and allergens to avoid repeated sinusitis attacks.

Practising good hand hygiene is also recommended to protect yourself against this condition's recurring attacks. Avoiding active smoking and second-hand smoke can help improve your respiratory health.

Some other recommendations for the treatment and prevention of sinusitis include:

- Stay away from people who have a common cold or any other respiratory infection
- Use a humidifier to moisten the air at your home and keep the air clean and free of pollutants and irritants
- Ensure your body receives a good supply of nutrients, including vitamins and minerals
- Eat antioxidant-rich foods and healthy fats to boost your immunity
- Maintain your air conditioning unit to prevent dust and mould from collecting
- Avoid exposure to allergens when possible
- Eat healthy foods, like fruits and vegetables
- Limit your exposure to harmful chemicals

- Wash your hands regularly, especially before and after eating and cooking

Conclusion

Sinusitis is a common condition that affects a large number of people. It can occur due to various factors. In most cases, symptoms of sinusitis are mild. Most patients can be treated with the simple and effective home remedies given above.

Natural Ways to Improve Your Eyesight

The eyes are the most precious sense organs of our body. Even the slightest impairment of vision could considerably impact our lives. Our vision can get affected due to the refractive errors of eyes like myopia, hyperopia, and astigmatism. Some severe conditions that may need surgical intervention include cataracts, macular degeneration, retinal detachment, retinal damage, and macular oedema.

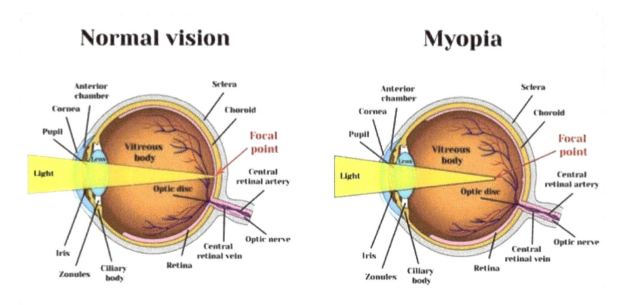

Luckily, there are a few ways to prevent or slow down the progress of these diseases and improve your vision. Here are some safe and effective natural ways to improve your eyesight.

Kale

A vegetable rich in vitamins and cancer-fighting antioxidants, kale could be a good friend for your eyes. It is a rich natural source of beta-carotene. It provides a perfect combo of lutein and zeaxanthin, both of which would protect your eyes from any form of damage and delay the decline of eyesight due to advancing age.

You can use kale in your salads or add it to any side dish. It can also be blended into a fruit smoothie or baked to make delicious kale chips.

Fish Oil

Fish oil is rich in omega-3 fatty acids called docosahexaenoic acid (DHA). It is present in high contractions in cold-water fish like krill, wild salmon, and cod. DHA is a powerful antioxidant that could protect your eyes from damages caused by UV radiation, free radicals, and age-related degenerative changes.

You may use fish oil in your regular diet in moderate amounts to improve your eyesight and prevent eye disorders.

Spinach

The nutrient-dense spinach packs a healthy dose of zeaxanthin and lutein. You can add spinach to wraps or sandwiches or use it to make green smoothies.

It is best to have them cooked as cooking the greens would help your body absorb lutein more easily.

Corn

Corn is not just a yummy side dish; it also contains zeaxanthin and lutein, including yellow to red pigments and a form of vitamin A called carotenoids.

Lutein and zeaxanthin are found in many vegetables other than corn, such as spinach and kale. These pigments are naturally present in the macula of our eyes.

A high concentration of these substances in the macula could help absorb excess light rays entering the eyes and thus, prevent damage to the eyes due to harmful UV radiation from sunlight.

They may also block light from reaching the retina, thereby reducing your risk of UV radiation-induced oxidative damage, which could lead to macular degeneration. Corn, being rich in these two pigments, would ensure the protection of our eyes and eyesight.

It is effortless to include corn in your diet. You can make a corn sandwich, add it to salads, or simply cook a corn web and eat it.

Exercise Your Eyes

Another effective way to improve your eyesight is to stimulate muscle growth, like exercising your abs and biceps to make them stronger and increase your stamina.

In fact, eye exercise is the key to optimal vision.

Here are some simple exercises you can practice to improve your vision:

- Warm up the eyes: Rub your hands against each other to create warmth, and put them over your eyes for a few seconds. Do this as and when you get time. The more you do, the better.

- Massage the temples: Massage your temples gently in small circles using the knuckles of the thumbs. You can do the movement 20 times in one direction and then 20 times in the opposite direction.

- Rolling the eyes: Start by looking up at the ceiling, and then move your eyes slowly in the clockwise direction five to ten times. Repeat the same in the counter-clockwise direction.

Give Adequate Rest to Your Eyes

Your eyes are working continuously at home or the workplace and while driving, walking, running, or even cooking. So, they need rest!

Make sure your eyes get a ten-minute rest after spending an hour reading, watching television, or working in front of a computer.

Allow them to relax by placing your cupped hands over the closed eyes while ensuring no light reaches them. Also, try to get at least 8 hours of sound sleep every night in a dark room with no distractions.

Keep Your Environment Safe

Environmental factors such as fluorescent lights, environmental allergens, computer screens, and chlorine in swimming pools could significantly contribute to poor vision. Even sitting in the air conditioning for too long, constant eye rubbing, and reading in dim lighting could diminish your vision.

The beneficial effect of including eye exercises and foods rich in zeaxanthin and lutein may negate eye damage to some extent if your eyes are exposed to these dangers. Hence, make sure you remove these factors from your immediate environment to protect your eyesight from deteriorating.

Ginkgo Biloba

Ginkgo biloba is a powerful medicinal herb that would improve blood circulation in the eye. IT supplies the required amounts of nutrients to the retina, macula, and other eye tissues.

In addition to improving your vision, Ginkgo biloba may also protect you against disorders like macular degeneration and glaucoma. It is also beneficial for patients suffering from retinopathy.

However, the use of this herb for children should be avoided. Also, people with diabetes need to consult their doctor before using it.

Bilberry

Bilberry is another potent herb for better vision and improved eye health. It can also be used to improve night vision. It is believed to work by stimulating the regeneration of purple components present in the retina.

Additionally, it offers protection against glaucoma, macular degeneration, and cataracts. It is considered beneficial for treating retinal problems caused due to diabetes and hypertension.

The best part is you can eat Bilberry as it is. No need for cooking or any tedious process! Simply take about half a cup of ripe bilberries in a bowl and relish it.

Conclusion

These home remedies would bring about a remarkable improvement in your eyesight and protect your eyes from age-related disorders. In some cases, they have been found to help people lead a life free from specs and lenses and allow them to see the beautiful world crystal clear!

Natural Treatment for Macular Degeneration

Macular degeneration (MD), also called age-associated macular degeneration (AMD), occurs due to the deterioration of the retina. This condition can impair vision severely.

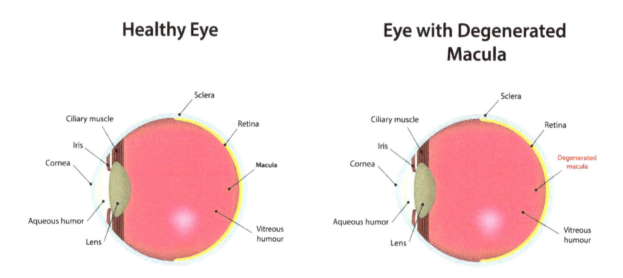

While there is no available cure for macular degeneration, it may be treated with vitamins, herbs, and vision aids.

Here is a brief discussion about what macular degeneration means and the natural ways to prevent or relieve its symptoms.

What Is Macular Degeneration?

It is an eye condition that often gets worse over time. It is the leading factor known to cause severe and permanent vision loss in people above 60 years of age.

It occurs when the tiny central region of the retina, called the macula, degenerates and wears down, resulting in a gradual loss of eyesight. The retina is composed of light-sensing nerve tissues located at the back of the eye.

Since this disease usually occurs as people get older, it can also be referred to as age-related macular degeneration. It does not always cause blindness, though it might cause severe problems with vision.

Another type of macular degeneration, known as Stargardt disease or juvenile macular degeneration, affects young adults and children.

What Are the Symptoms of Macular Degeneration?

Patients with macular degeneration may not develop any noticeable signs in the initial stages. The condition may not be diagnosed until degenerative changes have worsened or affected both eyes.

As the diseases progress, patients may develop some symptoms that may include:

- Vision blur
- Reduced vision clarity
- Difficulty in reading fine print or driving
- Dark or blurry areas at the centre of the vision
- Lack of correct colour perception

What Are the Causes of Macular Degeneration?

Macular degeneration tends to be more common in older men and women. Moreover, the risk is comparatively higher in women than in men. It is one of the leading causes of severe vision loss in adults above 60 years.

Macular degeneration may also have genetic links. It has been found that people who have a close family member suffering from macular degeneration have a higher risk of developing it.

Smoking, high blood pressure, obesity, high cholesterol, having a light complexion or eye colour, and the increased intake of saturated fats are also the risk factors for this condition.

How Is Macular Degeneration Diagnosed?

A routine eye examination can help detect age-related macular degeneration. The most common early sign of this condition is drusen or the appearance of tiny yellow spots under the retina and pigment clumping. The doctor can detect these signs during routine eye examinations.

The patient may also be asked to look at an Amsler grid, a pattern of lines resembling a checkerboard. Some of those straight lines tend to appear wavy, while some may seem missing. These could be the early signs of macular degeneration.

If the doctor suspects age-related macular degeneration, the patient may be advised to undergo an angiography or OCT procedure.

In angiography, the doctor would inject a small quantity of a dye into the arm's vein. Then, images are taken as the dye passes through the blood vessels and reaches the retina. If there are new blood vessels or any vessels leaking blood or fluid into the macula, the images will show their exact type and location.

OCT may also detect the presence of fluid and blood beneath the retina even without injecting the dye.

What Are the Treatments for Macular Degeneration?

There is no cure for this condition. However, regular treatment may help slow down the progress of macular degeneration or protect the patient from further loss of eyesight.

Some of the treatment options for patients with macular degeneration include:

- Anti-angiogenesis drugs, which work by blocking the creation of new blood vessels and preventing blood or fluid leakage from the vessels into the eye.

- Laser therapy with high-energy laser light that helps by destroying the abnormal blood vessels forming and growing in the affected eye.

- Photodynamic laser therapy that involves injecting a light-sensitive drug, usually verteporfin, into the bloodstream. Once it is absorbed by the abnormal vessels, the doctor releases laser rays at controlled pulses into the eye, causing the medication to destroy those vessels.

- Devices like low vision aids with special lenses and electronic systems that help create larger images of nearby things. These devices can help patients with vision difficulties due to macular degeneration to make the most of their remaining eyesight.

Prevention of Macular Degeneration

Some patients with macular degeneration show simprovement in symptoms after taking supplements containing vitamins C and E, zeaxanthin, zinc, lutein, and copper.

Other than these, patients diagnosed with macular degeneration and those at risk of developing it should also make appropriate dietary changes. It would help slow down the degenerative changes in the tissues of the eyes, especially the retina and macula.

Some other dietary steps that could be beneficial for preventing macular degeneration include:

- Avoiding excessive intake of beta carotene

- Eating vegetables, especially the leafy greens

- Reducing your sugar intake significantly

- Consuming foods containing omega-3 fatty acids, like avocado, flaxseeds, chia seeds, and olive oil
- Quitting smoking
- Limiting your alcohol intake
- Eating more fruits, especially high-fibre fruits

Moreover, regular exercise is also recommended to maintain blood pressure, reduce cholesterol levels, and prevent diabetes to reduce your risk of macular degeneration.

Maintaining healthy body weight, blood sugar level, blood pressure, and cholesterol level could reduce your risk of macular degeneration and slow down its progression to a great extent.

Natural herbal remedies that may help prevent the onset of vision loss include eyebright, Gingko Biloba, and Coleus. These herbs help by reducing fluid secretion in the eyes and inhibiting the formation of new capillaries.

Conclusion

Patients with age-related macular degeneration rarely lose their vision completely. Their central vision could be affected severely, but they can still perform most routine activities.

Undergoing regular eye examination can help detect vision decline and help you seek timely treatment to slow down the progression of this disease. The ageing population is the most vulnerable to the effect of impaired vision due to this condition.

Hence, consulting your eye doctor once or twice every year is considered the best defence for preventing vision loss.

The use of supplements containing essential nutrients that support eye health and slow down degenerative changes and herbal remedies that support regeneration is also recommended for improving the prognosis.

Common Skin Conditions and Their Natural Treatments

Eczema, pruritus, warts, and fungal infections are the common conditions that affect the skin. In rare cases, eczema may originate in adulthood.

It is a chronic condition that results in a red rash, constant itching, oozing, and skin irritation. There are no known specific causes for the disease, though it may be genetic in origin.

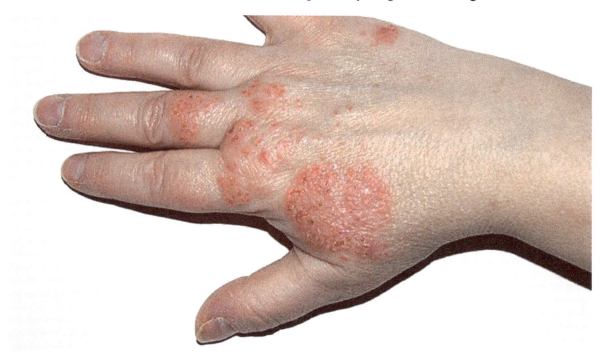

However, there are a few factors that could trigger the condition and cause a flare-up.

What Is Eczema?

The term eczema refers to the condition caused due to the inflammation of the skin or a state where the skin becomes red and looks like it has bubbles. Though the word eczema refers to skin inflammation in general, what is commonly referred to as eczema is really called Atopic Dermatitis (also called Atopic Eczema).

Atopic dermatitis is a chronic skin condition. Dermatitis refers to the inflammation of the skin, whereas atopic means a genetically-linked predisposition to a disease. Atopic dermatitis is usually associated with asthma and hay fever. It occurs due to the heightened response of the body's immune system to allergens in the environment.

Allergens could be detergents, dust mites, pollen, or even certain microbes.

These allergens irritate the skin and lead to itching and rash. In fact, intense itching is the hallmark sign of this disorder.

Contact dermatitis is another form of eczema that usually occurs due to the reaction of sensitive skin to substances, such as jewellery, that lies in direct contact with the skin.

What Are the Symptoms of Eczema?

Skin rashes associated with eczema tend to appear on any body part. Sometimes, the symptoms flare up on any part of the skin while they seem to be waning off from another region. There can be periods when the disease appears to be in control, only to flare up due to exposure to some trigger.

Exposure to some specific triggers often brings on frequent flaring-ups. The rashes lead to itching, and the skin starts oozing during a flare-up. The oozing can lead to an infection, which can exacerbate the condition leading to a cycle of further itching and scratching.

Sometimes, the itching could be so bad that it may lead to bleeding sores on the skin.

Some of the common symptoms of eczema include:

- Frequently rashes
- Dryness and itching of the skin
- Rough skin that has a "leathery" look
- Hypersensitive skin
- Red and scaly patches on the skin
- Oozing of colourless liquid from the affected part of the skin, referred to as weeping
- Red bumps on the skin

What Are the Causes of Eczema?

The exact cause of eczema is still not known. It is supposedly the result of a combination of genetic and environmental factors. Many people who suffer from eczema have a family history of the disease. It is closely associated with asthma and hay fever. A large percentage of children with eczema also suffer from asthma or hay fever. These conditions are associated with the immune system's allergic reaction to environmental factors. These conditions, too, have been found to run in families.

Eczema is also associated with an inherited skin condition known as Ichthyosis Vulgaris. This condition is caused due to a shortage of protein called Filaggrin in the body that results in excessive dryness of the skin.

Several gene variants have been linked to eczema. To date, about 31 different gene variants associated with this disease have been identified. Research has also indicated a genetic overlap between eczema and other skin diseases like asthma, rhinitis, and inflammatory bowel disease.

Some gene variants have been commonly found among children whose mothers have been exposed to secondhand smoke during pregnancy.

Recent research has also found that babies who have been treated with very high doses of certain antibiotics in the first year of their life could also have a higher risk of getting eczema.

Factors That Can Provide Relief From Eczema

The symptoms may vary from a slight rash that disappears quite soon to a severe rash that persists longer. Whatever be the manifestation of the disease, the main goal of the management of Eczema is to eliminate the dryness and itching.

If itching is left untreated, it could provoke other symptoms, which usually accompany the problem, like redness, blisters, oozing, crusting, thickening, and skin discolouration. Let us look at some effective relief methodologies for managing eczema.

The First Step

People attempt numerous medications for eczema to reduce the itch. They use over-the-counter drugs they get in a local drugstore. They also utilize prescription medicines they get from their skin specialists.

Though these treatments could be effective, the first step you have to take is to take good care of your skin to prevent dryness. Dryness is the symptom that triggers or aggravates other symptoms of eczema. Taking showers with lukewarm water and applying a moisturizing cream or lotion on the skin later could keep it from getting dry.

Avoid the Triggers

The sources of irritation are called the 'trigger factors'. Avoiding these sources of irritation could be an effective way to lessen the symptoms of eczema. You would have to figure out the trigger factors that aggravate your symptoms.

Here is a list of some factors that could act as an irritant for you:

- Fabric allergy: You may wear delicate garments that do not rub against or prick your skin. Also, avoid fabrics of fleece, nylon, or any firm material.

- Dryness: Try to keep your skin moist and avoid excessive scaling. The mantra is to moisturize!

- Sweat: If you sweat too much, try to keep your body cooler: Avoid exerting yourself, particularly during the hot times of the day. Try not to overheat the rooms, particularly your bedroom. Also, try to wear soft bedclothes.

- Dust and Pollen: If the itching occurs due to dust or pollen, take a prolonged shower bathing session or bathe in a tub. You may apply a moisturizing cream within 5 minutes of coming out of the shower. This routine would help 'lock in' the moisture and prevent excessive skin drying.

- Soft toys and pets: Carpet dust or pet-furs have been found to trigger eczema. If you have pets, keep them outside or at least off your beds, mats, and furniture. Change the covers of cushions and sleeping pads regularly. Make it a habit to wash your bedclothes in boiling water.

- Food allergy: If the allergy is caused due to foods, be methodical. The most likely guilty parties could be eggs, milk, peanuts, soy, wheat, and fish. Stop eating these foods. When the skin symptoms have cleared up, attempt eating them again one at a time. Look for indications of itching or redness in the two hours after eating that food. Once you have ascertained the allergen, avoid it.

- Stress: Coping with stress, depression, and anxiety is another factor that would help you overcome the symptoms of eczema. If you tend towards depression, consult a psychiatrist for advice. Staying happy and adopting an active lifestyle would help you overcome depression and cope with the symptoms of eczema better.

Here is a brief checklist of the tips to control eczema:

- Take baths with lukewarm water and use a mild soap or a non-soapy cleanser.

- Wear cotton clothes or ones with soft fabrics. Avoid rough fibres and skin-tight clothing.

- Moisturize your skin, including the affected area, every day.

- Apply a moisturizing cream immediately after bathing to retain the moisture in the skin.

- Do not rub your skin; instead, gently pat it with a soft towel.

- If possible, try to avoid the sudden changes in temperature and activities that make you sweat.

- Use a humidifier if you reside at a place with a dry and cold climate.
- Detect the triggers for your eczema and try to avoid them.
- If you have allergies to carpet dust or pet furs, avoid contact with them.
- Keep your fingernails short. It will prevent the breaking of the skin.

Natural Treatments for Eczema

Treatment strategies for eczema are aimed at strengthening the skin and promoting the skin's moisture-retaining capacity. Eczema treatment should also aim to reduce the itching and inflammation that develop due to infection or lead to an infection.

Alternative natural treatments such as using home remedies could be very effective for relieving the symptoms of eczema.

Home Remedies for Relieving the Symptoms of Eczema

Simple ingredients you can find in your kitchen would effectively relieve the symptoms of eczema. They moisturize the skin and reduce the intensity of itching and inflammation. The commonly used home remedies for eczema are given below:

Coconut Oil or Jojoba Oil

Oils such as coconut oil or jojoba oil can penetrate very quickly into the skin, fill in the intercellular spaces and prevent the skin from losing moisture, thereby keeping eczema under control.

Jojoba oil is a liquid wax that could do wonders to your skin, similar to the natural sebum secreted by the skin's oil glands. It would penetrate deep into the skin and improve its moisture-retaining capacity. These oils are also beneficial for improving the tone and texture of your skin compared to artificial alcohols such as isopropyl alcohol, benzyl alcohol, and methanol that are commonly added to most cosmetic products.

Using these oils is very simple. Just apply the oil on the affected part of the skin and massage gently for a few minutes. This routine helps the oil penetrate deep into the skin. For better results, you may apply the oil three times a day.

Homemade Butter

It is easier to soothe those dry, painful skin patches caused by eczema with the application of body butter. Make a healing butter by combining beeswax, jojoba oil, shea butter, and coconut oil in equal amounts.

Stearic and oleic acid contained in the shea butter possesses wonderful healing abilities. They would regulate the inflammatory processes and repair and soften the scratched skin.

Beeswax would also soften the skin and prevent further flare-ups. Moreover, jojoba oil and coconut oil also moisten the skin. For a pleasing fragrance, you may use lavender oil too.

Vegetable Glycerine

Pure vegetable glycerine can draw water towards it and seal the skin's moisture content. It would fill in the cracks in the dry skin by drawing more water from the deeper layers of the skin.

Mix vegetable glycerine and water in equal amounts and pour the mixture into a spray bottle. Shake it well and spray it on your skin at least 3 to 4 times a day.

Oats

Oatmeal would moisturize, soothe, and repair your damaged skin. It may also help reduce inflammation, ease the discomfort and relieve itching.

Ready a cup of oatmeal and a muslin cloth. Transfer the oatmeal into the muslin cloth and tie it just beneath the faucet. Run the tap water until the bathtub is filled with milky water. Then, soak yourself in the water for 10 to 15 minutes. Gently pat the skin dry with a thin cotton towel and apply a moisturizer. It may be a little painful initially, but it could give excellent results when continued for a week or two.

Honey

Honey would relieve the symptoms of eczema very efficiently. The anti-microbial property of honey would prevent bacterial infections and hasten the healing process. The anti-inflammatory property of honey may also reduce inflammation and the associated pain, redness, and swelling. It would also moisten the skin.

Just apply honey to the affected area and let it remain for about 20 to 30 minutes. Later, rinse it off with cool water and pat dry with a cotton cloth. Consider reapplying, if required.

Conclusion

These natural home remedies for eczema are worth trying, as they are not known to cause any harmful side effects. Along with these natural remedies, you can consider making small changes in your daily routine to reduce mental stress, which is one of the factors that could aggravate eczema.

For obtaining relief from eczema, it is also essential to make changes in your dietary habits. Consider having a diet rich in healthy fats and avoid taking processed foods containing preservatives and dyes. Taking probiotics and gelatin-rich foods would also help relieve the symptoms of eczema.

What Are the Symptoms, Causes, Risk Factors, and Treatment for Herpes

Herpes occurs due to the infection caused by the herpes simplex virus (HSV). It develops sores and blisters in or around the oral cavity and genitals, along with other symptoms.

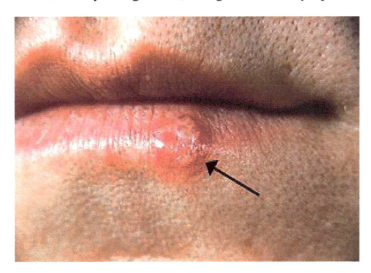

There are two basic forms of HSV as mentioned below:

- HSV-1, which causes oral herpes, usually affects the mouth and the surrounding skin.
- HSV-2, which causes genital herpes, is a sexually transmitted infection.

If a patient has an HSV infection, they will continue to have recurring attacks of symptoms for the rest of their life, although some patients never develop any signs of the condition. If the symptoms occur, they reflect the specific form of HSV the patient is suffering from based on the tissues affected.

Currently, there is no cure for the infection caused due to the herpes simplex virus. However, early diagnosis and treatment could help greatly relieve the symptoms and reduce the chances of them recurring in the future.

HSV is one of the most common viruses affecting humans. According to the World Health Organization (WHO), nearly 67% of patients worldwide suffer from the HSV-1 infection, while more than 10% of the global population suffers from the HSV-2 infection.

Here is a detailed description of oral and genital herpes symptoms, the best ways to treat them, and the methods to prevent this infection:

What Are the Symptoms of Herpes Infection?

Patients who develop symptoms of herpes infections may initially experience only tingling, itching, and burning. Then, they may notice the formation of sores and blisters around their mouth and genitals over a few days or weeks.

These symptoms tend to develop over 2 to 20 days after exposure to the herpes simplex virus.

Symptoms of Oral Herpes

The common symptoms of oral herpes include blisters, sometimes referred to as fever sores and cold sores. The blisters usually develop in and around the mouth and lips.

Sometimes, painful blisters may form on any part of the face or even the tongue, though rarely formed on any skin area.

The sores generally last for about two to three weeks at a time.

Symptoms of Genital Herpes

Sores in patients with genital herpes tend to develop on the skin of the penis, around the vagina, or the delicate mucus membrane inside the vagina. The sores may also form on the buttocks and anus, though they may also form on other parts of the skin.

Herpes simplex is known to cause intense pain while passing urine and abnormal changes in vaginal discharge.

The first time a patient develops these sores, they might last for about 2 to 6 weeks.

However, soon after the initial outbreak, the symptoms recur more frequently and even last longer. But, later, outbreaks might occur less often while the symptoms tend to be lesser in severity.

What Are the Primary Symptoms of Herpes Infection?

The primary symptoms of herpes infection occur when a patient develops the disease for the first time.

Alongside the sores and blisters, herpes infections may cause some other symptoms such as:

- Severe pain and itching
- Fatigue
- Fever
- Swollen lymph nodes

- A general feeling of being unwell

In some cases, the lesions may heal without any long-term scarring or damage.

What Are the Recurring Symptoms of Herpes Infection?

Research studies have suggested that more than 30% of patients with oral herpes and nearly 50% with genital herpes develop recurring symptoms.

The symptoms that reappear regularly are similar to the initial signs and symptoms, although they are usually less severe and last for a shorter period.

During each episode of recurrence, the symptoms of oral herpes last for about 8 to 10 days. Also, the signs of genital herpes recurrence usually last for about 10 to 12 days. Episodes of recurrences are marked by the formation of fewer sores than those in the initial stage. A patient may pass on genital herpes for about two to five days during the recurrence.

What Are the Causes of Herpes Infection?

When herpes simplex infection is present on the skin, it may easily pass from one person to another through contact with moist skin of the genital or mouth, including the anus or the tongue.

The virus might also spread through direct contact with other parts of the skin or the eyes.

A patient cannot simply contract this infection by touching the objects or the surfaces, such as towels or washbasin used by an infected person.

The infection may spread in the following ways:

- Sharing of sex toys
- Having anal or vaginal sex without using any form of barrier protection, like a condom
- Having oral and genital contact in any other form with a patient who has a herpes infection

This virus is the most contagious when symptoms appear for the first time and during healing. The patient may transmit the virus less commonly when the symptoms are not evident or have resolved entirely.

When a woman with genital herpes infection develops sores during pregnancy, she may pass the virus to the baby when the sores have persisted while giving birth.

The Association Between HSV and HIV

Patients with genital herpes often have a very high risk of contracting or passing on other sexually transmitted infections. The risk of HIV especially, as the sores on the skin facilitate the spread of the viruses to the other person.

HSV-2 has been found to increase the number of immune cells, called CD4 cells, in the mucosal lining of the genitals. This escalation may raise the risk of infection if a patient is exposed to HIV.

Also, patients with HIV often have a fragile immune system. This condition could further increase their risk of developing more severe complications of HIV/AIDS.

For example, suppose a patient has oral herpes and a weak immune system. In that case, they might have an increased risk of developing a type of eye inflammation called keratitis, serious complications such as encephalitis, and brain inflammation.

Additionally, suppose a patient has genital herpes and a weak immune system. In that case, they may also get an increased risk of developing life-threatening complications such as inflammation in the brain, oesophagus, eyes, lungs, and the liver, as well as a widespread infection affecting multiple organs and systems.

Treatment of Herpes Infection

There are several treatment options for relieving the symptoms of both oral and genital herpes infections, though this condition can not be cured completely.

Home Remedies for Herpes Infection

The following strategies can help relieve the symptoms of herpes infection in some patients:

- Dabbing a small amount of corn starch onto the affected area
- Applying aloe vera gel to the sores, and
- Squirting cold water from a bottle to the sores and blisters to ease pain, especially while urinating

A patient may also try some other home remedies such as:

- Soaking in a warm sitz bath
- Taking pain relief medications, like acetaminophen or ibuprofen, if the symptoms are severe
- Bathing in lightly salted water
- Applying a small amount of petroleum jelly to affected parts of the skin
- Wearing loose clothing, preferably cotton clothing, to avoid irritation

- Refraining from any sexual activities, even with protection, until the symptoms have resolved completely

Medications

There are no medications that can cure herpes virus infections. However, patients may be prescribed an antiviral drug, like acyclovir, to inhibit the virus from multiplying and causing more severe symptoms.

Meanwhile, some over-the-counter treatments for herpes, such as creams and other forms of topical medications, may help manage mild symptoms like itching, tingling, and pain.

It is advisable to begin the treatment within the initial 24 hours once the symptoms start, for example, immediately after the pain or tingling occurs to lessen the duration of outbreaks.

If a patient uses any antiviral medication, the symptoms may resolve more quickly by about one or two days than if they had received no treatment. Medications may also help reduce the severity of the symptoms.

Taking these medications regularly for a more extended period could significantly reduce their risk of passing the herpes infection to the partner, though it remains possible.

Prevention Tips for Herpes Infection

The following strategies might help reduce the risk of passing on or developing herpes infections:

- Avoiding sex when the symptoms are present
- Using barrier protection, like condoms, while having sex
- Avoiding oral sex or kissing when there are cold sores in and around the mouth or lips
- Washing the hands well, especially after touching any affected area, during an acute episode of symptoms

Some patients also find that mental stress, illness, being tired, skin friction, or sunbathing tend to trigger the recurrences of symptoms of this infection. Identifying these triggers and avoiding them could help reduce the number and severity of outbreaks.

Conclusion

Though there is no cure for herpes infections, taking proper precautions and regular treatment might help prevent the spread of the disease and reduce the severity of the outbreaks.

How To Manage the Symptoms of Allergies in a Safe and Natural Way?

Allergies are common disorders that tend to occur due to the immune system's exaggerated response to substances called allergens. It is an immunological disorder, which occurs in several forms, such as asthma, dermatitis, and rhinitis.

Prednisone is a form of steroids that acts as an immunosuppressant and helps relieve the symptoms of allergic and autoimmune diseases.

However, since allergic disorders are chronic, patients have to use Prednisone and other modern drugs for a longer duration. This response can increase the risk of side effects associated with these medicines. It is known to cause insomnia, sodium retention, increased body weight, and the stimulation of the catabolic or diabetogenic processes in the body.

The use of steroids is also associated with a high risk of osteoporosis, adrenal suppression, Cushing's syndrome, and immunosuppression.

These side effects could be avoided by reducing your dependence on Prednisone or other modern anti-allergic drugs and following natural ways to control allergies' attacks as described below.

Identifying the Allergens

Maintain a diary to note down the changes in soaps, detergents, foods consumed, and the changes in temperature and weather that could be linked to your allergy attacks. You can correlate the changes in your diet and the surrounding environment with the allergy attacks. This method would help you find the exact substances you are allergic to. Avoiding these substances would help you prevent the attacks.

Probiotics

Allergy attacks usually occur as a result of imbalances in the immune system. It is caused due to the abnormal response of the immune cells to specific allergens. The use of probiotics could improve the healthy microbial flora in your gut, which has been linked to the reduced incidence of allergies.

Fermented foods and drinks such as yoghurt, Kombucha, or Kefir would help boost the gut flora and minimise the attack of allergic diseases to a great extent.

Quercetin

Quercetin is a bioflavonoid that can stabilize the mast cells. It may help prevent the release of histamine, which is primarily responsible for triggering symptoms of allergic diseases like itching, skin rashes, swelling, and breathlessness.

Quercetin may also act as a potent antioxidant and reduce inflammation in the skin, nose, and lungs. The regular use of Quercetin would prevent swelling and inflammation in different tissues and thus, avoid the attacks of allergic disorders.

Avoid Pollen

A high pollen count in the atmosphere could precipitate the attacks of allergic rhinitis and asthma. Though it is not possible to reduce the pollen count in your surroundings, you can take steps to avoid your exposure to them through some simple ways such as:

- Installing an air filter on the air-conditioning system to minimise the entry of pollen into your home
- Keeping the doors and windows closed to protect indoor air
- Covering your nose and mouth with a mask while stepping out of the house

Conclusion

These simple methods would protect against repeated asthma attacks, allergic rhinitis, and allergic dermatitis. It would reduce the need to take prednisolone and other modern drugs and help you avoid the dangerous side effects of these medications.

Symptoms, Causes, Treatment, and Home Remedies for Candidiasis

Vaginal candidiasis infection is a common fungal infection affecting the genitals. It is known to cause inflammation, itching, irritation, and abnormal vaginal discharge. It commonly affects women, though even men can get infected with this fungus.

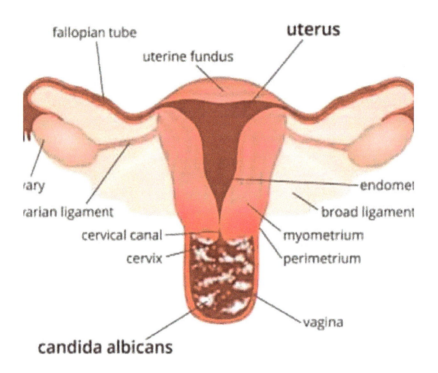

Following is a brief discussion about what candidiasis means, its symptoms, causes, and treatments.

What Is Candidiasis?

Vaginal candidiasis, sometimes called vaginal yeast infections and vulvovaginal candidiasis (VVC), is estimated to be experienced by nearly 3 out of 4 women in their lifetime. Most women experience a minimum of two to three episodes of this infection, especially during their childbearing age.

What Are the Symptoms of Candidiasis?

The most common symptoms of vaginal yeast infections include burning, itching, and abnormal vaginal discharge.

Symptoms of a vulvovaginal yeast infection may include:

- Itching, irritation, and burning of the vulva, which include the tissues surrounding the vagina, as well as the vaginal tissues
- Pain and soreness in the vaginal opening or vagina
- Vaginal burning during and after intercourse and urination
- A thick, whitish, odourless discharge resembling cottage cheese from the vagina
- An abnormal watery discharge from the vagina
- Rashes on the skin surrounding the vagina

Sometimes, a more complicated fungal infection may occur in the vagina, causing more severe symptoms. In some cases, four or more episodes of these infections may occur in just one year.

Women may develop symptoms like severe redness, itching, and swelling, leading to the formation of fissures or sores on the vagina or the skin surrounding it.

Some medical conditions that could cause complicated yeast infections include uncontrolled diabetes, pregnancy, having a weak immune system, or the presence of the alternate Candida fungi, as opposed to the Candida albicans.

In men, this condition usually affects the tip of the penis. Symptoms may include redness, discharge, and irritation. It may also affect the skin and the oral cavity.

What Are the Causes of Candidiasis?

Common yeast infections are usually caused by the yeast species called Candida albicans, though other species of Candida may also cause these infections.

The balanced bacteria and yeast levels are usually present in the woman's vagina. However, disturbances in the delicate balance may lead to the development of these infections.

Also, the Lactobacillus bacteria usually create an environment that does not encourage yeast overgrowth. But, when yeast becomes dominant, symptoms of fungal infections may emerge.

Vaginal fungal infections are not always linked to sexually transmitted infections (STIs). However, they often spread through oral-genital contact and during intercourse.

These infections are more common in women and men who are sexually active.

Factors that can increase the risk of a yeast infection in the vagina include:

- Excessive use of antibiotics, or corticosteroids, or both
- Being immune-compromised
- Use of contraceptive devices or hormonal contraceptives
- Pregnancy
- Uncontrolled diabetes

Any activity that could cause a change in normal vaginal flora, such as douching, could contribute to yeast infections. Poor diet, as well as mental stress and lack of sleep, can also increase the risk.

Treatment of Fungal Infections, Including Candidiasis

Vaginal or oral yeast infections are often treated according to the severity of the symptoms and complications.

Treatment of these infections also depends on whether the condition is complicated or uncomplicated.

Treatment of Uncomplicated Candidiasis or Yeast Infections

There are two basic ways to treat uncomplicated yeast infections: oral treatment or direct vaginal therapy.

While treating uncomplicated yeast infections, a short-term course of vaginal therapy would be sufficient. As these medications are oil-based, they weaken the latex diaphragms and condoms, potentially making them less effective or reliable. Hence, the use of non-latex condoms is recommended for contraception while patients are undergoing vaginal therapy to manage candidiasis.

Alternatively, oral anti-fungal agents such as fluconazole may be used as a single dose.

Treatment of Complicated Yeast Infections

The treatment usually includes long-course vaginal therapy and multi-dosage oral formulations in men and women with complicated yeast infections.

Maintenance medications are sometimes recommended. These medicines need to be taken regularly for preventing the infections from returning. The long-course vaginal therapy may include vaginal creams, ointments, tablets, or suppositories for about 7 to 15 days.

Sometimes, 2 to 3 doses of oral fungal agents such as fluconazole might be recommended instead of direct vaginal therapy.

If the symptoms are severe, a patient may be advised to use topical medications containing steroids to help ease the symptoms while the anti-fungal drug works.

Before using any anti-fungal medication, it is crucial to ensure that the symptoms are only due to the fungal infection. It should be noted that the overuse of anti-fungal medicines may increase the risk of yeast resistance, such that the medication may not work later when it is needed in the future.

When maintenance medications are needed, they may be used only after one of the treatment methods mentioned above is finished. It often includes a weekly treatment with oral drugs like fluconazole for about six months or a weekly treatment with clotrimazole administered vaginally.

If the sexual partner of the patient has the symptoms of candidiasis, they should also consider undergoing the treatment. The use of condoms is highly recommended to prevent the spread of infection.

Home Remedies for Candidiasis

Several alternative therapies can be used for treating vaginal candidiasis infection. These include using a boric acid vaginal suppository and yoghurt's vaginal or oral application.

Prevention of Candidiasis

Women who are susceptible to developing fungal infections are advised to follow the following methods for reducing their risk.

- Avoid douching
- Wear loose-fitting skirts and pants
- Avoid using feminine deodorant and deodorant tampons and pads
- Wear underwear made of natural fibres like cotton
- Wash underwear at a higher temperature
- Eat a healthy, balanced diet
- Avoid tight pantyhose or underwear
- Change wet clothing, like bathing suits, promptly
- Avoid hot baths and hot tubs

Conclusion

Taking precautions to avoid the spread of vaginal candidiasis, timely diagnosis, and treatment can help prevent the risk of complicated yeast infections. Women are advised to follow the prevention tips discussed above to protect themselves against these infections.

What Are the Causes of Hair Loss and How to Manage It Naturally?

Hair fall is a condition believed to have the maximum number of causes. Avoiding hair fall is nothing less than playing dodgeball. Hair loss can occur due to so many reasons that it is practically impossible to dodge or prevent each of them.

Some causes of hair loss are more dangerous and can lead to baldness, often requiring hair transplantation. Some causes of hair fall are relatively rare and can be controlled easily by making healthy changes in your diet and lifestyle.

Let us have a look at the most common causes of hair loss in men and women:

What Are the Causes of Hair Loss?

Male Pattern Baldness

Male pattern baldness is the most common cause of hair loss in men, which cannot be managed easily. It occurs due to the combination of your genes and excessive male sex hormones. It is hereditary and often follows a classic pattern of hair loss that begins from the temple, later leaving an M-shaped hairline.

A healthy diet is considered one of the most effective natural treatments for preventing male pattern baldness.

Heredity

Not just men, women too can suffer from hair loss due to hereditary factors. The female-pattern hair loss, also called the androgenic alopecia, is just the female version of the male pattern baldness.

If the women in your family had started to have hair loss at a particular age, you too might be vulnerable to it. However, unlike in men, the androgenic hair fall in women doesn't cause a receding hairline. Instead, it often causes a noticeable thinning of the hair from all over the scalp.

Stress

Stress and hair loss often coexist! Stress, physical or emotional, is bound to invite hair loss because it can disrupt your hair cycle, thus pushing more hair into the shedding phase. In short, you will be shedding off more hair than your scalp can regrow, making your hair look thinner.

Lack of Proteins

We all learned in school that proteins are the building blocks of our bodies. Proteins are required for the growth of the body's cells and tissues. So, if you are not getting enough proteins from your diet, your body is bound to preserve its source of proteins by shutting down the hair growth resulting in hair loss.

Excessive Vitamin A

Vitamins are good for our health! But, in the case of vitamin A, it is not the deficiency but an excess of it that can be the cause of your hair loss.

Taking a very high dose of vitamin A supplements for a long duration can trigger hair loss. Luckily, this cause is reversible. Once you stop taking the supplements, your hair should grow normally.

Hormonal Problems

The hormones in your body are meant to help it function efficiently. However, the same hormones can also create havoc when secreted in more or less than the average amounts.

Hair loss is also the most common symptom of hormonal imbalance in men and women.

Hormonal diseases could trigger hair fall, which include hypothyroidism, thyroiditis, polycystic ovarian disease (PCOD), and diabetes. Women may experience severe hair fall due to the hormonal changes occurring during puberty, pregnancy, and menopause or disorders like PCOD.

Over-Styling

Vigorous use of hair styling products over several years may cause hair to fall out. Examples of harmful hair-styling methods include hair weaving, tight braids, cornrows, and the use of chemical relaxers for straightening your hair.

Hot oil treatments can also cause damage to your hair follicles and make them brittle, causing your hair to fall out.

Drastic Weight Loss

If you are obese, losing weight is welcome! However, an unhealthy approach to weight loss, such as prolonged hours of starving, may lead to malnutrition and may trigger hair loss. The psychological stress to reduce weight can also lead to hair loss.

Side Effects of Medications

Hair fall can occur due to the side effects of some drugs like birth control pills, blood thinners, and cholesterol-reducing medicines.

Unfortunately, chemotherapy drugs used to manage cancer can also cause your hair to fall out.

Some of these causes of hair loss can be managed well if you take proper care of your scalp and hair. Eating a healthy diet, minimizing your exposure to harmful toxins, and avoiding the use of chemical-based hair care products may also help reduce hair fall.

Best Natural Ways to Prevent Hair Fall Naturally!

Pay attention to your diet. Your skin and hair are the reflections of your overall health. Shiny and voluminous hair indicates a healthy body and a happy mind. The beauty of the hair comes from within your mind and body. However, most people tend to ignore this fact and give more importance to their external beauty.

If you want to succeed in overcoming your hair loss, you must make efforts to maintain maximum physical and mental health.

Good physical health stems from a nutritious diet. Iron, vitamin E, and protein deficiency can worsen your hair loss. Make sure your diet comprises all the food groups, including proteins, vitamins, and minerals. Also, eat plenty of fresh fruits and vegetables so that your body gets complete nutrition.

You can also include cucumbers in your regular diet. Ayurveda recommends drinking a glass of cucumber juice at least twice or thrice a week to reduce hair loss. It contains sulphur and silicon that could help stop your hair fall and promote healthy and strong hair. Vitamin A, vitamin C, and silica contents of the cucumber juice would also help repair damaged hair and reduce hair thinning.

Believe me, whatever you eat will finally reflect on your hair and skin. Paying attention to what you eat would stop your hair loss and restore the lost mane.

Apply Onion Juice

Do you know what the best way to treat any disease is? It is to find its root cause and treat that first. This method is the most effective way to ensure faster and long-lasting results. The same rule applies to hair fall as well.

If you want hair fall to stop, you must find its root cause. For example, if you are over 40 years, the cause of your hair loss could be the reduced production of collagen in your scalp and hair roots. So, the only way to avoid this problem is to replenish the lost collagen.

Onion is one of the best natural remedies in this regard. It contains sulphur that can stimulate collagen production and support hair growth, thus improving your hair volume.

To use, chop one onion and squeeze out its juice. Apply this juice to your scalp and allow it to stay for about 10 to 15 minutes. Then, rinse with water.

Massage With Coconut Oil

There is nothing better than coconut oil to nourish and condition your hair. Coconut oil can promote your hair growth by providing essential healthy fats, proteins, and minerals.

Regular scalp massaging with coconut oil would reduce hair breakage and make your hair look shiny and voluminous. It may also reduce dandruff, one of the leading causes of hair loss.

An efficient way to use coconut oil for hair fall is to warm it slightly and then massage your scalp, starting from the hair roots to the tips. You can wash your hair after one hour. Alternatively, you may massage the scalp at night and wash it off in the morning.

Don't Ignore Your Mental Health

As revealed earlier, a happy mind is a necessity if you want to flaunt the beautiful tresses of hair. However, it would be challenging to stay satisfied when life is burdened with too many stressors like the pressure of improving your academic or professional performance, battling traffic daily, meeting deadlines and targets, strained personal relations, and so on.

These stressors are often the hidden factors responsible for your hair fall. You must fight these demons if you want to stay fit and prevent hair loss. Ayurveda advises men and women to regularly practice yoga, meditation, and breathing exercises to reduce stress and avoid affecting their health.

These stress-busting techniques are highly effective for preventing hair fall. They would also help improve your perception of the negativities surrounding you and help you emerge a positive and successful person!

Sleep Well

Lack of sleep could deprive your body of the time it needs to repair itself. Our hair and scalp are exposed to harmful toxins, pollutants, and dust throughout the day. These factors leave the hair strands and follicles damaged.

Your body tries to repair these damages through various healing processes. However, the body needs to be at rest to be able to carry out these processes efficiently.

Lack of sound sleep may deprive your body of this phase of rest and thus, prevent it from repairing the damaged hair. Over some time, your hair would become weaker and prone to breakage.

The best way to avoid these complications is to ensure you get a sound sleep for at least 8 hours every day.

Some More Tips to Reduce Hair Loss

- Avoid washing hair too often; once or twice a week is sufficient
- Limit your use of styling tools such as curling or straightening irons
- Avoid vigorous brushing
- Never fiddle with your hair
- Do not use a blow dryer to dry your hair
- Avoid chemical-based hair dyes
- Use a thick, wide-toothed comb to detangle your hair
- Avoid a hairstyle that pulls on your hair, like a very tight ponytail and buns
- Avoid perms and similar harsh chemical treatments

Conclusion

Natural treatments for hair loss are not just focused on reducing hair loss. The Ayurvedic treatments discussed above aim to treat you as a whole, considering your physical, emotional, and spiritual aspects. This method is why the results you can achieve by following these holistic natural treatments would last longer.

What to Expect During Wound Healing and Natural Ways to Accelerate Healing

A wound is an abnormal opening or a cut in the skin that breaches the continuity of tissues. It may be just a scratch or a larger cut.

An extensive abrasion, scrape or cut often occurs due to an accident, fall, or trauma. Surgical cuts made by healthcare providers during medical procedures are also types of wounds.

Our body has a complex mechanism that helps patch up the skin wounds and repair damaged tissues to restore the integrity of the skin. Wound healing occurs in several steps that together help repair the body's damaged tissues. Each stage of the wound healing process is vital for ensuring proper wound healing.

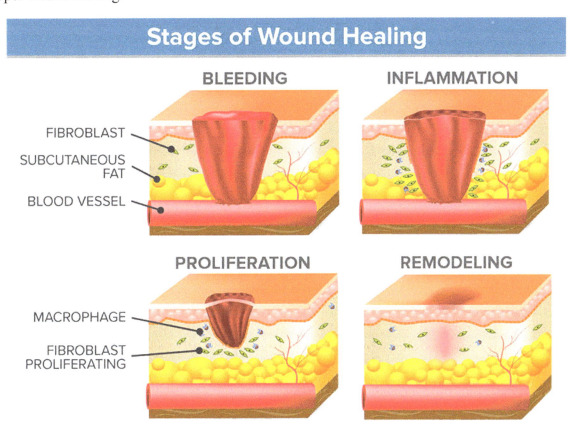

Here is a brief discussion about the types of wounds, the stages of wound healing, and the natural ways to accelerate healing.

What Are the Different Types of Wounds?

There are several different types of wounds, depending on certain factors, including the wound's source or the underlying issues that might have led to it. The type of wound may alter based on other factors involved in the healing processes or how the physician treats it.

Wounds are typically closed or open. Closed wounds refer to injuries that do not cause a break on the skin's surface, though they may cause damage to the underlying tissue. A bruise is one of the most common forms of a closed wound.

On the other hand, open wounds tend to cause a break on the skin's surface and could damage the underlying tissues.

Some common forms of open wounds are:

- Abrasions: These are the types of wounds that occur due to scraping or rubbing of the skin against any hard surfaces.
- Burns: These injuries result from contact with open flames, an intense heat source, exposure to severe cold, certain chemicals, and electricity.
- Punctures: These are tiny yet deeper holes that are caused due to long and pointed objects, like a nail.
- Lacerations: These are the deeper cuts that are caused due to sharp objects, like a knife and sharp edges.
- Avulsions: These are the types of injuries that result in the complete or partial tearing away of the skin and underlying tissues.

Chronic wounds might also cause a breakage in the skin that needs to heal to restore the normal structural integrity of affected tissues. These types of damages include pressure injuries like bedsores and diabetes-linked ulcers.

What Are the Stages of the Wound Healing Process?

The body heals the damaged tissues of a wound in four main stages. The phases of wound healing include:

1. Prevention of too much blood loss
2. Cleaning and defending the affected area
3. Healing and repairing

This list suggests that keeping the affected part of the wound clean and covered would help the body repair the damaged tissues most efficiently. Here is a detailed description of what happens during each stage of wound healing.

Stage 1: Haemostasis (Stopping the Bleeding)

When we get a scratch, cut, or any other wound on the skin, it usually starts to bleed. Hence, the first stage of the wound healing process is to inhibit the bleeding. This phase is called haemostasis.

Blood begins to form a clot within a few seconds to minutes after getting a wound. This process is a healthy or a good blood clot that helps prevent excessive blood loss. Blood clotting can also help close the wound by forming a scab while healing the tissues.

Stage 2: Clotting (Scabbing)

The scabbing or clotting phase has four primary steps:

1. The blood vessels around the tissues of the wound begin to narrow. This process can help stop further bleeding and reduce the risk of severe blood loss.

2. Platelets, the primary clotting cells in the blood, begin to clump together to form a 'plug' at the site of the wound.

3. Coagulation and clotting also include a protein known as fibrin. It is like a "blood glue" that can form a net to hold that platelet plug in place. This process leads to the formation of a scab that covers the wound.

4. Inflammation that involves healing and cleaning.

Once the wound is not bleeding anymore, the body's immune system can start the cleaning and healing processes. At first, the small blood vessels or capillaries around the wound site open slightly to allow more blood to flow to it. This step may make the area appear a little red, inflamed, and swollen. The affected part may also feel a bit warm. These are the signs that the healing mechanisms have started to occur efficiently.

The flow of fresh blood to the wound site improves oxygen supply and healing nutrients. The blood also includes white blood cells, known as macrophages, which help promote the cleaning and healing of the wound.

Macrophages clean the affected tissues by fighting against any infection. These cells also secrete chemical messengers known as growth factors, which help repair the tissues.

It may also result in clear fluid oozing in or around the area. This effect indicates that the white blood cells have started the process of defending or rebuilding the tissues.

Stage 3: Growth and Proliferation (Rebuilding)

Once the wound is stable and clean, our body begins rebuilding the site of injury. The oxygen-rich red cells flow to the site to form new tissues by stimulating the body to build materials using proteins and other nutrients.

At the same time, chemical signals in the body carry impulses to the cells around the wound site to form new elastic tissues known as collagen. Collagen acts like a scaffold on which other cells can build. The collagen also helps repair and heal the skin and other tissues in the wound.

You might see a fresh, raised, red scar at this stage in healing. The scar slowly fades in colour and looks flatter.

Stage 4: Strengthening (Maturation)

Even after the wound looks fully repaired or closed, it may still be in the stage of healing. It may look pinkish and puckered or stretched. You might also feel a mild tightness or itching over the parts. This reaction indicates the body's efforts to further strengthen and repair the area.

Natural Methods to Support Wound Healing Processes

- Keep the affected part of the skin clean and covered
- Change the dressing regularly
- Ensure your blood sugar levels are within normal limits
- Avoid excess intake of unhealthy fats and sugars, especially if the wound is larger and is expected to take longer to heal
- Eat food rich in proteins to support the tissue-building processes
- Maintain hygiene to prevent infection

Conclusion

Wound healing is a complicated process with many phases. From the moment the wound occurs until it is healed completely, the body undergoes numerous processes to restore the structural integrity of the tissues.

The proper treatment of wounds to prevent excessive bleeding and infections can help ensure faster healing of the affected part of the skin.

What Is Constipation and What Are the Natural Remedies to Avoid It?

Constipation is one of the most typical digestive problems affecting people of all age groups worldwide. It is defined as having hard stool and dry bowel movements and passing stools fewer than three times a week.

While constipation is not considered a significant health issue by most people, it can lead to severe consequences if not managed appropriately. Also, constipation can be a sign of an underlying condition. Hence, there is a need to be aware of constipation's causes and risk factors and seek appropriate treatment to improve bowel movements to restore healthy digestive functions and prevent long-term complications.

What Are the Common Symptoms Associated With Constipation?

The bowel habits of every person are different. However, a person may be considered constipated if they experience the following symptoms:

- Less than three bowel movements per week
- Severe pain during bowel movements
- Passing hard, lumpy, and dry stools
- A sensation of fullness, even after bowel movements
- Excessive straining while passing stoops

Healthcare experts recommend seeking medical advice if these symptoms do not go away or if any of the following signs develop:

- Bleeding from the rectum
- Presence of blood in the stool
- Persistent abdominal pain
- A feeling as if gas is trapped in the lower part of the abdomen
- Pain in the back
- Consistent vomiting
- Unexplained weight loss
- A sudden change in the bowel movements
- Fever

What Are the Causes of Constipation?

The primary function of the colon, part of the large intestines, is to absorb water from the residual food while it is passing through the digestive tract so that the remaining waste can be excreted from the body in the form of stools.

The colon muscles eventually help propel waste out of the body through the rectum to be eliminated via the anus. If the stools remain in the colon for too long, they may become hard, resulting in constipation or difficulty passing stools.

A poor diet can also cause constipation frequently. Dietary fibres and adequate intake of water are necessary to keep stools soft. The lack of fibre in the diet and reduced water intake are often the reasons why a person may develop chronic constipation.

Fibre-rich foods are often plant-based. Dietary fibres come in soluble as well as insoluble forms. Soluble fibres can easily dissolve in water, creating a soft, gel-like material while it passes through the digestive tract.

On the other hand, insoluble fibres retain most of their structure while passing through the digestive tract. These forms of fibres join with stool, thus increasing its size and weight whilst also softening it. This development makes the stools easier to pass through the rectum, improving bowel movements and preventing constipation. Hence, it is vital to enhance the intake of fibre-rich foods to avoid constipation.

Mental stress, changes in the daily routine, conditions that slow down muscle contractions in the colon, and delaying the urge to pass stools may also result in chronic constipation.

Some common causes and risk factors of constipation include:

- Older age
- A low fibre diet
- A diet high in milk, meat, and cheese
- Low exercise levels
- Dehydration
- Frequent travelling or changes in the routine
- Delaying the impulse to have bowel movements
- Side effects of medications, such as certain antacids, diuretics, pain medications, and some drugs used for the treatment of Parkinson's disease

Underlying health issues that can lead to constipation include:

- Misuse or overuse of laxatives
- Diseases affecting the colon and rectum, such as intestinal obstruction, diverticulosis, and

IBS

- Chronic diseases, such as Parkinson's disease, stroke, and diabetes
- Hormonal disturbances, including hypothyroidism (an underactive thyroid gland)

Management of Constipation Using Natural Home Remedies

Changing your diet to include fibre-rich foods and increasing your physical activities are the most efficient ways to prevent constipation.

Some other natural remedies that could help prevent constipation include the following:

- Drink at least 1.5 to 2 litres of water or other unsweetened fluids every day to hydrate the body.
- Include fibre-rich foods in your diets, such as fresh fruits, veggies, whole grains, bran cereals, beans, and prunes. Make sure your daily intake of fibre is around 20 to 35 grams.
- Limit your intake of alcohol and caffeinated drinks, as these beverages can cause severe dehydration.
- Avoid the intake of low-fibre foods, like milk, cheese, meat, and processed foods.
- Don't delay passing stools when you feel the urge to have bowel movements.
- Aim for at least 150 to 180 minutes of moderate exercises per week, aiming at least 30 minutes per day five times a week. Try simple exercises like walking, swimming, or biking in the beginning to avoid overexertion.
- Do not misuse or overuse laxatives. If you must, use them sparingly.
- Raise the knees by putting the feet on a footstool while having bowel movements

Conclusion

Constipation is a common digestive problem known to affect people of all ages. The problem may worsen as a person gets older or due to certain medicines. Constipation often occurs due to the lack of dietary fibres in the regular diet.

However, most cases of acute and chronic constipation are mild. They can easily be treated with some changes in diet and physical activities.

Natural Treatments for Haemorrhoids

Haemorrhoids, also referred to as piles, are swollen veins in the anus and the lower part of the rectum. These are dilated and tortuous veins similar to varicose veins that occur in the legs.

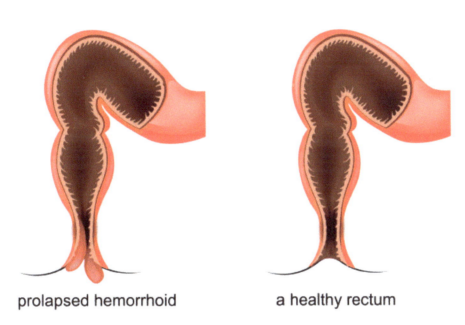

Haemorrhoids developing inside the rectum are called internal haemorrhoids, while those developing beneath the skin around the anal region are known as external haemorrhoids.

It is estimated that nearly 3 out of 4 adults suffer from haemorrhoids from time to time. Piles or haemorrhoids may occur due to several causes. Fortunately, several effective natural treatments are available for patients with haemorrhoids. Home treatments, including dietary and lifestyle changes, can play a crucial role in obtaining relief from symptoms of this condition.

Here is a brief discussion about what haemorrhoids are and the natural remedies to manage this condition.

What Are the Causes of Haemorrhoids?

Small veins around the anus begin to stretch when under pressure or straining and might swell or bulge. Haemorrhoids often develop from the rise in pressure in the lower part of the rectum associated with conditions such as:

- Straining for bowel movements
- Having chronic constipation or diarrhoea
- Sitting on the toilet for an extended period
- Being pregnant
- Anal intercourse
- Eating a low-fibre diet
- Being obese
- Regular lifting of heavy objects

The risk of haemorrhoids tends to increase as a person ages as the tissues supporting the veins in the rectum and anus start to become weaker and stretch. This issue may also happen in pregnancy in women, as the baby's weight can put extra pressure and strain on the anal region.

What Are the Symptoms of Haemorrhoids?

The signs and symptoms of piles usually depend on the specific type of haemorrhoids the patient suffers from.

External Haemorrhoids

These types of piles are located under the skin around the anus. The signs and symptoms caused due to external piles might include:

- Bleeding
- Itching and irritation in the anal region
- Swelling around the anus
- Pain and discomfort

Internal Haemorrhoids

The internal haemorrhoids are located inside the rectum. Patients usually cannot see or feel the internal piles, but they can cause severe discomfort. Also, patients may experience some symptoms while straining for passing stool.

The common signs and symptoms of internal piles include:

- Painless bleeding from the anus during bowel movements
- A lump of haemorrhoids pushing through the anal opening (protruding or prolapsed haemorrhoid), causing mild to moderate pain or irritation.

Thrombosed Piles

If blood pools into the external haemorrhoids, it may form a clot (thrombus), resulting in symptoms such as:

- Inflammation
- Severe pain
- A hard lump near the anus
- Swelling

What Are the Possible Complications of Haemorrhoids?

Complications of piles are rare but may include:

- Anaemia: In rare cases, chronic blood loss caused due to haemorrhoids may result in anaemia, a condition in which the patient's red blood cell count reduces. This issue may lead to loss of the ability of blood to carry oxygen to all the cells of the body efficiently.
- Strangulated haemorrhoids: If blood flow to the internal haemorrhoids is cut off, the haemorrhoids may become strangulated, causing intense pain.
- Blood clots: Occasionally, clots formed due to blood flow occlusion to the piles may lead to thrombosed haemorrhoids. Although usually not dangerous, it may become excruciatingly painful and need to be drained.

Prevention of Haemorrhoids

The most effective way to prevent haemorrhoids is to avoid constipation and keep the stools soft. Here are some tips and natural remedies that would help you prevent haemorrhoids or reduce their symptoms:

- Eat high-fibre foods: Eating a diet comprising fresh fruits, whole grains, and vegetables can soften the stools and increase the bulk. This step would help you avoid exerting pressure or straining during defecation, lowering your risk of haemorrhoids. Adding fibre-rich foods to your diet would also help prevent digestive problems like flatulence and bloating that exert pressure on the lower abdomen.

- Drink plenty of fluids: Aim to drink at least six to ten glasses of water every day to keep the stools soft and avoid constipation.

- Do not strain: Straining for stools and holding the breath while trying to pass the stools can create more pressure on the veins in the anus and rectum. Hence, it is advisable to avoid straining for stools.

- Avoid holding the urge: It is advisable to avoid waiting for too long to pass stools when you get an urge or experience bowel movements. Holding your urge for too long would cause the bowel movement to cease. As a result, the stools would dry out and become harder to pass.

- Avoid long periods of inactivity or sitting: A long period of inactivity or sitting or too long, especially on the toilet, could raise the pressure on the veins in the rectum and anus and cause piles.

- Exercise: Staying active would prevent constipation and reduce pressure on the veins caused due to prolonged periods of sitting or standing. Exercise would also help you lose excess weight and prevent obesity that could be contributing to the development and worsening of haemorrhoids.

Treatment of Piles

Mild pain, inflammation, and swelling caused due to haemorrhoids may be relieved with the help of simple home remedies given below:

- Topical treatment: Applying over-the-counter haemorrhoid creams and using suppositories containing hydrocortisone may provide significant relief from the symptoms of piles.

- Soak in a sitz bath or warm bath regularly: Soak the anal area in warm water for about 10 to 15 minutes two to three times a day. You can also try a sitz bath to derive relief from the symptoms. The sitz bath can fit over the toilet easily.

Conclusion

With these simple treatments and home remedies, haemorrhoid symptoms often go away within a few days to weeks. However, it is vital to seek a long-term approach by changing your dietary and lifestyle habits to prevent the recurrence of piles in the future.

Natural Home Remedies for the Management of Urinary Tract Infections

If you are experiencing a burning sensation while passing urine, you are probably suffering from a urinary tract infection. Symptoms may be accompanied by an increased frequency of urination and dull, aching pain in the lower part of the abdomen.

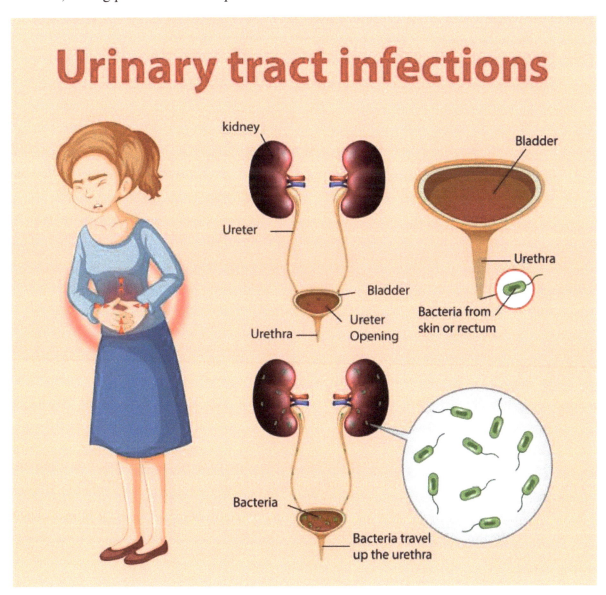

Here are some home remedies that can help you manage urinary tract infections safely and effectively.

Drink Plenty of Water

This one may not sound like an extraordinary remedy, but its effect is definitely extraordinary! In fact, drinking plenty of water is what you must do to prevent and treat your urinary tract infection.

When you drink more water, your kidneys tend to secrete more urine to be expelled out of the body. And along with this extra amount of urine, bacteria, viruses, and other toxins that cause infections and irritation in your urinary tract are also eliminated!

Drink 8 to 10 glasses of water or even more to flush out the bacteria from your body system and bounce back to good health rather quickly.

Celery Seeds

Celery seeds act as a natural diuretic, mainly due to the butylphthalide present in them. Chewing a handful of these seeds would increase the secretion of urine by the kidneys and help to flush out the harmful bacteria.

Boil a handful of celery seeds in one or two cups of water on medium heat until the liquid is reduced to half. Then, strain it and drink the liquid one or two times every day.

Alternatively, you may also snack on celery seeds. Apart from relieving your urinary tract infection, it will also help improve your digestion.

Parsley

Parsley not just makes a wonderfully refreshing drink but would also relieve urinary tract infections. It can speed up the healing processes by working as a diuretic. It would help increase the amount of urine secreted by the kidneys.

Increased secretion of urine would help flush out the bacteria from the body more efficiently and relieve your discomfort.

All you need to do is add about half a cup of fresh parsley leaves in one or two cups of water and bring this to a boil. You may also use dried parsley leaves if fresh leaves are not available. Reduce the heat and allow it to simmer. Let parsley infuse the water for about six to ten minutes. Then, strain out the leaves and drink the water.

Baking Soda

It has powerful medicinal properties that could help relieve the symptoms of several ailments, especially those arising due to the acidic pH in the body fluids, including urinary infections, heartburn, and gastritis.

The alkaline nature of baking soda would neutralize the acidity of your urine. It would ease the discomfort caused due to the burning sensation while passing urine and create an unfavourable environment for the bacteria to survive.

Stir in one tablespoon of baking soda in a glass of water and drink this once or twice daily for at least five to seven days. You may drink this once every day in the morning regularly if you tend to develop repeated episodes of urinary infections.

Indian Gooseberry

Indian Gooseberry contains a high amount of vitamin C, which would help treat urinary tract infections by inhibiting the growth of bacteria.

Simply add one teaspoon of Indian gooseberry powder and a pinch of turmeric powder to a cup of water and boil this solution for about 10 minutes. Drink the residue twice a day for four to five days.

Ginger Tea

When dealing with an infective or inflammatory condition, you just cannot skip ginger. The chemical make-up of this herb would help block prostaglandin synthesis, which would result in less pain and reduced inflammation.

You can make ginger tea by boiling grated ginger with your regular tea. Consume this two to three times a day.

Blueberries

Blueberries possess natural anti-bacterial and antioxidant properties, which would help reduce inflammation and infections in the urinary tract.

You can munch on berries for your snacking or breakfast, add them to a smoothie, or top your oatmeal with chopped berries.

Cucumbers

Cucumbers are rather a bland vegetable with no particular taste other than a slightly sour and watery finish. But, the cucumber's watery content could come in handy for managing urinary tract infections.

The high water content of cucumbers would increase urine output and force the bacteria out of your body system. You can add cucumber slices to your sandwiches or salads or just eat them raw.

Use Heating Pads

The best way to reduce pain and discomfort in the lower abdomen caused due to urinary infections is to use heating pads. The inflammation and irritation of the urinary bladder may cause a continuous, nagging discomfort, making passing urine a painful activity.

If you experience these symptoms, you can try applying a heating pad over your lower abdomen. The warmth would relieve the pain caused due to inflammation and also release the spasms of the bladder muscles.

4 C's You Must Avoid While Suffering From Urinary Infections:

- Chocolate: high-carb chocolates would create a favourable environment for the bacteria to grow, thus worsening your infection.

- Citrus fruits: The acidic nature of citric acid in these fruits may increase the burning sensation.

- Caffeine: Caffeine may increase the burning sensation and make it more difficult for you to pass urine.

- Carbonation: Fizzy carbonated drinks would irritate your bladder and aggravate your symptoms.

Conclusion

These home remedies are highly effective and would help you get rid of the symptoms of urinary infections safely and effectively. You may also use these remedies regularly to prevent urinary infections in the future.

Treatment of Kidney Stones Using Natural Remedies

Kidney stones, sometimes referred to as renal calculi, renal stones, nephrolithiasis, and urolithiasis, are the hard deposits made of salts and minerals which form inside the kidneys.

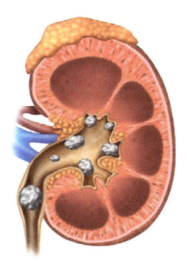

A diet comprising high amounts of certain substances such as oxalates, excess body weight, and the long-term use of some supplements and medicines are among the common causes of renal stones.

This condition can affect any part of the urinary system, from the kidneys to the bladder. The stones often form when urine becomes more concentrated, allowing minerals and salts to crystallise and then stick together, forming a stone.

The passage of kidney stones is often quite painful. However, kidney stones usually do not cause permanent damage to the urinary tract tissues, provided they are detected on time.

Patients with kidney stones may be advised treatments such as taking painkillers to relieve the pain that occurs when the stone tries to pass through the urinary tract. Other treatment is drinking lots of water for pushing the passage of the kidney stone so that it can be expelled from the body via urine.

In some cases, if the stone has lodged into the urinary tract, it could be associated with an infection. The result could be serious complications necessitating a surgical procedure or other treatments such as lithotripsy to remove the stone.

Ayurveda recommends following a healthy diet and making appropriate changes in your lifestyle to avoid the risk of renal stones. Here is a brief discussion about kidney stones' symptoms, causes, and risk factors and the natural ways to manage this condition.

What Are the Common Causes of Kidney Stones?

Kidney stones usually do not have any definite, single cause, though several factors could increase the risk of this condition.

Renal stones may form when the urine contains certain crystal-forming substances, including uric acid, calcium, and oxalates, in higher amounts causing urine to become more concentrated.

At the same time, renal stones may also be formed when the urine lacks substances that can prevent these excess minerals from sticking together or forming crystals, thus creating a favourable environment for this condition's pathogens.

What Are the Types of Kidney Stones?

Kidney stone treatment depends on the type of stone. Being aware of the renal stone type can help determine its cause and give clues on the proper ways to reduce the risk of developing more renal stones in the future.

Patients are often advised to try to save the kidney stone, if possible, when they pass one to be analysed in a laboratory to determine what it is composed of.

The common forms of kidney stones include:

Calcium Stone

Most renal stones are calcium stones, generally in the form of calcium oxalate crystals. Oxalate is a compound regularly formed in the liver or absorbed from the diet. Some fruits, vegetables, nuts, and chocolates have a very high oxalate content.

Including these foods in your diet could increase the risk of renal stones to a great extent. Moreover, using very high doses of vitamin D supplements, having intestinal bypass surgery, and some metabolic disorders may raise the concentrations of calcium and oxalate in the urine, thus triggering the development of stones.

Calcium stones might occur in the form of other compounds like calcium phosphate as well. This form of renal stone is common in patients with metabolic conditions, like renal tubular acidosis. It is usually associated with using certain medications prescribed to treat seizures and migraines, like topiramate.

Cystine Stones

These stones are usually formed in people with a hereditary condition known as cystinuria, characterised by the kidneys' excretion of more amounts of specific amino acids.

Uric Acid Stones

Uric acid stones often occur in people who lose excessive body fluid due to malabsorption and chronic diarrhoea, those who consume a protein-rich diet, and those with metabolic syndrome or diabetes. Some genetic factors might also increase the risk of uric acid stones.

Struvite Stones

These stones are usually formed in response to urinary tract infections. These stones often quickly grow and become very large, sometimes with little warning or few symptoms.

What Are the Risk Factors for Renal Stones?

- Family history and personal history: Patients who have someone in the family with a history of kidney stones are more likely to develop this condition. Also, people, who have had kidney stones in the past, are at an increased risk of developing renal stones in the future.

- Dietary factors: Eating a diet rich in proteins, salt (sodium), and sugars might increase the risk of some forms of kidney stones. This factor is specifically true with a high-salt diet. Too much salt intake could increase the amount of calcium the kidneys need to filter, thus significantly increasing your risk of renal stones.

- Dehydration: Lack of adequate water intake could increase the risk of renal calculi. People living in dry or warm climates and those who sweat more could be at a higher risk.

- Pre-existing medical conditions: cystinuria, overactive thyroid, renal tubular acidosis, and recurrent urinary infections could increase the risk of renal stones.

- Digestive surgery: Patients who have had gastric bypass surgery, chronic diarrhoea, or inflammatory bowel disease may develop abnormal digestive processes that could affect the absorption of water and calcium, thus increasing the amount of calculus-forming substances in the urine.

- Obesity: High body mass index (BMI), weight gain, and larger waist size have been linked to a higher risk of renal stones.

- Supplements and medicines: Long-term use of some supplements and medication, including vitamin C, laxatives, nutritional supplements, calcium-based antacid drugs, and drugs used for treating depression and migraines, could raise the risk of renal calculi.

What Are the Symptoms of Kidneys Stones?

Usually, a kidney stone does not cause any severe symptoms or pain until it moves through the kidneys or passes into the ureters, narrow tubes connecting the kidneys and urinary bladder.

If the stones get lodged into the ureters, it can block the urine flow, causing the kidneys to become swollen and the ureters to undergo spasmodic contractions. These complications can cause intense unbearable pain.

If patients develop these complications, they may experience some signs and symptoms such as:

- Severe and sharp pain in the back and side, especially below the ribs
- Pain coming in waves and fluctuating in intensity
- Pain radiating to the groin and lower abdomen
- Pain with burning sensation while passing urine
- Foul-smelling, cloudy urine
- Passing pinkish, brown, or red urine
- Passing urine more often than usual and a minimal amount of urine
- A persistent urge to urinate
- Fever and chills
- Nausea and vomiting

Pain caused due to a kidney stone might change in nature. It may also shift to a different location and increase intensity as it moves through the urinary tract.

Prevention and Treatment of Kidney Stones Using Simple Natural Remedies

- Drinking water throughout the day is highly recommended for patients having a history or family history of renal stones. Doctors usually recommend drinking at least litres of water every day to avoid the risk,
- People living in a hot and dry climate or who exercise frequently may need to increase their water intake accordingly. This ensures the kidneys produce enough urine to dilute the calculus-forming substances.
- Avoiding oxalate-rich foods such as rhubarb, beets, Swiss chard, okra, spinach, sweet potatoes, chocolate, nuts, tea, and black pepper can help reduce the risk of oxalate stones.
- It is advisable to choose a diet low in animal proteins and salt. Reducing the amount of salt and choosing non-animal protein sources, like legumes, could help prevent the risk of kidneys stones.
- Herbal remedies: Regular use of herbal remedies such as Holy Basil, Dandelion Root, and Horsetail could be beneficial for preventing the formation of stones in the urinary tract.

Conclusion

Identifying the type of renal stones and making appropriate changes in your diet and lifestyle are the keys to preventing more renal stones from forming in the future.

What Are the Causes, Symptoms, and Treatments for Gout?

Gout is a common joint disorder caused due to damage and inflammation. The common symptoms of this condition include severe pain in the affected joints that usually begins abruptly.

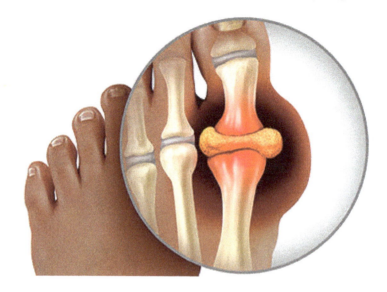

Why Does Gout Occur?

Gout is caused due to the deposition of tiny uric acid crystals within the joint tissues. The crystals are usually formed due to the excess of uric acid in the bloodstream precipitated in the joints, forming solid masses having sharp edges.

Gout usually affects the big toes and other small joints.

What Are the Symptoms of Gout?

The common signs and symptoms of gout are as follows:

- Severe pain and tenderness of the joints
- Redness and swelling of the joint
- Warmth of the skin overlying the joint
- Formation of nodules called tophi under the skin

Joint pains in patients with gout are usually severe, indicating the extent of inflammation. The joints may become sensitive to touch. The sensitivity is sometimes so high that patients complain of pain even when any object brushes against the affected area or pulls a bedcover over the joint.

Tophi formation is a characteristic sign of gout. Tophi refer to the hard nodules formed of uric acid crystals deposited under the skin. It is usually found in the big toe joints, upper ear cartilage, and elbows.

The formation of tophi indicates a substantially increased uric acid level in the blood and higher severity of the symptoms of this condition. Regular use of natural joint pain remedies could relieve the joint pains caused by gout and also prevent tophi formation.

What Are the Risk Factors for Gout?

- The risk of gout is higher in patients having a family history of this condition.
- Obesity and chronic renal dysfunctions are known to contribute to symptoms of gout.
- Side effects of certain medications such as diuretics are known to trigger the pathogenesis of gout.
- Other risk factors include severe dehydration, injury, and trauma.

How Is Gout Diagnosed?

The diagnosis of gout is usually made based on the specific involvement of the big toe, the tophi formation, and other characteristic symptoms the patient has developed.

The patient's medications, dietary habits, family history, and the abruptness of the onset of the attacks of joint pains may also provide clues to the diagnosis.

Physical examination of the affected joint and the results of a few blood tests could confirm the diagnosis. Usually, pathological tests to check the uric acid levels in the blood are recommended to assess the risk of gout.

In some cases, a small amount of fluid is removed from the joint tissues and examined in a laboratory to detect the presence of uric acid crystals. Imaging tests, magnetic resonance imaging (MRI), computed tomography scan (CT), and ultrasound of the affected joints may be recommended to confirm or rule out the diagnosis of this condition.

Effective Herbal Ingredients for the Treatment and Prevention of Gout

Gout is one of the most common and most painful diseases affecting the joints, especially the big toe. Pain caused due to gout usually comes suddenly and is severe, often preventing the person from performing any activity.

Patients suffering from gout or any similar arthritic condition that causes pain in the joints can derive significant relief from their symptoms by using natural herbal remedies given below. These herbs possess natural medical potential, which would help relieve the gout pain and ease the routine life of patients.

Bets Natural Herbs for Managing Gout

Sambucus chinensis

Sambucus Chinensis is revered for its ability to regulate the body's metabolic processes. Gout occurs due to metabolic disturbances that prevent the efficient uric acid elimination from the body by the kidneys during urination.

Sambucus Chinensis could promote kidney functions and improve metabolic processes, thereby eliminating the common causes of gout.

Moreover, it may also protect the joints against the pro-inflammatory substances released by the immune cells, such as cytokines and interleukins, reducing pain and redness in the joints occurring during the acute attacks of gout.

Dipsacus asper

What makes Dipsacus asper one of the best natural remedies for gout is the powerful antioxidant and anti-inflammatory compounds it possesses. It offers a rich source of phenolic and polyphenolic compounds that could protect the joints against damage by free radicals. It would also help ease pain and swelling by reducing inflammation in the affected joint tissues.

Dipsacus asper possesses anti-arthritic properties that could prevent and slow down the progress of gout. Regular use of the supplements containing Dipsacus asper could help minimise the frequency of acute gout attacks by keeping the joints protected against the damage caused due to toxins and inflammatory substances.

Angelica dahurica

Angelica dahurica would act as a natural pain-relieving agent. It may relieve joint pain and swelling, reducing the recovery time involved in acute gout attacks.

This herb may also produce an antioxidant action and prevent damage to the delicate joints in the toes, ankles, and knees, thereby slowing down the progress of this condition. It would help inhibit gout complications such as long-term disabilities and even the need for amputation.

Corydalis turtschaninovii

The medicinal compounds in corydalis turtschaninovii would provide faster relief from intense joint pains caused by gout. A plant alkaloid derived from this corydalis plant called DL-tetrahydropalmatine (DL-THP) possesses the potential to block the pain sensation by acting on specific receptor sites in the brain.

Another active compound in corydalis is known as dehydrocorybulbine (DHCB). It could also help control inflammation, pain, redness, and swelling in the joints, providing faster relief during acute gout attacks.

Vincetoxicum pycnostelma

Vincetoxicum pycnostelma could play a vital role in offering quick relief from gout symptoms. This herb also possesses the ability to prevent severe gout attacks.

The high antioxidant capacity of this herb could help minimise the inflammatory and oxidative responses produced by the enzyme called xanthine oxidase. Xanthine oxidase is responsible for causing a sharp rise in the body's uric acid levels. It can also contribute to the formation and deposition of urate crystals in the joints by promoting the conversion of hypoxanthine to xanthine and then to uric acid.

Vincetoxicum Pycnostelma has been found to act as a natural xanthine oxidase inhibitor. It would break the chain of metabolic events created by xanthine oxidase, reducing the uric acid level in your body. This effect could prevent the formation of urate crystals in the joints and lower the risk of gout.

Hence, Vincetoxicum Pycnostelma is highly recommended even for people at a higher risk of developing gout due to factors like family history and obesity.

Sargentodoxa cuneata

Sargentodoxa cuneata could produce a natural anti-inflammatory effect in the body's cells and tissues, including joints that are vulnerable to gout. It may reduce inflammatory damage to the joints caused due to the deposition of urate crystals and thus, minimise the risk of developing severe acute attacks of this condition.

This herb also possesses the ability to support the natural physiological processes occurring in the body. It would help lower the uric acid levels in the blood by enhancing metabolic functions and thus, prevent the risk of gout.

Morus alba

Morus alba would help you avoid severe gout attacks by regulating the metabolic functions involved in breaking certain substances and releasing uric acid.

This herb can reduce uric acid levels in the blood and promote its elimination from the kidneys. These effects could prevent the deposition of urate crystals in the joints effectively and inhibit the development of gout.

Morus alba may also improve your glycemic control by modifying the breakdown and assimilation of carbohydrates in the body. It would encourage the body's cells and tissues to utilise sugars. These effects might help lower your blood sugar levels, improve your glycemic control, and reduce the risk of complications linked to uncontrolled diabetes, including gout.

Glycyrrhiza glabra

Glycyrrhiza glabra is one of the most effective natural remedies for gout, thanks to its ability to inhibit the action of xanthine oxidase. It would block xanthine oxidase activities, thereby reducing uric acid levels in the blood. It may also reduce the risk of gout in the vulnerable group of patients.

Glycyrrhiza glabra is specifically suitable for gout patients who suffer from diabetes and obesity. It should be noted that these are the two common precursors to gout.

The chances of developing more intense gout attacks are higher in overweight patients or have uncontrolled diabetes. Glycyrrhiza Glabra might act as a natural anti-diabetic agent and help reduce blood sugar levels. It could also promote fat-burning processes and speed up weight loss.

These properties of glycyrrhiza glabra could be beneficial for avoiding both obesity and diabetes, which could otherwise contribute to the faster progression of gout.

Sarcandra glabra

Sarcandra glabra contains phenols and polyphenols that could produce an antioxidants effect in the body. These compounds would protect the joints against damage by free radicals and pro-inflammatory substances such as cytokines released by the immune system.

These properties of Sarcandra Glabra could effectively control joint damage and reduce the risk of developing repeated or severe gout attacks.

Sarcandra Glabra may also help improve the immune system functions and support the body's defence mechanisms against disease development. It might strengthen the functions of the immune cells and white blood cells involved in healing the damaged tissue of the joints.

This action would help the patients recover from an acute gout attack in a shorter duration. It would also help restore the optimum functioning or mobility of the affected joints and help a person move about with better ease and minimal discomfort.

Panax notoginseng

Panax notoginseng would play a unique role in improving the physical and emotional health of patients prone to developing repeated gout attacks. It contains plant saponins that have the potential to restore the healthy balance of hormones in the brain. This effect of Panax Notoginseng would be beneficial for reducing stress and anxiety that are common in patients with gout.

The repeated gout attacks and unpredictable nature of their occurrences often lead to anxiety patients experience even during periods of remission. Regular use of a supplement containing Panax notoginseng would ease anxiety and improve their emotional health.

Additionally, Panax notoginseng would also act as an anti-inflammatory and analgesic agent and relieve pain, swelling, and redness in the affected joints. It may help patients recover faster after the acute attacks while enabling them to resume their routine activities with better ease.

Saposhnikovia divaricata

Saposhnikovia divaricata has been widely studied for its natural anti-hyperuricemic potential. This herb can reduce the uric acid levels in the blood by modifying the processes involved in the breakdown of foods containing purines and blocking the mechanisms that lead to uric acid release.

It may also play a role in controlling blood sugar levels, making it a suitable remedy for diabetic patients at risk of gout and its complications. This herb would also regulate blood pressure and reduce mental stress.

These properties of Saposhnikovia divaricata can be beneficial for improving patients' general health and enable them to live a healthy life without the risk of serious complications linked to gout, including depression and anxiety disorders.

Phragmites australis

Phragmites australis may act as an antioxidant and minimise damages to the big toe and other joints vulnerable to gout. This effect of Phragmites australis is further complemented by its ability to strengthen the body's natural detoxification mechanisms.

It would act as a natural cleansing agent by improving kidney functions. This effect might promote an efficient removal of excess uric acid from the body, thereby preventing the deposition of urate crystals in the joints.

Regular use of supplements containing Phragmites australis has been found to lower the risk of gout. It may also reduce the frequency and intensity of gout attacks by reducing pain, redness, and swelling.

Tinospora sinensis

Tinospora sinensis is one of the commonly used herbal remedies for gout. It would act through various mechanisms, thus reducing the risk of gout and preventing the progression of this condition in those who are already affected.

It is believed to work by targeting xanthine oxidase enzymes, thereby reducing uric acid levels in the blood. Moreover, this herb may also regulate digestion and minimise the absorption of unwanted substances such as purines from foods. Tinospora Sinensis' unique action could play a key role in reducing the risk of gout in patients whose diet comprises a higher level of purine responsible for triggering severe attacks of this condition.

It may also help avoid the impact of factors such as obesity on the risk of developing gout. Tinospora sinensis would regulate the balance of some hormones, especially ghrelin and leptin, in the brain. These two hormones play a crucial role in controlling hunger and the sense of satiety after meals.

A favourable balance of these two hormones produced by Tinospora sinensis could help patients reduce their food intake and support their weight loss efforts. This effect is how Tinospora Sinensis could be helpful for gout patients who are likely to develop more severe attacks due to obesity. It would help them reduce weight and maintain a healthy weight, thus inhibiting the recurrence of painful episodes.

Nepeta tenuifolia

Nepeta tenuifolia could be a valuable addition to the list of natural gout remedies. It possesses a varied medicinal potential evident in its anti-inflammatory, analgesic, and antioxidant properties.

This herb's analgesic properties could provide rapid relief from joint pains occurring during acute gout attacks. It would also help restore the joint's mobility in a much shorter duration once the pain has subsided.

The antioxidant and anti-inflammatory effects produced by Nepeta tenuifolia could play a role in preventing damage to the affected joints due to pro-inflammatory toxins and free radicals. It would maintain joint mobility and inhibit the worsening of the condition.

Hence, regular use of Nepeta tenuifolia is highly recommended for preventing gout complications.

How to Prevent Gout?

Gout is a common disorder caused by the deposition of uric acid crystals in the joints, particularly of the big toe. This condition is known to cause abrupt, severe, acute attacks of pain, swelling, and redness in the affected joints.

With appropriate changes in the diet and lifestyle, it is possible to control the pain caused due to gout. Here is a brief discussion about the best ways to prevent gout and minimise the severity and frequency of its attacks.

Foods to Eat

Patients can avoid severe gout attacks by increasing their intake of low-fat dairy products, vitamin C-rich foods, and soy products. These foods could reduce uric acid levels, thereby preventing gout.

The intake of vitamin C-rich food may also help enhance the immune system functions. It has been found that the risk of gout is higher in patients suffering from autoimmune disorders like rheumatoid arthritis. Vitamin C would act as an antioxidant and regulate the functions of the immune system and thus, control the risk of developing an autoimmune disorder.

Patients with gout should also include fresh fruits in their regular diet. Fruits such as cherries might help prevent gout attacks by controlling uric acid levels in the blood and reducing inflammation.

Vegetables such as potatoes, eggplants, peas, mushrooms, and dark leafy vegetables are also suitable for patients with gout.

Foods to Avoid

Certain foods are known to trigger gout attacks by increasing uric acid levels in the blood. These triggering factors include foods that are rich in purines.

When your body metabolises purines, it releases uric acid as one of its waste products. Hence, foods containing purines must be avoided to lower uric acid levels.

Foods containing moderate to high purine count include red meats, seafood, organ meats, and alcohol, especially beer.

Besides these, patients should also avoid consuming foods and beverages containing increased amounts of carbohydrates, especially fructose. It has been found that carbonated and sugar-sweetened beverages often increase the risk and severity of gout attacks. These foods do not contain a very high amount of purines. However, they may still increase uric acid levels by interfering with specific cellular processes.

Additionally, refined carbs like cookies, white bread, and cakes should be avoided as they have a low nutritional content and might raise uric acid levels.

Lifestyle Strategies to Prevent Gout

Patients at a higher risk of developing gout should eat a healthy and balanced diet and exercise regularly to prevent this condition. They should also limit the consumption of alcohol, especially beer, as it can worsen gout symptoms by raising uric acid levels.

Smoking cessation is also linked with the reduced severity and frequency of gout attacks.

Overweight patients should try healthy weight loss methods like regular exercises and avoid junk food to lose weight effectively. Preventing obesity and maintaining a healthy weight would minimise inflammation in the joints, relieving gout symptoms.

Patients with gout should follow these strategies to prevent the attacks of this condition safely and effectively.

Conclusion

Though gout is incurable, it is possible to avoid its recurring attacks by using supplements containing natural herbs. These natural remedies could help reduce the intensity and frequency of gout attacks and even inhibit the progression of joint damage, thus allowing patients to live a healthy and active life for many years.

What Are Diuretic Agents?

Diuretic agents, referred to as water pills, are medications recommended for increasing the amount of salt and water eliminated from the body system as urine. There are three primary forms of diuretics often prescribed to patients who suffer from high blood pressure or any disorders affecting the kidneys. However, these medications are also used to treat some other conditions.

> **Diuretic**

- **A diuretic is any substance that promotes diuresis, the increased production of urine.**

- **All diuretics increase the excretion of water from bodies.**

What Are Diuretics Used For?

The most common disorder managed with diuretic agents is high blood pressure. These drugs help decrease the amount of water or fluid in the blood vessels to help lower blood pressure.

Other conditions treated with diuretic agents include congestive heart failure that keeps the heart from pumping blood effectively throughout the body. This effect often leads to excess fluid build-up in the body, leading to oedema. Diuretics would help reduce the fluid build-up and, thus, lower the risk of congestive cardiac failure.

What Are the Different Types of Diuretics?

There are three major types of diuretic medications including thiazide diuretics, loop diuretics, and potassium-sparing diuretics. These drugs help the body excrete more fluid in the form of urine.

Thiazide Diuretics

These are the most commonly used types of diuretics. They are often recommended for treating high blood pressure. These drugs reduce the fluid overload in the body and cause the blood vessels to relax, thereby lowering the blood pressure.

Sometimes, thiazides are used with other drugs to keep blood pressure in control. The common examples of thiazides include:

- Hydrochlorothiazide
- Chlorthalidone
- Indapamide
- Metolazone

Loop Diuretics

These types of diuretics are commonly used for the treatment of heart failure. Some examples of these medications include:

- Torsemide
- Bumetanide
- Furosemide

Potassium-Sparing Diuretics

These types of diuretics reduce the body's fluid level without causing it to lose potassium, which is an essential nutrient.

The other forms of diuretics cause the body to lose potassium leading to serious health issues such as arrhythmia. Potassium-sparing diuretics are usually prescribed to people at a higher risk of a low potassium level, including those who use other medications that could deplete potassium.

Potassium-sparing diuretics do not reduce blood pressure as effectively as the other forms of diuretics do. Hence, the patient may be prescribed potassium-sparing diuretics alongside other medications that can control blood pressure.

Some examples of potassium-sparing diuretics include:

- Eplerenone
- Amiloride
- Spironolactone
- Triamterene

What Are the Side Effects of Diuretics?

When used as prescribed, most diuretics are tolerated well. However, some may still cause a few side effects.

Common side effects of diuretics include:

- Increased potassium in the blood (when potassium-sparing diuretics are used)
- Too little potassium in your blood
- Headache
- Reduced sodium levels
- Increased thirst
- Dizziness
- Muscle cramps
- Increased blood sugar
- Skin rashes
- Increased cholesterol
- Diarrhoea
- Gout

Natural Herbs That Can Produce a Diuretic Action

Some natural herbs and spices are considered natural diuretics, thanks to their ability to promote the excretion of excess fluids from the body.

Here are some natural plants and herbs that can be used as diuretics to manage high blood pressure, congestive cardiac failure, and kidney ailments.

Hibiscus

This herb has shown to possess a significant diuretic potential that could benefit patients who suffer from symptoms like oedema and swelling due to water retention. Hibiscus may also help increase kidney filtration.

Hawthorn

This herb might produce a powerful diuretic action. It could reduce fluid build-up and improve congestive heart failure symptoms. Some studies have shown that this plant's nutrients may increase urinary flow and excretion to some extent and reduce oedema. Hawthorn berries also act as natural diuretics and could help treat renal problems.

Dandelion

Most people consider the dandelion as just a weed. However, research studies have found that one of the compounds in this plant can enhance the functions of the kidneys and increase the frequency of urination. Dandelion can be consumed in the form of a tea to derive its diuretic effect.

Horsetail

Horsetail extract has been found to produce a similar diuretic effect as some prescription medications but with fewer side effects. Horsetail could be an excellent alternative to prescription diuretics, especially for patients with a history of developing severe side effects. Horsetail is available as tea.

Black Tea or Green Tea

A hot cup of black tea or green tea might stimulate the flushing of excess fluids from the body system. Both black and green teas have shown immense potential as natural diuretics.

Juniper

This plant has been commonly used as a diuretic since medieval times. A few modern-day research studies have also proven juniper's health benefits. It has been shown to produce a significant diuretic effect, thereby increasing the urine volume.

Like most other natural diuretics, juniper does not seem to lower the potassium levels in the blood, making it a safer option for patients with a risk of electrolyte imbalances. Patients may add juniper as a flavouring agent to their dishes.

Parsley

Parsley is commonly used for garnishing dishes. This herb may also be helpful for patients who are having difficulty tolerating modern diuretic drugs. It has even been found to increase the urine volume and reduce oedema, thanks to its natural diuretic properties, and thus, lower blood pressure.

Best Diuretic Foods

Besides the natural diuretics we discussed above, cutting back on your sodium intake and regularly exercising are also effective strategies for reducing the fluid build-up in the body. Eating fresh fruits and vegetables could also produce a diuretic effect providing a safer and more effective solution for patients with conditions that cause urinary retention.

These foods include:

- Berries
- Watermelon
- Grapes
- Onions
- Asparagus
- Bell peppers
- Garlic

Conclusion

The use of natural herbs alone or together with modern diuretics could provide significant relief from the symptoms of water retention, such as high blood pressure. You can experience a reduced risk of renal failure and congestive cardiac failure. However, it is crucial to assess the kidney functions regularly and seek the advice of your physician before adopting natural or modern treatments for managing these conditions.

Postoperative Care

Postoperative care includes the care received by a patient following a surgical procedure. The type of postoperative care a patient needs would depend on the type of surgery they had and their health history. It usually includes wound care and pain management.

Postoperative care starts immediately after the surgical procedure. It lasts for the duration of the hospital stay and continues after the patient has been discharged. As a part of the postoperative care, your surgeon or healthcare provider would inform you about the potential adverse effects and complications related to the procedure.

Before a patient has surgery, they should ask the doctor about the postoperative care involved. This inquiry would give the patient some time to prepare beforehand. The doctor may also revise some instructions after the surgery, based on how the surgery went and how well the patient is recovering.

Preparing for Surgery Ahead of Time

Patients should ask the doctor as many questions as possible before the surgery. They should also ask for updated instructions before being discharged from the hospital. Most hospitals provide written discharge instructions to ensure patients follow them correctly.

You may ask your doctor questions like:

- Will I need any specific medications or supplies when I am discharged from the hospital?
- How long will I have to stay in the hospital?
- What do I need to do and avoid to support faster recovery?
- What are the complications I should watch out for?
- What are the adverse effects I may develop?
- Will I need a physical therapist or a caregiver when I go home?
- When will I be able to resume normal activities?

The answers to these queries would help you prepare ahead of time. If you expect to seek help from a caregiver, you may arrange for it before the surgery. It is also essential that you learn to recognise, prevent, and respond to possible complications.

Based on the type of surgery you have, there can be several potential complications that might arise. For instance, many surgeries are known to put patients at risk of infections, excessive bleeding at the site of surgery, and the formation of blood clots due to prolonged inactivity following the procedure. Prolonged inactivity may also cause patients to lose some muscle strength and develop mild to moderate respiratory complications.

The patients should ask the doctor for more information about the risk of potential complications for their specific procedure.

Postoperative Care in Hospital Settings

After the surgery, the patient is moved to the recovery room. They would probably need to stay in the recovery room for a couple of hours or until they wake up from anaesthesia. They may feel groggy or slightly disorientated when they wake up. Some patients also feel nauseated and vomit after regaining their consciousness after the effect of anaesthesia has waned off.

While in the recovery room, the medical staff monitors your blood pressure, breathing rate, pulse, and temperature. The doctor or nurse may also ask you to take deep breaths for assessing your lung functions. They would check the surgical site for signs of infection and bleeding. They would also watch for symptoms of an allergic reaction.

For some types of surgeries, general anaesthesia is needed. It may involve the risk of an allergic reaction to the anaesthetic agent.

Once the patient is stable, they would be moved to a hospital room if they stay overnight or transferred to any other healthcare facility area to begin the discharge process.

Outpatient Surgeries

Outpatient surgeries are also known as same-day surgeries. Unless you show any signs of postoperative complications, you will be discharged from the hospital on the same day of the procedure. You do not need to stay overnight for these surgeries.

Before you are discharged from the hospital, you must demonstrate signs of recovery. The doctors would ensure you can breathe, urinate and drink normally. You will not be allowed to drive immediately after the surgery, especially if you were given general anaesthesia. Hence, it is essential to ensure you have arranged the transportation back home ahead of time. You might feel a bit dizzy or weak the following day of the procedure.

In-patient surgeries

If you plan to undergo an in-patient surgery, you might need to stay in the hospital for a day or overnight to continue receiving postoperative care. You might need to wait for a few days or even longer.

Sometimes, patients initially scheduled for outpatient surgery tend to show the signs of complications. In these cases, they need to be admitted for ongoing care.

The postoperative care would continue after you have been transferred out of the recovery room. You may still have the intravenous (IV) catheter in the arm, a finger device used to measure the oxygen level in the blood, and a dressing to cover the wound at the surgical site.

Depending on the form of surgery you had, a heartbeat monitor, a breathing apparatus, and a tube in the nose, mouth, or bladder may be needed to monitor your health.

The hospital staff would continue to monitor your vital parameters. They may also administer pain relievers and other medications through the IV line, injections, or oral medications. Depending on your overall condition, they might ask you to sit up or walk around. You might need assistance in doing this. Moving around would help decrease your risk of developing abnormal blood clots. It may also help maintain muscle strength.

You might be asked to perform simple deep breathing exercises and forced coughing to prevent the risk of any respiratory complications.

Your surgeon and physician would decide when you'll be discharged from the hospital based on your recovery after the procedure. Make sure you ask for the discharge instructions to ensure you can follow the treatment and care at home and make relevant arrangements before the discharge.

Postoperative Care at Home

It is essential to follow the doctor's instructions after being discharged from the hospital. Patients should use the medications as prescribed and watch out for potential complications. They should also keep the follow-up appointments so that their progress can be regularly monitored until they have recovered completely or even thereafter, in some cases.

Patients should avoid physical overexertion during the recovery phase. They should also take adequate rest as instructed. However, they should also prevent neglecting physical activities entirely once advised.

They may start performing their daily activities as soon as they safely can. It is advisable to return to the regular routine gradually.

Conclusion

Appropriate follow-up care after surgery could help reduce the risk of complications and support the recovery process. Patients should ask their surgeon and physician about the instructions they need to follow before undergoing surgery and check for updates before leaving the hospital. They should also contact the doctor if they suspect they are experiencing any adverse effects or complications or if the recovery is not progressing as expected.

Management of HIV Infections

The human immunodeficiency virus (HIV) is one of the most dangerous viruses that can attack the immune system and cause widespread, long-lasting symptoms. If not treated, it can lead to a full-blown condition called AIDS or acquired immunodeficiency syndrome. Here is a brief discussion about what HIV infection means and the proper ways to prevent it.

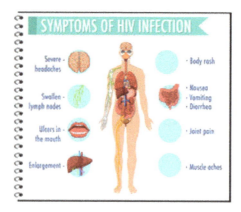

What Are the Symptoms of HIV Infection?

Some patients with HIV may have mild to moderate flu-like symptoms that occur within two to five weeks after the infection. This symptom is called acute HIV infection. It often lasts for a few days to weeks.

Some of the common initial symptoms of this infection include:

- Fever
- Chills
- Night sweats
- Sore throat
- Muscle aches
- Fatigue
- Rashes

- Mouth ulcers
- Swollen lymph nodes

However, some patients may not develop any symptoms during acute HIV infection. Hence, getting tested is the only way to confirm this condition's diagnosis.

Transmission of the HIV Infection

HIV is often transmitted through the exchange of body fluids from the infected person, like blood, semen, breast milk, and vaginal secretions. HIV may also be transferred from the mother to the child during pregnancy and labour. Ordinary day-to-day contact with an infected person, such as kissing, shaking hands, hugging, and sharing food, water, and personal objects, is not known to cause the spread of this infection.

It is essential to mention that patients with HIV undergoing treatments such as antiretroviral therapy (ART) and who are virally suppressed would not transmit HIV infection to their sexual partners.

What Are the Risk Factors for the HIV Infection?

- Having unprotected vaginal or anal sex
- Receiving unsafe blood transfusions, injections, tissue transplantation, or medical procedures, which involve unsterile piercing or cutting
- Having other sexually transmitted infections (STI) like syphilis, chlamydia, herpes, gonorrhoea, or bacterial vaginitis
- Sharing used or contaminated syringes, needles, and other injecting material or drug solutions while injecting medications
- Having accidental needle stick injuries, such as among healthcare workers

Prevention of the HIV Infection

It is possible to avoid the risk of HIV infection by limiting your exposure to the risk factors.

The critical approaches for the prevention of HIV best used in combination include the following:

- The use of male and female condoms during sex
- Counselling and testing for HIV and other STIs
- The use of antiretroviral drugs (ARVs) for the prevention
- Voluntary medical male circumcision (VMMC)

- Counselling and testing for the linkages to tuberculosis care
- Elimination of the mother-to-child transmission of HIV

Treatment of the HIV Infection

HIV infection could be managed with the help of treatment regimens composed of the combination of three or more antiretroviral (ARV) drugs. The current antiretroviral therapy (ART) does not help cure this infection. Still, it may suppress the viral replication highly, allowing the patient's immune system to recover, strengthen, and regain its capacity to fight opportunistic infections and some form of cancers.

Ayurvedic Treatment for the HIV infection

AIDs and HIV may be considered as Ojakshaya in Ayurveda. It means the loss of immunity or Vital Energy.

The Ojas is the essence of our body. It is explained as the Bala (immunity or strength) and "Dhatusara". Ojas is of two types: the "apara ojas" and the "para ojas". The ojas of the para (excellent) form has eight drops in quantity. It is located in the heart and causes poor heath when depleted. The other form, apara ojas, is also called the "sleshmaka ojas". The quantity of this form of ojas is described as the Ardha Anjali. It is distributed throughout our bodies. When this form of ojas is efficient, the body's organs are able to work normally.

In conditions such as HIV and AIDS, the loss of ojas is often the most prominent feature. It can make people susceptible to several other infections and diseases. Hence, the treatment of HIV and AIDS in Ayurveda aims to restore ojas.

The treatment primarily focuses on aspects such as:

- Inhibition of further viral replication for controlling the viral load and inducing the CD4 count improvement
- Restoration of the disrupted immune system for improving the overall well-being and enhancing the quality of life
- Treatment and prevention of the associated occasional or opportunistic infections as well as the other associated symptoms

Conclusion

HIV treatment should be aimed at strengthening the patient's immunity to protect the person against severe infections and other conditions such as cancer. Following a healthy diet and lifestyle based on the principles of Ayurveda could provide relief from HIV symptoms to some extent.

Management and Treatment of Influenza

Influenza is one of the most common viral infections that attack the respiratory system, including the nose, throat, and lungs. It is commonly known as the flu, though it is not the same as the stomach "flu" viruses, which cause vomiting and diarrhoea.

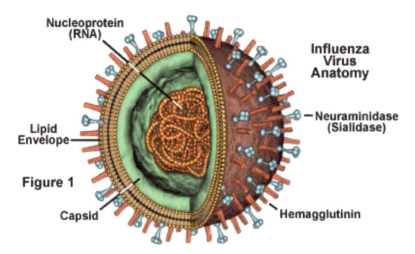

Figure 1

Here is a brief discussion about influenza's causes, risk factors, and symptoms, and the best ways to manage this infection.

What Are the Symptoms of Influenza?

Initially, the flu symptoms may appear like those of a common cold. Patients with influenza may develop symptoms like a runny nose, sore throat, and sneezing. But the signs of the common cold tend to develop slowly, while flu usually comes on suddenly.

The common signs and symptoms of influenza include:

- Fever
- Chills and sweats
- Headache
- Aching muscles
- Shortness of breath
- Dry and persistent cough

- Tiredness or weakness
- Running and stuffy nose
- Sore throat
- Eye pain
- Vomiting or diarrhoea

What Are the Risk Factors for Influenza?

For most patients, the symptoms of flu resolve spontaneously. However, sometimes, influenza may cause a few complications that could be life-threatening. Patients at a higher risk of developing flu complications include:

- Adults above 65 years of age
- Young patients under the age of five years, especially those below six months of age
- Residents of long-term care facilities such as the nursing homes
- People having a weakened immune system
- Pregnant women and women who are up to 2 to 4 weeks after giving birth to a baby
- Individuals who are obese, with a body mass index (BMI) of 40 or more
- Patients who suffer from chronic illnesses, like asthma, kidney diseases, heart disease, liver diseases, or diabetes
- Native Americans

What Are the Common Causes of Influenza?

Influenza viruses tend to travel through the air via tiny droplets. So, when a person with this infection sneezes, coughs, or talks, the other person close to them may inhale the droplets, thus acquiring the infection.

It is also possible to pick up the flu viruses from contaminated objects such as the telephone and computer keyboard. They may get transferred to the eyes, nose, and mouth, causing an infection.

Influenza viruses are constantly changing, with new strains appearing regularly. If you have contracted an influenza infection in the past, your body would have already formed antibodies for fighting that specific strain of the virus. So, if the future influenza virus you are exposed to is similar to the one you had encountered earlier, those antibodies would prevent the infection or lessen the severity. However, it should be noted that antibody levels often decline over time.

Prevention of Influenza

Taking the annual flu vaccination is recommended for all people above six months of age. The flu vaccine could reduce your risk of flu as well as its severity. It may also lower your risk of having severe complications due to the flu or the need to stay in a hospital.

Flu vaccination is vital during this season as the flu and coronavirus disease 2019 (COVID-19) have been found to cause similar symptoms. Flu vaccination would reduce the symptoms confused with those linked to COVID-19. The prevention of the flu infection and reducing its severity or the need for an advanced form of treatment is expected to lessen the total number of patients who require a hospital stay.

How to Manage Influenza at Home Using Ayurvedic Remedies?

According to Ayurveda, an imbalance in any of the three doshas – the vata, pitta, and the kapha – would cause an ailment such as influenza. In this case, the excess of pitta and the kapha dosha in the body is responsible for causing cough and nasal congestion.

Here are some Ayurvedic remedies that would help you manage the symptoms of influenza:

Tulsi

Tulsi is known as the Mother Medicine of Nature or the Queen of Herbs. Tulsi leaves would help improve the body's ability to fight the common cold and cough and relieve symptoms of influenza.

Honey

Loaded with strong antimicrobial properties, honey would not just clear the infection in a much shorter duration but also provide relief from sore throat. It also acts as a natural and effective cough suppressant.

Mulethi

Mulethi, also called the Sweet Wood, offers an effective natural treatment for relieving cough and other flu symptoms. Mulethi powder can alleviate sore throat and cough by reducing the excessive production of mucus secretions in the airways.

Cinnamon

This aromatic woody spice is loaded with numerous health benefits, providing relief from cough and cold. It would relieve a running nose, nose block, and sore throat.

Conclusion

The use of natural herbal remedies can provide significant relief from flu symptoms. It is also advisable to take flu vaccines to minimise the risk of developing severe symptoms of this condition.

Female Hormonal Status

Hormones are natural substances produced by the different glands in our bodies. Hormones help send messages between the cells and organs and affect several bodily functions.

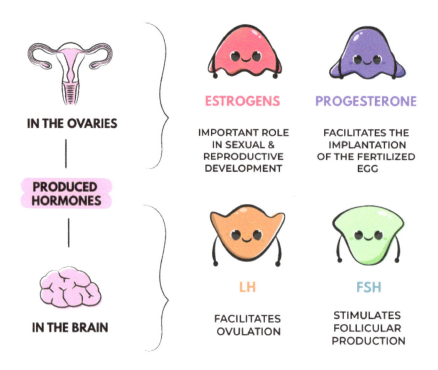

Here is a brief discussion on the female sex hormones and how they fluctuate throughout the life of women. We will also learn the common signs of hormonal imbalances in women.

The Types of Female Hormones

There are two main female hormones called oestrogen and progesterone. However, testosterone, considered a male sex hormone, is also produced in small amounts in women's bodies.

Oestrogen

Oestrogen is one of the most important female hormones. A large share of this hormone is secreted in the ovaries. The adrenal glands and fat cells also secrete small amounts of this hormone. During pregnancy, the placenta makes oestrogen to support the continuation of the pregnancy.

Oestrogen plays a vital role in several reproductive and sexual functions during puberty, pregnancy, menstruation, and menopause.

Oestrogen also affects the brain's functions, hair, musculoskeletal system, cardiovascular system, skin, and urinary tract.

Progesterone

The ovaries secrete the female sex hormone called progesterone after the ovulation phase. During pregnancy too, the placenta produces some amount of this hormone.

Progesterone's role includes preparing the uterus's inner lining for the implantation of the fertilised egg, supporting pregnancy, and suppressing oestrogen production after ovulation.

Testosterone

A small amount of testosterone is secreted in women's adrenal glands and ovaries. This hormone plays a vital role in a few body functions, including regulating menstrual cycles and supporting muscle and bone strength.

The roles these hormones play in normal body functions change over time during different phases of a woman's life.

These female sex hormones form an integral part of many body functions. However, the hormonal cycle changes as a girl leaves the childhood phase and enters puberty. The hormonal changes may also occur dramatically when a woman becomes pregnant, gives birth, or breastfeeds a child. They continue to change even during and after menopause. These changes in hormone levels are natural and expected.

What Happens When the Hormonal Levels Become Unbalanced?

- Polycystic ovarian syndrome (PCOS): PCOS is the most common endocrinal disorder affecting young women. PCOS is known to cause anovulation and irregular menstrual cycles, thus interfering with a woman's fertility.

- Androgen excess: Androgen excess refers to the overproduction of the male sex hormones. This effect could cause menstrual irregularities, acne, infertility, and even male pattern baldness.

- Hirsutism: Hirsutism refers to the abnormal increase in hair growth on the face, abdomen, chest, and back. It is usually caused due to the excessive secretion of male sex hormones and may sometimes be the most evident symptom of PCOS.

Some other underlying conditions that can lead to hormonal imbalances in women include:

- Hypogonadism that occurs due to the shortage of the female sex hormones

- Abnormal pregnancy
- A miscarriage
- Multiple pregnancies such as having twins, triplets, and more
- Ovarian tumour

Conclusion

The imbalances in the levels of female sex hormones can put women at risk of several health issues, including infertility. Hence, there is a need to check your hormonal levels at regular intervals. This especially applies if you are planning a pregnancy or suffering from menstrual irregularities or abnormal hair growth and seek appropriate treatment to restore the balance of hormones.

Fertility Boost for Men and Women With Infertility

Women facing fertility challenges usually feel like no one else suffers from this issue. Everywhere they turn, they see other families enjoying themselves with their children and are left wondering why they have been singled out for having this seemingly "rare" problem. The stigma associated with fertility issues in some communities and the feeling of inadequacy often leads to a sense of exclusion and isolation for couples, especially women. However, due to the advent of new treatment methods and changing attitudes, discussing and overcoming the challenge of infertility has become more accessible today.

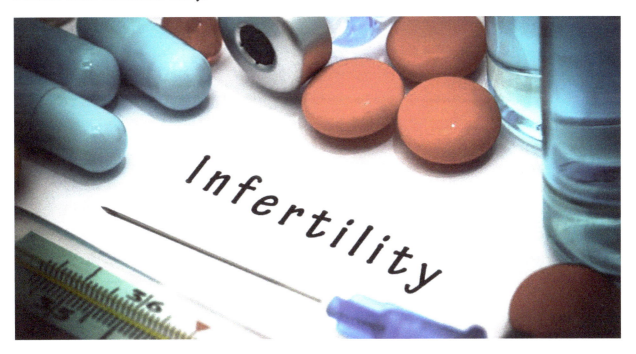

First of all, though it may seem that infertility is a rare problem, statistics show that almost 15%-20% of all couples face some form of fertility issue. Now, these statistics are only meant to keep you from feeling that you are the only one. Several others around you face the same problem and its consequences, including the emotional repercussions.

If you look around, you would also find plenty of couples who faced this problem earlier but managed to conquer it. Today, they are living happily with their own child. You can be one of them!

You can manage this problem with a step-by-step approach, and the first step is understanding what infertility means and its causes.

What Is Infertility?

The generally accepted definition of infertility is the inability of a woman to conceive or get pregnant after attempting for 12 months or more. This standard definition is derived from a statistical analysis.

A woman attempting to conceive usually has a 20% chance of getting pregnant in any given month, provided the conditions are favourable. Accordingly, you would not be considered suffering from infertility until you have tried for at least six months. Besides, since optimal conditions may or may not be favourable always and since they may also remain unbeknownst to you, a 12-month period is required to assume there could be a problem with conception.

If you have already tried for 12 months or more, you will have to look into the different causes of infertility and evaluate what could be the reason that is preventing conception in you.

It should be noted here that female factors contribute to infertility in 50% of the cases, and male factors contribute to infertility in about 40%. The remaining 10% are categorised as 'unexplained' as the cause could not be identified or attributed to one of the partners.

Let's look at the male and female factors that could contribute to infertility in couples:

What Are the Causes of Male Infertility?

The common underlying factor responsible for causing infertility in men includes the low sperm count, which can be defined as a sperm count of less than 20 million per ml.

The other prevalent cause is varicocele (relaxed or enlarged veins of the spermatic cord). Varicocele affects the circulation or movement of the sperm resulting in a low sperm count.

Men can also have blocked or damaged sperm ducts due to the anatomical pressure, the effect of varicocele, or scarring caused by an untreated sexually transmitted disease (like gonorrhoea and chlamydia).

Hormonal abnormalities that can impede the development of sperm can also cause infertility. In some men, the testicles are non-responsive to hormones or do not respond appropriately to signals that lead to sperm development and maturation. In some cases, men have antibodies that attack other body cells, including their own sperm, causing damage and rendering them ineffective for fertilising an egg and causing a pregnancy.

Certain environmental and occupational factors may affect the production of sperm in men. Additionally, prolonged exposure to lead, other heavy metals, and pesticides are common causes of male infertility. Some other environmental factors include excessive exposure to heat, ultrasound or microwave radiation, and the presence of other health hazards like diabetes, hypertension, and high cholesterol.

Age can also be a factor responsible. The levels of testosterone fall, and the concentration and volume of sperm may change as men age resulting in infertility.

What Are the Causes of Female Infertility?

Age

A woman's fertility reduces as she ages into the fourth decade of her life (age 35-39 years). A woman's fertility peaks in the third decade of her life and reduce beyond 40 years.

Ovulation Problems

An ovulation problem occurs when a mature egg is prevented from developing in the ovaries. Possible symptoms include the absence of or infrequent periods and abnormally heavy or light bleeding. A few drugs like Clomiphene Citrate could help manage this problem. These drugs work by inducing ovulation.

Endometriosis

Endometriosis occurs when the endometrial tissue (tissue forming the uterine lining) grows outside the uterus, usually in the pelvic or abdominal cavity. While most women with endometriosis have no symptoms, some may develop painful menstrual periods, pain or discomfort during intercourse, heavy bleeding, unusual spotting, and pelvic pain.

Up to 40% of women conceive naturally or with treatment after undergoing surgery to remove the abnormal endometrial tissue.

Polycystic Ovarian Syndrome or PCOS

PCOS is a prevalent cause of infertility. It is a condition in which immature follicles in the ovaries do not develop into larger, mature follicles, which handle the release of eggs. This condition is characterised by imbalances in hormonal levels and unpredictable ovulation patterns. Women with this disorder often have irregular periods, acne, excessive hair growth, and obesity.

Lifestyle modifications with appropriate changes in diet and exercise and the use of fertility drugs could help restore regular ovulation in women with this condition and help them conceive.

Pelvic Inflammatory Disease (PID)

Sexually transmitted diseases, such as chlamydia and gonorrhoea, are often associated with pelvic inflammatory diseases that cause damage to the fallopian tubes, resulting in an inability to conceive. It usually affects women in their reproductive years and contributes to infertility in a large percentage of them.

Tubal Factors

Blockage in the fallopian tubes could prevent sperm from reaching the egg and prevent a fertilised egg from reaching the uterus. The common causes of tubal abnormalities include sexually transmitted infections (like chlamydia), pelvic inflammatory disease, and previous sterilisation surgery.

The possible solution to this factor could be surgery to open the tubes. The success rate depends on the severity and location of the blockage and the amount of scar tissue developed after the surgery.

Some Other Common Causes of Infertility in Men and Women

Smoking can cause infertility in both men and women. Nicotine in cigarettes has been shown to block the production of sperm in men and reduce the size of their testicles. In women, tobacco affects the characteristics of the cervical mucus, thus reducing the possibility of the sperm reaching the egg.

Marijuana is known to disrupt a woman's ovulation cycles. It also affects men by reducing their sperm count and the quality of sperm. Cocaine, heroin, and crack cocaine induce similar effects.

In women, excessive alcohol consumption is more related to the complications occurring during pregnancy than causing infertility. Nevertheless, chronic alcoholism can lead to ovulation disorders and interfere with fertility. Excessive alcohol consumption by men can affect the synthesis of testosterone and reduce sperm concentration. Alcoholism can also delay a man's sexual response resulting in impotence (inability to have an erection).

The Importance of the Time of Intercourse While Trying to Conceive

Time is everything. And when it comes to getting pregnant, it becomes essential that you know when to have sex to increase your chances. The sperm can live in your uterus for only three to six days, and the egg can live for an even lesser time, for only 12 to 24 hours.

So, the sperm and the egg have a brief period, during which they must fertilise to cause pregnancy. Hence, to increase your likelihood of conception, it is crucial that you have sex more often during the period when the eggs are produced and can stay viable in your body.

The best approach is to have sex one or two days before ovulation and also on the day of ovulation. This approach will ensure the sperm have more chances of meeting an egg in the fallopian tube and fertilising it.

The time of ovulation depends on the average duration of your menstrual cycles. If your menses are relatively regular, you should have ovulation about 14 days before your subsequent periods.

So, if you have a 28-day cycle, your ovulation will occur at around mid-cycle or on the 14th day, whereas if you have a 35-day cycle, you will ovulate on the 21st day of your menses, considering the first day of your menses as the first day of the cycle. You can arrive at the exact day after deducting 14 from the average number of days in your cycle.

There is a problem with this method of calculation. If your periods are not regular, it could be difficult for you to predict when you will get the next period. This means you will not be able to know your fertile days with exact precision. The irregular menses may occur due to diseases like polycystic ovarian syndrome, thyroid disorders, ovarian dysfunction, or even seemingly benign issues like mental stress, heavy exercises, and sudden weight loss or gain.

Finding the underlying cause of irregular menses and taking appropriate measures to tackle it would help you overcome such hurdles in the management of infertility.

Besides these, there are a few other signs of ovulation. Let us learn about them to be better equipped with knowing your fertile days.

Changes in the Basal Body Temperature

Charting of basal body temperature is the most commonly used method of tracking ovulation. Basal body temperature is the temperature of the body taken when at rest. It rises by a tiny percentage during ovulation and stays elevated for one or two days after ovulation. Take your temperature every morning to detect this temperature rise. Do this preferably at the same time every morning, such as before you get out of bed. Make a note of the temperature in a diary. The day you find a slight elevation in the temperature, you can almost be certain that you are ovulating.

Changes in the Cervical Mucus

The amount and consistency of your cervical mucus change as ovulation approaches. When you are not ovulating, cervical mucus appears creamy and sticky. It may also be entirely absent. It would become more abundant and take on an egg-white-like consistency as ovulation approaches. The mucus can be stretched up to an inch or more between your fingers. By paying careful attention to these changes, you can predict your fertile days.

Tenderness in the Breasts

You may experience mild tenderness in the breasts just before ovulation. This effect may occur due to the rush of hormones in the body meant to prepare itself for the potential pregnancy.

Saliva Ferning

Checking for the ferning pattern of your saliva is a unique and uncommon way of detecting ovulation. The ferning looks like the frost on the windowpane. It occurs 24-48 hours before ovulation.

Ovulation Predictor Tests

Ovulation predictor kits require you to dip a test paper into a cup of collected urine or pee on the test stick, once daily, for a week before the roughly expected date of ovulation.

The test strip has two lines; the test line and the control line. The test is considered positive when the test line becomes darker than the control line.

Increased Sexual Desire

You may experience an increased sexual desire during your fertile days. This libido boost might come one or two days before ovulation. And when you start experiencing this, it could be a sign of that being the right time to have sex to get pregnant. This method often works for women planning to conceive.

Timing your intercourse on the days you are most fertile can increase your chances of getting pregnant. These signs of ovulation are not difficult to notice once you are clear about what to look for. Though each of these methods is reliable, don't try to use all of them. That might make things more stressful and complicated for you! Try just two or three of them, whichever you find comfortable and convenient to pinpoint your days of ovulation.

Coping with Fertility Problems

Infertility is often a medical problem that can touch every aspect of your life, including how you feel about yourself, your overall perspective on living, and even your relationship with your partner. It could be highly stressful as it can create a great deal of uncertainty, resulting in severe, emotional upheavals in a couple's day-to-day life. If you have been struggling with infertility, you are indeed no stranger to stress and anxiety. But even though your situation may seem overwhelming at times, there are several ways to reduce the stress. Here are ten simple tips from experts to help you focus your attention on your body and mind and bring about a positive and calmer perspective to your life.

Know Why You Must Get Rid of Stress

You need to understand why reducing stress is so important. That's because stress can severely affect the functioning of your hypothalamus – the gland responsible for regulating your emotions and the production of hormones that signal your ovaries to release eggs. So, if you're stressed out, there are chances that you will ovulate later in the cycle or not ovulate at all. So if you're having sex only around day 14 of your cycle, thinking it's the time when you ovulate, you are bound to miss the opportunity to conceive.

Hopefully, you have understood why it's essential to feel relaxed and positive and are eager to know how to reduce the stress that's causing a major roadblock in your goal of getting pregnant.

Identify the Cause of Stress

Just like how infertility can occur due to a particular reason, which has to be tackled to get pregnant, stress too has a cause. And you need to identify that reason and learn to tackle it to get rid of your stress. This method is easier said than done, but it's definitely not impossible. Keep track of when you felt stressed out and relate the stress to events that have occurred during or before that period.

For example, if you felt stressed out before leaving from office, the cause of your stress could be traffic or the chores you need to finish off upon reaching home, and if you felt stressed before leaving for office, it could be the pressure from your boss to improve your performance. Keeping track of these events will help you know what's causing stress and take steps to work around the problem.

Change How You Respond to the Situations

When faced with a stressful situation, you can only control one thing: how you respond to it. Do pay attention to your reaction to the stressful situation. Introspect whether you turn it over in your head for long after the crisis is over, or do you create scary visions of what could happen in the future due to the situation?

Answers to these questions would help you control your reactions and help you reduce the significant impact of what happens inside your body. This step might take some practice and attention.

Don't Blame Yourself

You do not have to get angry at yourself for not being able to conceive. Resist the temptation to listen to the little voice in your head that says, "I shouldn't have waited for so long; I'm being punished for giving more importance to my career" or so on. This negative pattern of thinking could only make matters worse. Instead of criticising yourself, look forward to how you will manage the situation.

When you feel like you "could have" or "should have" done something, remind yourself that your fertility is not your fault. Even if you could have taken any different decision in the past, it is all behind you now. Instead, work as a team with your partner and concentrate on your future.

Acknowledge Your Feelings

To get rid of stress, it's essential to understand that what you are feeling is entirely normal. Going through infertility treatment procedures, for cycles after cycles, could be physically, emotionally, and financially draining. And the feeling that you have no control over the ultimate outcome of your treatments could be highly debilitating for any person.

Infertility may have shattered your dream of having your baby, but it's just that your goals have been put on hold temporarily. It's nature's way of allowing you some time to make you aware of your medical issues and prepare yourself better so that your baby gets optimum benefits.

Develop Hobbies or Habits That Reduce Stress

Some habits or practices can help reduce the harmful effect of stress on your health. Some of such routines are:

- Making sure you get enough sleep
- Prayer
- Getting healthy exercises daily
- Meditating daily
- Practising yoga and breathing exercises
- Taking warm baths
- Reading a book or watching your favourite TV show (preferably a humorous one that will evoke a lot of laughter)

Communicate With Your Partner

Infertility often takes a toll on the relationship between the couple. It often causes unspoken resentment, sexual pressure, feelings of inadequacy, and tension between both of you. What's more, you and your partner may respond differently to the crisis, as men tend to be emotionally distant while women usually show their emotions more freely. This issue might create a rift between you and your partner.

Hence, it's crucial you talk to your partner and share your feelings. Confide in about what you feel or are going through emotionally and assure each other that you will be together in all the ups and downs through the infertility treatment. This unconditional support from your partner will help you be more confident and improve your chances of success.

Share Your Fears

When dealing with infertility, it can help to have people around you who can be sensitive to your feelings, answer your questions, and understand your fears. You can speak to a counsellor or join an infertility support group. By meeting other couples struggling with the same problem, you will be assured that you are not alone. And above all, you would meet other like-minded people who can share your feelings and concerns.

Stay Connected to Family and Friends

Build a bridge back to your close friends and family. It would allow those closest to you to offer their love and support. If you keep your friends and relatives uninformed about your problem, you will end up feeling more stressed. Instead, confide in them about what you are going through and let them know how you want to be treated.

Stress can interfere with your chances of conception. In most cases, stress is the root cause of infertility. In fact, if you're having a hard time getting pregnant, your friends and relatives may have already told you, "Just relax, and it will happen." You may find this odd, but there's a kernel of truth to it.

Just follow the tips given here to reduce your stress, and you will be amazed to see how relaxed you feel after that. This method would significantly impact how your body functions, resulting in the regularisation of several processes, including hormone production, and lead you to your dream of getting pregnant quietly without even letting you know. It would boost your fertility and make your journey towards parenthood much easier.

Treatment Approach: Medications, IUI and IVF, Surrogacy

Fertility treatments are grouped into three categories:

- Medications that improve fertility that can be used alone or in addition to assisted conception

- Surgical treatments helpful in cases where the cause of infertility, such as endometriosis, is found and can be corrected by doing a surgery

- The assisted conception that includes methods like intrauterine insemination (IUI), in vitro fertilisation (IVF), intracytoplasmic sperm injection (ICSI), and gamete intra-fallopian transfer (GIFT)

Medicines

Some highly effective medications help with ovulation. The most commonly used medicine for women having anovulation is clomiphene that works by blocking the feedback mechanisms to the pituitary gland, which results in the gland producing and releasing more of the gonadotropin hormone. This excess gonadotropin hormone helps by stimulating the ovaries to ovulate and produce healthier eggs.

Medicines containing gonadotropins are used for treating anovulation in some women. These are available in the form of injections. They are used if clomiphene does not work. It is also used before IUI and IVF treatments to induce ovulation. Gonadotropin injections can also be given to men to improve their sperm count.

Women can also be treated with gonadotropin-releasing hormone medicines, which works by stimulating the pituitary gland to release more gonadotropins.

Metformin has proven to be highly effective in women with polycystic ovary syndrome (PCOS). Though it is primarily an anti-diabetic medication, it has been found to improve fertility in women with PCOS when used in addition to clomiphene. It works by lowering the levels of male hormones in women with PCOS, resulting in ovulation.

Talk to your doctor before taking any medicine for infertility. The success rate of each medication varies among different women depending upon the cause of infertility. Ask your doctor about the potential side effects of the drug and which side effects need immediate medical attention so that you don't panic if you develop any.

Surgical Treatments

The conditions where surgery may be an option include:

- Fallopian tube disorders
- Endometriosis
- Polycystic ovary syndrome

Assisted Conception

The current techniques for assisted conception are described below. Your doctor will advise you about the feasible options for your particular cause and explain the chance of success.

Intrauterine Insemination (IUI)

This treatment is a process in which the sperm is placed into the uterus with the help of a fine plastic tube passed through the cervix into the uterus. This method ensures that the sperm has reached the uterus. The procedure can be timed to coincide with ovulation.

Women having problems with ovulation can be given ovulation-inducing medications beforehand to maximise the chances of ovulation.

Women who opt for this procedure need healthy fallopian tubes to allow the eggs to get into the womb from the ovaries. The sperm used for this procedure can be obtained from the male partner or a donor if the male partner's sperm count is too low.

Gamete Intra-Fallopian Transfer (GIFT)

In GIFT, the eggs and sperm are collected in the same way as IVF. The eggs are then mixed with the sperm, and the mixture is placed into the fallopian tubes. So, unlike IVF, the sperm is allowed to fertilise the egg directly inside the woman's fallopian tube and not outside the body in a laboratory dish.

In Vitro Fertilization (IVF)

In vitro means outside of the body. In vitro fertilisation means fertilisation that occurs outside the body, which is literally in a glass – a test tube or a laboratory dish. IVF is recommended for couples whose cause of infertility is blocked fallopian tubes or not determined.

IVF treatment involves taking fertility medications for stimulating the ovaries to make more eggs. When the eggs are formed, a small operation is performed to harvest them. This method is known as egg retrieval. Later, each egg is mixed with a sperm obtained from the male partner or donor. The mixture of egg and sperm is left in a laboratory dish for a few days so that the sperm can fertilise the egg and form embryos.

One or two embryos that have formed are placed into the woman's uterus with the help of a plastic tube passed through the cervix. Your chances of success with IVF treatment are higher if you are under the age of 39 and your body mass index (BMI) is between 19 and 30.

Intracytoplasmic Sperm Injection (ICSI)

This method involves injecting an individual sperm directly into an egg. It is called such as the sperm is injected into the outer part of the egg, which is called the cytoplasm. The egg containing the sperm is later placed in the uterus in the same way as IVF.

This method bypasses the natural barriers that could prevent fertilisation from taking place. It is used in cases where the sperm cannot penetrate the egg's outer layer. ICSI is also used when the sperm count of the male partner is meagre, as just one sperm is required for this procedure.

A small operation can be performed to obtain sperm from the man's testis if needed. This step is required when the sperm cannot be obtained by masturbation because the male partner has had a vasectomy earlier or has blocked vas deferens. ICSI is usually recommended for couples in whom IVF has failed or when IVF is less likely to be successful due to the low sperm count of the male partner.

Getting aquatinted with these treatment options and their pros and cons is essential for making the right decisions for infertility treatment.

Besides these, another method has helped several couples realise their dream: surrogacy. Surrogacy is an arrangement that allows a woman to carry a baby for another couple; she later hands over the child to the couple after delivery. A surrogate mother does not have legal rights over the baby born out of a surrogate agreement.

Surrogacy treatment is often the last option for couples who have not achieved any results with other treatments. The advancing age also makes their chances of achieving their dream much dimmer. The couples also have the option of adopting a child; which is a lovely thought of giving love and support to an innocent child whose eyes are searching for a mother and father in the world they feel lost in.

Effective Herbs and Spices to Boost Fertility

While you are undergoing these treatments, you may try some herbs to increase your chances of conception. It is no secret that the rich heritage of Ayurveda, the ancient Indian system of medicine, has provided us with the knowledge of valuable herbs and spices that can help you fight the causes of infertility and get pregnant.

Using herbs is a simple and effective process that could assist in establishing a pregnancy with the help of safe and time-tested plants that balance the female hormones and sexual desire.

Here are some of the most effective herbs you can use while undergoing the other treatments to achieve your dream of getting pregnant with better ease.

Red Clover

Red clover works excellent as a fertility herb due to its high magnesium and calcium. These two minerals are thought to be of high importance in affecting the ability of a woman to conceive.

Red clover contains the trace elements needed by the body for the conception to occur. This alkalising herb also helps balance the hormones and maintains the body's PH levels, including the uterus, thereby favouring conception.

Brew your red clover tea together with mint leaves. Drink this mixture as and when desired once it has cooled down.

Stinging Nettle

This plant is a highly effective herb for promoting fertility. It would tone and nourish the uterus and also strengthen the adrenal glands. If you cannot conceive due to the hormonal imbalance arising from the lack of proper communication between the pituitary gland and the adrenals, you may try this herb.

The health of the adrenal gland is essential when you are trying to get pregnant. This gland acts as a messenger centre for the body and regulates the production and release of different hormones. By correcting this gland's functions, stinging nettle brings you closer to getting pregnant.

Drinking two or more cups of mineral tea prepared from this herb will go a long way in preparing your body for conception and sustaining the embryo when fertilisation occurs.

Alchemilla vulgaris

This herb has been used successfully for centuries for treating various feminine disorders. This herb's natural hormones and properties would help modify the hormonal balance. It is specifically helpful for women having naturally impaired fertility, cervical disorders, uterine fibroids, the absence of menses, and irregular menstrual cycle. It may also strengthen the uterine wall and prepare it for conception.

Ashwagandha Root (Withania somnifera)

This herb would support the overall endocrinal functions of the body and promote proper immune response, thereby correcting autoimmune fertility issues. The immuno-modulating properties of this herb are beneficial for managing autoimmune-related fertility issues like recurrent miscarriages that may occur as a result of the abnormal immunological response of the mother's body, causing the immune cells to attack and reject the foetus.

Damiana (Turnera diffusa)

It can be tough to conceive when you live a stressful life or have reduced libido. If you find that your sex life lacks a spark, you may consider using herbs like turnera diffusa that have been found to increase the woman's sexual desire.

This herb works as an excellent female aphrodisiac. Damiana has also been used for centuries to increase blood circulation in the reproductive organs and regulate menses.

Achillea millefolium

This herb is highly recommended for a series of female ailments. It would help restore a woman's fertility status. Its medicinal properties are beneficial for tackling abnormal menstrual cycles, toning the uterine walls, and improving the blood supply of the reproductive organs.

Furthermore, its antiseptic action could help clear out vaginal and cervical infections. It might also help create favourable uterine conditions for the implantation of fertilised eggs.

Red Raspberry

Red raspberry leaves are high in calcium. Red raspberry leaves can act as a soothing tonic for the uterus. The fertility-promoting effect of red raspberry can be enhanced further by combining it with red clover.

Make a powerful infusion of this herb by using 1/2 ounce of red raspberry and 1/2 ounce of red clover in one cup of hot water for 15 minutes. Drink it once it cools down.

Glycyrrhiza glabra

This herb stimulates fertility, thanks to its oestrogen-like effect that could counteract the harmful effects of xenoestrogens on the body and create a hormonal balance suitable for pregnancy to occur.

Capsella bursa-pastoris

The active ingredients in this herb are highly efficient for managing menstrual irregularities like excessive menstrual flow.

The haemostatic and astringent actions of this herb could help restore the normal functions of the female reproductive organs. It also offers an effective treatment for women with uterine fibroids. It could help tone up the uterine walls and increase the chances of conceiving and maintaining a pregnancy.

Oenothera biennis

This herb has an amazing impact on the fertility of women. It improves the conditions of the uterus and the cervix, thereby creating a suitable environment for the sperm and egg to fertilise and induce conception.

Black Haw (Viburnum prunifolium)

This herb is specifically meant for women having a history of repeated miscarriages. It is highly effective in reducing uterine contractions by preventing spasms of the uterine muscles.

Use this herb regularly for at least six to eight months before your next treatment cycle to reduce the risk of miscarriage. It would act as a tonic for the uterus and strengthen the uterine walls. It may also be helpful when a woman is experiencing abnormal bleeding or passing of blood clots in the first trimester of pregnancy.

The herbs and spices mentioned above are just a few among the plentitude of plants that our mother nature yields for women trying to conceive.

Including these herbs and spices in your regular diet could play a role in preventing infertility and increasing your chances of getting pregnant. These fertility-boosting herbs may also help nourish your body as a whole and the female reproductive system, in particular, thus facilitating conception.

Conclusion

Pregnancy is a miracle! It is truly a glorious and fantastic time in a woman's life. Women are gifted with the ability to create an entirely new human being from just one cell!

Women who have difficulty getting pregnant can try the treatment options discussed here. Each infertility treatment has a few ups and downs. Also, it may take some time for you to conceive with these treatment options. You will also have to follow the trial and error method as no single treatment is 100% successful in all women.

Yet, determination and consistency are two common ingredients in all infertility treatments. Be consistent with your healthy dietary and lifestyle habits, as they will slowly and surely improve your general health and boost your fertility.

Being healthy would also increase your chances of conception with the treatment method you opt, whether IVF, IUI, or herbal remedies.

Also, make sure you avoid mental stress. Stress and anxiety are the biggest enemies that can create significant obstacles in your ability to get pregnant. Do not let stress creep into your mind, as it can lower your chances of conception even with the advanced modern treatments. It would also reduce your sexual desire, affect your general health and hormonal balance, and keep you from getting pregnant.

Importance of Improving Nutritional Support and General Health Before and During Pregnancy

If you have decided to get pregnant, you must be emotionally prepared to have a baby. But you also need to consider whether your body is ready for the challenges ahead. You need to assess whether your health is optimal for baby-making. For instance, if you are underweight or overweight, stressed, or sleep-deprived, you will have to take some dedicated steps to bring your health back on the right track before you begin your journey towards conception and pregnancy.

If you are trying to become pregnant, it is imperative that you prepare your body for the upcoming challenges. You need to prepare your body by toning up the muscles and making some lifestyle and dietary changes to make you healthier and eliminate the health issues that could create difficulties in conception despite trying.

Here are some tips that will help you prepare your body by providing adequate nutritional and dietary support for the journey of bringing a new life into the world.

Check Your Weight

Overweight or underweight, both are not conducive for a pregnancy to occur. If you are overweight, control your diet and exercise regularly to reduce weight. And if you are underweight, make sure your diet comprises all the essential nutrients, including minerals and vitamins.

Clean Up Your Diet

When you are planning to start a family but cannot get pregnant, the hurdle could be your health, which has resulted from your poor, nutrition-less diet. The first thing you can do is remove all unhealthy foods from your diet and add many healthy foods.

Here's how you can look at it: A gardener prepares the soil and nourishes it before planting precious seeds because he knows the healthier the earth is, the more vibrantly the seeds will grow.

Our body is similar: the healthier you are physically, the better the circumstances will be to conceive and maintain a healthy pregnancy.

To eat healthily, start with eliminating harmful carbohydrates from your diet. Refined carbohydrates like pasta, white bread, and white rice can short-change your body and reduce your chances of pregnancy. The refining process strips the critical nutrients from these grains.

Instead, eat foods that boost fertility, such as those containing antioxidants, vitamins, and iron. Pack your diet with as many nutrient-rich foods as possible. Think of produce as the multivitamin from Mother Nature. Fruits and vegetables deliver a wealth of minerals and vitamins and are overflowing with free-radical-scavenging phytochemicals and antioxidants.

Get the best nutritional bang by eating brightly coloured fruits and vegetables like blueberries, kale, and red peppers. Remember one thing: the more vivid the hue of the fruit or vegetable, the more nutrient-packed will it be.

Eat Iron-Rich Foods

Iron deficiency anaemia is a prevalent cause of infertility. Besides, bleeding every month during menstruation can also lead to iron depletion from your body. You can fill up your body's depleting iron reserves by eating iron-rich foods like apples and beetroot.

Exercise Regularly

The benefits of exercising are multifold. Regular exercises will keep you in the best health, making your body conditions favourable for conception. Exercises are also a great way to reduce stress, another prevalent cause of infertility.

A short walk for half an hour after a stressful day will help you unwind and feel more energetic. Exercises will help you maintain your weight and control the medical conditions you may be suffering from, like diabetes and hypertension.

Exercising doesn't necessarily mean following a strict gym routine. You can make your exercise program interesting and enjoyable by doing fun activities like playing outdoor games.

Limit Your Exposure to Toxins

A research study has found the presence of nearly 287 toxic chemicals in the umbilical cord blood of newborn babies. Of these, around 180 chemicals are known to cause cancer, and 218 are extremely harmful to the development of the brain and nervous system. About 210 of these chemicals are known to cause congenital disabilities.

These findings are alarming. You must minimise your exposure to toxins to safeguard the health and well-being of your baby.

Make Space in Your Life

When our life is full, there is no room left for anything new to enter. Too much of things in the limited space of our life and time can also make us feel anxious and stressed. We are so pressed for time with too many responsibilities that we hardly get any breathing space to think about the goodness of life.

Due to this, we feel stressed, resulting in the body refusing to accept anything new, even a baby. It's only by allowing for the presence of some space in your life that you will be able to give birth to a new life within you.

Create this space by removing unnecessary clutter from your life. Minimise the time you spend with your gadgets and surfing through social media posts. Learn to manage your time well by planning your days well in advance. Make provision for some "me" time with yourself and your loved ones.

Curb Caffeine

Caffeine can affect your fertility. Though one or two mugs of coffee a day won't get in your way of getting pregnant, you would be better off by cutting out caffeine altogether if you're having difficulty in conceiving.

Avoid Alcohol

Though some experts believe that drinking sparingly does not lower your chances of conception, I would advise you and your partner to stop drinking alcohol altogether as most people never know when they cross the limits of healthy drinking.

Excessive alcohol consumption can also affect the sperm count in men and egg production in women. So, the best bet when you are trying hard to conceive is to say "no" to alcohol.

Manage Your Current Medical Conditions

If you suffer from a chronic medical condition like diabetes, asthma, or hypertension, make sure it is under control before you conceive. Inform the doctor about your plans to conceive. They may advise a change in the medications that could be harmful to the foetus.

You and your partner may also be taking some drugs that can cause infertility and prevent you from getting pregnant. Some medicines may lower the sperm count and reduce the ability of a man to get an erection. Consulting a doctor is recommended to ensure the medications you or your partner are using would not affect your chances of having a smooth and healthy pregnancy.

From losing weight to getting fit, from eating nutritious foods to giving up your addictions, this rundown of the things would surely improve your chances of conception and keep you in the best health that's favourable for a smooth pregnancy and delivery.

Essential Nutrients for a Smooth and Healthy Pregnancy

We already discussed that one of the most important things you have to consider before trying for a baby is making sure that your body is ready for it. Even if you are fit, healthy, and young, there may still be many factors to consider to prepare your body for pregnancy.

Here are some dietary recommendations that pregnant women can follow to ensure they do not experience any nutritional deficiencies that could create health issues during pregnancy for them or the baby.

Essential Nutrients for a Healthy Pregnancy

Eating a proper diet is vital when you are preparing for pregnancy. Here are some important dietary and nutritional guidelines for pregnant women as well as women planning a pregnancy:

- It is essential to eat a properly balanced diet. The six elements of carbohydrates, fats, vitamins, minerals, proteins, and water should be consumed in appropriate quantities.

- One of the most important things you need to remember is to include plenty of folic acid or folate in your diet. Folic acid is a B vitamin, which plays an integral part in developing the baby's brain and the spinal column.

- It would be best to continue eating plenty of foods rich in folic acid before conception until at least up to the third month of pregnancy, which is when the brain and the spine develop.

- This step is necessary to avoid congenital disabilities in the baby. Foods rich in folic acids are fortified breakfast cereals, dried beans and peas, and green leafy vegetables. However, it is difficult to get the necessary amount of folic acid from diet alone.

- Hence, it is advisable to use multivitamin supplements regularly when preparing for pregnancy and later until you deliver the baby.

- It is advisable to consume at least 1000 mg of calcium every day when preparing for pregnancy. Low-fat milk, yoghurt, and cheese are good options.

- You also need to increase the amount of iron in your diet. Include iron-rich and iron-fortified foods in your diet. Red meat, fish, poultry, beans, and lentils are rich in iron. In addition, eat foods rich in vitamin C as it helps your body absorb iron.

- If you find it difficult to conceive without any apparent reason, try removing gluten from your diet. This removal increases the chances of conception.

- According to recent nutritional guidelines, you should eat plenty of fruits like oranges, strawberries, bananas, peaches, apricots, etc. Veggies like dark green leafy vegetables, orange veggies, beans, and peas are also beneficial. You can eat fresh or frozen fruits and veggies but avoid juices.

- Nuts and dry fruits are healthy snacks to eat during the pre-pregnancy days as they supply calories and nutrients.

- You should limit the amount of sodium in your diet. Most sodium comes from junk and processed foods, which should be avoided. On the other hand, you should increase the amount of potassium in your diet by including foods like bananas.

- While too much fat is bad for conception, your diet should include some amount of unsaturated fats. Ensure that you get no more than 25% to 30% of your total daily calories from fats.

- Fishes are high in lean proteins, and omega-3 fatty acids are low in fat. You should include plenty of fish in your diet. However, avoid swordfish, mackerels, and the fishes caught in streams known to have high mercury levels.

Some More Guidelines for Healthy Conception and Smooth Pregnancy

- You should stop smoking as soon as you decide to have a baby. Moreover, it is recommended that your partner also stop smoking around you because secondary smoke can be equally harmful.

- Alcohol intake should be avoided because it leads to severe developmental disorders in the baby.

- While there is no absolute number of calories you can consume during pregnancy, you should adjust the number to maintain a healthy weight.

- Avoid plastic wraps when you microwave your food. Studies indicate that some plastics contain phthalate, which can leach out when you put them in the microwave. This issue may lead to congenital disabilities in the baby.

- Avoid all drugs, including prescription drugs, when trying to get pregnant. If you have to take any medication, you should consult your doctor first.

- Avoid undercooked meat as it may cause toxoplasmosis and lead to congenital disabilities.

Other Fitness Considerations

In addition to the proper diet, here are some other fitness considerations that you should keep in mind when you decide to enter parenthood:

It has been noticed that having an average weight or being slightly overweight could be suitable for conception. However, you should avoid crash diets when trying for a baby.

Exercise is recommended during this period. It helps control your weight and is the best way to get rid of stress. Exercise releases feel-good hormones or endorphins, which can help you fight stress. Light impact exercises are most recommended before and during pregnancy. Additionally, swimming is excellent during this period. Other light impact exercises include walking, aerobics, dancing, and biking. These exercises would keep you fit and control your weight without putting unnecessary strain on your joints.

On the other hand, you should also avoid exercises like skiing, horse riding, water skiing, and mountain biking. These activities can be harmful, especially if you are already pregnant. Weight training is a good toning exercise, but it should not be started during pregnancy.

Pelvic exercises are an essential group of exercises that should be performed when you start planning for a baby. The pelvic floor refers to the sling-like muscles in the lower portion of the body that supports all your abdominal organs. These muscles lose their elasticity and become stretched during pregnancy and labour. Hence, it is necessary to perform pelvic floor exercises to maintain its tone. The Kegel exercises are the most crucial group of pelvic floor exercises. In this set, you need to squeeze your pelvic muscles, hold the contraction for five to ten seconds and then, release. Do not tense the muscles of your tummy or thighs when you perform this exercise. You can increase the duration of holding the muscles to about 10 to 20 seconds over a period. Regular pelvic exercises can help avoid post-delivery complications such as incontinence.

Getting rid of stress is one of the priorities for women trying of getting pregnant. Make sure you are getting plenty of sleep. Reading a good book, a relaxing bath, meditation, nature walk, getting a massage, or keeping a journal can also be highly relaxing.

Yoga and Pilates help make the body flexible and supple. Yoga can significantly help you deal with issues like back pain and improve your posture.

Many people recommend acupuncture in the pre-pregnancy days. It would help you get rid of stress, improve ovarian functions, regulate hormonal balance, and increase the blood flow to the uterus.

Conclusion

It is best not to start any strenuous exercise or dietary regime during the conception phase. Instead, you can take up the activities you enjoy and let nature take its course.

Following a nutrient-dense diet and regular exercise would help you stay fit and healthy and allow you to enjoy a smooth pregnancy as well as faster recovery after birth.

Pregnancy is something that should be enjoyed and celebrated! The same is also true for the process of getting pregnant. The methods may be a bit difficult for some couples. However, you can follow these steps to avoid health issues that may come up on your way while trying to conceive or during pregnancy.

Pregnancy and Birth Defects

Congenital disabilities are the primary cause of concern for all pregnant women and gynaecologists. Not all congenital disabilities are preventable. However, women can increase the chances of having a healthy baby by managing their health conditions and adopting a nutritional diet and healthy lifestyle habits before they become pregnant.

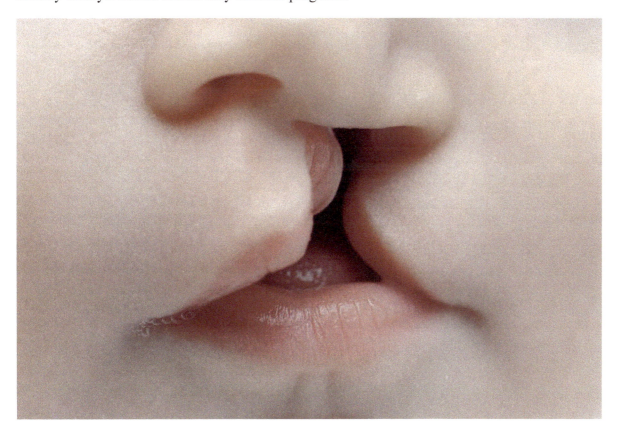

It is vital for women to commit themselves to becoming healthier before and during pregnancy by actively planning, avoiding harmful substances, choosing a healthy lifestyle, and talking with their healthcare provider.

Here is a brief discussion about the precautions women can take to reduce the risk of congenital disabilities in the child.

Plan in Advance

Women can plan in advance and talk to their healthcare provider about the body's nutritional needs. It is advisable to get 400 micrograms of folic acid, a form of vitamin B, daily during pregnancy. A woman, who has enough folic acid in the body for at least one month before conception and during the pregnancy until childbirth, is less likely to develop significant congenital disabilities in the baby.

It would help prevent brain and spine development defects, thereby avoiding the risk of anencephaly and spina bifida.

It is possible to get folic acid from fortified foods. Women can also use supplements, in addition to a varied diet that is rich in foods containing folate. It is also essential to see a healthcare provider regularly while planning a pregnancy and later, during the duration of pregnancy.

Women should see the doctor while planning a pregnancy and start prenatal care as soon as they get pregnant.

Avoid Harmful Substances

Avoiding the intake of alcohol while planning a pregnancy at any time during all three trimesters of pregnancy is highly important. Alcohol consumed by a person can enter the bloodstream, which passes to the developing foetus via the umbilical cord.

It should be noted that there is no known safe limit for alcohol usage during pregnancy and while trying to become pregnant. There is also no safer period during pregnancy when women can drink alcohol without the risk of developing any complications for themselves or the baby. All forms of alcohol, including beer and wine, are considered equally harmful for the mother and the child.

The intake of alcohol during pregnancy could cause stillbirth, miscarriage, and a wide range of lifelong behavioural, physical, or intellectual disabilities in the child. This concern indicates why women must stop drinking alcohol while pregnant or are trying to get pregnant. The disabilities that tend to occur in the children when the mother consumes alcohol during pregnancy are called the foetal alcohol spectrum disorders (FASDs).

Quit Smoking

Women should also avoid other unhealthy habits such as smoking. Avoiding smoking is essential for ensuring the proper growth and development of the baby. The adverse effects of smoking by the mother during pregnancy include specific congenital disabilities such as cleft lip and cleft palate, preterm birth, and infant death.

Also, active smoking and even passive smoking can increase the risk of these congenital disabilities. Being around tobacco smoke could put a woman and her baby at risk of severe complications. Quitting smoking before you get pregnant is the most effective way to protect your child against serious complications.

For women who are already pregnant, quitting at the earliest, i.e. once they know they are pregnant or become aware of the harmful impact of smoking, may still help protect them and the baby against some health issues.

Avoid Marijuana

Avoiding marijuana and other drugs is essential for ensuring women do not develop any serious complications during pregnancy. Women who use marijuana or any other drugs during pregnancy are at risk of having a baby born preterm. The risk of having a low birth weight baby and other health problems like congenital disabilities is also higher in women who use these recreational drugs during pregnancy.

Since there is no known safe level for the intake of marijuana during pregnancy, women planning to enter motherhood and those who are already pregnant should altogether avoid using marijuana. Also, women who use marijuana for any medical reason should consult their physician about alternative therapies with pregnancy-specific safety data without any risks for the mother and the baby.

Protect Against Infections

Preventing infections is essential for pregnant women as some infections could be harmful to the developing foetus. It may even increase the risk of congenital disabilities.

Avoid Overheating

Avoiding overheating and promptly treating fever is highly recommended for women planning a pregnancy or those who are already pregnant. During pregnancy, they should prevent overheating and treat fever promptly.

Overheating may occur due to a fever or exposure to very high temperatures (such as getting into a hot tub). These activities may increase the core temperature of the body. Overheating could increase the risk of having a child with congenital disabilities substantially.

Maintain Normal Blood Sugar Levels

It is advisable to keep diabetes under control as poor glycaemic control and high blood sugar levels during pregnancy can increase the risk for congenital disabilities in the baby and other complications in the mother. Proper healthcare assessment before and during pregnancy could help prevent congenital disabilities and poor outcomes.

Maintain a Healthy Weight

Women should strive to attain and maintain healthy body weight during pregnancy. Women, who are obese with a body mass index (BMI) of 30 or higher than 30 before pregnancy, usually have a higher risk of developing complications.

Obesity may also increase pregnant women's risk of having a baby with severe congenital disabilities. Even women who are not actively planning a pregnancy should try to maintain a healthy weight to improve their general health and mood.

Women who are obese and overweight should consult a doctor about the proper ways to attain a healthy weight before becoming pregnant.

Talk With the Healthcare Provider

Women are advised to talk to their healthcare provider about using any medications while planning a pregnancy. Some medicines are known to cause congenital disabilities in the baby when the mother uses them during pregnancy.

Also, the safety of some medications taken by pregnant women is difficult to determine or not yet established. However, despite the limited data related to the safety of some drugs for pregnant women, some medications may be needed to manage severe conditions. So, when a woman is planning a pregnancy or is already pregnant, she should not stop using the medicines she needs or start taking any new medications without talking to the healthcare provider.

This rule also includes prescription medications, over-the-counter medications, and dietary and herbal products.

Take Vaccinations

Women can consult their healthcare provider about vaccinations they need to take before or during pregnancy. Most vaccinations are safe for mothers during pregnancy. In contrast, some vaccinations like the flu vaccine and the Tdap vaccine (administered to prevent adult tetanus, diphtheria, and acellular pertussis) are specifically recommended to be taken by women during pregnancy.

Some vaccines can help protect pregnant women against serious infections that could otherwise cause congenital disabilities. Having the correct vaccination at the right time could help keep the woman and the baby safe and healthy and avoid the risk of congenital disabilities.

Women should also talk to the doctor about which vaccines are necessary and recommended during pregnancy.

Pregnant women are often more prone to develop severe illnesses from infections like the flu. They may require hospitalisation for the management of these infections. If not managed properly, they may develop life-threatening complications, increasing mortality risk. Also, pregnant women with influenza have a higher risk of severe complications during pregnancy, such as preterm birth and congenital disabilities.

Getting a flu vaccine is considered the first and the most important step women need to take for protecting themselves against these infections. The flu shot can be given during pregnancy, which protects the mother and the baby from the infection for up to six months after delivery.

Conclusion

Pregnancy is an exciting phase in the life of women. However, it can also be highly stressful. Knowing how to take care of yourself and the proper ways to avoid the chances of having congenital disabilities in the baby can allow women to overcome the risks and enjoy the journey. It can also help them be prepared for the pregnancy and stay healthier during pregnancy while giving the baby a healthier start in life.

Best Natural Herbs That Can Reduce the Signs of Ageing

There is no harm in having wrinkles and fine lines on the face. Yet, it is no secret that almost everyone prefers to keep these signs of ageing in check and have youthful and glowing skin even during older age.

Most people believe that it could be challenging to reduce the appearance of wrinkles without advanced surgical or medical intervention once they have developed them. However, using some herbal remedies combined with a few lifestyle changes could slow down the appearance of wrinkles and fine lines and help you look younger. Let's take a closer look at the best ways to help reduce wrinkles.

Protect From the Sun

Exposure to the sun can cause immense damage to the skin, leading to the appearance of premature wrinkles and other signs of ageing.

Regular use of sunscreen lotions could slow down the signs of ageing skin. To protect the skin from the sun's damaging ultraviolet (UV) rays, you can apply a cream or lotion that has an SPF of between 30 and 50 every time you step out in the sun.

Also, UV rays can penetrate the clouds. Hence, it is advisable not to skip the sunscreen routine even when the weather is cool or not too sunny.

You can wear a wide-brimmed hat, light-coloured, long-sleeved clothes, and sunglasses for extra sun protection.

Retinoids

Retinoids derived from vitamin A can produce a natural anti-ageing effect by protecting the skin against the impact of sun exposure. Retinoids can also improve collagen production in the skin, making it appear smoother and plumper.

Retinoids may encourage the regeneration of the skin cells and promote the formation of new blood vessels, thus improving the skin's overall tone, texture, and appearance.

Moisturiser

A moisturiser would help hydrate and nourish the skin. This routine is essential because as we get older, our skin becomes drier, making it prone to wrinkles.

The application of a moisturiser containing hyaluronic acid and vitamin C is especially recommended for preventing wrinkles.

Some other lifestyle habits that can reduce wrinkles and fine lines include:

- Drinking plenty of water to stay hydrated
- Eating vitamin-rich foods
- Sleeping on your back
- Avoiding smoking
- Keeping your facial muscles relaxed and avoid repeated facial movements such as squinting, pursing of the lips, and frowning

Herbal Remedies for Reducing Wrinkles

Cinnamon

Cinnamon possesses natural anti-ageing properties. It would help reduce the signs of ageing by promoting the formation of collagen and elastin in the skin, thereby improving its elasticity and firmness.

You can boil a few cinnamon sticks in a glass of water and brew it for about five minutes. Then, strain the liquid and drink it. Do this once or twice a week to derive noticeable results.

Cucumber

Applying cucumber slices on the face, especially under the eyes, could help the skin look soft and supple and lighten its tone. The cucumber's water content would hydrate and nourish the skin and improve its elasticity, allowing you to look younger and more attractive.

Aloe Vera

Applications of fresh aloe vera gel on the skin could offer great results for reducing the sign of ageing. You can cut an aloe vera leaf and extract a small quantity of the juice. Apply this juice on your face forming a thin layer, and leave it for about 10 to 15 minutes. Then, wash it off with cold water.

You would see an immediate improvement in the glow on your skin. With regular use, it would help to reduce wrinkles and fine lines to a great extent.

Conclusion

Following a healthy lifestyle and the regular use of these herbs could protect the skin against the impact of ageing and reduce the appearance of wrinkles and fine lines.

Common Ailments Affecting Children

All children deserve timely medical care. Parents need to be aware of the most common ailments affecting children to ensure their child gets the best possible care. Here is a list of some of the most common illnesses affecting children.

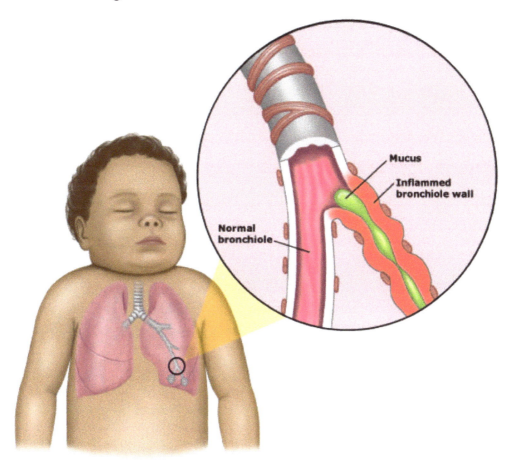

Sore Throat

Sore throat is extremely common in young children. It can be excruciating, often making children cranky and restless. Parents should keep in mind that a sore throat, which is caused due to an infection by a virus, should not be treated with antibiotics. In such cases, no specific treatment is required. The child would get better in five to seven days without any active medical interaction.

In the case of bacterial infections, your paediatrician might recommend antibiotics to relieve the symptoms and clear the infection. Gargling with warm salt water is also an effective home remedy to relieve the symptoms of this condition.

Ear Pain

Ear pain in children can occur due to several causes, such as otitis media (ear infection), swimmer's ear, pressure due to the cold and sinus infections, and toothache radiating to the ear.

A paediatrician's examination of the child's ear would help confirm the diagnosis, based on which appropriate treatment can be recommended.

Urinary Tract Infections

Urinary tract infections occur when harmful bacteria build up in the kidneys or other urinary tract tissues. It can affect children from infancy through their teen years and even into adulthood.

UTI's symptoms include pain and burning sensation during urination and the need to pass urine frequently and urgently. Some children may experience bedwetting and accidents even when they know how to use the toilet.

Skin Infections

In most paediatric patients with skin infections, skin tests that involve taking a swab of the affected tissues and testing it in a laboratory may be needed to determine the correct diagnosis and treatment.

Parents should inform the doctor if the kid has a history of staphylococcal infection, methicillin-resistant staphylococcus aureus (MRSA), or any other condition due to the resistant strains of bacteria. They should also inform the physician if the child has had close contact with any person having an infection with resistant bacteria recently.

Bronchitis

Chronic bronchitis refers to an infection affecting the larger airways of the lungs. While this condition is more common in adults, it may sometimes affect children resulting in serious complications.

Parents should consult a physician at the earliest if their child develops bronchitis symptoms such as persistent cough, fever, wheezing in the chest, and difficulty in breathing.

Bronchiolitis

Bronchiolitis is more common in young children and infants during the winter season. It may cause wheezing sounds in the chest.

Bronchiolitis is usually caused due to a virus that does not require treatment with antibiotics. Most treatment recommendations aim to make the child comfortable with continuous monitoring to assess the change in symptoms like breathing difficulties, cough, and the signs of dehydration.

Other Respiratory Infections

Other respiratory infections like the common cold caused by viral infections are common in young children. Many children, especially those who have recently started going to a child care facility or school, get bouts of common cold nearly five to seven times a year. The symptoms of a cold include running nose, congestion in the nose, sneezing, and cough. These symptoms usually last for up to five to ten days.

Sinusitis caused due to the bacteria accumulated in the sinuses is also common in children. Sinusitis is often suspected when flu-like symptoms like nasal discharge and daytime cough last for more than ten days without any signs of improvement.

Pain

Children may complain of pain due to common injuries like a sprained ankle. They may also become restless due to pain caused by an infection in the ears, stomach, skin, or throat.

Conclusion

Parents should pay attention to these common ailments' signs in their kids and consult a paediatrician to seek appropriate treatment. Timely diagnosis and medical intervention can help the child avoid severe complications if the symptoms persist for too long.

References

Dudhamal, T. S., Gupta, S. K., & Bhuyan, C. (2010). Role of honey (Madhu) in the management of wounds (Dushta Vrana). International journal of Ayurveda research, 1(4), 271–273. https://doi.org/10.4103/0974-7788.76793

Dorai A. A. (2012). Wound care with traditional, complementary and alternative medicine. *Indian journal of plastic surgery : official publication of the Association of Plastic Surgeons of India*, *45*(2), 418–424. https://doi.org/10.4103/0970-0358.101331

Sizar O, Khare S, Goyal A, et al. Vitamin D Deficiency. [Updated 2021 Jul 21]. In: StatPearls [Internet]. Treasure Island (FL): StatPearls Publishing; 2022 Jan. Available from: https://www.ncbi.nlm.nih.gov/books/NBK532266/

Darnton-Hill I. (2019). Public Health Aspects in the Prevention and Control of Vitamin Deficiencies. *Current developments in nutrition*, *3*(9), nzz075. https://doi.org/10.1093/cdn/nzz075

Turner J, Parsi M, Badireddy M. Anemia. [Updated 2022 Jan 9]. In: StatPearls [Internet]. Treasure Island (FL): StatPearls Publishing; 2022 Jan-. Available from: https://www.ncbi.nlm.nih.gov/books/NBK499994/

Cappellini, M. D., & Motta, I. (2015). Anemia in Clinical Practice-Definition and Classification: Does Hemoglobin Change With Aging?. *Seminars in hematology*, *52*(4), 261–269. https://doi.org/10.1053/j.seminhematol.2015.07.006

Harter, K., Levine, M., & Henderson, S. O. (2015). Anticoagulation drug therapy: a review. The western journal of emergency medicine, 16(1), 11–17. https://doi.org/10.5811/westjem.2014.12.22933

Umerah Co, Momodu II. Anticoagulation. [Updated 2021 Dec 27]. In: StatPearls [Internet]. Treasure Island (FL): StatPearls Publishing; 2022 Jan. Available from: https://www.ncbi.nlm.nih.gov/books/NBK560651/

Sridharan, K., Mohan, R., Ramaratnam, S., & Panneerselvam, D. (2011). Ayurvedic treatments for diabetes mellitus. The Cochrane database of systematic reviews, (12), CD008288. https://doi.org/10.1002/14651858.CD008288.pub2

The Art of Living. (2022). *Natural Home remedies for Diabetes | Ayurvedic Tips for Diabetes*. Art of Living (India). https://www.artofliving.org/in-en/ayurveda/ayurvedic-remedies/home-remedies-for-diabetes

Kubala, M. J. S. (2020, September 3). *Can Ayurvedic Medicine Help Lower Cholesterol?* Healthline. https://www.healthline.com/nutrition/ayurvedic-medicine-for-cholesterol

Rana, W. B. S. (2017, September 7). *5 Ayurvedic Remedies for Malaria that Will Help You Recover Quickly*. NDTV.Com. https://www.ndtv.com/food/5-ayurvedic-remedies-for-malaria-that-will-help-you-recover-quickly-1747344

Binu, S. (2021, May 5). *Respiratory Health: 5 Incredible Herbs To Boost Your Lung Power*. Netmeds. https://www.netmeds.com/health-library/post/respiratory-health-5-incredible-herbs-to-boost-your-lung-power

IANS. (2020, December 11). *Protect your lungs by these Ayurvedic home remedies | Lifestyle Health | English Manorama*. OnManorama. https://www.onmanorama.com/lifestyle/health/2020/12/11/protect-lungs-ayurvedic-home-remedies.html

QuikDr Healthcare. (2020, December 11). *Ayurvedic Home Remedies to Cure Respiratory Problems*. Health and Fitness Tips | QuikDr HealthCare Blog. https://quikdr.com/healthtips/ayurveda-for-asthma-and-respiratory-problems/

Midwest Allergy Relief Centers. (2019, November 1). *6 Best Herbs to Protect Your Respiratory System*. Holistic Allergy Treatment Center in the Midwest. https://www.midwestallergyrelief.com/6-best-herbs-to-protect-your-respiratory-system/

Mohiuddin, A. (2019). Natural Foods and Indian herbs of cardiovascular interest. *Pharmacy & Pharmacology International Journal*, 7(2). https://doi.org/10.15406/ppij.2019.07.00235

Mashour, N. H., Lin, G. I., & Frishman, W. H. (1998). Herbal Medicine for the Treatment of Cardiovascular Disease. *Archives of Internal Medicine*, 158(20), 2225. https://doi.org/10.1001/archinte.158.20.2225

Shaito, A., Thuan, D., Phu, H. T., Nguyen, T., Hasan, H., Halabi, S., Abdelhady, S., Nasrallah, G. K., Eid, A. H., & Pintus, G. (2020). Herbal Medicine for Cardiovascular Diseases: Efficacy, Mechanisms, and Safety. *Frontiers in pharmacology*, 11, 422. https://doi.org/10.3389/fphar.2020.00422

Rastogi, S., Pandey, M. M., & Rawat, A. K. (2016). Traditional herbs: a remedy for cardiovascular disorders. *Phytomedicine : international journal of phytotherapy and phytopharmacology*, 23(11), 1082–1089. https://doi.org/10.1016/j.phymed.2015.10.012

Bharat, D. (2021, March 8). *Ayurveda For Varicose Veins: Fantastic Herbal Remedies To Heal*

Swollen Legs And Blood Clots. Netmeds. https://www.netmeds.com/health-library/post/ayurveda-for-varicose-veins-fantastic-herbal-remedies-to-heal-swollen-legs-and-blood-clots

Seladi-Schulman, J. (2021, March 5). *Ayurvedic Treatment for Varicose Veins: Does it Work?* Healthline. https://www.healthline.com/health/ayurvedic-treatment-for-varicose-veins

Cancer Research UK. (2019a). *Herbal medicine | Complementary and alternative therapy | Cancer Research UK*. https://www.cancerresearchuk.org/about-cancer/cancer-in-general/treatment/complementary-alternative-therapies/individual-therapies/herbal-medicine

Whitmer, M. (2022). *Is Herbal Medicine Safe for Cancer Patients?* Asbestos. https://www.asbestos.com/treatment/alternative/herbal-medicine/

Cancer Council Victoria. (2022). *Therapies using herbs and plants | Cancer Council Victoria*. Cancer Council Victoria. https://www.cancervic.org.au/living-with-cancer/common-side-effects/complementary-therapies/herbs-plants.html

Shareef, M., Ashraf, M. A., & Sarfraz, M. (2016). Natural cures for breast cancer treatment. *Saudi pharmaceutical journal : SPJ : the official publication of the Saudi Pharmaceutical Society*, *24*(3), 233–240. https://doi.org/10.1016/j.jsps.2016.04.018

Laskar, Y. B. (2020, March 25). *Chapter: Herbal Remedies for Breast Cancer Prevention and Treatment*. In Tech Open. https://www.intechopen.com/chapters/70593

Wigutow, C. (2016). *Cancer Fighting Herbs and Spices*. Memorial Healthcare System. https://www.mhs.net/news/2016/09/cancer-fighting-herbs-and-spices

Rafatjah, S. (2021, May 25). *10 Natural Treatments for Alzheimer's Disease & Dementia*. PrimeHealth Denver. https://primehealthdenver.com/alzheimers-natural-treatment/

Agarwal, P., Alok, S., Fatima, A., & Singh, P. P. (2013). HERBAL REMEDIES FOR NEURODEGENERATIVE DISORDER (ALZHEIMER'S DISEASE): A REVIEW. *International Journal of Pharmaceutical Sciences and Research*, *4*(9). https://doi.org/10.13040/ijpsr.0975-8232.4(9).3328-40

Chang, D., Liu, J., Bilinski, K., Xu, L., Steiner, G. Z., Seto, S. W., & Bensoussan, A. (2016). Herbal Medicine for the Treatment of Vascular Dementia: An Overview of Scientific Evidence. *Evidence-Based Complementary and Alternative Medicine*, *2016*, 1–15. https://doi.org/10.1155/2016/7293626

Holland, K. (2017, February 9). *Alternative Treatments for Alzheimer's Disease*. Healthline. https://www.healthline.com/health/alzheimers-disease/alternative-treatments

Kubala, M. J. S. (2021, July 30). *11 Herbs and Supplements to Help Fight Depression*. Healthline. https://www.healthline.com/nutrition/herbs-supplements-for-depression

Galan, R. N. N. (2019, February 26). *8 herbs and supplements for depression*. Medical News Today. https://www.medicalnewstoday.com/articles/314421

Mayo Foundation for Medical Education and Research. (2018, September 11). *Natural remedies for depression: Are they effective?* Mayo Clinic. https://www.mayoclinic.org/diseases-conditions/depression/expert-answers/natural-remedies-for-depression/faq-20058026

Bruce, D. F. (2008a, June 2). *Alternative Treatments for Depression*. WebMD. https://www.webmd.com/depression/guide/alternative-therapies-depression

Villines, Z. (2021, February 2). *What natural treatments are there for MS?* Medical News Today. https://www.medicalnewstoday.com/articles/multiple-sclerosis-natural-treatment

Mojaverrostami, S., Bojnordi, M. N., Ghasemi-Kasman, M., Ebrahimzadeh, M. A., & Hamidabadi, H. G. (2018). A Review of Herbal Therapy in Multiple Sclerosis. *Advanced pharmaceutical bulletin*, *8*(4), 575–590. https://doi.org/10.15171/apb.2018.066

Wong, C. (2021, November 5). *How Alternative Therapies Can Be Used to Treat Alcohol Addiction*. Verywell Health. https://www.verywellhealth.com/natural-support-for-alcoholism-treatment-89263

Lu, L., Liu, Y., Zhu, W., Shi, J., Liu, Y., Ling, W., & Kosten, T. R. (2009). Traditional medicine in the treatment of drug addiction. *The American journal of drug and alcohol abuse*, *35*(1), 1–11. https://doi.org/10.1080/00952990802455469

Harold, L. (2022, February 22). *Natural Remedies to Help You Quit Smoking*. Verywell Mind. https://www.verywellmind.com/natural-remedies-to-quit-smoking-89997

Story, C. M. (2021, July 29). *The 7 Best Herbs for ADHD Symptoms*. Healthline. https://www.healthline.com/health/adhd/herbal-remedies

Dresden, D. (2018, September 21). *Are there natural remedies for ADHD?* WebMD. https://www.medicalnewstoday.com/articles/315239

Bhandari, S. (2020, February). *Natural Remedies for ADHD*. WebMD. https://www.webmd.com/add-adhd/ss/slideshow-adhd-natural-remedies

Story, C. M. (2019, March 22). *6 Natural Remedies for ADHD*. Healthline. https://www.healthline.com/health/adhd/natural-remedies

St. Luke's Hospital. (2022). *Herbs and Supplements for Down's syndrome | Complementary and Alternative Medicine | St. Luke's Hospital*. St. Luke's Hospital. https://www.stlukes-stl.com/health-content/medicine/33/002462.htm

Chauhan, M. (2019, April 24). *Down Syndrome*. Planet Ayurveda. https://www.planetayurveda.com/library/down-syndrome/

Choices Market. (2021, June 2). *Natural Remedies to Aid Digestion: Herbal Medicine*. https://www.choicesmarkets.com/health-article/digestive-aids-back-to-the-basics-with-herbal-medicine/

Huizen, J. (2020, January 11). *Home and natural remedies for upset stomach*. WcbMD. https://www.medicalnewstoday.com/articles/322047

Dabur. (2022). *Home Remedies for Indigestion*. One of the Best Ayurvedic Companies in India | Dabur. https://www.dabur.com/?aspxerrorpath=/article.aspx

Harley, J. (2020). *10 Best Natural Home Remedies for IBS*. Mindset Health. https://www.mindsethealth.com/matter/10-best-natural-home-remedies-for-ibs

Comar, K. M., & Kirby, D. F. (2005). Herbal remedies in gastroenterology. *Journal of clinical gastroenterology*, *39*(6), 457–468. https://doi.org/10.1097/01.mcg.0000165650.09500.3a

Babaeian, M., Naseri, M., Kamalinejad, M., Ghaffari, F., Emadi, F., Feizi, A., Hosseini Yekta, N., & Adibi, P. (2015). Herbal Remedies for Functional Dyspepsia and Traditional Iranian Medicine Perspective. *Iranian Red Crescent medical journal*, *17*(11), e20741. https://doi.org/10.5812/ircmj.20741

Kelber, O., Bauer, R., & Kubelka, W. (2017). Phytotherapy in Functional Gastrointestinal Disorders. *Digestive Diseases*, *35*(Suppl. 1), 36–42. https://doi.org/10.1159/000485489

Kim, Y. S., Kim, J. W., Ha, N. Y., Kim, J., & Ryu, H. S. (2020). Herbal Therapies in Functional Gastrointestinal Disorders: A Narrative Review and Clinical Implication. *Frontiers in Psychiatry*, *11*. https://doi.org/10.3389/fpsyt.2020.00601

Thompson Coon, J., & Ernst, E. (2002). Herbal medicinal products for non-ulcer dyspepsia. *Alimentary Pharmacology & Therapeutics*, *16*(10), 1689–1699. https://doi.org/10.1046/j.1365-2036.2002.01339.x

Zingone, F., Capone, P., & Ciacci, C. (2010). Celiac disease: Alternatives to a gluten free diet. *World journal of gastrointestinal pharmacology and therapeutics*, *1*(1), 36–39. https://doi.org/10.4292/wjgpt.v1.i1.36

Chedid, V., Dhalla, S., Clarke, J. O., Roland, B. C., Dunbar, K. B., Koh, J., Justino, E., Tomakin,

E., & Mullin, G. E. (2014). Herbal therapy is equivalent to rifaximin for the treatment of small intestinal bacterial overgrowth. *Global advances in health and medicine*, *3*(3), 16–24. https://doi.org/10.7453/gahmj.2014.019

Christiansen, S. (2021, July 12). *Non-Celiac Gluten Sensitivity Treatment Options*. Verywell Health. https://www.verywellhealth.com/how-non-celiac-gluten-sensitivity-is-treated-4691924

Liu, Y., Sun, M., Yao, H., Liu, Y., & Gao, R. (2017). Herbal Medicine for the Treatment of Obesity: An Overview of Scientific Evidence from 2007 to 2017. *Evidence-Based Complementary and Alternative Medicine*, *2017*, 1–17. https://doi.org/10.1155/2017/8943059

Koithan, M., & Niemeyer, K. (2010). Using Herbal Remedies to Maintain Optimal Weight. *The journal for nurse practitioners : JNP*, *6*(2), 153–154. https://doi.org/10.1016/j.nurpra.2009.12.005

Teng, L., Lee, E. L., Zhang, L., & Barnes, J. (2020). Herbal preparations for weight loss in adults. *The Cochrane Database of Systematic Reviews*, *2020*(4), CD013576. https://doi.org/10.1002/14651858.CD013576

Issa, R. (2018). Use of Herbal Remedies, Conventional Medicine, Diet andExercise for Weight Loss: Case Study of University Students inJordan. *Pakistan Journal of Nutrition*, *17*(2), 76–88. https://doi.org/10.3923/pjn.2018.76.88

Vorvick, L. (2022). *A guide to herbal remedies*. Medline Plus. https://medlineplus.gov/ency/patientinstructions/000868.htm

Dugdale, D. (2022). *Herbal remedies and supplements for weight loss*. Medline Plus. https://medlineplus.gov/ency/patientinstructions/000347.htm

Alok, S., Jain, S. K., Verma, A., Kumar, M., & Sabharwal, M. (2013). Pathophysiology of kidney, gallbladder and urinary stones treatment with herbal and allopathic medicine: A review. *Asian Pacific Journal of Tropical Disease*, *3*(6), 496–504. https://doi.org/10.1016/S2222-1808(13)60107-3

Prasad S, Aggarwal BB. Turmeric, the Golden Spice: From Traditional Medicine to Modern Medicine. In: Benzie IFF, Wachtel-Galor S, editors. Herbal Medicine: Biomolecular and Clinical Aspects. 2nd edition. Boca Raton (FL): CRC Press/Taylor & Francis; 2011. Chapter 13. Available from: https://www.ncbi.nlm.nih.gov/books/NBK92752/

Anthony, K. (2019, October 9). *Relieving Gallbladder Pain Naturally*. Healthline. https://www.healthline.com/health/gallbladder-pain-relief

Huizen, J. (2018, May 9). *How to get rid of yellow eyes*. Medical News Today. https://www.medicalnewstoday.com/articles/321746

Kriegermeier, A., & Green, R. (2020). Pediatric Cholestatic Liver Disease: Review of Bile Acid Metabolism and Discussion of Current and Emerging Therapies. *Frontiers in Medicine*, 7. https://doi.org/10.3389/fmed.2020.00149

Cruz Martínez, C., Diaz Gómez, M., & Oh, M. S. (2017). Use of traditional herbal medicine as an alternative in dental treatment in Mexican dentistry: a review. *Pharmaceutical biology*, *55*(1), 1992–1998. https://doi.org/10.1080/13880209.2017.1347188

Kumar, G., Jalaluddin, M., Rout, P., Mohanty, R., & Dileep, C. L. (2013). Emerging trends of herbal care in dentistry. *Journal of clinical and diagnostic research : JCDR*, *7*(8), 1827–1829. https://doi.org/10.7860/JCDR/2013/6339.3282

Guo, J., Low, K. S., Mei, L., Li, J. H., Qu, W., & Guan, G. (2020). Use of traditional medicine for dental care by different ethnic groups in New Zealand. *BMC Oral Health*, *20*(1). https://doi.org/10.1186/s12903-020-01272-7

Anushya, P., Priya, J., & Arivarasu, L. (2020). ROLE OF HERBAL MEDICINE IN DENTAL HEALTH- A DETAILED REVIEW. *European Journal of Molecular & Clinical Medicine*, *07*(01).

Tewari, D., Samoilă, O., Gocan, D., Mocan, A., Moldovan, C., Devkota, H. P., Atanasov, A. G., Zengin, G., Echeverría, J., Vodnar, D., Szabo, B., & Crişan, G. (2019). Medicinal Plants and Natural Products Used in Cataract Management. *Frontiers in pharmacology*, *10*, 466. https://doi.org/10.3389/fphar.2019.00466

Ige, M., & Liu, J. (2020). Herbal Medicines in Glaucoma Treatment. *The Yale journal of biology and medicine*, *93*(2), 347–353.

Kelly, J. P. (2005). Recent Trends in Use of Herbal and Other Natural Products. *Archives of Internal Medicine*, *165*(3), 281. https://doi.org/10.1001/archinte.165.3.281

Ekor, M. (2014). The growing use of herbal medicines: issues relating to adverse reactions and challenges in monitoring safety. *Frontiers in Pharmacology*, *4*. https://doi.org/10.3389/fphar.2013.00177

Gudgel, D. T. (2021, September 17). *Get Rid of Pink Eye Fast With These Home Remedies*. American Academy of Ophthalmology. https://www.aao.org/eye-health/diseases/pink-eye-quick-home-remedies

Johnson, J. (2020, April 27). *Are there any home remedies for pneumonia?* Medical News Today. https://www.medicalnewstoday.com/articles/320881

Thomas, L. (2020, June 10). *Natural Remedies: Reversing Vision Loss | Florida Eye.* Florida Eye Specialists & Cataract Institute. https://floridaeye.org/eye-health/natural-remedies-to-reverse-vision-loss-fact-or-fiction/

Shenefelt PD. Herbal Treatment for Dermatologic Disorders. In: Benzie IFF, Wachtel-Galor S, editors. Herbal Medicine: Biomolecular and Clinical Aspects. 2nd edition. Boca Raton (FL): CRC Press/Taylor & Francis; 2011. Chapter 18. Available from: https://www.ncbi.nlm.nih.gov/books/NBK92761/

Frothingham, S. (2018, July 12). *Skin Allergy Home Remedies*. Healthline. https://www.healthline.com/health/skin-allergy-home-remedy

Berry, J. (2021, November 19). *Top 12 natural remedies for eczema*. Medical News Today. https://www.medicalnewstoday.com/articles/324228

American Academy Of Dermatology Association. (2022). *What's the difference between eczema and psoriasis?* AAD. https://www.aad.org/public/diseases/eczema/childhood/child-have/difference-psoriasis

Ali, B., Al-Wabel, N. A., Shams, S., Ahamad, A., Khan, S. A., & Anwar, F. (2015). Essential oils used in aromatherapy: A systemic review. *Asian Pacific Journal of Tropical Biomedicine*, *5*(8), 601–611. https://doi.org/10.1016/j.apjtb.2015.05.007

Cleveland Clinic. (2022). *Dry Skin: Eczema, Itchy Skin, Causes, Treatments, Relief, Types*. Cleveland Clinic. https://my.clevelandclinic.org/health/diseases/16940-dry-skinitchy-skin

Chapman, J. A. (2006). Food allergy: a practice parameter. *ANNALS OF ALLERGY, ASTHMA & IMMUNOLOGY*, *96*. https://www.aaaai.org/Aaaai/media/MediaLibrary/PDF%20Documents/Practice%20and%20Parameters/food-allergy-2006.pdf

Tabassum, N., & Hamdani, M. (2014). Plants used to treat skin diseases. *Pharmacognosy reviews*, *8*(15), 52–60. https://doi.org/10.4103/0973-7847.125531

McDermott, A. (2019, April 17). *8 Natural Remedies to Reduce Eczema Symptoms*. Healthline. https://www.healthline.com/health/natural-remedies-to-reduce-eczema-symptoms

Jaradat, N., & Zaid, A. N. (2019). Herbal remedies used for the treatment of infertility in males and females by traditional healers in the rural areas of the West Bank/Palestine. *BMC complementary and alternative medicine*, *19*(1), 194. https://doi.org/10.1186/s12906-019-2617-2

Lans, C., Taylor-Swanson, L., & Westfall, R. (2018). Herbal fertility treatments used in North America from colonial times to 1900, and their potential for improving the success rate of assisted reproductive technology. *Reproductive biomedicine & society online*, *5*, 60–81. https://doi.org/10.1016/j.rbms.2018.03.001

Jaradat, N., & Zaid, A. N. (2019). Herbal remedies used for the treatment of infertility in males and females by traditional healers in the rural areas of the West Bank/Palestine. *BMC Complementary and Alternative Medicine*, *19*(1). https://doi.org/10.1186/s12906-019-2617-2

Sissons, B. (2020, May 22). *Can you unblock fallopian tubes with natural remedies?* Medical News Today. https://www.medicalnewstoday.com/articles/natural-treatment-for-blocked-fallopian-tubes

Brown, M. J. (2020, August 13). *16 Natural Ways to Boost Fertility*. Healthline. https://www.healthline.com/nutrition/16-fertility-tips-to-get-pregnant

Fazly Bazzaz, B. S., Darvishi Fork, S., Ahmadi, R., & Khameneh, B. (2021). Deep insights into urinary tract infections and effective natural remedies. *African Journal of Urology*, *27*(1). https://doi.org/10.1186/s12301-020-00111-z

Pathak, N. (2021). *Do You Have a Hormone Imbalance?* WebMD. https://www.webmd.com/women/ss/slideshow-hormone-imbalance

Bruce, D. F. (2008b, September 22). *Normal Testosterone and Estrogen Levels in Women*. WebMD. https://www.webmd.com/women/guide/normal-testosterone-and-estrogen-levels-in-women

Medanta. (2019, January 2). *5 Common Childhood Illnesses and Their Treatment*. https://www.medanta.org/patient-education-blog/5-common-childhood-illnesses-and-their-treatments/

HealthyChildren.Org. (2022). *10 Common Childhood Illnesses and Their Treatments*. HealthyChildren.Org. https://www.healthychildren.org/English/health-issues/conditions/treatments/Pages/10-Common-Childhood-Illnesses-and-Their-Treatments.aspx

CPSIA information can be obtained
at www.ICGtesting.com
Printed in the USA
LVHW070756240522
719581LV00002B/18